PEARSON CUSTOM LIBRARY

AMERICAN HISTORY

HIST 105
America in the 20th and 21st Centuries
CAYUGA COMMUNITY COLLEGE

PEARSON

ISBN 10: 1-269-23190-1
ISBN 13: 978-1-269-23190-9

Table of Contents

The Age of Reform

From Chapter 21 of *American Destiny: Narrative of a Nation*, Combined Volume, Fourth Edition. Mark C. Carnes and John A. Garraty. Copyright © 2012 by Pearson Education, Inc. Published by Pearson Prentice Hall. All rights reserved.

The Age of Reform

(((●—[Hear the Audio at myhistorylab.com

Are college students apathetic?

SOME THINK SO. IN 2007 *NEW YORK TIMES* COLUMNIST THOMAS Friedman proposed that they be known as Generation Q—for Quiet. That generation, he reported, was "too quiet, too online, for its own good, and for the country's own good."

In 2010 Gabrielle Grow, a senior at the University of California at Davis, offered an explanation in the *Huffington Post*: "From those who deem us apathetic, we have not only inherited a country up to its neck in debt but a society and lifestyle in which we are constantly expected to outperform each other. . . [An] intense course load combined with little free time leaves little room for political inquiry or investigation."

Other students challenged Friedman's stereotype through civic engagement of the old-fashioned sort, by rolling up their sleeves and helping out. In a 2009 UCLA survey, two-thirds of college seniors reported that they "occasionally" or "frequently" performed volunteer work. Over three-fourths said that they voted in the 2008 presidential election. In 2009 AmeriCorps, a federally sponsored public-service plan, received twice as many applications from college graduates as the previous year. That same year, more than 168,000 college students worked for Habitat for Humanity, far more than a decade earlier.

Today's college-age volunteers in many ways resemble their counterparts during the "age of reform" a century ago. Then, large numbers of young adults worked to improve society in various ways. They investigated tenements, factories, schools, municipal governments, and consumer goods. They promoted legislation to protect children from exploitative employers and to secure voting rights for women. They advocated conservation of natural resources. They swelled the ranks of the Socialist party, the Progressive party, and of more radical movements. In response to this sea change among younger voters, the Republican and Democratic parties embraced reforms that earlier generations had regarded as wild-eyed radicalism.

Roots of Progressivism

The progressives were never a single group seeking a single objective. The movement sprang from many sources. One was the fight against corruption and inefficiency in government, which began with the Liberal Republicans of the Grant era and was

Orchard Street, a tenement in lower Manhattan in New York City. The unpaved street, ankle-deep in mud, is lined with garbage. But while reformers deplored life in such slums, many who lived there enjoyed the sociability of the congested streets.

continued by the mugwumps of the 1880s. The struggle for civil service reform was only the first skirmish in this battle; the continuing power of corrupt political machines and the growing influence of large corporations and their lobbyists on municipal and state governments outraged thousands of citizens and led them to seek ways to make the machinery of government at all levels responsive to the majority rather than to special-interest groups.

Progressivism also had roots in the effort to regulate and control big business, which characterized the Granger and Populist agitation of the 1870s and 1890s. The failure of the Interstate Commerce Act to end railroad abuses and of the Sherman Antitrust Act to check the growth of large corporations became increasingly apparent after 1900. The return of prosperity after the depression of the 1890s encouraged reformers by removing the fear, so influential in the 1896 presidential campaign, that an assault on the industrial giants might lead to the collapse of the economy.

Between 1897 and 1904 the trend toward concentration in industry accelerated. Such new giants as Amalgamated Copper (1899), U.S. Steel (1901), and International Harvester (1902) attracted most of the attention, but even more alarming were the overall statistics. In a single year (1899) more than 1,200 firms were absorbed in mergers, the resulting combinations being capitalized at $2.2 billion. By 1904 there were 318 industrial combinations in the country with an aggregate capital of $7.5 billion. People who considered bigness inherently evil demanded that the huge new "trusts" be broken up or at least strictly controlled.

America was becoming more urban, more industrial, more mechanized, more centralized—in short, more complex. This trend put a premium on efficiency and cooperation. It seemed obvious to the progressives that people must become more socially minded, and the economy more carefully organized.

By attracting additional thousands of sympathizers to the general cause of reform, the return of prosperity after 1896 fueled the progressive movement. Good times made people more tolerant and generous. As long as profits were on the rise, the average employer did not object if labor improved its position too. Middle-class Americans who had been prepared to go to the barricades in the event of a Bryan victory in 1896 became conscience-stricken when they compared their own comfortable circumstances with those of the "huddled masses" of immigrants and native-born poor.

Giant industrial and commercial corporations undermined not so much the economic well-being as the ambitions and sense of importance of the middle class. The growth of large labor organizations worried such types. In general, character and moral values seemed less influential; organizations—cold, impersonal, heartless—were coming to control business, politics, and too many other aspects of life.

The middle classes could support reform measures without feeling that they were being very radical because they were resisting change and because the intellectual currents of the time harmonized with their ideas of social improvement and the welfare state. The new doctrines of the social scientists, the Social Gospel religious leaders, and the philosophers of pragmatism provided a salubrious climate for progressivism. Many of the thinkers who had formulated these doctrines in the 1880s and 1890s turned to the task of putting them into practice in the new century. Their number included the economist Richard T. Ely, the philosopher John Dewey, and the Baptist clergyman Walter Rauschenbusch, a civic reformer who wrote many books extolling the Social Gospel.

The Muckrakers

As the diffuse progressive army gradually formed its battalions, a new journalistic fad brought the movement into focus. For many years magazines had been publishing articles discussing current political, social, and economic problems. In the fall of 1902, *McClure's* began two particularly hard-hitting series of articles, one on Standard Oil by Ida Tarbell, the other on big-city political machines by Lincoln Steffens. When the editor, S. S. McClure, decided to include in the January 1903 issue an attack on labor gangsterism in the coal fields along with installments of the Tarbell and Steffens series, he called attention to the circumstance in a striking editorial.

Something was radically wrong with the "American character," McClure wrote. These articles showed that large numbers of American employers, workers, and politicians were fundamentally immoral. Lawyers were becoming tools of big business, judges were permitting evildoers to escape justice, the churches were materialistic, and educators seemed incapable of understanding what was happening.

McClure's editorial caused a sensation. The issue sold out quickly. Thousands of readers found their own vague apprehensions brought into focus. Some became active in progressive movements; still more lent passive support.

Other editors jumped to adopt the McClure formula. A small army of professional writers soon flooded the periodical press with denunciations of the insurance business, the drug business, college athletics, prostitution, sweatshop labor, political corruption, and dozens of other subjects. This type of article inspired Theodore Roosevelt, with his gift for vivid language, to compare the journalists to "the Man with the Muck-Rake" in John Bunyan's *Pilgrim's Progress*, whose attention was so fixed on the filth at his feet that he could not notice the "celestial crown" that was offered him in exchange. Roosevelt's characterization grossly misrepresented the literature of exposure, but the label *muckraking* was thereafter affixed to the type. Despite its literal connotations, **muckraker** became a term of honor.

The Progressive Mind

Unlike many earlier reformers, progressives believed that the source of society's evils lay in the structure of its institutions, not in the weaknesses or sinfulness of individuals. Therefore local, state, and national government must be made more responsive to the will of citizens who stood for the traditional virtues. In the South, many people who considered themselves progressives even argued that poll taxes and other measures designed to deny blacks the vote were reforms because they discouraged a class of people they considered unthinking and shiftless from voting.

When government had been thus reformed, then it must act; whatever its virtues, laissez-faire was obsolete. Businessmen, especially big businessmen, must be compelled to behave fairly, their acquisitive drives curbed in the interests of justice and equal opportunity for all. The weaker elements in society—women, children, the poor, the infirm—must be protected against unscrupulous power.

Despite its fervor and democratic rhetoric, progressivism was paternalistic, moderate, and often softheaded. Typical reformers of the period oversimplified complicated issues and treated their personal values as absolute standards of truth and morality. Thus progressives often acted at cross-purposes; at times some were even at war with themselves. This accounts for the diffuseness of the movement.

The progressives never challenged the fundamental principles of capitalism, nor did they attempt a basic reorganization of society. They would have little to do with the socialist brand of reform. Many progressives were anti-immigrant, and only a handful had anything to offer blacks, surely the most exploited group in American society.

A good example of the relatively limited radicalism of most progressives is offered by the experiences of progressive artists. Early in the century a number of painters, including Robert Henri, John Sloan, and George Luks, tried to develop a distinctively American style. They turned to city streets and the people of the slums for their models, and they depended more on inspiration and inner conviction than on careful craftsmanship to achieve their effects.

These artists of the **Ashcan School** were individualists, yet they supported political and social reform and were caught up in the progressive movement. Sloan was a socialist; Henri claimed to be an anarchist. Most saw themselves as rebels. But artistically the Ashcan painters were not very advanced. Their idols were long-dead European masters such as Hogarth, Goya, and Daumier. They were uninfluenced by the outburst of post-impressionist activity then taking place in Europe. To their dismay, when they included canvases by Matisse, Picasso, and other European artists in a show of their own works at the Sixty-Ninth Regiment Armory in New York City in 1913, the "advanced" Europeans got all the attention.

In 1900, Ashcan artist George Luks portrayed corporate monopolies and franchises as a monster preying on New York City.

"Radical" Progressives: The Wave of the Future

The hard times of the 1890s and the callous reactions of conservatives to the victims of that depression pushed many toward Marxian socialism. In 1900 the labor leader Eugene V. Debs ran for president on the Socialist ticket. He polled fewer than 100,000 votes. When he ran again in 1904 he got more than 400,000, and in later elections still more. Labor leaders hoping to organize unskilled workers in heavy industry were increasingly frustrated by the craft orientation of the American Federation of Labor, and some saw in socialism a way to win rank-and-file backing.

In 1905 Debs, William "Big Bill" Haywood of the Western Federation of Miners, Mary Harris "Mother" Jones (a former organizer for the United Mine Workers), Daniel De Leon of the Socialist Labor party, and a few others organized a new union: the **Industrial Workers of the World (IWW)**. The IWW was openly anticapitalist. The preamble to its constitution began: "The working class and the employing class have nothing in common."

But the IWW never attracted many ordinary workers. Haywood, its most prominent leader, was usually a general in search of an army. His forte was attracting attention to spontaneous strikes by unorganized workers, not the patient recruiting of workers and the pursuit of practical goals. In 1912 he was closely involved in a bitter and, at times, bloody strike of textile workers in Lawrence, Massachusetts, which was settled with some benefit to the strikers; he was also involved in a failed strike the following winter and spring by silk workers in Paterson, New Jersey.

Other "advanced" European ideas affected the thinking and behavior of some important progressive intellectuals. Sigmund Freud's psychoanalytical theories attracted numbers of Americans. Many picked up enough of the vocabulary of psychoanalysis to discourse impressively about the significance of slips of the tongue, sublimation, and infant sexuality.

Some saw in Freud's ideas reason to effect a "revolution of manners and morals" that would have shocked (or at least embarrassed) Freud, who was personally quite conventional. They advocated easy divorce, trial marriage, and doing away with the double standard in all matters relating to sex. They rejected Victorian reticence and what they incorrectly identified as "puritan" morality out of hand, and they called for programs of sex education, especially the dissemination of information about methods of birth control.

Most large cities boasted groups of these "bohemian" thinkers, by far the most famous being the one centered in New York City's Greenwich Village. The dancer Isadora Duncan, the photographer Alfred Stieglitz, the novelist Floyd Dell, several of the Ashcan artists, and the playwright Eugene O'Neill rubbed shoulders with Big Bill Haywood of the IWW, the anarchist Emma Goldman, the psychoanalyst A. A. Brill, the militant feminist advocate of birth control Margaret Sanger, Max Eastman, and John Reed, a young Harvard graduate who was soon to become famous for his eyewitness account of the Russian Revolution in *Ten Days That Shook the World*.

Goldman, Haywood, Sanger, and a few others in this group were genuine radicals who sought basic changes in bourgeois society, but most of the Greenwich Village intellectuals were as much concerned with aesthetic as social issues. Nearly all of them came from middle-class backgrounds. They found the far-different world of the Italian and Jewish immigrants of the Village and its surrounding neighborhoods charming. But they did not become involved in the immigrants' lives the way the settlement house workers did. Their influence on their own times, therefore, was limited. They are historically important, however, because many of them were genuinely creative people and because many of the ideas and practices they advocated were adopted by later generations.

The creative writers of the era, applying the spirit of progressivism to the realism they had inherited from Howells and the naturalists, tended to adopt an optimistic tone. The poet Ezra Pound, for example, at this time talked grandly of an American renaissance and fashioned a new kind of poetry called imagism, which, while not appearing to be realistic, rejected all abstract generalizations and concentrated on concrete word pictures to convey meaning. "Little" magazines and experimental theatrical companies sprang to life by the dozen, each convinced that it would revolutionize its art. The poet Carl Sandburg, the best-known representative of the Chicago school, denounced the local plutocrats but sang the praises of the city they had made: "Hog Butcher for the World," "City of the Big Shoulders."

Most writers eagerly adopted Freudian psychology without understanding it. Freud's teachings seemed only to mean that they should cast off the restrictions of Victorian prudery; they ignored his essentially dark view of human nature. Theirs was an "innocent rebellion," exuberant and rather muddleheaded.

Rural Socialism Socialist strength extended far beyond the cities. Socialists in rural areas called for tenants to be allowed to work on state-owned plots of land. In 1912, Socialist candidates received nearly half the vote in southern Oklahoma.

EMMA GOLDMAN

In January 1886 a sixteen-year-old Jewish girl named Emma Goldman arrived in New York City from St. Petersburg, Russia, where her parents ran a grocery store. As soon as immigration officials had approved her entry into the United States, she hurried on to Rochester, New York, where her half-sister lived. Like most immigrants she expected the United States to be a kind of paradise on earth.

After moving in with her half-sister's family, Emma got a job in a factory sewing coats and earning $2.50 a week. She paid her sister $1.50 a week for room and board and spent sixty cents a week to get to her job. But when she asked her employer for more money he told her to "look for work elsewhere. " She found a job at another factory that paid $4 a week.

In 1887 she married Jacob Kirshner, another Russian immigrant, but they soon divorced. In 1889 she took up with a group of radicals, most of them either socialists or anarchists. By this time Goldman was herself an ardent anarchist, convinced by her experiences that *all* governments repressed individual freedom and should be abolished.

In New York Emma fell in love with another Russian-born radical, Alexander Berkman. They started a kind of commune. Emma worked at home sewing shirts. Alexander found a job making cigars. They never married.

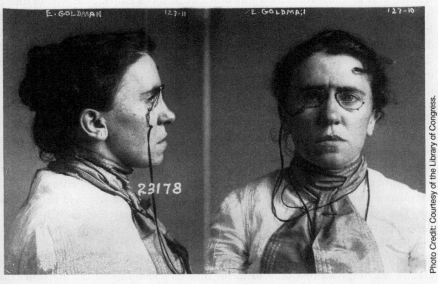

Photo Credit: Courtesy of the Library of Congress.

A "mug shot" of Emma Goldman, 1901. She was arrested so often that she took to carrying a book with her everywhere so that she would have something to read in jail if she were arrested.

The couple moved to New Haven, where Emma started a cooperative dressmaking shop. Then they moved to Springfield, Massachusetts, where, with Berkman's cousin, an artist, they opened a photography studio. When this business failed, they opened an ice cream parlor.

Nearly all immigrants of that period retained their faith in the promise of American life even after they discovered that the streets were not paved with gold. But Emma was so disappointed that she became a radical.

In 1892 when she and Berkman learned of the bloody battle between Pinkertons and strikers during the Homestead steel strike, they closed the ice cream parlor and plotted to assassinate Henry Clay Frick, the archvillain of the Homestead drama. Berkman went to Pittsburgh, where, posing as a representative of an agency that provided strikebreakers, he got into Frick's office. Pulling a pistol, Berkman aimed for Frick's head but the shot went wide and hit Frick in the shoulder. Berkman then stabbed Frick, but still the Homestead boss survived. Convicted of the attempt on Frick's life, Berkman was imprisoned for fourteen years.

The next year Goldman was herself arrested and sentenced to a year in jail for making an "incendiary" speech urging unemployed workers to distrust politicians. Upon her release, Goldman went to Vienna, where she trained as a nurse. When she returned to America, she worked as a midwife among the New York poor, an experience that made her an outspoken advocate of birth control. She also helped organize a theatrical group, managed a touring group of Russian actors, and lectured on theatrical topics. In 1901, Goldman was arrested on charges of inspiring Leon Czolgosz to assassinate President McKinley. Czolgosz had attended one of Goldman's lectures, but there was no direct connection between the two, and the charges against her were dropped.

In 1906 Goldman founded *Mother Earth*, an anarchist journal. When Alexander Berkman was released from prison later that year, she made him its editor. *Mother Earth* denounced governments, organized religion, and private property. By this time Goldman had become a celebrity. "She was considered a monster, an exponent of free love and bombs," recalled Margaret Anderson, editor of a literary magazine.

Now Goldman campaigned for freedom of speech and lectured in support of birth control. In 1915, after Margaret Sanger was arrested for disseminating information on birth control, Goldman did the same in public speeches. She was arrested and spent two weeks in jail.

Goldman regarded the Great War—and especially American entry in it—as a calamity beyond measure. In 1917 Goldman and Berkman were convicted of conspiring to persuade men not to register for the draft. They served two years in federal prison. In 1919 they were deported to Russia. Two years later, disillusioned with the Bolsheviks, Goldman left the Soviet Union.

"Red Emma" Goldman was not a typical American, but she was in many ways a typical American immigrant. She learned English and quickly became familiar with American ways. She worked hard and developed valuable skills. Gradually she moved up the economic ladder. And while she was critical of the United States, she was a typical immigrant also in insisting that she was an American patriot. "The kind of patriotism we represent," she said during her trial in 1917, "is the kind of patriotism which loves America with open eyes."

Questions for Discussion

- Why did most immigrants, on learning of the gap between the promise of America and its reality, not become radicals?
- Was Goldman a radical by birth or by acculturation?

Political Reform: Cities First

To most "ordinary" progressives, political corruption and inefficiency lay at the root of the evils plaguing American society, nowhere more obvious than in the nation's cities. Urban life's anonymity and complexity help explain why slavery did not flourish in cities, but also why the previously named vices did flourish. As the cities grew, their antiquated and boss-ridden administrations became more and more disgraceful.

City reformers could seldom destroy the machines without changing urban political institutions. Some cities obtained "home rule" charters that gave them greater freedom from state control in dealing with local matters. Many created research bureaus that investigated government problems in a scientific and nonpartisan manner. A number of middle-sized communities (Galveston, Texas, was the prototype) experimented with a system that integrated executive and legislative powers in the hands of a small elected commission, thereby concentrating responsibility and making it easier to coordinate complex activities. Out of this experiment came the city manager system, under which the commissioners appointed a professional manager to administer city affairs on a non-partisan basis. Dayton, Ohio, which adopted the plan after a flood devastated the town in 1913, offers the best illustration of the city manager system in the Progressive Era.

Once the political system had been made responsive to the desires of the people, the progressives hoped to use it to improve society itself. Many cities experimented with "gas and water socialism," taking over public utility companies and operating them as departments of the municipal government. Under "Golden Rule" Jones, Toledo established a minimum wage for city employees, built playgrounds and golf courses, and moderated its harsh penal code. Mayor Seth Low improved New York's public transportation system and obtained passage of the tenement house law of 1901. Mayor Tom Johnson forced a fare cut to three cents on the Cleveland street railways.

Political Reform: The States

To carry out this kind of change required the support of state legislatures since all municipal government depends on the authority of a sovereign state. Such approval was often difficult to obtain—local bosses were usually entrenched in powerful state machines, and rural majorities insensitive to urban needs controlled most legislatures. Therefore the progressives had to strike at inefficiency and corruption at the state level too.

During the first decade of the new century, Robert M. La Follette, one of the most remarkable figures of the age, transformed Wisconsin. He had served three terms as a Republican congressman (1885–1891) and developed a reputation as an uncompromising foe of corruption before being elected governor in 1900. That the people would always do the right thing if properly informed and inspired was the fundamental article of his political faith. "Machine control is based upon misrepresentation and ignorance," La Follette said. "Democracy is based upon knowledge."

Despite the opposition of railroad and lumbering interests, Governor La Follette obtained a direct primary system for nominating candidates, a corrupt practices act, and laws limiting campaign expenditures and lobbying activities. In power he became something of a boss himself. He made ruthless use of patronage, demanded absolute loyalty of his subordinates, and often stretched, or at least oversimplified, the truth when presenting complex issues to the voters.

La Follette was a consummate showman who never rose entirely above rural prejudices. He was prone to see a nefarious "conspiracy" organized by "the interests" behind even the mildest opposition to his proposals. But he was devoted to the cause of honest government. Realizing that some state functions called for specialized technical knowledge, he used commissions and agencies to handle such matters as railroad regulation, tax assessment, conservation, and highway construction. Wisconsin established a legislative reference library to assist lawmakers in drafting bills. For work of this kind, La Follette called on the faculty of the University of Wisconsin, enticing top-notch economists and political scientists into the public service and drawing freely on the advice of such outstanding social scientists as Richard T. Ely, John R. Commons, and E. A. Ross.

The success of these policies, which became known as the Wisconsin Idea, led other states to adopt similar programs. Reform administrations swept into office in Iowa and Arkansas (1901); Oregon (1902); Minnesota, Kansas, and Mississippi (1904); New York and Georgia (1906); Nebraska (1909); and New Jersey and Colorado (1910). In some cases the reformers were Republicans, in others Democrats, but in all the example of Wisconsin was influential. By 1910, fifteen states had established legislative reference services, most of them staffed by personnel trained in Wisconsin. The direct primary system, in which candidates were selected by voters rather than party bosses, became almost universal.

Some states went beyond Wisconsin in striving to make their governments responsive to the popular will. In 1902 Oregon began to experiment with the initiative, a system by which a bill could be forced on the attention of the legislature by popular petition, and the referendum, a method for allowing the electorate to approve measures rejected by their representatives and to repeal measures that the legislature had passed. Eleven states, most of them in the West, legalized these devices by 1914.

State Social Legislation

The first state laws aimed at social problems long preceded the Progressive Era, but most were either so imprecise as to be unenforceable or, like the Georgia law "limiting" textile workers to eleven hours a day, so weak as to be ineffective. In 1874 Massachusetts restricted the working hours of women and children to ten per day, and by the 1890s many other states, mostly in the East and Midwest, had followed suit. Illinois passed an eight-hour law for women workers in 1893.

As part of this trend, some states established special rules for workers in hazardous industries. In the 1890s several states limited the hours of railroad workers on the grounds that fatigue sometimes caused railroad accidents. Utah restricted miners to eight hours in 1896. In 1901 New York finally enacted an effective tenement house law, greatly increasing the area of open space on building lots and requiring toilets for each apartment, better ventilation systems, and more adequate fireproofing.

Before 1900 the collective impact of such legislation was not impressive. Powerful manufacturers and landlords often succeeded in defeating the bills or rendering them innocuous. The federal system further complicated the task of obtaining effective legislation.

The Fourteenth Amendment to the Constitution, although enacted to protect the civil rights of blacks, imposed a revolutionary restriction on the states by forbidding them to "deprive any person of life, liberty, or property without due process of law." Since much state social legislation represented new uses of coercive power that conservative judges considered dangerous and unwise, the Fourteenth Amendment gave such judges

On March 25, 1911, as scores of young factory girls leaped to their deaths from the eighth, ninth, and tenth stories of the Triangle Shirtwaist Factory in New York City, eighteen-year-old Victor Gatto watched in horror. Thirty-three years later he painted this rendering of his nightmare, the bodies of the dead girls placed in order at the base of the building. Source: Victor Joseph Gatto (1893–1965), *Triangle Fire: March 25, 1911*. c. 1944 (depicting 1911), oil on canvas, 19 × 28", Gift of Mrs. Henry L. Moses, 54.75. The Museum of the City of New York.

an excuse to overturn the laws that deprived employers of the "liberty" to choose how long their employees should work or the conditions of the workplace.

As stricter and more far-reaching laws were enacted, many judges, fearing a trend toward socialism and regimentation, adopted an increasingly narrow interpretation of state authority to regulate business. In 1905 the U.S. Supreme Court declared in the case of *Lochner v. New York* that a New York ten-hour act for bakers deprived the bakers of the liberty of working as long as they wished and thus violated the Fourteenth Amendment. Justice Oliver Wendell Holmes, Jr., wrote a famous dissenting opinion in this case. If the people of New York believed that the public health was endangered by bakers working long hours, he reasoned, it was not the Court's job to overrule them.

Nevertheless, the progressives continued to battle for legislation to use state power against business. Women played a particularly important part in these struggles.

Little Spinner in Globe Cotton Mill at **myhistorylab.com**

Sparked by the National Child Labor Committee, organized in 1904, reformers over the next ten years obtained laws in nearly every state banning the employment of young children and limiting the hours of older ones. Many of these laws were poorly enforced, yet when Congress passed a federal child labor law in 1916, the Supreme Court, in *Hammer v. Dagenhart* (1918), declared it unconstitutional.[1]

---

[1]A second child labor law, passed in 1919, was also thrown out by the Court, and a child labor amendment, submitted in 1924, failed to achieve ratification by the necessary three-quarters of the states.

By 1917 nearly all the states had placed limitations on the hours of women industrial workers, and about ten had set minimum wage standards for women. But once again federal action that would have extended such regulation to the entire country did not materialize. A minimum wage law for women in the District of Columbia was overturned by the Court in *Adkins v. Children's Hospital* (1923).

The passage of so much state social legislation sent conservatives scurrying to the Supreme Court for redress. Such persons believed that no government had the power to deprive either workers or employers of the right to negotiate any kind of labor contract they wished. The decision of the Supreme Court in *Lochner v. New York* seemed to indicate that the justices would adopt this point of view. When an Oregon law limiting women laundry workers to ten hours a day was challenged in *Muller v. Oregon* (1908), Florence Kelley and Josephine Goldmark of the Consumers' League persuaded Louis D. Brandeis to defend the statute before the Court.

The Consumers' League, whose slogan was "investigate, agitate, legislate," was probably the most effective of the many women's reform organizations of the period. With the aid of league researchers, Brandeis prepared a remarkable brief stuffed with economic and sociological evidence indicating that long hours damaged both the health of individual women and the health of society. This nonlegal evidence greatly impressed the justices, who upheld the constitutionality of the Oregon law.

Political Reform: The Woman Suffrage Movement

On the national level the Progressive Era saw the culmination of the struggle for **woman suffrage**. The shock occasioned by the failure of the Fourteenth and Fifteenth Amendments to give women the vote after the Civil War continued to embitter most-leaders of the movement. But it resulted in a split among feminists. One group, the American Woman Suffrage Association (AWSA), focused on the vote question alone. The more radical National Woman Suffrage Association (NWSA), led by Elizabeth Cady Stanton and Susan B. Anthony, concerned itself with many issues of importance to women as well as suffrage. The NWSA put the immediate interests of women ahead of everything else. It was deeply involved in efforts to unionize women workers, yet it did not hesitate to urge women to be strikebreakers if they could get better jobs by doing so.

See the **Map**

Woman Suffrage Before the 19th Century at **myhistorylab.com**

Aside from their lack of unity, feminists were handicapped in the late nineteenth century by widely held Victorian ideals: Sex was a taboo topic, and women were to be "pure" guardians of home and family. Even under the best of circumstances, dislike of male-dominated society is hard enough to separate from dislike of men. Most feminists, for example, opposed contraception, insisting that birth control by any means other than continence would encourage what they called masculine lust.

These ideas and prejudices enticed feminists into a logical trap. If women were morally superior to men—a tempting conclusion—giving women the vote would improve the character of the electorate. Society would benefit because politics would become less corrupt, war a thing of the past. "City housekeeping has failed," said

Another argument in support of woman suffrage claimed that women were intrinsically *better* than men. Note that this woman in the turn-of-the-century poster, crowned by a halo, has her clothes arranged in the shape of a cross.

Jane Addams of Hull House in arguing for the reform of municipal government, "partly because women, the traditional housekeepers, have not been consulted."

By the early twentieth century there were signs of progress. In 1890 the two major women's groups combined as the **National American Woman Suffrage Association (NAWSA).** Stanton and Anthony were the first two presidents of the association, but new leaders were emerging, the most notable being Carrie Chapman Catt, a woman who combined superb organizing abilities and political skills with commitment to broad social reform. The NAWSA made winning the right to vote its main objective and concentrated on a state-by-state approach. Wyoming gave women the vote in 1869, and Utah, Colorado, and Idaho had been won over to woman suffrage by 1896.

The burgeoning of the progressive movement helped as middle-class recruits of both sexes adopted the suffrage cause. The 1911 referendum in California was crucial. Fifteen years earlier, California voters had rejected the measure. But in 1911, despite determined opposition from saloonkeepers, the proposal barely passed. Within three years, most other Western states fell into line. For the first time, large numbers of working-class women began to agitate for the vote. In 1917, bosses at New York City's Tammany Hall, who had engineered the defeat of woman suffrage in that state two years earlier, concluded that passage was inevitable and threw their support to the measure, which passed. The suffragists then shifted the campaign back to the national level, the lead taken by a new organization, the Congressional Union, headed by Alice Paul and the wealthy reformer Alva Belmont. When President Wilson refused to support the idea of a constitutional amendment granting women the vote, militant women picketed the White House. A number of them were arrested and sentenced to sixty days in the workhouse. This roused a storm of criticism, and Wilson quickly pardoned the picketers. After some hesitation the NAWSA stopped concentrating on the state-by-state approach and began to campaign for a constitutional amendment. Pressure on Congress mounted steadily. The amendment finally won congressional approval in 1919. By 1920 the necessary three-quarters of the states had ratified the Nineteenth Amendment; the long fight was over.

Woman Suffrage, 1896–1914

States that adopted full
woman suffrage, 1869–1896

States that adopted full
woman suffrage, 1910–1914

States that had not adopted
full woman suffrage by 1914

Woman Suffrage Resolution
May 21, 1919, House
of Representatives

Yes
No
Not voting
Unsettled

Boston
New York City
Philidelphia
Baltimore
Detroit

The Advance of Woman Suffrage In 1869 Wyoming, still a territory, voted to give women the vote. The next year, after Mormon leader Brigham Young endorsed woman suffrage, Utah followed. Then came Colorado (1893) and Idaho (1896), frontier states that sought to attract women settlers. In 1911, by a margin of 3,587 votes, California endorsed woman suffrage, and within three years the remainder of the western states had done so, too. World War I stimulated support for the Woman Suffrage (Nineteenth) Amendment. The May 21, 1919, vote in the House of Representatives shows that most of the opposing votes came from southern congressmen who believed that woman suffrage would be the first step toward securing the vote for blacks.

Theodore Roosevelt: Cowboy in the White House

On September 6, 1901, an anarchist named Leon Czolgosz shot President McKinley during a public reception at the Pan-American Exposition at Buffalo, New York. Eight days later McKinley died and Theodore Roosevelt became president of the United States. His ascension to the presidency marked the beginning of a new era in national politics.

Although only forty-two, by far the youngest president in the nation's history up to that time, Roosevelt brought solid qualifications to the office. Son of a well-to-do New York merchant, he had graduated from Harvard in 1880 and studied law briefly at Columbia, though he did not obtain a degree. In addition to political experience that included three terms in the New York assembly, six years on the U.S. Civil Service Commission, two years as police commissioner of New York City, another as assistant secretary of the navy, and a term as governor of New York, he had been a rancher in the Dakota Territory and a soldier in the Spanish-American War. Politically, he had always been a loyal Republican. He rejected the mugwump heresy in 1884, and during the tempestuous 1890s he vigorously denounced populism, Bryanism, and "labor agitators."

Nevertheless, Roosevelt's elevation to the presidency alarmed many conservatives, and not without reason. He did not fit their conception, based on a composite image of the chief executives from Hayes to McKinley, of a president. He seemed too undignified, too energetic, too outspoken, too unconventional. It was one thing to have operated a cattle ranch, another to have captured a gang of rustlers at gunpoint; one thing to have run a metropolitan police force, another to have roamed New York slums in the small hours to catch patrolmen fraternizing with thieves and prostitutes; and one thing to have commanded a regiment, another to have killed a Spaniard personally.

Roosevelt worshiped aggressiveness and was extremely sensitive to any threat to his honor as a gentleman. When another young man showed some slight interest in Roosevelt's fiancée, he sent for a set of French dueling pistols. His teachers found him an interesting student, for he was intelligent and imaginative, if annoyingly argumentative.

Few individuals have rationalized or sublimated their feelings of inferiority as effectively as Roosevelt and to such good purpose. And few have been more genuinely warmhearted, more full of spontaneity, more committed to the ideals of public service and national greatness. As a political leader he was energetic and hard-driving. Conservatives and timid souls, sensing his aggressiveness even

Theodore Roosevelt addressing a crowd in Evanston, Illinois, in the early 1900s.

Photo Credit: Getty Images.

when he held it in check, distrusted Roosevelt's judgment. In fact his judgment was nearly always sound; responsibility usually tempered his aggressiveness.

When Roosevelt was first mentioned as a running mate for McKinley in 1900, he wrote, "The Vice Presidency is a most honorable office, but for a young man there is not much to do." As president it would have been unthinkable for him to preside over a caretaker administration devoted to maintaining the status quo. However, the reigning Republican politicos, basking in the sunshine of the prosperity that had contributed so much to their victory in 1900, distrusted anything suggestive of change.

Had Roosevelt been the impetuous hothead that conservatives feared, he would have plunged ahead without regard for their feelings and influence. Instead he moved slowly and often got what he wanted by using his executive power rather than by persuading Congress to pass new laws. His domestic program included some measure of control of big corporations, more power for the Interstate Commerce Commission (ICC), and the conservation of natural resources. By consulting congressional leaders and following their advice not to bring up controversial matters like the tariff and currency reform, he obtained a modest budget of new laws.

The Newlands Act (1902) funneled the proceeds from land sales in the West into federal irrigation projects. The Department of Commerce and Labor, which was to include a Bureau of Corporations with authority to investigate industrial combines and issue reports, was established. The Elkins Railroad Act of 1903 strengthened the ICC's hand against the railroads by making the receiving as well as the granting of rebates illegal and by forbidding the roads to deviate in any way from their published rates.

Roosevelt and Big Business

Roosevelt soon became known as a trustbuster, and in the sense that he considered the monopoly problem the most pressing issue of the times, this was accurate to an extent. But he did not believe in breaking up big corporations indiscriminately. Regulation seemed the best way to deal with large corporations because, he said, industrial giantism "could not be eliminated unless we were willing to turn back the wheels of modern progress."

With Congress unwilling to pass a stiff regulatory law, Roosevelt resorted to the Sherman Act to get at the problem. Although the Supreme Court decision in the Sugar Trust case (*E.C. Knight* [1895]) seemed to have emasculated that law, in 1902 he ordered the Justice Department to bring suit against the Northern Securities Company.

He chose his target wisely. The Northern Securities Company controlled the Great Northern, the Northern Pacific, the Chicago, the Burlington, and the Quincy railroads. It had been created in 1901 after a titanic battle on the New York Stock Exchange between the forces of J. P. Morgan and James J. Hill and those of E. H. Harriman, who was associated with the Rockefeller interests. In their efforts to obtain control of the Northern Pacific, the rivals had forced its stock up to $1,000 a share, ruining many speculators and threatening to cause a panic.

Neither side could win a clear-cut victory, so they decided to put the stock of all three railroads in a holding company owned by the two groups. Since Harriman already controlled the Union Pacific and the Southern Pacific, the plan resulted in a virtual monopoly of western railroads. The public had been alarmed, for the merger seemed to typify the rapaciousness of the tycoons.

The announcement of the suit caused consternation in the business world. Morgan rushed to the White House. "If we have done anything wrong," he said to the president, "send your man to my man and they can fix it up." Roosevelt was not fundamentally opposed to this sort of agreement, but it was too late to compromise in this instance. Attorney General Philander C. Knox pressed the case vigorously, and in 1904 the Supreme Court ordered the dissolution of the Northern Securities Company.

Roosevelt then ordered suits against the meat packers, the Standard Oil Trust, and the American Tobacco Company. His stock among progressives rose, yet he had not embarrassed the conservatives in Congress by demanding new antitrust legislation.

The president went out of his way to assure cooperative corporation magnates that he was not against size per se. At a White House conference in 1905, Roosevelt and Elbert H. Gary, chairman of the board of U.S. Steel, reached a "gentlemen's agreement" whereby Gary promised "to cooperate with the Government in every possible way." The Bureau of Corporations would conduct an investigation of U.S. Steel, Gary allowing it full access to company records. Roosevelt in turn promised that if the investigation revealed any corporate malpractices, he would allow Gary to set matters right voluntarily, thereby avoiding an antitrust suit. He reached a similar agreement with the International Harvester Company two years later.

There were limits to the effectiveness of such arrangements. Standard Oil agreed to a similar détente and then reneged, refusing to turn over vital records to the bureau. The Justice Department brought suit against the company under the Sherman Act, and eventually the company was broken up at the order of the Supreme Court. Roosevelt would have preferred a more binding kind of regulation, but when he asked for laws giving the government supervisory authority over big combinations, Congress refused to act.

Roosevelt and the Coal Strike

Roosevelt made remarkable use of his executive power during the anthracite coal strike of 1902. In June the United Mine Workers (UMW), led by John Mitchell, laid down their picks and demanded higher wages, an eight-hour day, and recognition of the union. Most of the anthracite mines were owned by railroads. Two years earlier the miners had won a 10 percent wage increase in a similar strike, chiefly because the owners feared that labor unrest might endanger the election of McKinley. Now the coal companies were dead set against further concessions; when the men walked out, they shut down the mines and prepared to starve the strikers into submission.

The strike dragged on through summer and early fall. The miners conducted themselves with great restraint, avoiding violence and offering to submit their claims to arbitration. As the price of anthracite soared with the approach of winter, sentiment in their behalf mounted.

Roosevelt shared the public's sympathy for the miners, and the threat of a coal shortage alarmed him. Early in October he summoned both sides to a conference in Washington and urged them as patriotic Americans to sacrifice any "personal consideration" for the "general good." His action enraged the coal owners, for they believed he was trying to force them to recognize the union. They refused even to speak to the UMW representatives at the conference and demanded that Roosevelt end the strike by force and bring suit against the union under the Sherman Act. Mitchell, aware of the immense prestige that Roosevelt had conferred on the union by calling the conference, cooperated fully with the president.

Table 1 Major Supreme Court Rulings during the Progressive Era

Northern Securities Case	1904	Upheld antitrust ruling against railroad conglomerate
Lochner v. New York	1905	Overturned (progressive) New York law restricting the hours bakers could work; invoked the Fourteenth Amendment to protect bakers' "right" to work as long as they wished
Muller v. Oregon	1908	Affirmed the right of Oregon to limit the hours worked by women in laundries

The attitudes of management and of the union further strengthened public support for the miners. Even former president Grover Cleveland, who had used federal troops to break the Pullman strike, said that he was "disturbed and vexed by the tone and substance of the operators' deliverances." Encouraged by this state of affairs, Roosevelt took a bold step: He announced that unless a settlement was reached promptly, he would order federal troops into the anthracite regions, not to break the strike but to seize and operate the mines.

The threat of government intervention brought the owners to terms. A Cabinet member, Elihu Root, worked out the details with J. P. Morgan, whose firm had major interests in the Reading and other railroads. The miners would return to the pits and all issues between them and the coal companies would be submitted for settlement to a commission appointed by Roosevelt. Both sides accepted the arrangement, and the men went back to work. In March 1903 the commission granted the miners a 10 percent wage increase and a nine-hour workday.

To the public the incident seemed a perfect illustration of the progressive spirit—in Roosevelt's words, everyone had received a **Square Deal**. In fact the results were by no means so clear-cut. The miners gained relatively little and the companies lost still less. The president was the main winner. The public acclaimed him as a fearless, imaginative, public-spirited leader. Without calling on Congress for support, he had expanded his own authority and hence that of the federal government. His action marked a major forward step in the evolution of the modern presidency.

TR's Triumphs

By reviving the Sherman Act, settling the coal strike, and pushing moderate reforms through Congress, Roosevelt ensured that he would be reelected president in 1904. Despite his resentment at Roosevelt's attack on the Northern Securities Company, J. P. Morgan contributed $150,000 to the Republican campaign. Other tycoons gave with equal generosity. Roosevelt swept the country, carrying even the normally Democratic border states of Maryland and Missouri.

Encouraged by the landslide and the increasing militancy of progressives, Roosevelt pressed for more reform legislation. His most imaginative proposal was a plan to make the District of Columbia a model progressive community. He suggested child labor and factory inspection laws and a slum clearance program, but Congress refused to act. Likewise, his request for a minimum wage for railroad workers was rejected.

Early in the twentieth century, when malnutrition was common, companies such as this one advertised that its pills could make people fatter. The Pure Food and Drug Act of 1906 fined manufacturers who made false claims for their products. A century later, in 2010, the *Seattle Post Intelligencer*, under the headline "Too Fat to Fight," reported that over a fourth of eighteen to twenty-four-year-old potential army recruits were rejected as unfit.

GET FAT ON LORINGS FAT-TEN-U AND CORPULA FOODS.

With progressive state governors demanding federal action and farmers and manufacturers, especially in the Midwest, clamoring for relief against discriminatory rates, Roosevelt was ready by 1905 to make railroad legislation his major objective. The ICC should be empowered to fix rates, not merely to challenge unreasonable ones. It should have the right to inspect the private records of the railroads since fair rates could not be determined unless the true financial condition of the roads were known.

Because these proposals struck at rights that businessmen considered sacrosanct, many congressmen balked. But Roosevelt applied presidential pressure, and in June 1906 the Hepburn bill became law. It gave the commission the power to inspect the books of railroad companies, to set maximum rates (once a complaint had been filed by a shipper), and to control sleeping car companies, owners of oil pipelines, and other firms engaged in transportation. Railroads could no longer issue passes freely—an important check on their political influence. In all, the **Hepburn Act** made the ICC a more powerful and more active body. Congress also passed meat inspection and pure food and drug legislation. In 1906 Upton Sinclair published *The Jungle*, a devastating exposé of the filthy conditions in the Chicago slaughterhouses. Sinclair was more interested in writing a socialist tract than he was in meat inspection, but his book, a best seller, raised a storm against the packers. After Roosevelt read *The Jungle* he sent two officials to Chicago to investigate. Their report was so shocking, he said, that its publication would "be well-nigh ruinous to our export trade in meat." He threatened to release the report unless Congress acted. After a fight, the meat inspection bill passed. The Pure Food and Drug Act, forbidding the manufacture and sale of adulterated and fraudulently labeled products, rode through Congress on the coattails of this measure.

●●●─[Read the Document

"Inside the Packinghouse" from Upton Sinclair's *The Jungle* at **myhistorylab.com**

To advanced liberals Roosevelt's achievements seemed limited when placed beside his professed objectives and his smug evaluations of what he had done. How could he be a reformer and a defender of established interests at the same time? Roosevelt found no difficulty in holding such a position. As one historian has said, "He stood close to the center and bared his teeth at the conservatives of the right and the liberals of the extreme left."

Roosevelt Tilts Left

As the progressive movement advanced, Roosevelt advanced with it. He never accepted all the ideas of what he called its "lunatic fringe," but he took steadily more liberal positions. He always insisted that he was not hostile to business interests, but when those interests sought to exploit the national domain, they had no more implacable foe. **Conservation** of natural resources was dear to his heart and probably his most significant achievement as president. He placed some 150 million acres of forest lands in federal reserves, and he strictly enforced the laws governing grazing, mining, and lumbering.

As Roosevelt became more liberal, conservative Republicans began to balk at following his lead. The sudden panic that struck the financial world in October 1907 speeded the trend. Government policies had no direct bearing on the panic, which began with a run on several important New York trust companies and spread to the Stock Exchange when speculators found themselves unable to borrow money to meet their obligations. In the emergency Roosevelt authorized the deposit of large amounts of government cash in New York banks. He informally agreed to the acquisition of the Tennessee Coal and Iron Company by U.S. Steel when the bankers told him that the purchase was necessary to end the panic. In spite of his efforts, conservatives insisted on referring to the financial collapse as "Roosevelt's panic," and they blamed the president for the depression that followed on its heels.

Roosevelt, however, turned left rather than right. In 1908 he came out in favor of federal income and inheritance taxes, stricter regulation of interstate corporations, and reforms designed to help industrial workers. He denounced "the speculative folly and the flagrant dishonesty" of "malefactors of great wealth," further alienating conservative, or Old Guard, Republicans. When the president began criticizing the courts, the last bastion of conservatism, he lost all chance of obtaining further reform legislation. As he said himself, during his last months in office "stagnation continued to rage with uninterrupted violence."

William Howard Taft: The Listless Progressive, or More Is Less

But Roosevelt remained popular and politically powerful; before his term ended, he chose William Howard Taft, his secretary of war, to succeed him and easily obtained Taft's nomination. William Jennings Bryan was again the Democratic candidate. Campaigning on Roosevelt's record, Taft carried the country by well over a million votes, defeating Bryan 321 to 162 in the Electoral College.

Taft was intelligent, experienced, and public spirited; he seemed ideally suited to carry out Roosevelt's policies. Born in Cincinnati in 1857, educated at Yale, he had served as an Ohio judge, as solicitor general of the United States under Benjamin Harrison, and

"GOODNESS GRACIOUS! I MUST HAVE BEEN DOZING!"

A hapless Taft is entangled in governmental yarn, while a disapproving Roosevelt looks on. "Goodness gracious! I must have been dozing," reads the caption, a reference to Taft's penchant for naps.

then as a federal circuit court judge before accepting McKinley's assignment to head the Philippine Commission in 1900. His success as civil governor of the Philippines led Roosevelt to make him secretary of war in 1904.

Taft supported the Square Deal loyally. This, together with his mentor's ardent endorsement, won him the backing of most progressive Republicans. Yet the Old Guard liked him too; although outgoing, he had none of the Roosevelt impetuosity and aggressiveness. His genial personality and his obvious desire to avoid conflict appealed to moderates.

However, Taft lacked the physical and mental stamina required of a modern chief executive. Although not lazy, he weighed over 300 pounds and needed to rest this vast bulk more than the job allowed. Campaigning bored him; speech making seemed a useless chore. The judicial life was his real love; intense partisanship dismayed and confused him. He was too reasonable to control a coalition and not ambitious enough to impose his will on others. He supported many progressive measures, but he never absorbed the progressive spirit.

Taft honestly wanted to carry out most of Roosevelt's policies. He enforced the Sherman Act vigorously and continued to expand the national forest reserves. He signed the Mann-Elkins Act of 1910, which empowered the ICC to suspend rate increases without waiting for a shipper to complain and established the Commerce Court to speed the settlement of railroad rate cases. An eight-hour day for all persons engaged in work on government contracts, mine safety legislation, and several other reform measures received his approval. He even summoned Congress into special session specifically to reduce tariff duties—something that Roosevelt had not dared to attempt.

But Taft had been disturbed by Roosevelt's sweeping use of executive power. "We have got to work out our problems on the basis of law," he insisted. Whereas Roosevelt had excelled at maneuvering around congressional opposition and at finding ways to accomplish his objectives without waiting for Congress to act, Taft adamantly refused to use such tactics. His restraint was in many ways admirable, but it reduced his effectiveness.

In 1910 Taft got into difficulty with the conservationists. Although he believed in husbanding natural resources carefully, he did not like the way Roosevelt had circumvented Congress in adding to the forest reserves. He demanded, and eventually obtained, specific legislation to accomplish this purpose. The issue that aroused the conservationists concerned the integrity of his secretary of the interior, Richard A. Ballinger. A less than ardent conservationist, Ballinger returned to the public domain certain waterpower sites that the Roosevelt administration had withdrawn on the legally questionable ground that they were to become ranger stations. Ballinger's action alarmed Chief Forester Gifford Pinchot, the darling of the conservationists. When Pinchot learned that Ballinger intended to validate the shaky claim of mining interests to a large tract of coal-rich land in Alaska, he launched an intemperate attack on the secretary.

In the Ballinger-Pinchot controversy Taft felt obliged to support his own man. The coal lands dispute was complex, and Pinchot's charges were exaggerated. It was certainly unfair to call Ballinger "the most effective opponent the conservation policies have yet had." When Pinchot, whose own motives were partly political, persisted in criticizing Ballinger, Taft dismissed him. He had no choice under the circumstances, but a more adept politician might have found some way of avoiding a showdown.

Breakup of the Republican Party

One ominous aspect of the Ballinger-Pinchot affair was that Pinchot was a close friend of Theodore Roosevelt. After Taft's inauguration, Roosevelt had gone off to hunt big game in Africa, bearing in his baggage an autographed photograph of his protégé and a touching letter of appreciation, in which the new president said, "I can never forget that the power I now exercise was a voluntary transfer from you to me." As soon as he emerged from the wilderness in March 1910, bearing more than 3,000 trophies, including nine lions, five elephants, and thirteen rhinos, he was caught up in the squabble between the progressive members of his party and its titular head. Pinchot met him in Italy, laden with injured innocence and a packet of angry letters from various progressives. TR's intimate friend Senator Henry Cabot Lodge, essentially a conservative, barraged him with messages, the gist of which was that Taft was lazy and inept and that Roosevelt should prepare to become the "Moses" who would guide the party "out of the wilderness of doubt and discontent" into which Taft had led it.

Roosevelt hoped to steer a middle course, but Pinchot's complaints impressed him. Taft had decided to strike out on his own, he concluded. Taft sensed the former president's coolness and was offended. He was egged on by his ambitious wife, who wanted him to stand clear of Roosevelt's shadow and establish his own reputation.

Perhaps the resulting rupture was inevitable. The Republican party was dividing into two factions, the progressives and the Old Guard. Forced to choose between them, Taft threw in his lot with the Old Guard. Roosevelt backed the progressives. Speaking at Osawatomie, Kansas, in August 1910 he came out for a comprehensive program of social legislation, which he called the **New Nationalism**. Besides attacking "special privilege" and the "unfair money-getting"

●●●─[Read the Document
Roosevelt, *The New Nationalism*
at **myhistorylab.com**

practices of "lawbreakers of great wealth," he called for a broad expansion of federal power. "The betterment we seek must be accomplished," he said, "mainly through the National Government."

The final break came in October 1911 when Taft ordered an antitrust suit against U.S. Steel. He was prepared to enforce the Sherman Act "or die in the attempt." But this initiative angered Roosevelt because the lawsuit focused on U.S. Steel's absorption of the Tennessee Coal and Iron Company, which Roosevelt had unofficially authorized during the panic of 1907. The government's antitrust brief made Roosevelt appear to have been either a proponent of the monopoly or, far worse, a fool who had been duped by the steel corporation. Early in 1912 he declared himself a candidate for the Republican presidential nomination.

Roosevelt plunged into the preconvention campaign with typical energy. He was almost uniformly victorious in states that held presidential primaries, carrying even Ohio, Taft's home state. However, the president controlled the party machinery and entered the national convention with a small majority of the delegates. Since some Taft delegates had been chosen under questionable circumstances, the Roosevelt forces challenged the right of 254 of them to their seats. The Taft-controlled credentials committee, paying little attention to the evidence, gave all but a few of the disputed seats to the president, who then won the nomination on the first ballot.

Roosevelt was understandably outraged by the ruthless manner in which the Taft "steamroller" had overridden his forces. When his leading supporters urged him to organize a third party, and when two of them, George W. Perkins, formerly a partner of the banker J. P. Morgan, and the publisher Frank Munsey, offered to finance the campaign, Roosevelt agreed to make the race.

In August, amid scenes of hysterical enthusiasm, the first convention of the Progressive party met at Chicago and nominated him for president. Announcing that he felt "as strong as a bull moose," Roosevelt delivered a stirring "confession of faith," calling for strict regulation of corporations, a tariff commission, national presidential primaries, minimum wage and workers' compensation laws, the elimination of child labor, and many other reforms.

Watch the Video
Bull Moose Campaign Speech
at **myhistorylab.com**

The Election of 1912

The Democrats made the most of the opportunity offered by the Republican schism. Had they nominated a conservative or allowed Bryan a fourth chance, they would probably have ensured Roosevelt's election. Instead, they nominated Woodrow Wilson, who had achieved a remarkable liberal record as governor of New Jersey.

Although as a political scientist Wilson had criticized the status quo and taken a pragmatic approach to the idea of government regulation of the economy, he had objected strongly to Bryan's brand of politics. In 1896 he voted for the Gold Democratic party candidate instead of Bryan. But by 1912, influenced partly by ambition and partly by the spirit of the times, he had been converted to progressivism. He called his brand of reform the **New Freedom**.

The federal government could best advance the cause of social justice, Wilson reasoned, by eradicating the special privileges that enabled the "interests" to flourish. Where

1912: Divided Republicans, Democratic Victory In 1912, when Theodore Roosevelt chose to run as a Progressive, he took away millions of votes from the Republican Taft. This ensured Democrat Woodrow Wilson's landslide election.

1912

▢ Democratic (Wilson)
▢ Progressive (T. Roosevelt)
▢ Republican (Taft)

Roosevelt had lost faith in competition as a way of protecting the public against monopolies, Wilson insisted that competition could be restored. The government must break up the great trusts, establish fair rules for doing business, and subject violators to stiff punishments. Thereafter, the free enterprise system would protect the public from exploitation without destroying individual initiative and opportunity.

Roosevelt's reasoning was perhaps theoretically more sound. He called for a New Nationalism. Laissez-faire made less sense than it had in earlier times. The complexities of the modern world seemed to call for a positive approach, a plan, the close application of human intelligence to social and economic problems.

But being more in line with American experience than the New Nationalism, Wilson's New Freedom had much to recommend it. The danger that selfish individuals would use the power of the state for their own ends had certainly not disappeared, despite the efforts of progressives to make government more responsive to popular opinion. Any considerable expansion of national power, as Roosevelt proposed, would increase the danger and probably create new difficulties. Managing so complicated an enterprise as an industrialized nation was sure to be a formidable task for the federal government. Furthermore, individual freedom of opportunity merited the toleration of a certain amount of inefficiency.

To choose between the New Nationalism and the New Freedom, between the dynamic Roosevelt and the idealistic Wilson, was indeed difficult. Taft got the hard-core Republican vote but lost the progressive wing of the GOP to Roosevelt. Wilson had the solid support of both conservative and liberal Democrats. As a result, Wilson won an easy victory in the Electoral College, receiving 435 votes to Roosevelt's 88 and Taft's 8. The popular vote was Wilson, 6,286,000; Roosevelt, 4,126,000; and Taft, 3,484,000.

If partisan politics had determined the winner, the election was nonetheless an overwhelming endorsement of progressivism. The temper of the times was shown by the 897,000 votes for Eugene Debs, who was again the Socialist candidate. Altogether, professed liberals amassed over 11 million of the 15 million ballots cast. Wilson was a minority president, but he took office with a clear mandate to press forward with further reforms.

Wilson: The New Freedom

No one ever rose more suddenly or spectacularly in American politics than Woodrow Wilson. In the spring of 1910 he was president of Princeton University; he had never held or even run for public office. In the fall of 1912 he was president-elect of the United States. Yet if his rise was meteoric, in a very real sense he had devoted his life to preparing for it. As a student he became interested in political theory, dreaming of representing his state in the Senate. He studied law solely because he thought it the best avenue to public office, and when he discovered that he did not like legal work, he took a doctorate at Johns Hopkins in political science.

For years Wilson's political ambitions appeared doomed to frustration. He taught at Bryn Mawr, then at Wesleyan, and finally at his alma mater, Princeton. He wrote several influential books, among them *Congressional Government* and *The State*, and achieved an outstanding reputation as a teacher and lecturer. In 1902 he was chosen president of Princeton and soon won a place among the nation's leading educators. In time Wilson's educational ideas and his overbearing manner of applying them got him in trouble with some of Princeton's alumni and trustees. Although his university career was wrecked, the controversies, in which he appeared to be championing democracy and progress in the face of reactionary opponents, brought him at last to the attention of the politicians. Then, in a great rush, came power and fame.

Wilson was an immediate success as president. Since Roosevelt's last year in office, Congress had been almost continually at war with the executive branch and with itself. Legislative achievements had been few. Now a small avalanche of important measures received the approval of the lawmakers. In October 1913 the **Underwood Tariff** brought the first significant reduction of duties since before the Civil War. To compensate for the expected loss of revenue, the act provided for a graduated tax on personal incomes.

Two months later the **Federal Reserve Act** gave the country a central banking system for the first time since Jackson destroyed the Bank of the United States. The measure divided the nation into twelve banking districts, each under the supervision of a Federal Reserve bank, a sort of bank for bankers. All national banks in each district and any state banks that wished to participate had to invest 6 percent of their capital and surplus in the reserve bank, which was empowered to exchange paper money, called Federal Reserve notes, for the commercial and agricultural paper that member banks took in as security from borrowers. The volume of currency was no longer at the mercy of the supply of gold or any other particular commodity.

The nerve center of the system was the Federal Reserve Board in Washington, which appointed a majority of the directors of the Federal Reserve banks and had some control over rediscount rates. The board provided a modicum of public control over the banks, but the effort to weaken the power of the great New York banks by decentralizing the system proved ineffective. Nevertheless, a true central banking system was created.

When inflation threatened, the reserve banks could raise the rediscount rate, discouraging borrowing and thus reducing the amount of money in circulation. In bad times it could lower the rate, making it easier to borrow and injecting new dollars into the economy. Much remained to be learned about the proper management of the money supply, but the nation finally had a flexible yet safe currency.

In 1914 Congress passed two important laws affecting corporations. One created the Federal Trade Commission (FTC) to replace Roosevelt's Bureau of Corporations. In addition to investigating corporations and publishing reports, this nonpartisan board could issue cease-and-desist orders against "unfair" trade practices brought to light through its research. The law did not define the term *unfair*, and the commission's rulings could be taken on appeal to the federal courts, but the FTC was nonetheless a powerful instrument for protecting the public against the trusts.

The second measure, the **Clayton Antitrust Act**, made certain specific business practices illegal, including price discrimination that tended to foster monopolies; "tying" agreements, which forbade retailers from handling the products of a firm's competitors; and the creation of interlocking directorates as a means of controlling competing companies. The act exempted labor unions and agricultural organizations from the antitrust laws and curtailed the use of injunctions in labor disputes. The officers of corporations could be held individually responsible if their companies violated the antitrust laws.

The Democrats controlled both houses of Congress for the first time since 1890 and were eager to make a good record, but Wilson's imaginative and aggressive use of presidential power was decisive. He called the legislators into special session in April 1913 and appeared before them to lay out his program; he was the first president to address Congress in person since John Adams. Then he followed the course of administration bills closely. Administration representatives haunted the cloakrooms and lobbies of both houses. Cooperative congressmen began to receive notes of praise and encouragement, whereas recalcitrant ones received stern demands for support, often pecked out on the president's own portable typewriter.

Wilson explained his success by saying, only half humorously, that running the government was child's play for anyone who had managed the faculty of a university. Responsible party government was his objective; he expected individual Democrats to support the decisions of the party majority, and his idealism never prevented him from awarding the spoils of office to city bosses and conservative congressmen, as long as they supported his program. Nor did his career as a political theorist make him rigid and doctrinaire. In practice the differences between his New Freedom and Roosevelt's New Nationalism tended to disappear. The FTC and the Federal Reserve system represented steps toward the kind of regulated economy that Roosevelt advocated.

Table 2   Progressive Legislation (Federal)

Newlands Act	1902	Funneled revenues from sale of public lands to irrigation projects
Elkins Act	1903	Strengthened the ICC by making it illegal for railroads to deviate from published rates, such as by granting rebates
Hepburn Act	1906	Gave ICC the power to fix rates of railroads and other corporations involved in interstate commerce (such as corporations operating oil pipelines)
Pure Food and Durg Act	1906	Prohibited the fraudulent advertising, manufacturing, and selling of impure foods and drugs
Mann-Elkins Act	1910	Empowered ICC to suspend rate increases for railroads or telephone companies
Underwood Tariff	1913	Lowered tariff rates; introduced graduated tax on personal incomes
Federal Reserve Act	1913	Established federal supervision of banking system
Sixteenth Amendment	1913	Authorized federal income tax
Clayton Antitrust Act	1914	Exempted labor unions from antitrust laws and curtailed injunctions against labor leaders
Nineteenth Amendment	1920	Established woman suffrage

There were limits to Wilson's progressivism. He objected as strenuously to laws granting special favors to farmers and workers as to those benefiting the tycoons. When a bill was introduced in 1914 making low-interest loans available to farmers, he refused to support it. He considered the provision exempting unions from the antitrust laws equally unsound. Nor would he push for a federal law prohibiting child labor; such a measure would be unconstitutional, he believed. He also refused to back the constitutional amendment giving the vote to women.

By the end of 1914 Wilson's record, on balance, was positive but distinctly limited. The president believed that the major progressive goals had been achieved; he had no plans for further reform. Many other progressives thought that a great deal more remained to be done.

The Progressives and Minority Rights

On one important issue, race relations, Wilson was distinctly reactionary. With a mere handful of exceptions, the progressives exhibited strong prejudices against nonwhite people and against certain categories of whites as well. Many were as unsympathetic to immigrants from Asia and eastern and southern Europe as any of the "conservative" opponents of immigration in the 1880s and 1890s.

American Indians were also affected by the progressives' racial attitudes. Where the sponsors of the Dawes Act (1887) had assumed that Indians were inherently capable of adopting the ways of "civilized" people, in the progressive period the tendency was to write Indians off as fundamentally inferior and to assume that they would make second-class citizens at best. Francis Leupp, Theodore Roosevelt's commissioner of Indian affairs, put it this way in a 1905 report: "If nature has set a different physical stamp upon different races of men it is fair to assume that the variation . . . is manifested in mental and moral traits as well. . . . Nothing is gained by trying to undo nature's work." A leading muckraker, Ray Stannard Baker, who was far more sympathetic to blacks than most progressives, dismissed Indians as pathetic beings, "eating, sleeping, idling, with no more thought of the future than a white man's child."

In 1902 Congress passed the Dead Indian Land Act, which made it easier for Indians to sell allotments that they had inherited, and in 1906 another law further relaxed restrictions on land sales. Efforts to improve the education of Indian children continued, but most progressives assumed that only vocational training would help them. Theodore Roosevelt knew from his experiences as a rancher in the Dakota Territory that Indians could be as energetic and capable as whites, but he considered these "exceptional." As for the rest, it would be many generations before they could be expected to "move forward" enough to become "ordinary citizens," Roosevelt believed.

To say that African Americans did not fare well at the hands of progressives would be a gross understatement. White southerners, furious at Populist efforts to unite white and black farmers, imposed increasingly repressive measures after 1896. Segregation became more rigid, white opposition to black voting more monolithic. In 1900 the body of a Mississippi black was dug up by order of the state legislature and reburied in a segregated cemetery; in Virginia in 1902 the daughter of Robert E. Lee was arrested for riding in the black section of a railroad car.

Photo Credit: Courtesy of the Library of Congress.

On May 15, 1916, after deliberating for one hour, an all-white jury in Waco, Texas, found seventeen-year-old Jesse Washington guilty of bludgeoning a white woman to death. A mob rushed him out of the courtroom, chained him to a tree, and burned him to death. The story was chronicled by Patricia Bernstein in *The First Waco Horror* (2005).

Many progressive women, still smarting from the insult to their sex entailed in the Fourteenth and Fifteenth Amendments and eager to attract southern support for their campaign for the vote, adopted racist arguments. They contrasted the supposed corruption and incompetence of black voters with their own "purity" and intelligence. Southern progressives of both sexes argued that disfranchising blacks would reduce corruption by removing from unscrupulous white politicians the temptation to purchase black votes!

The typical southern attitude toward the education of blacks was summed up in a folk proverb: "When you educate a Negro, you spoil a good field hand." In 1910 only about 8,000 black children in the entire South were attending high schools. Despite the almost total suppression of black rights, lynchings persisted; between 1900 and 1914 more than 1,100 blacks were murdered by mobs, most (but not all) in the southern states. In the rare cases in which local prosecutors brought the lynchers to trial, juries almost without exception brought in verdicts of not guilty.

●●●─┤Read the Document

"Events in Paris, Texas," from Ida B. Wells, *A Red Record* at **myhistorylab.com**

Booker T. Washington was shaken by this trend, but he could find no way to combat it. The times were passing him by. He appealed to his white southern "friends" for help but got nowhere. Increasingly he talked about the virtues of rural life, the evils of big cities, and the uselessness of higher education for black people. By the turn of the century a number of young, well-educated blacks, most of them Northerners, were breaking away from his accommodationist leadership.

Black Militancy

William E. B. Du Bois was the most prominent of the militants. Du Bois was born in Great Barrington, Massachusetts, in 1868. His father, a restless wanderer of Negro and French Huguenot stock, abandoned the family, and young William grew up on the edge of poverty. Neither accepted nor openly rejected by the overwhelmingly white community, he devoted himself to his studies, showing such brilliance that his future education was ensured by scholarships: to Fisk University, then to Harvard, and then to the University of Berlin. In 1895 Du Bois became the first American black to earn a PhD in history from Harvard; his dissertation, *The Suppression of the African Slave Trade* (1896), remains a standard reference.

Like Washington, Du Bois wanted blacks to lift themselves up by their own bootstraps. They must establish their own businesses, run their own newspapers and colleges, and write their own literature; they must preserve their identity rather than seek to amalgamate themselves into a society that offered them only crumbs and contempt. At first he cooperated with Washington, but in 1903, in the essay "Of Mr. Booker T. Washington and Others," he subjected Washington's "attitude of adjustment and submission" to polite but searching criticism. Washington had asked blacks to give up political power, civil rights, and the hope of higher education, not realizing that "voting is necessary to modern manhood, that . . . discrimination is barbarism, and that black boys need education as well as white boys." Washington "apologizes for injustice," Du Bois charged. "He belittles the emasculating effects of caste distinctions, and opposes the higher training and ambitions of our brightest minds." Du Bois deemed this totally wrong: "The way for a people to gain their reasonable rights is not by voluntarily throwing them away."

Du Bois was not an uncritical admirer of the ordinary American black. He believed that "immorality, crime, and laziness" were common vices. He blamed the weaknesses of blacks on the treatment afforded them by whites, but his approach to the solution of racial problems was frankly elitist. "The Negro race," he wrote, "is going to be saved by its exceptional men," what he called the "talented tenth" of the black population. Whatever his prejudices, Du Bois exposed both the weaknesses of Washington's strategy and the callousness of white American attitudes. Accommodation was not working. Washington was praised, even lionized by prominent southern whites, yet when Theodore Roosevelt invited him to a meal at the White House they exploded with indignation, and Roosevelt, although not personally prejudiced, meekly backtracked, never repeating his "mistake." He defended his record by saying, "I have stood as valiantly for the rights of the negro as any president since Lincoln." That, sad to relate, was true enough.

Not mere impatience but despair led Du Bois and a few like-minded blacks to meet at Niagara Falls in July 1905 and to issue a stirring list of demands: the unrestricted right to vote, an end to every kind of segregation, equality of economic opportunity, higher education for the talented, equal justice in the courts, and an end to trade-union discrimination. This **Niagara movement** did not attract mass support, but it did stir the consciences of some whites, many of them the descendants of abolitionists, who were also becoming disenchanted by the failure of accommodation to provide blacks with real opportunity.

> Watch the Video
>
> *The conflict between Booker T. Washington & W.E.B Du Bois* at **myhistorylab.com**

In 1909, the centennial of the birth of Abraham Lincoln, a group of these liberals, including the newspaperman Oswald Garrison Villard (grandson of William Lloyd Garrison), the social worker Jane Addams, the philosopher John Dewey, and the novelist William Dean Howells, founded the **National Association for the Advancement of Colored People (NAACP)**. The organization was dedicated to the eradication of racial discrimination. Its leadership was predominantly white in the early years, but Du Bois became a national officer and the editor of its journal, *The Crisis*.

A turning point had been reached. After 1909 virtually every important leader, white and black alike, rejected the Washington approach. More and more, blacks turned to the study of their past in an effort to stimulate pride in their heritage. In 1915 Carter G. Woodson founded the Association for the Study of Negro Life and History; the following year he began editing the *Journal of Negro History*, which became the major publishing organ for scholarly studies on the subject.

This militancy produced few results in the Progressive Era. Theodore Roosevelt behaved no differently than earlier Republican presidents; he courted blacks when he thought it advantageous, and turned his back when he did not. When he ran for president on the Progressive ticket in 1912, he pursued a "lily-white" policy, hoping to break the Democrats' monopoly in the South. By trusting in "[white] men of justice and of vision," Roosevelt argued in the face of decades of experience to the contrary, "the colored men of the South will ultimately get justice."

The southern-born Wilson was actively hostile to blacks. During the 1912 campaign he appealed to them for support and promised to "assist in advancing the interest of their race" in every possible way. Once elected, he refused even to appoint a privately financed commission to study the race problem. Southerners dominated his administration and Congress; as a result, blacks were further degraded.

These actions stirred such a storm that Wilson backtracked a little, but he never abandoned his belief that segregation was in the best interests of both races. "Wilson . . . promised a 'new freedom,'" one newspaperman complained. "On the contrary we are given a stone instead of a loaf of bread." Even Booker T. Washington admitted that his people were more "discouraged and bitter" than at any time in his memory.

Du Bois, who had supported Wilson in 1912, attacked administration policy in *The Crisis*. In November 1914 the militant editor of the *Boston Guardian*, William Monroe Trotter, a classmate of Du Bois at Harvard and a far more caustic critic of the Washington approach, led a delegation to the White House to protest the segregation policy of the government. When Wilson accused him of blackmail, Trotter lost his temper, and an ugly confrontation resulted. The mood of black leaders had changed completely.

By this time the Great War had broken out in Europe. Soon every American would feel its effects, blacks perhaps more than any other group. In November 1915, a year almost to the day after Trotter's clash with Wilson, Booker T. Washington died. One era had ended; a new one was beginning.

Many of the young Americans who had participated in the various crusades of the "age of reform" would soon embark on another crusade—but one of a very different character.

Milestones

1890	National American Woman Suffrage Association is founded	1908	*Muller v. Oregon* upholds law limiting women's work hours
1900	Robert La Follette is elected governor of Wisconsin		William Howard Taft is elected president
	McKinley is reelected president	1909	NAACP is founded
1901	McKinley is assassinated; Theodore Roosevelt becomes president	1910	Ballinger-Pinchot Affair deepens Roosevelt–Taft rift
1902	Roosevelt helps settle anthracite coal strike	1911	Roosevelt gives New Nationalism speech
	Oregon adopts initiative system for proposing legislation	1912	Roosevelt runs for president on Progressive ticket
1904	Northern Securities case revives Sherman Antitrust Act		Woodrow Wilson is elected president
	National Child Labor Committee is established	1913	Sixteenth Amendment authorizes federal income taxes
	Theodore Roosevelt is elected president		Seventeenth Amendment provides for direct election of U.S. senators
1905	Anticapitalist Industrial Workers of the World (IWW) is founded		Underwood Tariff Act reduces duties and imposes personal income tax
1906	Hepburn Act strengthens Interstate Commerce Commission		Federal Reserve Act gives the United States a central banking system again
	Upton Sinclair exposes Chicago slaughterhouses in *The Jungle*	1914	Federal Trade Commission is created to protect against trusts
1907	U.S. Steel absorbs Tennessee Coal and Iron Company		Clayton Antitrust Act regulates business
1908	Theodore Roosevelt convenes National Conservation Conference	1920	Nineteenth Amendment guarantees women the right to vote

✓•─ **Study** and **Review** at **www.myhistorylab.com**

Review Questions

1. The introduction to this chapter compares volunteers today to young reformers early in the twentieth century. What were the similarities and differences?

2. List the ideas of the various progressive-thinking leaders and their movements. What attitudes and values did they share? Were these sufficiently coherent to constitute a "Progressive movement"?

3. How did the attitudes of the reformers and political activists compare with those of the people whose lives they meant to improve? How did immigrants, Native Americans, and workers respond to Progressive reforms?

4. In what ways was the Progressive Era especially challenging for African Americans?

5. How did the relationship between business and government change during the presidencies of Roosevelt, Taft, and Wilson? Did business oppose government regulation or favor it as a means of controlling competition and weakening radicalism?

Key Terms

Ashcan School
Clayton Antitrust Act
Conservation
Federal Reserve Act
Hepburn Act
Industrial Workers of the World (IWW)

muckraker
National American Woman Suffrage Association (NAWSA)
National Association for the Advancement of Colored People (NAACP)

New Freedom
New Nationalism
Niagara movement
Progressivism
Square Deal
Underwood Tariff
woman suffrage

From Isolation to Empire

From Isolation to Empire

Can you find Afghanistan on a map?

DURING THE PRESIDENTIAL CAMPAIGN OF 2000, REPUBLICAN CANDIDATE George W. Bush chastised the Clinton administration for sending troops to Haiti and the Balkans. "If we don't stop extending our troops all around the world in nation-building missions," Bush declared, "then we're going to have a serious problem coming down the road."

Few could have imagined that within two years, following the 9/11 attacks on the World Trade Center and the Pentagon, thousands of American troops would be patrolling the high mountains of the Hindu Kush, fighting enemies at places named Tora Bora and Mazar-e Sharif, and working to install a new government in Afghanistan. A National Geographic Society survey found that nearly half of Americans aged 18 to 24 knew that the fictional island for the *Survivor* TV series was located in the South Pacific, but five in six could not find Afghanistan on a map.

Yet by the summer of 2010, President Barack Obama had increased American troops in Afghanistan to nearly 100,000. "If I thought for a minute that America's vital interests were not at stake here in Afghanistan," he told American soldiers, "I would order all of you home right away." These vital interests in many ways originated during the late nineteenth and early twentieth centuries.

Until then, Americans had given little thought to foreign affairs. In 1888 Benjamin Harrison articulated a widely held belief when he said that the United States was "an apart nation" and should remain so.

But sentiment was shifting. Intellectuals and many others cited "Darwinian" principles, such as "survival of the fittest," to justify American expansion abroad. Missionaries called on Americans to help impoverished and ill-educated peoples elsewhere in the world. American businessmen, increasingly confident of their own powers, craved access to foreign resources and markets. Such factors converged in Cuba, prompting the United States to go to war with Spain.

In 1898 tens of thousands of American troops were dispatched to Cuba and, within a year, to the Philippines. For years thereafter, Americans at home would struggle to locate on globes and in atlases battle sites in places such as Balangiga, Pulang Lupa, and Kandahar. They still do.

Isolation or Imperialism?

If Americans had little concern for what was going on far beyond the seas, their economic interest in Latin America was great and growing, and in East Asia only somewhat less so. Whether one sees isolation or expansion as the hallmark of American foreign policy after 1865 depends on what part of the world one looks at.

The disdain of the people of the United States for Europe rested on several historical foundations. Faith in the unique character of American civilization—and the converse of that belief, suspicion of Europe's supposedly aristocratic and decadent society—formed the chief basis of this **isolationism**. Bitter memories of indignities suffered during the Revolution and the Napoleonic Wars and anger at the hostile attitude of the great powers toward the United States during the Civil War strengthened it. In an era before airplanes, the United States was virtually invulnerable to European attack and at the same time incapable of mounting an offensive against any European power. In turning their backs on Europe, Americans were taking no risk and passing up few opportunities.

Origins of the Large Policy: Coveting Colonies

The nation's interests elsewhere in the world gradually increased. During the Civil War, France had established a protectorate over Mexico, installing the Archduke Maximilian of Austria as emperor. In 1866 Secretary of State William H. Seward demanded that the French withdraw, and the United States moved 50,000 soldiers to the Rio Grande. While fear of American intervention was only one of many reasons for their action, the French pulled their troops out of Mexico during the winter of 1866–1867. Mexican nationalists promptly seized and executed Maximilian. In 1867, at the instigation of

Photo Credit: REUTERS/Hugh Gentry/ Landov.

Midway Island, an inhospitable atoll acquired in 1867, was valuable as a military base located midway between Pearl Harbor, another naval station, and East Asia. The acquisition of a Pacific empire during these years was a reason why Pearl Harbor and Midway became pivotal during the war in the Pacific in World War II.

Seward, the United States purchased Alaska from Russia for $7.2 million, ridding the continent of another foreign power.

In 1867 Seward acquired the Midway Islands in the western Pacific. He also made overtures toward annexing the Hawaiian Islands, and he looked longingly at Cuba. In 1870 President Grant submitted to the Senate a treaty annexing the Dominican Republic. He applied tremendous pressure in an effort to obtain ratification, thus forcing a "great debate" on extracontinental expansion. The distance of the Dominican Republic from the continent and its population of what one congressman called "semi-civilized, semi-barbarous men who cannot speak our language" made annexation unattractive. The treaty was rejected.

The internal growth that preoccupied Americans eventually led them to look outward. By the late 1880s the country was exporting a steadily increasing share of its agricultural and industrial output. Exports, only $450 million in 1870, passed the billion-dollar mark early in the 1890s. Imports increased at a rate only slightly less spectacular.

The character of foreign trade was also changing: Manufactures loomed ever more important among exports until in 1898 the country shipped abroad more manufactured goods than it imported. By this time American steelmakers could compete with producers anywhere in the world. When American industrialists became conscious of their ability to compete with Europeans in far-off markets, they took more interest in world affairs, particularly during periods of depression.

Shifting intellectual currents further altered the attitudes of Americans. Darwin's theories, applicable by analogy to international relations, gave the concept of manifest destiny a new plausibility. Darwinists like the historian John Fiske argued that the American democratic system of government was so clearly the world's "fittest" that it was destined to spread peacefully over "every land on the earth's surface." In *Our Country* (1885) Josiah Strong found racist and religious justifications for American expansionism, again based on the theory of evolution. The Anglo-Saxon race, centered now in the United States, possessed "an instinct or genius for colonization," Strong claimed.

The completion of the conquest of the American West encouraged Americans to consider expansion beyond the seas. "For nearly 300 years the dominant fact in American life has been expansion," declared Frederick Jackson Turner, propounder of the frontier thesis. "That these energies of expansion will no longer operate would be a rash prediction." Turner and writers who advanced other expansionist arguments were much influenced by foreign thinking. European liberals had tended to disapprove of colonial ventures, but in the 1870s and 1880s many of them were changing their minds. English liberals in particular began to talk and write about the "superiority" of English culture, to describe the virtues of the "Anglo-Saxon race," to stress a "duty" to spread Christianity among the heathen, and to advance economic arguments for overseas expansion.

European ideas were reinforced for Americans by their observation of the imperialist activities of the European powers in what would today be called underdeveloped areas. "While the great powers of Europe are steadily enlarging their colonial domination in Asia and Africa," James G. Blaine said in 1884, "it is the especial province of this country to improve and expand its trade with the nations of America." While Blaine emphasized commerce, the excitement and adventure of overseas enterprises appealed to many people even more than the economic possibilities or any sense of obligation to fulfill a supposed national, religious, or racial destiny.

Finally, military and strategic arguments were advanced to justify adopting a "large" policy. The powerful Union army had been demobilized rapidly after Appomattox; in the 1880s only about 25,000 men were under arms, their chief occupation fighting Indians in the West.

Half the navy, too, had been scrapped after the war, and the remaining ships were obsolete. While other nations were building steam-powered iron warships, the United States still depended on wooden sailing vessels. In 1867 a British naval publication accurately described the American fleet as "hapless, broken-down, tattered [and] forlorn."

Although no foreign power menaced the country, the decrepit state of the navy vexed many of its officers and led one of them, Captain Alfred Thayer Mahan, to develop a startling theory about the importance of sea power. According to him, history proved that a nation with a powerful navy and the overseas bases necessary to maintain it would be invulnerable in war and prosperous in time of peace. Applied to the current American situation, this meant that in addition to building a modern fleet, the United States should obtain a string of coaling stations and bases in the Caribbean, annex the Hawaiian Islands, and cut a canal across Central America. A more extensive colonial empire might follow, but these bases and the canal they would protect were essential first steps to ensure America's future as a great power.

Mahan attracted many influential disciples. One was Congressman Henry Cabot Lodge of Massachusetts, a prominent member of the Naval Affairs Committee. Lodge had married into a navy family and was close with the head of the new Naval War College, Commodore Stephen B. Luce. In 1883 he helped push through Congress an act authorizing the construction of three steel warships, and he consistently advocated expanding and modernizing the fleet. Elevated to the Senate in 1893, Lodge pressed for expansionist policies, basing his arguments on the strategic concepts of Mahan. Lodge's friend Theodore Roosevelt was another ardent supporter of the "large" policy, but he had little influence until McKinley appointed him assistant secretary of the navy in 1897.

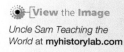

View the **Image**

Uncle Sam Teaching the World at **myhistorylab.com**

Toward an Empire in the Pacific

The interest of the United States in the Pacific and East Asia began in the late eighteenth century, when the first American merchant ship dropped anchor in Canton harbor. After the Treaty of Wanghia (1844), American merchants in China enjoyed many privileges and trade expanded rapidly.

The Hawaiian Islands were an important way station on the route to China, and by 1820 merchants and missionaries were making contacts there. As early as 1854 a movement to annex the islands existed, although it foundered because Hawaii insisted on being admitted to the Union as a state. Commodore Perry's expedition to Japan led to the signing of a commercial treaty (1858) that opened several Japanese ports to American traders.

American influence in Hawaii increased steadily; the descendants of missionary families, most of them engaged in raising sugar, dominated the Hawaiian monarchy. While they made no overt effort to make the islands an American colony, all the expansionist ideas of the era—manifest destiny, Darwinism, Josiah Strong's racist and religious assumptions, and the relentless force of American commercial interests—pointed them in that direction. In 1875 a reciprocity treaty admitted Hawaiian sugar to the United

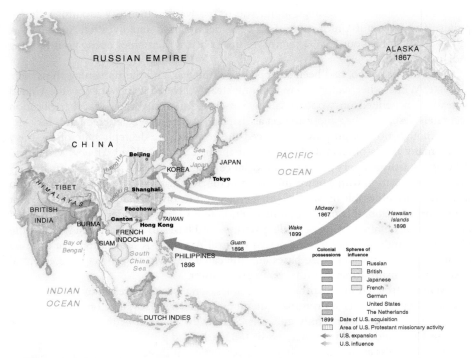

The Course of Empire, 1867–1901 China was the focus of American imperial visions: Missionaries, most of them women, flocked into China, and American manufacturers craved access to the huge China market.

States free of duty in return for a promise to yield no territory to a foreign power. When this treaty was renewed in 1887, the United States obtained the right to establish a naval base at Pearl Harbor. In addition to occupying Midway, America obtained a foothold in the Samoan Islands in the South Pacific.

During the 1890s American interest in the Pacific area steadily intensified as a result of the situation in Hawaii. The McKinley Tariff Act of 1890, discontinuing the duty on raw sugar and compensating American producers of cane and beet sugar by granting them a bounty of two cents a pound, struck Hawaiian sugar growers hard, for it destroyed the advantage they had gained in the reciprocity treaty.

The following year the death of King Kalakaua brought Queen Liliuokalani, a determined nationalist, to the throne. Placing herself at the head of a "Hawaii for the Hawaiians" movement, she abolished the existing constitution under which the white

Iolani Palace, Hawaii at **myhistorylab.com**

minority had pretty much controlled the islands and attempted to rule as an absolute monarch. The resident Americans then staged a coup. In January 1893, with the connivance of the U.S. minister, John L. Stevens, who ordered 150 marines into Honolulu, they deposed Queen Liliuokalani and set up a provisional government. Stevens recognized their regime at once, and the new government sent a delegation to Washington to seek a treaty of annexation.

In the closing days of the Harrison administration such a treaty was negotiated and sent to the Senate, but when Cleveland took office in March, he withdrew it.

The new president disapproved of the way American troops had been used to over-throw the monarchy and attempted to restore Queen Liliuokalani. But by now the new regime, backed by American businessmen, was firmly entrenched. Cleveland found himself unable to do anything.

Finally, in July 1898, after the outbreak of the Spanish-American War, Congress annexed the islands by joint resolution, a procedure requiring only a simple majority vote.

Toward an Empire in Latin America

Most of the arguments for extending American influence in the Pacific applied more strongly to Central and South America, where the United States had much larger economic interests and where the strategic importance of the region was clear.

As early as 1869 President Grant had come out for an American-owned canal across the isthmus of Panama, in spite of the fact that the United States had agreed in the Clayton-Bulwer Treaty with Great Britain (1850) that neither nation would "obtain or maintain for itself any exclusive control" over an inter-oceanic canal. In 1880, when the French engineer Ferdinand de Lesseps organized a company to build a canal across the isthmus, President Hayes announced that the United States would not permit a European power to control such a waterway.

When Cleveland returned to power in 1893, the possibility of trouble in Latin America seemed remote, for he had always opposed imperialistic ventures. Yet scarcely two years later the United States was again on the verge of war in South America as a result of a crisis in Venezuela, and before this issue was settled Cleveland had made the most powerful claim to American hegemony in the hemisphere ever uttered. The tangled borderland between Venezuela and British Guiana had long been in dispute, Venezuela demanding more of the region than it was entitled to and Great Britain making exaggerated claims and refusing to submit the question to arbitration. What made a crisis of the controversy was the political situation in the United States. With his party rapidly deserting him because of his stand on the silver question, and with the election of 1896 approaching, President Cleveland desperately needed a popular issue.

There was considerable anti-British feeling in the United States. By taking the Venezuelan side in the boundary dispute, Cleveland would be defending a weak neighbor against a great power, a position certain to evoke a popular response.

In July 1895 he ordered Secretary of State Richard Olney to send a near ultimatum to the British. By occupying the disputed territory, Olney insisted, Great Britain was invading Venezuela and violating the Monroe Doctrine. Unless Great Britain responded promptly by agreeing to arbitration, the president would call the question to the attention of Congress.

The note threatened war, but the British ignored it for months. They did not take the United States seriously as a world power. The American navy, although expanding, could not hope to stand up against the British, who had fifty battleships, twenty-five armored cruisers, and many smaller vessels. When Lord Salisbury, the prime minister and foreign secretary, finally replied, he rejected outright the argument that the Monroe Doctrine had any status under international law and refused to arbitrate what he called the "exaggerated pretensions" of the Venezuelans.

Cleveland was furious. On December 17, 1895, he asked Congress for authority to appoint an American commission to determine the correct line between British Guiana and Venezuela. When that had been done, he added, the United States should "resist by every means in its power" the appropriation by Great Britain of any territory "we have determined of right belongs to Venezuela." Congress responded at once, unanimously appropriating $100,000 for the boundary commission. Popular approval was almost universal.

In Great Britain government and people suddenly awoke to the seriousness of the situation. No one wanted a war with the United States over a remote patch of tropical real estate. In Europe, Britain was concerned about German economic competition and the increased military power of that nation. The immense potential strength of the United States could no longer be ignored. Why make an enemy of a nation of 70 million, already the richest industrial power in the world?

Great Britain agreed to arbitrate the boundary, and the war scare subsided. When the boundary tribunal awarded nearly all the disputed region to Great Britain, whatever ill feeling the surrender may have occasioned in that country faded away. Instead of leading to war, the affair marked the beginning of an era of Anglo-American friendship. It had the unfortunate effect, however, of adding to the long-held American conviction that the nation could get what it wanted in international affairs by threat and bluster—a dangerous illusion.

The Cuban Revolution

On February 10, 1896, scarcely a week after Venezuela and Great Britain had signed the treaty ending their dispute, General Valeriano Weyler arrived in Havana from Spain to take up his duties as governor of Cuba. His assignment to this post was occasioned by the guerrilla warfare that Cuban nationalist rebels had been waging for almost a year. Weyler, a tough and ruthless soldier, began herding the rural population into wretched **"reconcentration" camps** to deprive the rebels of food and recruits. Resistance in Cuba hardened.

The United States had been interested in Cuba since the time of John Quincy Adams and, were it not for Northern opposition to adding more slave territory, might well have obtained the island one way or another before 1860. When the Cubans revolted against Spain in 1868, considerable support for intervening on their behalf developed. Hamilton Fish, Grant's secretary of state, resisted this sentiment, and Spain managed to pacify the rebels in 1878 by promising reforms. But change was slow in coming—slavery was not abolished until 1886. The worldwide depression of the 1890s hit the Cuban economy hard, and when an American tariff act in 1894 jacked up the rate on Cuban sugar by 40 percent, thus cutting off Cuban growers from the American market, the resulting distress precipitated another revolt.

Public sympathy in the United States went to the Cubans, who seemed to be fighting for liberty and democracy against an autocratic Old World power. Most newspapers supported the rebels; labor unions, veterans' organizations, many Protestant clergymen, a great majority of American blacks, and important politicians in both major parties demanded that the United States aid their cause. Rapidly increasing American investments in Cuban sugar plantations, now approaching $50 million, were endangered by the fighting and by the social chaos sweeping across the island.

In April 1896 Congress adopted a resolution suggesting that the revolutionaries be granted the rights of belligerents. Since this would have been akin to formal recognition, Cleveland would not go that far, but he did exert diplomatic pressure on Spain to remove the causes of the rebels' complaints, and he offered the services of his government as mediator. The Spanish rejected the suggestion. For a time the issue subsided. The election of 1896 deflected American attention from Cuba, and then McKinley refused to take any action that might disturb Spanish-American relations. In Cuba General Weyler made some progress toward stifling rebel resistance.

American expansionists, however, continued to demand intervention, and the press kept resentment alive with tales of Spanish atrocities. McKinley remained adamant. Although he warned Spain that Cuba must be pacified, his tone was friendly and he issued no ultimatum. A new government in Spain relieved the situation by recalling Weyler and promising partial self-government to the Cubans. In a message to Congress in December 1897, McKinley urged that Spain be given "a reasonable chance to realize her expectations" in the island.

His hopes were doomed. The fighting in Cuba continued. When riots broke out in Havana in January 1898, McKinley ordered the battleship *Maine* to Havana harbor to protect American citizens.

Shortly thereafter Hearst's *New York Journal* printed a letter written to a friend in Cuba by the Spanish minister in Washington, Dupuy de Lôme. The letter had been stolen by a spy. De Lôme, an experienced but arrogant diplomat, failed to appreciate McKinley's efforts to avoid intervening in Cuba. In the letter he characterized the president as a *politicastro*, or "small-time politician," which was a gross error, and a "bidder for the admiration of the crowd," which was equally insulting though somewhat closer to the truth. Americans were outraged, and de Lôme's hasty resignation did little to soothe their feelings.

Then, on February 15, the *Maine* exploded and sank in Havana harbor, 260 of the crew perishing in the disaster. Interventionists in the United States accused Spain of having destroyed the ship and clamored for war. The willingness of Americans to blame Spain indicates the extent of anti-Spanish opinion in the United States by 1898. No one has ever discovered what actually happened. A naval court of inquiry decided that the vessel had been sunk by a submarine mine, but it now seems more likely that an internal explosion destroyed the *Maine*. The Spanish government could hardly have been foolish enough to commit an act that would probably bring American troops into Cuba.

Watch the Video

Burial of the *Maine* Victims at **myhistorylab.com**

With admirable courage, McKinley refused to panic; but he could not resist the wishes of millions of citizens that something be done to stop the fighting and allow the Cubans to determine their own fate. Spanish pride and Cuban patriotism had taken the issue of peace or war out of the president's hands. Spain could not put down the rebellion, and it would not yield to the nationalists' increasingly extreme demands. The Cubans, sensing that the continuing bloodshed aided their cause, refused to give the Spanish regime room to maneuver. After the *Maine* disaster, Spain might have agreed to an armistice had the rebels asked for one, and in the resulting negotiations it might well have given up the island. The rebels refused to make the first move. The fighting continued, bringing the United States every day closer to intervention.

The president faced a dilemma. Most of the business interests of the country, to which he was particularly sensitive, opposed intervention. Congress, however, seemed

The explosion of the *Maine* in Havana harbor, killing 260 men, caused much speculation in the newspapers and across the nation. Many Americans accused Spain of destroying the ship, a reaction that typified American sentiment toward the Spanish in 1898. What really caused the explosion remains unknown.
Source: ICHi-08428/Kurz & Allison/Chicago History Museum.

determined to act. When he submitted a restrained report on the sinking of the *Maine*, the Democrats in Congress, even most of those who had supported Cleveland's policies, accused him of timidity. Vice President Garret A. Hobart warned him that the Senate could not be held in check for long; should Congress declare war on its own, the administration would be discredited.

Finally, early in April, the president drafted a message asking for authority to use the armed forces "to secure a full and final termination of hostilities" in Cuba.

At the last moment the Spanish government seemed to yield; it ordered its troops in Cuba to cease hostilities. McKinley passed this information on to Congress along with his war message, but he gave it no emphasis and did not try to check the march toward war. To seek further delay would have been courageous but not necessarily wiser. Merely to stop fighting was not enough. The Cuban nationalists now insisted on full independence, and the Spanish politicians were unprepared to abandon the last remnant of their once-great American empire. If the United States took Cuba by force, the Spanish leaders might save their political skins; if they meekly surrendered the island, they were done for.

The "Splendid Little" Spanish-American War

On April 20, 1898, Congress, by joint resolution, recognized the independence of Cuba and authorized the use of the armed forces to drive out the Spanish. An amendment proposed by Senator Henry M. Teller disclaiming any intention of adding Cuban territory to the United States passed without opposition. Four days after passage of the **Teller Amendment**, Spain declared war on the United States.

Photo Credit: The Granger Collection, New York.

Sailors on the USS *Oregon* watch the destruction of the Spanish cruiser, *Cristobal Colon*, during the Battle of Santiago, Cuba, July 3, 1898.

The Spanish-American War was fought to free Cuba, but the first action took place on the other side of the globe, in the Philippine Islands. Weeks earlier, Theodore Roosevelt, at the time assistant secretary of the navy, had alerted Commodore George Dewey, who was in command of the United States Asiatic Squadron located at Hong Kong, to move against the Spanish base at Manila if war came. Dewey had acted promptly, drilling his gun crews, taking on supplies, giving his gleaming white ships a coat of battle-gray paint, and establishing secret contacts with the Filipino nationalist leader, Emilio Aguinaldo. When word of the declaration of war reached him, Dewey steamed from Hong Kong across the South China Sea with four cruisers and two gunboats. On the night of April 30 he entered Manila Bay, and at daybreak he opened fire on the Spanish fleet at 5,000 yards. His squadron made five passes, each time reducing the range; when the smoke had cleared, all ten of Admiral Montojo's ships had been destroyed. Not a single American was killed in the engagement.

Dewey immediately asked for troops to take and hold Manila, for now that war had been declared, he could not return to Hong Kong or any other neutral port. McKinley took the fateful step of dispatching some 11,000 soldiers and additional naval support. On August 13 these forces, assisted by Filipino irregulars under Aguinaldo, captured Manila.

Watch the Video

Roosevelt's Rough Riders
at **myhistorylab.com**

Meanwhile, in Cuba, the United States had won a total victory. When the war began, the U.S. regular army consisted of about 28,000 men. This tiny force was bolstered by 200,000 hastily enlisted volunteers. Aggressive units like the regiment of "Rough Riders" raised by Theodore Roosevelt, who had resigned his Navy Department post to become a lieutenant colonel of volunteers, scrambled for space and supplies, shouldering aside other units to get what they needed.

Since a Spanish fleet under Admiral Pascual Cervera was known to be in Caribbean waters, no invading army could safely embark until the fleet could be located. On May 29 American ships found Cervera at Santiago harbor, on the eastern end of Cuba, and established a blockade. In June a 17,000-man expeditionary force landed at Daiquiri, east of Santiago, and pressed quickly toward the city. The Americans sweated through Cuba's torrid summer in heavy wool winter uniforms, ate "embalmed beef" out of cans, and fought mostly with old-fashioned rifles using black powder cartridges that marked the position of each soldier with a puff of smoke whenever he pulled the trigger. On July 1 they broke through undermanned Spanish defenses and stormed San Juan Hill, the intrepid Roosevelt in the van.

With Santiago harbor in range of American artillery, Admiral Cervera had to run the blockade. On July 3 his black-hulled ships, flags proudly flying, steamed forth from the harbor and fled westward along the coast. Five American battleships and two cruisers, commanded by Rear Admiral William T. Sampson and Commodore Winfield Scott Schley, ran them down. In four hours the entire Spanish force was destroyed. Damage to the American ships was superficial; only one American seaman lost his life in the engagement.

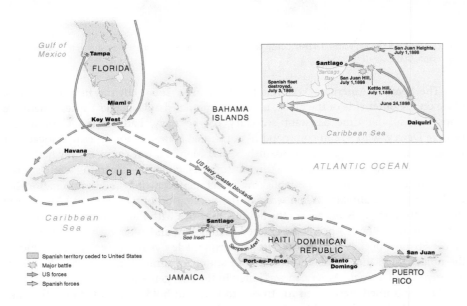

Spanish-American War: Caribbean Theater, 1898 After boarding in Tampa, American soldiers landed near Santiago, Cuba. They swiftly overran Spanish fortifications on the heights to the east of the city. When U.S. troops came within artillery range of Santiago Bay, the Spanish fleet fled. Soon the Spanish ships were intercepted and destroyed by the American navy.

The end then came abruptly. Santiago surrendered on July 17. A few days later, other U.S. troops completed the occupation of Puerto Rico. On August 12, one day before the fall of Manila, Spain agreed to get out of Cuba and to cede Puerto Rico and an island in the Marianas (Guam) to the United States. The future of the Philippines was to be settled at a formal peace conference, convening in Paris on October 1.

Developing a Colonial Policy

Although the Spanish resisted surrendering the Philippines at Paris, they had been so thoroughly defeated that they had no choice. The decision hung rather on the outcome of a conflict over policy within the United States. The war, won at so little cost militarily, produced problems far larger than those it solved.[1] The nation had become a great power in the world's eyes. European leaders had been impressed by the forcefulness of Cleveland's diplomacy in the Venezuela boundary dispute and by the efficiency displayed by the navy in the war. The annexation of Hawaii and other overseas bases intensified their conviction that the United States was determined to become a major force in international affairs.

But were the American people determined to exercise that force? The debate over taking the Philippine Islands throws much light on their attitudes. It was titillating for Americans to think of a world map liberally sprinkled with American flags and of the economic benefits that colonies might bring, but most citizens were not prepared to join in a worldwide struggle for power and influence. They entered blithely on adventures in far-off regions without facing the implications of their decision.

Since the United States had abjured any claim to Cuba, even though the island had long been desired by expansionists, logic dictated that a similar policy be applied to the Philippines. But expansionists were eager to annex the entire archipelago. Even before he had learned to spell the name, Senator Lodge was saying that "the Phillipines [sic] mean a vast future trade and wealth and power," offering the nation a greater opportunity "than anything that has happened . . . since the annexation of Louisiana."

President McKinley adopted a more cautious stance, but he too favored "the general principle of holding on to what we can get." A speaking tour of the Midwest in October 1898, during which he experimented with varying degrees of commitment to expansionism, convinced him that the public wanted the islands. Business opinion had shifted dramatically during the war. Business leaders were now calling the Philippines the gateway to the markets of East Asia.

The Anti-Imperialists

The war had produced a wave of unifying patriotic feeling. It greatly furthered reconciliation between the North and the South. But victory raised new divisive questions. An important minority objected strongly to the U.S. acquisition of overseas possessions.

The anti-imperialists insisted that since no one would consider statehood for the Philippines, it would be unconstitutional to annex them. It was a violation of the spirit of

---

[1]More than 5,000 Americans died as a result of the conflict, but fewer than 400 fell in combat. The others were mostly victims of yellow fever, typhoid, and other diseases.

While the good children (the states) sit at their seats, with the Indian off to the side, the unruly blacks—"Cuba," "Puerto Rico," "Hawaii," and "Philippines"—are lectured by Uncle Sam. Racist anti-imperialists argued, as did this cartoon in *Puck* in 1899, that the inclusion of other peoples would weaken the American nation.

the Declaration of Independence to govern a foreign territory without the consent of its inhabitants, Senator George Frisbie Hoar of Massachusetts argued; by taking over "vassal states" in "barbarous archipelagoes" the United States was "trampling . . . on our own great Charter, which recognizes alike the liberty and the dignity of individual manhood."

McKinley was not insensitive to this appeal to idealism and tradition, which was the fundamental element in the anti-imperialist argument. But he rejected it for several reasons.

Public opinion would not sanction restoring Spanish authority in the Philippines or allowing some other power to have them. That the Filipinos were sufficiently advanced and united socially to form a stable government if granted independence seemed unlikely. Senator Hoar believed that "for years and for generations, and perhaps for centuries, there would have been turbulence, disorder and revolution" in the islands if they were left to their own devices.

The president searched the depths of his soul and could find no solution but annexation. The state of public feeling made the decision easier, and he probably found the idea of presiding over an empire appealing. Certainly the commercial possibilities did not escape him. In the end it was with a heavy sense of responsibility that he ordered the American peace commissioners to insist on acquiring the Philippines. To salve the feelings of the Spanish the United States agreed to pay $20 million for the archipelago, but it was a forced sale, accepted by Spain under duress.

The peace treaty faced a hard battle in the U.S. Senate, where a combination of partisan politics and anticolonialism made it difficult to amass the two-thirds majority necessary for ratification. McKinley had shrewdly appointed three senators, including one

Democrat, to the peace commission. This predisposed many members of the upper house to approve the treaty, but the vote was close. William Jennings Bryan, titular head of the Democratic party, could probably have prevented ratification had he urged his supporters to vote nay. Although he was opposed to taking the Philippines, he did not do so. To reject the treaty would leave the United States technically at war with Spain and the fate of the Philippines undetermined; better to accept the islands and then grant them independence. The question should be decided, Bryan said, "not by a minority of the Senate but by a majority of the people" at the next presidential election. Perplexed by Bryan's stand, a number of Democrats allowed themselves to be persuaded by the expansionists' arguments and by McKinley's judicious use of patronage; the treaty was ratified in February 1899 by a vote of fifty-seven to twenty-seven.

The Philippine Insurrection

The national referendum that Bryan had hoped for never materialized. Bryan himself confused the issue in 1900 by making free silver a major plank in his platform, thereby driving conservative anti-imperialists into McKinley's arms. Moreover, early in 1899 the Filipino nationalists under Aguinaldo, furious because the United States would not withdraw, took up arms. A savage guerrilla war resulted, one that cost far more in lives and money than the "splendid little" Spanish-American conflict.

Neither side displayed much regard for the "rules" of war. Goaded by sneak attacks and instances of cruelty to captives, American soldiers, most of whom had little respect for Filipinos to begin with, responded in kind. (See American Lives, "Frederick Funston".) Civilians were rounded up, prisoners tortured, and property destroyed. Horrifying tales of rape, arson, and murder by U.S. troops filtered into the country, providing ammunition for the anti-imperialists. In fact, far more than 8,000 Filipinos lost their lives during the conflict, which raged for three years. More than 70,000 American soldiers had to be sent to the islands before the resistance was crushed, and about as many of them lost their lives as had perished in the Cuban conflict.

In 1900 McKinley sent a commission headed by William Howard Taft, a federal judge, to establish a government. Taft took an instant liking to the

Read the Document

Twain, *Incident in the Philippines* at **myhistorylab.com**

View the Image

Filipino Guerrillas at **myhistorylab.com**

Emilio Aguinaldo, shown here with his young son, commanded Filipino insurgents who worked with Commodore Dewey to help overthrow Spanish rule of the Philippines in 1898. He later took up arms against the United States in a brutal three-year struggle when President McKinley opposed granting independence to the islands.

Filipinos, and his policy of encouraging them to participate in the territorial government attracted many converts. In July 1901 he became the first civilian governor of the Philippines.

Actually, the reelection of McKinley in 1900 settled the Philippine question so far as most Americans were concerned. Anti-imperialists still claimed that it was unconstitutional to take over territories without the consent of the local population. Their reasoning, while certainly not unsound, was unhistorical. No American government had seriously considered the wishes of the American Indians, the French and Spanish settlers in Louisiana, the Eskimos of Alaska, or the people of Hawaii when it had seemed in the national interest to annex new lands.

Cuba and the United States

Nevertheless, grave constitutional questions arose as a result of the acquisitions that followed the Spanish-American War. McKinley acted with remarkable independence in handling the problems involved in expansion. He set up military governments in Cuba, Puerto Rico, and the Philippines without specific congressional authority. The Supreme Court, in what became known as the "insular cases," granted Congress permission to act toward the colonies much as it pleased.

While the most heated arguments raged over Philippine policy, the most difficult colonial problems concerned the relationship between the United States and Cuba. Despite the desire of most Americans to get out of Cuba, an independent government could not easily be created.

The insurgent government was feeble, corrupt, and oligarchic, the Cuban economy in a state of collapse, and life was chaotic. The first Americans entering Havana found the streets littered with garbage and the corpses of horses and dogs. All public services were at a standstill; it seemed essential for the United States, as McKinley said, to give "aid and direction" until "tranquillity" could be restored.

The problems were indeed knotty, for no strong local leader capable of uniting Cuba appeared. Even Senator Teller, father of the Teller Amendment, expressed concern lest "unstable and unsafe" elements gain control of the country. European leaders expected that the United States would eventually annex Cuba; and many Americans, including General Leonard Wood, who became military governor in December 1899, considered this the best solution. The desperate state of the people, the heavy economic stake of Americans in the region, and its strategic importance militated against withdrawal.

In the end the United States did withdraw, after doing a great deal to modernize sugar production, improve sanitary conditions, establish schools, and restore orderly administration. In November 1900 a Cuban constitutional convention met at Havana and proceeded without substantial American interference or direction to draft a frame of government. The chief restrictions imposed by this document on Cuba's freedom concerned foreign relations; at the insistence of the United States, it authorized American intervention whenever necessary "for the preservation of Cuban independence" and "the maintenance of a government adequate for the protection of life, property, and individual liberty." Cuba had to promise to make no treaty with a foreign power compromising its independence and to grant naval bases on its soil to the United States.

The Cubans, after some grumbling, accepted this arrangement, known as the **Platt Amendment**. It had the support of most American opponents of imperialism. The amendment was a true compromise: It safeguarded American interests while granting to the Cubans real self-government on internal matters. In May 1902 the United States turned over the reins of government to the new republic. The next year the two countries signed a reciprocity treaty tightening the economic bonds between them.

●◆●▪Read the Document

The Platt Amendment at myhistorylab.com

True friendship did not result. Although American troops occupied Cuba only once more, in 1906, and then at the specific request of Cuban authorities, the United States repeatedly used the threat of intervention to coerce the Cuban government. American economic penetration proceeded rapidly and without regard for the well-being of the Cuban peasants, many of whom lived in a state of peonage on great sugar plantations. Nor did the Americans' good intentions make up for their tendency to consider themselves innately superior to the Cubans and to overlook the fact that Cubans did not always wish to adopt American customs and culture.

The United States in the Caribbean and Central America

If the purpose of the Spanish-American War had been to bring peace and order to Cuba, the Platt Amendment was a logical step. The same purpose soon necessitated a further extension of the principle, for once the United States accepted the role of protector and stabilizer in parts of the Caribbean and Central America, it seemed desirable to supervise the entire region.

The Caribbean and Central American countries were economically underdeveloped, politically unstable, and desperately poor. Most of the people were uneducated peasants, many of whom were little better off than slaves. Rival cliques of wealthy families struggled for power, force being the usual method of effecting a change in government. Most of the meager income of the average Caribbean state was swallowed up by the military or diverted into the pockets of the current rulers.

Cynicism and fraud poisoned the relations of most of these nations with the great powers. European merchants and bankers systematically cheated their Latin American customers, who in turn frequently refused to honor their obligations. Foreign bankers floated bond issues on outrageous terms, while revolutionary governments in the region annulled concessions and repudiated debts with equal disdain for honest business dealing.

In 1902, shortly after the United States had pulled out of Cuba, trouble erupted in Venezuela, where a dictator, Cipriano Castro, was refusing to honor debts owed the citizens of European nations. To force Castro to pay up, Germany and Great Britain established a blockade of Venezuelan ports and destroyed a number of Venezuelan gunboats and harbor defenses. Under American pressure the Europeans agreed to arbitrate the dispute. For the first time, European powers had accepted the broad implications of the Monroe Doctrine. By this time Theodore Roosevelt had become president of the United States, and he quickly capitalized on the new

FREDERICK FUNSTON

On the night of March 22, 1901, as rain battered his campsite in the deep jungles of Luzon Island in the Philippines, Frederick Funston pondered what awaited him the next day. Ten miles to the north lay his prey, Emilio Aguinaldo, President of the Philippine Republic. For two years, the American army had been trying to capture Aguinaldo. But repeatedly Aguinaldo had slipped away. This time Funston was close. His ruse was working.

It had been a wild idea, something out of a boy's adventure story. He conceived it after capturing a Filipino messenger carrying coded documents. Funston's interrogation of the courier had been successful. The courier confirmed that Aguinaldo's secret headquarters was located in a remote area of Luzon.

Funston had chosen eighty Filipino scouts from the Macabebes, a tribe hostile to Aguinaldo. He outfitted them in the uniforms of Aguinaldo's army and trained them to pretend to be Filipino nationalists. These "nationalists" would escort five American "prisoners" (including Funston) for presentation to Aguinaldo.

Funston longed to be a hero. Ever since he was a child, he worried that he failed to measure up to his father. Edward "Foghorn" Funston had been an artillery officer during the Civil War and a fiery Republican congressman afterward. At six feet two and 200 pounds, he was regarded by all as an exemplar of nineteenth-century manhood. But Frederick, born in 1864, was only five feet four and slightly built. He compensated with bravado displays of martial manliness. He craved a military career, but though his father was a congressman, West Point rejected him: His grades were mediocre, and he was too small.

In 1886 he enrolled at the University of Kansas but didn't fit in. He devoted himself to the pursuit of the most desirable women on campus, all of whom spurned him. Increasingly he retreated from social situations, preferring to drink alone in his room, periodically bursting out in a drunken rage.

He dropped out of college. First, he explored an unmapped section of Death Valley in California. Then he volunteered to gather botanical samples in Alaska for the Department of Agriculture. When the department proposed that he command an entire expedition for the purpose, he flatly turned them down. Alone, he trekked into the frigid wastes of northern Alaska and remained there for the better part of a year. When he ran out of food he ate his sled dogs.

During those long, silent nights, Funston realized that he could hardly prove that he measured up if no one were around to take the measurements. He decided to become a soldier, not caring much against whom he fought. In 1895 he contacted a recruiter for the cause of Cuban independence and accepted a commission as an artillery officer in the rebel army.

In Cuba he was given command of a Hotchkiss cannon; he made up for his lack of gunnery skill by sneaking his cannon absurdly close to Spanish fortifications at night, often within 400 yards. As the sun rose, the Spaniards, aghast at what was sitting on their doorstep, fired everything they had at Funston's cannon. Funston calmly adjusted the sights, pulled the lanyard, and climbed upon the parapet, shouting

Frederick Funston: hero or antihero?

"Viva Cuba libre!" He was repeatedly wounded; once, a bullet pierced his lungs. When a severe hip wound became infected, he returned to the United States for medical assistance.

But he was not done with war. In 1898 Funston was given command of the Kansas regiments that had volunteered against Spain. To his dismay, they were sent to the Philippines, where the Spaniards had already ceased fighting. But after President McKinley decided to annex the Philippines, war broke out between the Americans and the Filipino nationalists. Funston finally got what he craved: sweeping charges, glorious victories, and newspaper feature stories. Yet the jokes persisted. Behind his back, his men called him the "Bantam General." The *New York Times,* in its coverage of a battle in which he won a Congressional Medal of Honor, ran the headline: "Daring Little Colonel Funston." The opening paragraph attributed Funston's courage to the fact that he was too small to hit.

But now, if he captured Aguinaldo, Funston, the little man, would become a great one.

On March 23, 1901, Funston's Macabebes and their five American "prisoners" met up with a contingent of Aguinaldo's army. Deceived, Aguinaldo's troops escorted Funston's band into the town of Palanan. Aguinaldo watched from a window above. When shots rang out, thinking the troops were firing a salute, he shouted, "Stop that foolishness. Don't waste ammunition!"

Then Funston burst into Aguinaldo's compound: "I am General Funston. You are a prisoner of war of the Army of the United States of America."

Dazed, Aguinaldo replied, "Is this not some joke?" Funston seized Aguinaldo, dragged him through the jungle to the coast, where the USS *Vicksburg* was waiting. It took them to American headquarters in Manila.

After being subjected to intense pressure by American officials, Aguinaldo renounced the Filipino revolution, swore allegiance to the United States, and called on his followers to do likewise. The Philippine-American conflict was virtually over. Frederick Funston had almost single-handedly won the war.

For a time, Funston was a sensation. He was promoted to brigadier general. Newspaper editors and politicians championed him for governor of Kansas or for vice president on a ticket headed by Theodore Roosevelt in 1904. But within a few years Funston all but vanished. Anti-imperialists pointed out that Funston's men had surrendered and then fired their weapons, and that the Macabebes had been wearing enemy uniforms; both actions violated international law. Worse, several reporters and some of his soldiers claimed that Funston had ordered the execution of Filipino prisoners. He was ordered to an inconsequential command in San Francisco.

One hundred years after Funston's capture of Aguinaldo, U.S. troops would again be tracking a rebel fugitive: Osama bin Laden, mastermind of the September 11, 2001, attacks on the World Trade Center and Pentagon. That virtually no one recalled Funston's single-handed pursuit and capture of Aguinaldo was one measure of how completely he had slipped from view.

But Funston's name resurfaced in 2010, after major earthquakes had triggered widespread looting in Haiti and Chile. The *New York Times* observed that when the 1906 earthquake destroyed much of San Francisco, General Frederick Funston had immediately marched his troops into the city and taken charge; sometimes, the *Times* noted, leaders must act decisively.

Question for Discussion

■ To catch Aguinaldo, Funston employed tactics of doubtful legality. A century later Americans have been accused of using torture and other unsavory methods to win "the war on terror." Are such techniques morally or legally wrong? Why or why not?

The United States in the Caribbean and Central America Puerto Rico was ceded by Spain to the United States after the Spanish-American War; the Virgin Islands were bought from Denmark; the Canal Zone was leased from Panama. The ranges of dates shown for Cuba, the Dominican Republic, Haiti, Nicaragua, and Panama cover those years during which the United States either had troops in occupation or in some other way (such as financial) had a protectorate relationship with that country.

European attitude. In 1903 the Dominican Republic defaulted on bonds totaling some $40 million. When European investors urged their governments to intervene, Roosevelt announced that under the Monroe Doctrine the United States could not permit foreign nations to intervene in Latin America. But, he added, Latin American nations should not be allowed to escape their obligations.

The president did not want to make a colony of the Dominican Republic. He therefore arranged for the United States to take charge of the Dominican customs service—the one reliable source of revenue in that poverty-stricken country. Fifty-five percent of the customs duties would be devoted to debt payment, the remainder turned over to the Dominican government to care for its internal needs. Roosevelt defined his policy, known as the Roosevelt Corollary to the Monroe Doctrine, in a message to Congress in December 1904. "Chronic wrongdoing" in Latin America, he stated with his typical disregard for the subtleties of complex affairs, might require outside intervention. Since, under the Monroe Doctrine, no other nation could step in, the United States must "exercise . . . an international police power."

In the short run this policy worked. Dominican customs were honestly collected for the first time and the country's finances put in order. The presence of American warships in the area provided a needed measure of political stability. In the long run, however, the Roosevelt Corollary caused a great deal of resentment in Latin America.

See the Map

Activities of the United States in the Caribbean at **myhistorylab.com**

The Open Door Policy in China

The insular cases, the Platt Amendment, and the Roosevelt Corollary established the framework for American policy both in Latin America and in East Asia. Coincidental with the Cuban rebellion of the 1890s, a far greater upheaval had convulsed the ancient empire of China. In 1894–1895 Japan easily defeated China in a war over Korea. Alarmed by Japan's aggressiveness, the European powers hastened to carve out for themselves new spheres of influence along China's coast. After the annexation of the Philippines, McKinley's secretary of state, John Hay, urged on by business leaders fearful of losing out in the scramble to exploit the Chinese market, tried to prevent the further absorption of China by the great powers.

For the United States to join in the dismemberment of China was politically impossible because of anti-imperialist feeling, so Hay sought to protect American interests by clever diplomacy. In a series of "Open Door" notes (1899) he asked the powers to agree to respect the trading rights of all countries and to impose no discriminatory duties within their spheres of influence.

The replies to the Open Door notes were at best noncommittal, yet Hay blandly announced in March 1900 that the powers had "accepted" his suggestions! Thus he could claim to have prevented the breakup of the empire and protected the right of Americans to do business freely in its territories. In reality nothing had been accomplished; the imperialist nations did not extend their political control of China only because they feared that by doing so they might precipitate a major war among themselves. Nevertheless, Hay's action marked a revolutionary departure from the traditional American policy of isolation, a bold advance into the complicated and dangerous world of international power politics.

Within a few months of Hay's announcement the **Open Door policy** was put to the test. Chinese nationalists, angered by the spreading influence of foreign governments, launched the so-called Boxer Rebellion. They swarmed into Peking and drove foreigners behind the walls of their legations, which were placed under siege. For weeks, until an international rescue expedition (which included 2,500 American soldiers) broke through to free them, the fate of the foreigners was unknown. Fearing that the Europeans would use the rebellion as a pretext for further expropriations, Hay sent off another round of Open Door notes announcing that the United States believed in the preservation of "Chinese territorial and administrative entity" and in "the principle of equal and impartial trade with all parts of the Chinese Empire." This broadened the Open Door policy to include all China, not merely the European spheres of influence.

Hay's diplomacy was superficially successful. But once again European jealousies and fears rather than American cleverness were responsible. When the Japanese, mistrusting Russian intentions in Manchuria, asked Hay how he intended to implement his policy, he replied meekly that the United States was "not prepared . . . to enforce these views." The United States was being caught up in the power struggle in East Asia without having faced the implications of its actions.

In time the country would pay a heavy price for this unrealistic attitude, but in the decade following 1900 its policy of diplomatic meddling worked fairly well. Japan attacked Russia in a quarrel over Manchuria, smashing the Russian fleet in 1905 and winning a series of battles on the mainland. Japan was not prepared for a long war,

Photo Credit: Courtesy of the Divinity School Library, Yale University.

Grace Service, a YMCA missionary, explained that these porters worked at the base of Mount Omei in Szechwan, China, a favorite site for Buddhist pilgrims. Upper-class Chinese women's feet were bound to keep them small. The deformities that resulted limited the distance they could walk, so they hired men such as these to carry them to the summit.

however, and suggested to President Roosevelt that an American offer to mediate would be favorably received.

Eager to preserve the balance of power in East Asia, which enabled the United States to exert influence without any significant commitment of force, Roosevelt accepted the hint. In June 1905 he invited the belligerents to a conference at Portsmouth, New Hampshire. At the conference the Japanese won title to Russia's sphere around Port Arthur and a free hand in Korea, but when they demanded Sakhalin Island and a large money indemnity, the Russians balked. Unwilling to resume the war, the Japanese settled for half of Sakhalin and no money.

The Treaty of Portsmouth was unpopular in Japan, and the government managed to place the blame on Roosevelt, who had supported the compromise. Ill feeling against Americans increased in 1906 when the San Francisco school board, responding to local opposition to the influx of cheap labor from Japan, instituted a policy of segregating Asian children in a special school. Japan protested, and President Roosevelt persuaded the San Franciscans to abandon segregation in exchange for his pledge to cut off further Japanese immigration. He accomplished this through a "Gentlemen's Agreement" (1907) in which the Japanese promised not to issue passports to laborers seeking to come to America. Discriminatory legislation based specifically on race was thus avoided. However, the atmosphere between the two countries remained charged. Japanese resentment at American racial prejudice was great; many Americans talked fearfully of the "yellow peril."

Roosevelt did not appreciably increase American naval and military strength in East Asia, nor did he stop trying to influence the course of events in the area, and he took no step toward withdrawing from the Philippines. He sent the fleet on a world cruise to demonstrate its might to Japan but knew well that this was mere bluff. "The 'Open Door' policy," he advised his successor, "completely disappears as soon as a powerful nation determines to disregard it." Nevertheless he allowed the belief to persist in the United States that the nation could influence the course of East Asian history without risk or real involvement.

The Panama Canal

In the Caribbean region American policy centered on building an interoceanic canal across Central America. The first step was to get rid of the old Clayton-Bulwer Treaty with Great Britain, which barred the United States from building a canal on its own. In 1901 Lord Pauncefote, the British ambassador, and Secretary of State John Hay negotiated an agreement abrogating the Clayton-Bulwer pact and giving the United States the right to build and defend a canal connecting the Pacific Ocean with the Caribbean Sea.

One possible canal route lay across the Colombian province of Panama, where the French-controlled New Panama Canal Company had taken over the franchise of the old De Lesseps company. Only fifty miles separated the oceans in Panama. The terrain, however, was rugged and unhealthy. While the French company had sunk much money into the project, it had little to show for its efforts aside from some rough excavations. A second possible route ran across Nicaragua. This route was about 200 miles long but was relatively easy since much of it traversed Lake Nicaragua and other natural waterways.

President McKinley appointed a commission to study the alternatives. It reported that the Panamanian route was technically superior, but recommended building in

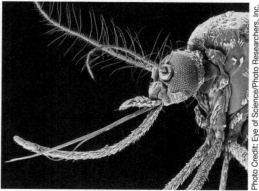

An electron microscopic photo of a mosquito that carried yellow fever. Major Walter Reed of the U.S. army proved that yellow fever was not spread directly among humans, but from the bites of infected mosquitoes. The virus then multiplied in the human bloodstream. Headache, backache, fever, and vomiting ensued. Liver cells were destroyed, resulting in jaundice—thus the name "yellow fever." American surgeon William Crawford Gorgas worked to eliminate yellow fever by destroying the breeding grounds of these mosquitoes. The last yellow fever outbreak in the United States struck New Orleans and parts of the South in 1905.

Photo Credit: Eye of Science/Photo Researchers, Inc.

The U.S. Panama Canal Following many negotiations, construction of the Panama Canal began in 1904. After many delays and hardships, it was completed in 1914.

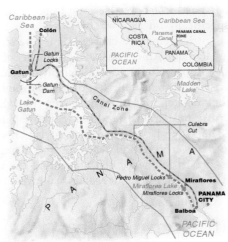

Nicaragua because the New Panama Canal Company was asking $109 million for its assets, which the commission valued at only $40 million. Lacking another potential purchaser, the French company lowered its price to $40 million, and after a great deal of clever propagandizing by Philippe Bunau-Varilla, a French engineer with heavy investments in the company, President Roosevelt settled on the Panamanian route.

In January 1903 Secretary of State Hay negotiated a treaty with Colombia. In return for a ninety-nine-year lease on a zone across Panama six miles wide, the United States agreed to pay Colombia $10 million and an annual rent of $250,000. The Colombian senate, however, unanimously rejected this treaty. It demanded $15 million directly from the United States, plus one-fourth of the $40 million U.S. payment to the New Panama Canal Company.

A little more patience might have produced a mutually satisfactory settlement, but Roosevelt looked on the Colombians as highwaymen who were "mad to get hold of the $40,000,000 of the Frenchmen." When Panamanians, egged on by the French company, staged a revolution against Colombia in November 1903, he ordered the cruiser *Nashville* to Panama. Colombian government forces found themselves looking down the barrels of the guns of the *Nashville* and shortly thereafter eight other American warships. The revolution succeeded.

Roosevelt instantly recognized the new Republic of Panama. Secretary Hay and the new "Panamanian" minister, Bunau-Varilla, then negotiated a treaty granting the United States a zone ten miles wide in perpetuity, on the same terms as those rejected by Colombia. Within the Canal Zone the United States could act as "the sovereign of the territory . . . to the entire exclusion of . . . the Republic of Panama." The United States guaranteed the independence of the republic. The New Panama Canal Company then received its $40 million, including a substantial share for Bunau-Varilla.

Historians have condemned Roosevelt for his actions, and with good reason. It was not that he fomented the Panamanian revolution, for he did not. Separated from the government at Bogotá by an impenetrable jungle, the people of Panama province had long wanted to be free of Colombian rule. He sinned, rather, in his disregard of Latin American sensibilities. He referred to the Colombians as "dagoes" and insisted that he was defending "the interests of collective civilization" when he overrode their opposition to his plans.

If uncharitable, Roosevelt's analysis was not entirely inaccurate, yet it did not justify his haste in taking Panama under his wing. Throughout Latin America, especially as nationalist sentiments grew stronger, Roosevelt's intolerance and aggressiveness in the canal incident bred resentment and fear.

Table 1 Path to Empire, 1885–1901

Josiah Strong, *Our Country*	1885	Applied social Darwinism—"survival of the fittest"—to justify American expansion
A. T. Mahan, *The Influence of Seapower upon History*	1890	Endorsed naval power to ensure prosperity and national security
United States helped sugar planters depose Queen Liliuokalani	1893	Major step toward annexation of Hawaii
United States intervened in British dispute with Venezuela over land claims	1895	Reaffirmed the Monroe Doctrine claim to American supervision of Latin America
USS *Maine* exploded in Havana harbor	1898	Generated public pressure for war against Spain
Defeat of Spain	1898	Opened former Spanish colonies to U.S. annexation and economic penetration
U.S. annexation of Philippines	1899	United States became formal empire
"Open Door" Policy	1899	United States asserted trading rights in China
Roosevelt intervened on behalf of Panamanian independence	1903	Advanced expansive rights in Central America
Roosevelt Corollary	1904	Asserted U.S. right to military intervention in Latin America
Taft's Dollar Diplomacy	1909–1913	Encouraged U.S. government-supported investment abroad
Panama Canal opened	1914	Allowed U.S. warships to travel swiftly between Atlantic and Pacific

The first vessels passed through the canal in 1914—and American hegemony in the Caribbean expanded. Yet even in that strategically vital area there was more show than substance to American strength. The navy ruled Caribbean waters largely by default, for it lacked adequate bases in the region. In 1903, as authorized by the Cuban constitution, the United States obtained an excellent site for a base at Guantanamo Bay, but before 1914 Congress appropriated only $89,000 to develop it.

The tendency was to try to influence outlying areas without actually controlling them. Roosevelt's successor, William Howard Taft, called this policy **dollar diplomacy**, his reasoning being that economic penetration would bring stability to underdeveloped areas and power and profit to the United States without the government's having to commit troops or spend public funds.

Under Taft the State Department won a place for American bankers in an international syndicate engaged in financing railroads in Manchuria. When Nicaragua defaulted on its foreign debt in 1911, the department arranged for American bankers to reorganize Nicaraguan finances and manage the customs service. Although the government truthfully insisted that it did not "covet an inch of territory south of the Rio Grande," dollar diplomacy provoked further apprehension in Latin America. Efforts to establish similar arrangements in Honduras, Costa Rica, and Guatemala all failed. In Nicaragua orderly administration of the finances did not bring internal peace. In 1912, 2,500 American marines and sailors had to be landed to put down a revolution.

Economic penetration proceeded briskly. American investments in Cuba reached $500 million by 1920, and smaller but significant investments were made in the Dominican Republic and in Haiti. In Central America the United Fruit Company accumulated large holdings in banana plantations, railroads, and other ventures. Other firms plunged heavily into Mexico's rich mineral resources.

Imperialism without Colonies

If one defines imperialism narrowly as a policy of occupying and governing foreign lands, American imperialism lasted for an extremely short time. With trivial exceptions, all the American colonies—Hawaii, the Philippines, Guam, Puerto Rico, the Guantanamo base, and the Canal Zone—were obtained between 1898 and 1903. In retrospect it seems clear that the urge to own colonies was only fleeting; the legitimate questions raised by the anti-imperialists and the headaches connected with the management of overseas possessions soon produced a change of policy.

The objections of protectionists to the lowering of tariff barriers, the shock of the Philippine insurrection, and a growing conviction that the costs of colonial administration outweighed the profits affected American thinking. Hay's Open Door notes marked the beginning of the retreat from imperialism as thus defined, while the Roosevelt Corollary and dollar diplomacy signaled the consolidation of a new policy. Elihu Root summarized this policy as it applied to the Caribbean nations in 1905: "We do not want to take them for ourselves. We do not want any foreign nations to take them for themselves. We want to help them."

Yet imperialism can be given a broader definition. Although the United States did not seek colonies, it pursued a course that promoted American economic penetration of underdeveloped areas without the trouble of owning and controlling them. American statesmen regarded American expansion as beneficial to all concerned. They genuinely believed that they were exporting democracy along with capitalism and industrialization.

Dollar diplomacy had two main objectives, the avoidance of violence and the economic development of Latin America; it paid small heed to how peace was maintained and how the fruits of development were distributed. The policy was self-defeating, for in the long run stability depended on the support of local people, and this was seldom forthcoming.

By the eve of World War I the United States had become a world power and had assumed what it saw as a duty to guide the development of many countries with traditions far different from its own. The national psychology, if such a term has any meaning, remained fundamentally isolationist. Americans understood that their wealth and numbers made their nation strong and that geography made it virtually invulnerable. Thus they proceeded to do what they wanted to do in foreign affairs, limited more by their humanly flexible consciences than by any rational analysis of the probable consequences. This policy seemed safe enough—in 1914.

See the **Map**

World Colonial Empires, 1900
at **myhistorylab.com**

Milestones

1850	Britain and United States sign Clayton-Bulwer Treaty concerning interoceanic canal	1898	Theodore Roosevelt leads Rough Riders at Battle of San Juan Hill
			United States annexes Hawaii
1858	Commercial treaty with Japan opens several ports to American trade	1899	Hay's Open Door policy safeguards United States' access to China trade
1867	United States buys Alaska from Russia		United States annexes Philippines and becomes an empire
1871	Treaty of Washington settles *Alabama* claims	1900	Platt Amendment gives United States naval stations and right to intervene in Cuba
1875	Reciprocity treaty increases U.S. influence in Hawaii		
1885	Josiah Strong justifies expansionism in *Our Country*	1901	Hay-Pauncefote Treaty gives United States rights to build interoceanic canal
1890	A. T. Mahan fuels American imperialism in *The Influence of Sea Power*		Supreme Court's insular cases give Congress free reign over colonies
1893	United States helps sugar planters depose Queen Liliuokalani of Hawaii	1902	Europeans accept Monroe Doctrine during Venezuela bond dispute
1895	United States supports Venezuela in European border dispute over British Guiana	1904	Roosevelt Corollary to Monroe Doctrine gives United States "international police power"
1898	*Maine* explodes in Havana harbor	1907	"Gentlemen's Agreement" curtails Japanese immigration
	Spanish-American war breaks out		
	Dewey defeats Spanish fleet at Manila Bay	1914	Panama Canal opens

✓●─⌐Study and Review at www.myhistorylab.com

Review Questions

1. The introduction to this chapter holds that American soldiers are fighting in Afghanistan in part because of American imperialism after 1890. Could Americans then have avoided imperial expansion? What factors impelled them to support imperialism?

2. On what issues did the anti-imperialists and the imperialists agree? And how did they differ?

3. How did American involvement in the Caribbean differ from the United States' approach to China and East Asia?

4. Why did McKinley choose to annex the Philippines? Was his decision a wise one?

5. How did the Roosevelt Corollary modify the Monroe Doctrine? How did Taft's policies differ from those of Roosevelt?

6. Was American imperialism from 1890–1910 chiefly beneficial or harmful to other nations? To the United States?

Key Terms

dollar diplomacy
isolationism
Open Door policy

Platt Amendment
"reconcentration"
  camps

Teller Amendment

Woodrow Wilson and the Great War

((•—[Hear the Audio at myhistorylab.com

Do you know someone with TBI?

IN 2008 TOGGLE, A CHARACTER IN GARY TRUDEAU'S *DOONESBURY* comic strip, was driving a Humvee in Iraq when it was blown up by an improvised explosive device (IED). Toggle was hospitalized with traumatic brain injury (TBI), a buffeting of the brain caused by the shock waves of an explosion. By 2010 over 5,000 service members had been diagnosed with TBI, about a quarter of all combat casualties. "The Iraq war," the *Washington Post* observed, "has brought back one of the worst afflictions of World War I trench warfare: shell shock."

During World War I millions of men hunkered down in trenches surrounded by thickets of barbed wire. Before a major offensive, attacking armies hurled millions of artillery shells to pulverize such defenses. The casualties were staggering; many of the wounded suffered from shell shock—some 80,000 in the British army alone. Most never returned to active duty.

Just as American soldiers at the outset of the twenty-first century could not have imagined that they would be the victims of powerful explosions in Afghanistan and Iraq, few Americans in the early twentieth century thought it possible that they would get caught up in a war in Europe. To be sure, in the early 1900s Americans heard ominous rumblings from across the Atlantic Ocean. But even as European rivals spoke of war, none of it had much to do with American imperial interests in the Pacific and the Caribbean. But history unfolds in unpredictable ways.

In 1914 a spark ignited the powder keg of ethnic tensions in the Balkans. Soon, much of Europe was in flames. As the armies of the major powers became bogged down in a bloody stalemate, nonbelligerent nations were drawn into the conflagration. Woodrow Wilson, who had campaigned as a peace candidate, later called on the United States to go to war. Eventually he embraced it with an almost religious zeal. He recruited workers, farmers, financiers, manufacturers, minorities, and women to help in the war effort. He stamped out dissent. He also sought to take advantage of the transformations wrought by the war to promote various reforms—including the creation of an international body to mediate future conflicts. The tragedy of the Wilson years was that none of it turned out quite as he had imagined.

From Chapter 23 of *American Destiny: Narrative of a Nation*, Combined Volume, Fourth Edition. Mark C. Carnes and John A. Garraty. Copyright © 2012 by Pearson Education, Inc. Published by Pearson Prentice Hall. All rights reserved.

Wilson's "Moral" Diplomacy

Wilson did not lead the nation to war; both he and the nation stumbled into it without meaning to. Part of the reason was that Wilson's foreign relations, though well-intentioned, were often confused. He knew that the United States had no wish to injure any foreign state and assumed that all nations would recognize this fact and cooperate. Like nineteenth-century Christian missionaries, he wanted to spread the gospel of American democracy, to lift and enlighten the unfortunate and the ignorant—but in his own way.

Wilson set out to raise the moral tone of American foreign policy by denouncing dollar diplomacy. To seek special economic concessions in Latin America was "unfair" and "degrading." The United States would deal with Latin American nations "upon terms of equality and honor."

Yet Wilson sometimes failed to live up to his promises. Because of the strategic importance of the Panama Canal, he was unwilling to tolerate "unrest" anywhere in the Caribbean. Within months of his inauguration he was pursuing the same tactics employed by Roosevelt and Taft. The Bryan-Chamorro Treaty of 1914, which gave the United States an option to build a canal across Nicaragua, made that country virtually an American protectorate and served to maintain in power an unpopular dictator, Adolfo Díaz.

A much more serious example of missionary diplomacy occurred in Mexico. In 1911 a liberal coalition overthrew the dictator Porfirio Díaz, who had been exploiting the resources and people of Mexico for the benefit of a small class of wealthy landowners, clerics, and military men since the 1870s. Francisco Madero became president.

Perhaps inspired by progressive reforms in the United States, Madero proposed a liberal constitution for Mexico. But British oil magnates, who controlled most of Mexico's chief export, conspired with Victoriano Huerta, a general in Madero's army. In 1913 Huerta assassinated Madero and seized power. Britain promptly recognized Huerta's government.

The American ambassador urged Wilson to do so too, but he refused. His sympathies were with the government of Madero, whose murder had horrified him. "I will not recognize a government of butchers," he said. Wilson instead brought enormous pressure to bear against Huerta. He demanded that Huerta hold free elections as the price of American mediation in the continuing civil war. Huerta refused. The tense situation exploded in April 1914, when a small party of American sailors was arrested in the port of Tampico, Mexico. Wilson used the affair as an excuse to send troops into Mexico.

The invasion took place at Veracruz, where Winfield Scott had launched the

Photo Credit: The Granger Collection, New York.

In 1911, Francisco Madero overthrew Mexican dictator Porfirio Diaz and established a constitutional government.

assault on Mexico City in 1847. Instead of surrendering the city, the Mexicans resisted, suffering 400 casualties before falling back. This bloodshed caused dismay throughout Latin America. Huerta, hard-pressed by Mexican opponents, fled from power.

Wilson now made a monumental blunder. He threw his support to Francisco "Pancho" Villa, one of Huerta's generals. But Villa was little more than an ambitious bandit whose only objective was personal power. In October 1915, realizing his error, Wilson abandoned Villa and backed another Mexican rebel, who drove Villa to the northern border of Mexico. In 1916 Villa stopped a train in northern Mexico and killed sixteen American passengers in cold blood. Then he crossed into New Mexico and burned the town of Columbus, killing nineteen.

Having learned the perils of intervening in Mexican politics, Wilson would have preferred to bear even this assault in silence; but public opinion forced him to send American troops under General John J. Pershing across the border in pursuit of Villa.

Villa proved impossible to catch. Cleverly he drew Pershing deeper and deeper into Mexico, which challenged Mexican sovereignty. Several clashes occurred between Pershing's men and Mexican regulars, and for a brief period in June 1916 war seemed imminent. Wilson now acted bravely and wisely. Early in 1917 he recalled Pershing's force, leaving the Mexicans to work out their own destiny.

Missionary diplomacy in Mexico had produced mixed, but in the long run beneficial, results. His bungling bred anti-Americanism in Mexico; but his opposition to Huerta strengthened the real revolutionaries, enabling the constitutionalists to consolidate power.

Europe Explodes in War

On June 28, 1914, in the Austro-Hungarian provincial capital of Sarajevo, Gavrilo Princip, a young student, assassinated the Archduke Franz Ferdinand, heir to the imperial throne. Princip was a member of the Black Hand, a Serbian terrorist organization. He was seeking to further the cause of Serbian nationalism. Instead his rash act precipitated a general European war. Within little more than a month, following a complex series of diplomatic challenges and responses, two great coalitions, the **Central Powers** (chiefly Germany, Austria-Hungary, and Ottoman Turkey) and the **Allied Powers** (chiefly Great Britain, France, and Russia), were locked in a brutal struggle that brought one era in world history to a close and inaugurated another.

Watch the Video

The outbreak of WWI at **myhistorylab.com**

The outbreak of this Great War caught Americans psychologically unprepared; few understood its significance. President Wilson promptly issued a proclamation of neutrality and asked the nation to be "impartial in thought." The almost unanimous reaction of Americans, aside from dismay, was that the conflict did not concern them.

Although most Americans hoped to keep out of the war, nearly everyone was partial to one side or the other. People of German or Austrian descent, about 8 million in number, and the nation's 4.5 million Irish Americans, motivated chiefly by hatred of the British, sympathized with the Central Powers. The majority of the people, however, influenced by bonds of language and culture, preferred an Allied victory, and when the Germans launched a mighty assault across neutral Belgium in an effort to outflank the French armies, many Americans were outraged.

As the war progressed, the Allies—especially Britain—cleverly exploited American prejudices by publishing exaggerated tales of German atrocities against Belgian civilians. A supposedly impartial study of these charges by the widely respected James Bryce, author of *The American Commonwealth*, portrayed the Germans as ruthless barbarians. The Germans also conducted a propaganda campaign in the United States, but they labored under severe handicaps and won few converts.

Freedom of the Seas

Propaganda did not basically alter American attitudes; far more important were questions arising out of trade and commerce. Under international law, neutrals could trade freely with any belligerent. Americans were prepared to do so, but because the British fleet dominated the North Atlantic, they could not. The situation was similar to the one that had prevailed during the Napoleonic Wars. The British declared nearly all commodities, even foodstuffs, to be contraband of war. They forced neutral merchant ships into British or French ports in order to search them for goods headed for the enemy. Many cargoes were confiscated, often without payment. American firms that traded with the Central Powers were "blacklisted," which meant that no British subject could deal with them. When Americans protested, the British answered that in a battle for survival, they dared not adhere to old-fashioned rules of international law.

Had the United States insisted that Great Britain abandon these "illegal" practices, as the Germans demanded, no doubt it could have had its way. The British foreign secretary, Sir Edward Grey, later admitted, "The ill-will of the United States meant certain defeat. The object of diplomacy, therefore, was to secure the maximum of blockade that could be enforced without a rupture with the United States." It is ironic that an embargo, which failed so ignominiously in Jefferson's day, would have been almost instantly effective if applied at any time after 1914, for American supplies were vital to the Allies.

Wilson faced a dilemma. To allow the British to make the rules meant siding against the Central Powers. Yet to insist on the old rules meant siding against the Allies because that would have deprived them of much of the value of their naval superiority. *Nothing* the United States might do would be truly impartial.

The immense expansion of American trade with the Allies made an embargo unthinkable. While commerce with the Central Powers fell to a trickle, that with the Allies soared from $825 million in 1914 to over $3.2 billion in 1916. An attempt to limit this commerce would have raised a storm; to have eliminated it would have caused a catastrophe. Munitions makers and other businessmen did not want the United States to enter the war. Neutrality suited their purposes admirably.

Britain and France soon exhausted their ready cash, and by early 1917 they had borrowed well over $2 billion. Although these loans violated no principle of international law, they fastened the United States more closely to the Allies' cause.

During the first months of the Great War, the Germans were not especially concerned about neutral trade or American goods because they expected to crush the Allied armies quickly. When their first swift thrust into France was blunted along the Marne River, only twenty miles from Paris, and the war became a bloody stalemate, they began to challenge the Allies' control of the seas. Unwilling to risk their battleships and cruisers against the much larger British fleet, they resorted to a new weapon, the submarine, commonly known as the U-boat (for *Unterseeboot*). German submarines played a role in World War I not unlike that of American privateers in the Revolution and the War of 1812: They ranged the seas stealthily in search of merchant ships. However, submarines could not operate under the ordinary rules of war, which required that a raider stop its prey, examine its papers and cargo, and give the crew and passengers time to get off in lifeboats before sending it to the bottom. U-boats when surfaced were vulnerable to the deck guns that many merchant ships carried; they could even be sunk by ramming, once they had stopped and put out a boarding party. Therefore, they commonly launched their torpedoes from below the surface without warning, often resulting in a heavy loss of life.

In February 1915 the Germans declared the waters surrounding the British Isles a zone of war and announced that they would sink without warning all enemy merchant ships encountered in the area. Since Allied vessels sometimes flew neutral flags to disguise their identity, neutral ships entering the zone would do so at their own risk. This statement was largely bluff, for the Germans had only a handful of submarines at sea; but they were feverishly building more.

Wilson—perhaps too hurriedly, considering the importance of the question—warned the Germans that he would hold them to "strict accountability" for any loss of American life or property resulting from violations of "acknowledged [neutral] rights on the high seas." He did not distinguish clearly between losses incurred through the destruction of *American* ships and those resulting from the sinking of other vessels. If he meant to hold the Germans responsible for injuries to Americans on *belligerent* vessels, he was changing international law as arbitrarily as the Germans were. Secretary of State Bryan, who opposed Wilson vigorously on this point, stood on sound legal ground when he said, "A ship carrying contraband should not rely upon passengers to protect her from attack—it would be like putting women and children in front of an army."

Correct or not, Wilson's position reflected the attitude of most Americans. It seemed barbaric to them that defenseless civilians should be killed without warning; Americans refused to surrender their "rights" as neutrals to cross the North Atlantic on any ship they wished. The depth of their feeling was demonstrated when, on May 7, 1915, the submarine *U-20* sank the British liner *Lusitania* off the Irish coast. This caused a profound and emotional reaction in the United States. The sinking of the *Lusitania* evoked the sinking of HMS *Titanic* three years earlier, after it had struck an iceberg in

NOTICE!

TRAVELLERS intending to embark on the Atlantic voyage are reminded that a state of war exists between Germany and her allies and Great Britain and her allies; that the zone of war includes the waters adjacent to the British Isles; that, in accordance with formal notice given by the Imperial German Government, vessels flying the flag of Great Britain, or of any of her allies, are liable to destruction in those waters and that travellers sailing in the war zone on ships of Great Britain or her allies do so at their own risk.

IMPERIAL GERMAN EMBASSY
WASHINGTON, D. C., APRIL 22, 1915.

Photo Credit: Brown Brothers.

Three weeks before the *Lusitania* was torpedoed, this notice appeared in the classified sections of Washington newspapers.

Titanic

James Cameron's *Titanic* (1997) was a blockbuster. He made audiences feel what it was like to be on the ship. What sent a shiver down the spine was the knowledge that real people had experienced what was being depicted on the screen.

Cameron well understood the audience's craving to relive a true story. The movie opens with footage of the actual HMS *Titanic* on the floor of the Atlantic, fish gliding silently through its barnacle-encrusted wreckage. Cameron also spent scores of millions of dollars devising computer-enhanced techniques to ensure that his *Titanic* looked like the one that went down in the North Atlantic on the night of April 14–15, 1912.

But Cameron's *Titanic* was more than a disaster movie. It was also the story of two young people who fall in love. The romance begins when Jack (Leonardo DiCaprio), a struggling artist, spots Rose (Kate Winslet), a wealthy socialite, climbing over the railing and peering despondently into the water below. Obliged to marry a contemptuous (and contemptible) snob, she is miserable. Jack, from a lower deck, scrambles up and persuades her to forgo the plunge.

As a reward for saving Rose, Jack is invited to dine with Rose's table. At dinner, Rose appraises Jack more carefully—and is impressed. He looks good in a tuxedo, displays plenty of moxie, and possesses artistic talent ("Jack, you see things!").

When the ship has its close encounter of the icy kind, Jack—young, vital, alive—perishes in the frigid waters. But he has imparted to Rose a gift of love, and thus of life. This tale of young lovers, held apart by society, is a nautical "Romeo and Juliet," a brief, pure instant of love, tragically ended by death.

If Cameron's *Titanic* is a love story for the ages, it was also frozen in a particular place and in a particular time. Much as Cameron spent millions to show the ship as it really was, he took similar pains to give a convincing rendering of New York society, especially its clothing, silverware, and social conventions.

Of the latter, the most significant for the story are the elaborate rituals of Victorian courtship. Rose seeks to break free from her impending marriage partly because she despises her fiancé, but also because marriage to him constitutes the final, irreversible step into the gilded cage of a society lady. Jack's presence at dinner with the "best" of society underscores the shallow materialism of this upper crust and its preoccupation with wealth, its absurd rules of etiquette, and its repressive attitudes toward sexuality. Viewers of the movie, looking through Rose's eyes, may wonder how such rituals ever came to be.

Some had existed for centuries. The idealization of courtly love and pure womanhood was a commonplace of medieval literature. In the early nineteenth century novelist Jane Austen described the subtle interplay of money and romance in England. But the rituals of New York society in the Gilded Age were characterized by sumptuous and public displays of wealth—glittering balls and extravagant "Grand Tours" of Europe.

This new mode of courtship was largely the creation of Mrs. John Jacob Astor, wife of one of New York's wealthiest businessmen, and her friends. After the Civil War, industrialization and urbanization were generating new wealth and destroying the old at a dizzying pace. While prominent businessmen and investment bankers were devising institutions to impose order on this creative industrial chaos, their wives were regulating its social elite. They endeavored to determine who should be admitted to New York's "best" families—and who should not. They concluded that it was not enough to be rich; the elite of the nation must also adhere to high standards of etiquette and decorum. Society women possessed immense power.

Leonardo DiCaprio and Kate Winslet as lovers on the *Titanic*.

Although the system was created and supervised by mature women, it demanded the compliance of adolescent girls. The process began when a wealthy mother took her daughter on a round of visits to society women, to whom they would present their "calling cards." If mother and daughter were judged suitable, they would be invited in for tea; if the girl behaved with decorum (and if her father's assets proved sound), she would be invited to balls and other formal events. At or near her sixteenth birthday, her parents would hold a ball in her honor—in New York the event usually took place at Delmonico's restaurant—marking her "debut" into society. She wore a white gown symbolizing her virginity. A male relative presented her formally to the prominent women. Now she could accept male suitors from "society."

This highly stylized—almost tribal—ritual brought young women to the threshold of womanhood. Marriage awaited beyond the door. Many eagerly anticipated the acquisition of adult status and the social power it entailed. Others regarded this rite with terror. (Novelist Edith Wharton remembered her debut as a "long cold agony of shyness.") In the early twentieth century, some young women began to rebel. Elsie Clews, daughter of a Wall Street banker, refused to wear corsets. When her mother wasn't looking, she took off her veil and white gloves. She subsequently scandalized Newport—the fashionable Rhode Island summer resort for society's wealthy—by going swimming with a young man without a chaperone (but not without a bathing suit).

To her mother's dismay, Clews delayed marriage and went to Barnard College; eventually she became a respected anthropologist (Elsie Clews Parsons).

Kate Winslet's "Rose" was, like Elsie Clews, a prematurely "modern" woman. But Clews dispensed with the rituals of courtship, not its substance. Even in the waning years of the Victorian era, few wealthy young women succumbed to impoverished men, however earnest and appealing.

Victorian courtship was necessarily protracted. Young women did not unburden themselves to strangers; and even to friends, especially of the opposite sex, the process of revealing one's inner feelings unfolded slowly, often after a series of tests and trials. One person's tentative disclosure invited a reciprocal response. Letters and diaries show that, over time, these personal revelations often led to sexual intimacies. Nowadays many people regard Victorian marriages as unfeeling and stiff, but many Victorians maintained that their personal intimacies were the more delicious for having been long delayed.

Cameron's *Titanic* looks like the past; but the heart of the movie is Jack and Rose's whirlwind romance. While Rose's story addresses some of the anxieties of young society women, it more closely resembles the courtship patterns of Hollywood today than the experiences of young people at the beginning of the last century.

Questions for Discussion
- Jack and Rose "hooked up," to use modern slang. Why was such behavior improbable among young women of wealthy families in the late nineteenth century?
- What other behaviors in the film seem anachronistic?

Photo Credit: © Mary Evans Picture Library/The Image Works.

The *Titanic* carried only twenty lifeboats, a reason why so many perished in 1912. The *Lusitania* (above) carried forty-eight lifeboats, but it sank so quickly that many went unused.

the northern Atlantic; first-person accounts rendered the tragedy all the more vivid to Americans. When it was learned that nearly 1,200 persons, including 128 Americans, lost their lives when the *Lusitania* went down (nearly as many as had perished on the *Titanic*), Americans were outraged. (For more on the *Titanic*, see Re-Viewing the Past.)

Wilson demanded that Germany disavow the sinking, indemnify the victims, and promise to stop attacking passenger vessels. When the Germans quibbled about these points, he responded with further diplomatic correspondence rather than with an ultimatum.

In one sense this was sound policy. The Germans pointed out that they had published warnings in American newspapers saying they considered the *Lusitania* subject to attack, that the liner was carrying munitions, and that on past voyages it had flown the American flag to deceive German U-boat captains. However, after dragging the controversy out for nearly a year, Germany apologized and agreed to pay an indemnity. After the torpedoing of the French channel steamer *Sussex* in March 1916 had produced another stiff American protest, the Germans at last promised, in the *Sussex* pledge, to stop sinking merchant ships without warning.

Theodore Roosevelt urged Wilson to commit the United States to war with Germany; Wilson's refusal to do so incensed him. In November 1915 Wilson, in a belated nod to such criticisms, pressed for increased military and naval expenditures.

The Election of 1916

Wilson had won the presidency in 1912 only because the Republican party had split in two. In late 1915 he sought to broaden his support by winning over the progressives. In January 1916 he appointed Louis D. Brandeis to the Supreme Court. In addition to being an advanced progressive, Brandeis was the first Jewish Justice appointed to the Court. Wilson's action won him many friends among people who favored fair treatment for minority groups. In July Wilson bid for the farm vote by signing the Farm Loan Act to provide low-cost loans based on agricultural credit. Shortly thereafter, he approved the Keating-Owen Child Labor Act barring goods manufactured by the labor of children under 16 from interstate commerce, and a workers' compensation act for federal employees. He persuaded Congress to pass the Adamson Act, establishing an eight-hour day for railroad workers, and he modified his position on the tariff by approving the creation of a tariff commission.

Each of these actions represented a sharp reversal. In 1913 Wilson had considered Brandeis too radical even for a Cabinet post. The new farm, labor, and tariff laws were all examples of the kind of "class legislation" he had refused to countenance in 1913 and 1914. Wilson was putting into effect much of the progressive platform of 1912. Although the progressive convention came out for the Republican nominee, Associate Justice Charles Evans Hughes, who had compiled a record as a progressive governor of New York, many other progressives supported Wilson.

The key issue in the campaign was American policy toward the warring powers. Wilson intended to stress preparedness, which he was now wholeheartedly supporting. However, during the Democratic convention, the delegates shook the hall with cheers whenever orators referred to the president's success in keeping the country out of the war. "He Kept Us Out of War" became the Democratic slogan.

The combination of progressivism and the peace issue placed the Democrats on substantially equal terms with the Republicans. In the end, personal factors probably tipped the balance. Hughes was very stiff and an ineffective speaker; he offended a number of important politicians, especially in crucial California, where he inadvertently snubbed the popular progressive governor, Hiram Johnson; and he equivocated on a number of issues. Nevertheless, on election night he appeared to have won, having carried nearly all the East and Midwest. Late returns gave Wilson California, however, and with it victory by the narrow margin of 277 to 254 in the Electoral College. He led Hughes in the popular vote, 9.1 million to 8.5 million.

The Road to War

Wilson's own feelings were more genuinely neutral than at any other time during the war, for the Germans had stopped sinking merchant ships without warning and the British had irritated him repeatedly by their arbitrary restrictions on neutral trade. He drafted a note to the belligerents asking them to state the terms on which they would agree to lay down their arms. Unless the fighting ended soon, he warned, neutrals and belligerents alike would be so ruined that peace would be meaningless.

When neither side responded encouragingly, Wilson, on January 22, 1917, delivered a moving speech aimed at "the people of the countries now at war" more than at their governments. Any settlement imposed by a victor, he declared, would breed hatred and more wars. There must be "peace without victory," based on the principles that all nations were equal and that every nationality should determine its own form of government. He mentioned, albeit vaguely, disarmament and freedom of the seas, and he suggested the creation of some kind of international organization to preserve world peace. This noble appeal met a tragic fate. The Germans had already decided to renounce the Sussex pledge and unleash their submarines against all vessels headed for Allied ports. After February 1, any ship in the war zone would be attacked without warning. Possessed now of more than 100 U-boats, the German military leaders had convinced themselves that they could starve the British people into submission and reduce the Allied armies to impotence by cutting off the flow of American supplies. The United States would probably declare war, but the Germans believed that they could overwhelm the Allies before the Americans could get to the battlefields in force. In 1917, after the German military leaders had made this decision, events moved relentlessly, almost uninfluenced by the actors who presumably controlled the fate of the world:

● Watch the Video

American entry into WWI at **myhistorylab.com**

February 3: Housatonic is torpedoed. Wilson announces to Congress that he has severed diplomatic relations with Germany.

February 24: Walter Hines Page, United States ambassador to Great Britain, transmits to the State Department an intercepted German dispatch (the "Zimmermann telegram") revealing that Germany has proposed a secret alliance with Mexico; Mexico will receive, in the event of war with the United States, "the lost territory in Texas, New Mexico, and Arizona."

February 25: Cunard liner *Laconia* is torpedoed; two American women perish.

February 26: Wilson asks Congress for authority to arm American merchant ships.

March 1: Zimmermann telegram is released to the press.

March 4: President Wilson takes oath of office, beginning his second term.

March 9: Wilson, acting under his executive powers, orders the arming of American merchantmen.

March 12: Revolutionary provisional government is established in Russia. *Algonquin* is torpedoed.

March 15: Czar Nicholas II of Russia abdicates.

March 16: City of Memphis, *Illinois*, and *Vigilancia* are torpedoed.

March 21: New York World, a leading Democratic newspaper, calls for declaration of war on Germany. Wilson summons Congress to convene in a special session on April 2.

March 25: Wilson calls up the National Guard.

April 2: Wilson asks Congress to declare war. Germany is guilty of "throwing to the winds all scruples of humanity," he says. America must fight, not to conquer, but for "peace and justice. . . . The world must be made safe for democracy."

April 4, 6: Congress declares war—the vote, 82–6 in the Senate, 373–50 in the House.

●●● Read the Document

United States Declaration of War (1917) at **myhistorylab.com**

●●● Read the Document

President Wilson's War Message to Congress (1917) at **myhistorylab.com**

The bare record conceals Wilson's agonizing search for an honorable alternative to war. To admit that Germany posed a threat to the United States meant confessing that interventionists had been right all along. To go to war meant, besides sending innocent Americans to their deaths, allowing "the spirit of ruthless brutality [to] enter into the very fibre of our national life."

The president's Presbyterian conscience tortured him. He lost sleep, appeared gray and drawn. In the end Wilson could salve his conscience only by giving intervention an idealistic purpose: the war had become a threat to humanity. Unless the United States threw its weight into the balance, Western civilization itself might be destroyed.

Mobilizing the Economy

America's entry into the Great War determined its outcome. The Allies were running out of money and supplies; their troops, decimated by nearly three years in the trenches, were exhausted, disheartened, and rebellious. In February and March 1917, U-boats sent over a million tons of Allied shipping to the bottom of the Atlantic. The outbreak of the Russian Revolution in March 1917, at first lifting the spirits of the Western democracies, led to the Bolshevik takeover under Lenin. The Russian armies collapsed; by December 1917 Russia was out of the war and the Germans were moving masses of men and equipment from the eastern front to France. Without the aid of the United States, the Allies would likely have sued for peace according to terms dictated from Berlin. Instead American men and supplies helped contain the Germans' last drives and then push them back to final defeat.

It was a close thing, for the United States entered the war little better prepared to fight than it had been in 1898. The conversion of American industry to war production had to be carried out without prearrangement. Confusion and waste resulted. The hurriedly designed shipbuilding program was an almost total fiasco. The gigantic Hog Island yard in Maine, which employed at its peak over 34,000 workers, completed its first vessel only after the war ended. Airplane, tank, and artillery construction programs developed too slowly to affect the war. The big guns that backed up American soldiers in 1918 were made in France and Great Britain; of the 8.8 million rounds of artillery ammunition fired by American troops, a mere 8,000 were manufactured in the United States. Congress authorized the manufacture of 20,000 airplanes, but only a handful, mostly British-designed planes made in America, got to France.

The problem of mobilization was complicated. It took Congress six weeks of hot debate merely to decide on conscription. Only in September 1917, nearly six months after the declaration of war, did the first draftees reach the training camps, and it is hard to see how Wilson could have speeded this process. He wisely supported the professional soldiers, who insisted that he resist the appeals of politicians who wanted to raise volunteer units, even rejecting, at considerable political cost, Theodore Roosevelt's offer to raise an entire army division.

"Enlist"—a poster by Fred Spear, published in June 1915 by the Boston Committee of Public Safety— evoked the drowning deaths of women and children on the *Lusitania*.

Wilson was a forceful and inspiring war leader once he grasped what needed to be done. He displayed both determination and unfailing patience in the face of frustration and criticism. Raising an army was only a small part of the job. The Allies had to be supplied with food and munitions, and immense amounts of money had to be collected.

After several false starts, Wilson placed the task in the hands of the **War Industries Board (WIB)**. The board was given almost dictatorial power to allocate scarce materials, standardize production, fix prices, and coordinate American and Allied purchasing. Evaluating the mobilization effort raises interesting historical questions. The antitrust laws were suspended and producers were encouraged, even compelled, to cooperate with one another. Government regulation went far beyond what the New Nationalists had envisaged in 1912.

As for the New Freedom variety of laissez-faire, it had no place in a wartime economy. The nation's railroads, strained by immensely increased traffic, became progressively less efficient. A monumental tie-up in December and January 1917–1918 finally persuaded Wilson to appoint Secretary of the Treasury William G. McAdoo director-general of the railroads, with power to run the roads as a single system. McAdoo's Railroad Administration pooled all railroad equipment, centralized purchasing, standardized accounting practices, and raised wages and passenger rates.

Wilson accepted the kind of government-industry agreement that he had denounced in 1912. Prices were set by the WIB at levels that allowed large profits—U.S. Steel, for example, despite high taxes, cleared over half a billion dollars in two years. It is at least arguable that producers would have turned out just as much even if compelled to charge lower prices.

Mobilization required close cooperation between business and the military. However, the army, suspicious of civilian institutions, resisted cooperating with them. Wilson finally compelled the War Department to place officers on WIB committees, laying the foundation for what was later to be known as the "industrial-military complex," an alliance between business and military leaders.

The history of industrial mobilization was the history of the entire home-front effort in microcosm: Marvels were performed, but the task was so gigantic and unprecedented that a full year passed before an efficient system had been devised, and many unforeseen results occurred.

The problem of mobilizing agricultural resources was solved more quickly, and this was fortunate because in April 1917 the British had on hand only a six-week supply of food Wilson appointed as food administrator Herbert Hoover; Hoover, a mining engineer, had headed the Belgian Relief Commission earlier in the war. Acting under powers granted by the Lever Act of 1917, Hoover set the price of wheat at $2.20 a bushel in order to encourage production. He established a government corporation to purchase the entire American and Cuban sugar crops, which he then doled out to American and British refiners. To avoid rationing he organized a campaign to persuade consumers to conserve food voluntarily. One slogan ran "If U fast U beat U boats"; another, "Serve beans by all means."

Without subjecting its own citizens to serious inconvenience, the United States increased food exports from 12.3 million tons to 18.6 million tons. Farmers, of course, profited greatly. Their real income went up nearly 30 percent between 1915 and 1918.

Workers in Wartime

With the army siphoning so many men from the labor market and with immigration reduced to a trickle, unemployment disappeared and wages rose. Although the cost of living soared, imposing hardships on people with fixed incomes, the boom produced unprecedented opportunities.

Americans, always a mobile people, pulled up their roots in record numbers. Disadvantaged groups, especially African Americans, were particularly attracted by jobs in big-city factories. Early in the conflict, the government began regulating the wages and hours of workers building army camps and manufacturing uniforms. In April 1918 Wilson created the National War Labor Board, headed by former president Taft and Frank P. Walsh, a prominent lawyer, to settle labor disputes. The board considered more than 1,200 cases and prevented many strikes. The War Labor Policies Board, chaired by Felix Frankfurter of the Harvard Law School, set wages-and-hours standards for each major war industry. Since these were determined in consultation with employers and representatives of labor, they speeded the unionization of workers by compelling management, even in antiunion industries like steel, to deal with labor leaders. Union membership rose by 2.3 million during the war.

However, the wartime emergency roused the public against strikers. While he opposed strikes that impeded the war effort, Wilson set great store in preserving the individual worker's freedom of action. It would be "most unfortunate . . . to relax the laws by which safeguards have been thrown about labor," he said. "We must accomplish the results we desire by organized effort rather than compulsion."

Paying for the War

Wilson managed the task of financing the war effectively. The struggle cost the United States about $33.5 billion, not counting pensions and other postwar expenses. About $7 billion of this was lent to the Allies,[1] but since this money was spent largely in America, it contributed to the national prosperity.

Over two-thirds of the cost of the war was met by borrowing. Five Liberty and Victory Loan drives, spurred by advertising, parades, and other appeals to patriotism, persuaded people to open their purses. Industrialists, eager to instill in their employees a sense of personal involvement in the war effort, conducted campaigns in their plants. In addition to borrowing, the government collected about $10.5 billion in taxes during the war. A steeply graduated income tax took more than 75 percent of the incomes of the wealthiest citizens. A 65 percent excess-profits tax and a 25 percent inheritance tax were also enacted. Thus although many individuals made fortunes from the war, its cost was distributed far more equitably than during the Civil War.

Americans also contributed generously to philanthropic agencies engaged in war work. Most notable, perhaps, was the great 1918 drive of the United War Work Council, an interfaith religious group, which raised over $200 million mainly to finance recreational programs for the troops overseas.

---

[1]In 1914 Americans owed foreigners about $3.8 billion. By 1919 Americans were owed $12.5 billion by Europeans alone.

Propaganda and Civil Liberties

Wilson was preeminently a teacher and preacher, a specialist in the transmission of ideas and ideals. He excelled at mobilizing public opinion and inspiring Americans to work for the better world he hoped would emerge from the war. In April 1917 he created the Committee on Public Information (CPI), headed by the journalist George Creel. Soon 75,000 speakers were deluging the country with propaganda prepared by hundreds of CPI writers. They pictured the war as a crusade for freedom and democracy, the Germans as a bestial people bent on world domination.

A large majority of the nation supported the war enthusiastically. But thousands of persons—German Americans and Irish Americans, for example; people of pacifist leanings such as Jane Addams, the founder of Hull House; and some who thought both sides in the war were wrong—still opposed American involvement. Creel's committee and a number of unofficial "patriotic" groups allowed their enthusiasm for the conversion of the hesitant to become suppression of dissent. People who refused to buy war bonds were often exposed to public ridicule and even assault. Those with German names were persecuted without regard for their views; some school boards outlawed the teaching of the German language; sauerkraut was renamed "liberty cabbage." A cartoonist pictured Senator Robert La Follette, who had opposed entering the war, receiving an Iron Cross from the German militarists, and the faculty of his own University of Wisconsin voted to censure him.

●◄─ Read the Document

Buffington, *Friendly Words to the Foreign Born* at **myhistorylab.com**

Although Wilson spoke in defense of free speech, his actions opposed it. He signed the **Espionage Act** of 1917, which imposed fines of up to $10,000 and jail sentences ranging to twenty years on persons convicted of aiding the enemy or obstructing recruiting, and he authorized the postmaster general to ban from the mails any material that seemed treasonable or seditious.

In May 1918, again with Wilson's approval, Congress passed the **Sedition Act,** which made "saying anything" to discourage the purchase of war bonds a crime, with the proviso that investment counselors could still offer "bona fide and not disloyal advice" to clients. The law also made it illegal to "utter, print, write, or publish any disloyal, profane, scurrilous, or abusive language" about the government, the Constitution, or the uniform of the army or navy. Socialist periodicals such as The Masses were suppressed, and Eugene V. Debs, formerly a candidate for president, was sentenced to ten years in prison for making an anti-war speech. Ricardo Flores Magón, an anarchist, was sentenced to twenty

Eugene V. Debs ("Convict #9653") was imprisoned for speaking against the war. In 1920 he ran as the Socialist candidate for president from the Atlanta federal prison, receiving nearly a million votes.

Photo Credit: Eugene V. Debs Foundation.

Table 1 Suppression of Liberties during World War I

Federal Action	Year	Consequence
Espionage Act	1917	Prohibited words or actions that would aid the enemy or obstruct recruiting efforts
Sedition Act	1918	Prohibited people from "saying anything" that might discourage purchase of war bonds or otherwise undermine the federal government or the Constitution
Schenck v. United States	1919	Supreme Court upheld limitations on free speech during times of "clear and present danger" to the nation

years in jail for publishing a statement criticizing Wilson's Mexican policy, an issue that had nothing to do with the war.

These laws went far beyond what was necessary to protect the national interest. Citizens were jailed for suggesting that the draft law was unconstitutional and for criticizing private organizations like the Red Cross and the YMCA.

The Supreme Court upheld the constitutionality of the Espionage Act in *Schenck v. United States* (1919), a case involving a man who had mailed circulars to draftees urging them to refuse to report for induction into the army. Free speech has its limits, Justice Oliver Wendell Holmes, Jr., explained. When there is a "clear and present danger" that a particular statement would threaten the national interest, it can be repressed by law. In peacetime Schenck's circulars would be permissible, but not in time of war.

The "clear and present danger" doctrine did not prevent judges and juries from interpreting the espionage and sedition acts broadly, and although in many instances higher courts overturned their decisions, this usually did not occur until after the war. The wartime repression far exceeded anything that happened in Great Britain and France. In 1916 the French novelist Henri Barbusse published *Le Feu (Under Fire)*, a graphic account of the horrors and purposelessness of trench warfare. In one chapter Barbusse described a pilot flying over the trenches on a Sunday, observing French and German soldiers at Mass in the open fields, each worshiping the same God. Yet *Le Feu* circulated freely in France and even won the coveted Prix Goncourt.

Wartime Reforms

The American mobilization experience was part and product of the Progressive Era. Many progressives believed that the war was creating the sense of common purpose that would stimulate the people to act unselfishly to benefit the poor and to eradicate social evils. Patriotism and public service seemed at last united. Secretary of War Newton D. Baker, a prewar urban reformer, expressed this attitude in supporting a federal child labor law: "We cannot afford, when we are losing boys in France, to lose children in the United States."

Men and women of this sort worked for a dozen causes only remotely related to the war effort. The women's suffrage movement was brought to fruition, as was the campaign against alcohol. Both the Eighteenth Amendment, outlawing alcoholic beverages, and the Nineteenth, giving women the vote, were adopted at least in part because of the war. Reformers began to talk about health insurance. The progressive campaign against prostitution and venereal disease gained strength, winning the enthusiastic support both of persons worried about inexperienced local girls being seduced by the soldiers and of those concerned lest prostitutes lead innocent soldiers astray. One of the latter type claimed to have persuaded "over 1,000 fallen women" to promise not to go near any army camps.

The effort to wipe out prostitution around military installations was a cause of some misunderstanding with the Allies, who provided licensed facilities for their troops as a matter of course. When the premier of France offered to supply prostitutes for American units in his country, Secretary Baker is said to have remarked, "For God's sake . . . don't show this to the President or he'll stop the war." Apparently Baker had a rather peculiar sense of humor. After a tour of the front in France, he assured an American women's group that life in the trenches was "far less uncomfortable" than he had thought and that not a single American doughboy was "living a life which he would not be willing to have [his] mother see him live."

Women and Blacks in Wartime

Although a number of prominent feminists were pacifists, most supported the war enthusiastically, moved by patriotism and the belief that opposition to the war would doom their hopes of gaining the vote. They also expected that the war would open up many kinds of high-paying jobs to women. To some extent it did; about a million women replaced men in uniform, but the numbers actually engaged in war industries were small (about 6,000 found jobs making airplanes, for example), and the gains were fleeting. When the war ended, most women who were engaged in industrial work either left their jobs voluntarily or were fired to make room for returning veterans. Some women went overseas as nurses, and a few served as ambulance drivers and YMCA workers.

Most unions were unsympathetic to the idea of enrolling women, and the government did little to encourage women to do more for the war effort than prepare bandages, knit warm clothing for soldiers, participate in food conservation programs, and encourage people to buy war bonds. The final report of another wartime agency, issued in 1919, admitted that

Women workers at the Dupont factory in Old Hickory, Tennessee, in 1917, form smokeless gunpowder into long strips, which will then be cut for use in artillery shells and other armaments.

Photo Credit: Photograph courtesy of the Hagley Museum and Library, Wilmington, Delaware.

few women war workers had been paid as much as men and that women had been promoted more slowly than men, were not accepted by unions, and were discharged promptly when the war ended.

The wartime "great migration" of southern blacks to northern cities where jobs were available brought them important economic benefits. Between 1870 and 1890 only about 80,000 blacks moved to northern cities. Compared with the influx from Europe and from northern farms, this number was inconsequential. The black proportion of the population of New York City, for example, fell from over 10 percent in 1800 to under 2 percent in 1900.

Watch the Video

The Great Migration at **myhistorylab.com**

Around the turn of the century, as the first postslavery generation reached maturity and as southern repression increased, the northward movement quickened—about 200,000 blacks migrated between 1890 and 1910. Then, after 1914, the war boom drew blacks north in a flood. Agents of northern manufacturers flocked into the cotton belt to recruit them in wholesale lots. Half a million made the move between 1914 and 1919. The African American population of New York City rose from 92,000 to 152,000; that of Chicago from 44,000 to 109,000; and that of Detroit from 5,700 to 41,000.

Life for the newcomers was difficult; many whites resented them; workers feared them as potential strikebreakers yet refused to admit them into their unions. In East St. Louis, Illinois, where employers had brought in large numbers of blacks in an attempt to discourage local unions from striking for higher wages, a bloody riot erupted during the summer of 1917 in which nine whites and an undetermined number of blacks were killed. As in peacetime, the Wilson administration was at worst antagonistic and at best indifferent to blacks' needs and aspirations.

Nevertheless, the blacks who moved north during the war were, as a group, infinitely better off than those they left behind. Many earned good wages and were accorded at least some human rights. They were not treated by the whites as equals, or even in most cases entirely fairly, but they could vote, send their children to decent schools, and within reasonable limits do and say what they pleased without fear of humiliation or physical attack.

There were two black regiments in the regular army and a number of black national guard units when the war began, and once these outfits were brought up to combat strength, no more volunteers were accepted. At first no blacks were conscripted; Southerners in particular found the thought of giving large numbers of guns to blacks and teaching them how to use them most disturbing. However, blacks were soon drafted, and once they were, a larger proportion of them were taken than whites. One Georgia draft board exempted more than 500 of 815 white registrants and only 6 of the 202 blacks in its jurisdiction before its members were relieved of their duties. After a riot in Texas in which black soldiers killed seventeen white civilians, black recruits were dispersed among many camps for training to lessen the possibility of trouble.

In the military service, all blacks were placed in segregated units. Only a handful were commissioned as officers. Despite the valor displayed by black soldiers in the Civil War and the large role they played in the Spanish-American War, where five blacks had won the Congressional Medal of Honor, most even those sent overseas, were assigned to labor battalions working as stevedores and common laborers. But many fought and died for their country. Altogether about 200,000 served overseas.

W. E. B. Du Bois supported the war wholeheartedly. He praised Wilson for making, at last, a strong statement against lynching, which had increased to a shocking extent during the previous decade. He even went along with the fact that the handful of black officer candidates were trained in a segregated camp. "Let us," he wrote in the Crisis, "while the war lasts, forget our special grievances and close ranks shoulder to shoulder with our fellow citizens and the allied nations that are fighting for democracy."

Many blacks condemned Du Bois's accommodationism, but most saw the war as an opportunity to demonstrate their patriotism and prove their worth. For the moment the prevailing mood was one of optimism. If winning the war would make the world safe for democracy, surely blacks in the United States would be better off when it was won. Whether or not this turned out to be so was (and still is) a matter of opinion.

Americans: To the Trenches and Over the Top

All activity on the home front had one ultimate objective: defeating the Central Powers on the battlefield. This was accomplished. The navy performed with special distinction. In April 1917, German submarines sank more than 870,000 tons of Allied shipping; after April 1918, monthly losses never reached 300,000 tons. The decision to send merchant ships across the Atlantic in convoys screened by destroyers made the reduction possible. Checking the U-boats was essential because of the need to transport American troops to Europe. Slightly more than 2 million soldiers made the voyage safely. Those who crossed on fast ocean liners were in little danger as long as the vessel maintained high speed and followed a zigzag course, a lesson learned from the *Lusitania*, whose

The Western Front, 1918 The Germans launched their great offensive in the spring and summer of 1918 with the goal of taking Paris. American troops helped hold the line at Château-Thierry and Belleau Woods. Several months later, a half million American soldiers participated in the counteroffensive that drove the Germans back to the Meuse River.

captain had neglected both precautions. Those who traveled on slower troop transports benefited from the protection of destroyers and also from the fact that the Germans concentrated on attacking supply ships. They continued to believe that inexperienced American soldiers would not be a major factor in the war.

The first units of the American Expeditionary Force (AEF), elements of the regular army commanded by General John J. Pershing, reached Paris on Independence Day, 1917. They took up positions on the front near Verdun in October. Not until the spring of 1918, however, did the "doughboys" play a significant role in the fighting, though their mere presence boosted French and British morale.

In March 1918 the Germans launched a great spring offensive, their armies strengthened by thousands of veterans who had been freed from the eastern front by the collapse of Russia. By late May they had reached a point on the Marne River near the town of Château-Thierry, only fifty miles from Paris. Early in June the AEF fought its first major engagements, driving the Germans back from Château-Thierry and Belleau Wood.

In this fighting only about 27,500 Americans saw action, and they suffered appalling losses. Nevertheless, when the Germans advanced again in the direction of the Marne in mid-July, 85,000 Americans were in the lines that withstood their charge. Then, in the major turning point of the war, the Allied armies counterattacked. Some 270,000 Americans participated, helping to flatten the German bulge between Reims and Soissons. By late August the American First Army, 500,000 strong, was poised before the Saint-Mihiel bulge, a deep extension of the German lines southeast of Verdun. On September 12 this army, buttressed by French troops, struck and in two days wiped out the salient.

Late in September began the greatest American engagement of the war. No fewer than 1.2 million doughboys plunged into the Argonne Forest. For over a month of indescribable horror they inched ahead through the tangle of the Argonne and the formidable defenses of the Hindenburg line, while to the west, French and British armies staged similar drives. In this one offensive the AEF suffered 120,000 casualties. Finally, on November 1, they broke the German center and raced toward the vital Sedan-Mézières railroad. On November 11, with Allied armies advancing on all fronts, the Germans signed the armistice, ending the fighting.

Preparing for Peace

The fighting ended on November 11, 1918, but the shape of the postwar world remained to be determined. European society had been shaken to its foundations. Confusion reigned. People wanted peace yet burned for revenge. Millions faced starvation. Other millions were disillusioned by the seemingly purposeless sacrifices of four years of horrible war. Communism—to some an idealistic promise of human betterment, to others a commitment to rational economic and social planning, to still others a danger to individual freedom, toleration, and democracy—having conquered Russia, threatened to envelop Germany and much of the defunct Austro-Hungarian Empire, perhaps even the victorious Allies. How could stability be restored? How could victory be made worth its enormous cost?

Woodrow Wilson had grasped the significance of the war while most statesmen still thought that triumph on the battlefield would settle everything automatically. As early as January 1917 he had realized that victory would be wasted if the winners permitted themselves the luxury of vengeance. Such a policy would disrupt the balance of power and lead to economic and social chaos. The victors must build a better society, not punish those they believed had destroyed the old one.

In a speech to Congress on January 8, 1918, Wilson outlined a plan, known as the **Fourteen Points**, designed to make the world "fit and safe to live in." The peace treaty should be negotiated in full view of world opinion, not in secret. It should guarantee the freedom of the seas to all nations, in war as in peacetime. It should tear down barriers to international trade, provide for a drastic reduction of armaments, and establish a colonial system that would take proper account of the interests of the native peoples concerned. European boundaries should be redrawn so that no substantial group would have to live under a government not of its own choosing.

More specifically, captured Russian territory should be restored, Belgium evacuated, Alsace-Lorraine returned to France, the heterogeneous nationalities of Austria-Hungary accorded autonomy. Italy's frontiers should be adjusted "along clearly recognizable lines of nationality," the Balkans made free, Turkey divested of its subject peoples, and an independent Polish state (with access to the Baltic Sea) created. To oversee the new system, Wilson insisted, "a general association of nations must be formed under specific covenants for the purpose of affording mutual guarantees of political independence and territorial integrity to great and small states alike."

Wilson's Fourteen Points for a fair peace lifted the hopes of people everywhere. After the guns fell silent, however, the vagueness and inconsistencies in his list became apparent. Complete national self-determination was impossible in Europe; there were too many regions of mixed population for every group to be satisfied. Self-determination, like the war itself, also fostered the spirit of nationalism that Wilson's dream of international organization, a league of nations, was designed to de-emphasize. Furthermore, the Allies had made territorial commitments to one another in secret treaties that ran counter to the principle of self-determination, and they were not ready to give up all claims to Germany's colonies. Freedom of the seas in wartime posed another problem; the British flatly refused to accept the idea. In every Allied country, millions rejected the idea of a peace without indemnities. They expected to make the enemy pay for the war.

Wilson assumed that the practical benefits of his program would compel opponents to fall in line. He had the immense advantage of seeking nothing for his own country and the additional strength of being leader of the one important nation to emerge from the war richer and more powerful than it had been in 1914.

Yet this combination of altruism, idealism, and power was his undoing; it intensified his tendency to be overbearing and undermined his judgment. He had never found it easy to compromise. Now, believing that the fate of humanity hung on his actions, he was unyielding. Always a preacher, he became in his own mind a prophet—almost, one fears, a kind of god.

In the last weeks of the war Wilson proved to be a brilliant diplomat, first dangling the Fourteen Points before the German people to encourage them to overthrow Kaiser Wilhelm II and sue for an armistice, then sending Colonel House to Paris to persuade Allied leaders to accept the Fourteen Points as the basis for the peace. When the Allies raised objections, House made small concessions, but by hinting that the United States might make a separate peace with Germany, he forced them to agree. Under the armistice, Germany had to withdraw behind the Rhine River and surrender its submarines, together with quantities of munitions and other materials. In return it received the assurance of the Allies that the Wilsonian principles would prevail at the Paris peace conference.

Wilson then came to a daring decision: He would personally attend the conference as a member of the United States Peace Commission. This was a precedent-shattering step, for no president had ever left American territory while in office.

Wilson probably erred in going to Paris, but not because of the novelty or possible illegality of the act. By going, he was turning his back on obvious domestic problems. Western farmers believed that they had been discriminated against during the war, since wheat prices had been controlled while southern cotton had been allowed to rise unchecked from seven cents a pound in 1914 to thirty-five cents in 1919. The administration's drastic tax program had angered many businessmen. Labor, despite its gains, was restive in the face of reconversion to peacetime conditions.

Wilson had increased his political difficulties by making a partisan appeal for the election of a Democratic Congress in 1918. Republicans, who had in many instances supported his war program more loyally than the Democrats, considered the action a gross affront. The appeal failed; the Republicans won majorities in both houses. Wilson appeared to have been repudiated at home at the very moment that he set forth to represent the nation abroad. Most important, Wilson intended to break with the isolationist tradition and bring the United States into a league of nations. Such a revolutionary change would require explanation; he should have undertaken a major campaign to convince the American people of the wisdom of this step.

The Paris Peace Conference and the Versailles Treaty

Wilson arrived in Europe a world hero. When the conference settled down to its work, control quickly fell into the hands of the so-called Big Four: Wilson, Prime Minister David Lloyd George of Great Britain, Premier Georges Clemenceau of France, and Prime Minister Vittorio Orlando of Italy. Wilson stood out in this group but did not dominate it. His principal advantage in the negotiations was his untiring industry. He alone of the leaders tried to master all the complex details of the task.

The seventy-eight-year-old Clemenceau cared only for one thing: French security. He viewed Wilson cynically, saying that since mankind had been unable to keep God's Ten Commandments, it was unlikely to do better with Wilson's Fourteen Points. Lloyd George's approach was pragmatic and almost cavalier.

Europe before the Great War In 1914, five countries dominated Europe: the German Empire, France, Great Britain, Austria-Hungary, and Russia.

Europe after the Great War The Versailles Treaty and other postwar settlements punished the losers, especially Germany and Austria-Hungary, transferring their lands to newly-created nations in eastern Europe, such as Poland, Czechoslovakia, and Yugoslavia.

He sympathized with much that Wilson was trying to accomplish but found the president's frequent sermonettes about "right being more important than might, and justice being more eternal than force" incomprehensible. "If you want to succeed in politics," Lloyd George advised a British statesman, "you must keep your conscience well under control." Orlando, clever, cultured, a believer in international cooperation but inflexible where Italian national interests were concerned, was not the equal of his three colleagues in influence. He left the conference in a huff when they failed to meet all his demands.

The conference labored from January to May 1919 and finally brought forth the Versailles Treaty. American liberals whose hopes had soared at the thought of a peace based on the Fourteen Points found the document abysmally disappointing.

The peace settlements failed to carry out the principle of self-determination completely. They gave Italy a large section of the Austrian Tyrol, though the area contained 200,000 people who considered themselves Austrians. Other German-speaking groups were incorporated into the new states of Poland and Czechoslovakia.

The victors forced Germany to accept responsibility for having caused the war—an act of senseless vindictiveness as well as a gross oversimplification—and to sign a "blank check," agreeing to pay for all damage to civilian properties and even future pensions and other indirect war costs. This reparations bill, as finally determined, amounted to $33 billion. Instead of attacking imperialism, the treaty attacked German imperialism; instead of seeking a new international social order based on liberty and democracy, it created a great-power entente designed to crush Germany and to exclude Bolshevik Russia from the family of nations.

Wilson himself backtracked on his pledge to honor the right of self-determination. For centuries, most Arabs had lived under the Turkish rulers of the Ottoman Empire. When the Ottoman Empire joined Germany and Austria-Hungary in World War I, Arab nationalists looked to the Allies and eventually worked out a deal with Britain. In return for Arab military support against the Ottoman Empire and the Germans, Britain would endorse Arab independence after the war. Wilson seemingly concurred, for Point Twelve of his Fourteen Points called for the "autonomous development" of Arab peoples. But in 1917 the British issued the Balfour Declaration in support of "a national home" for the Jewish people in Palestine, land mostly occupied by Palestinian Arabs. How could Palestinian Arabs be granted independence if Palestine was to become the home of Jewish settlers?

In the postwar negotiations, Britain retreated from its earlier promise to the Arabs. Wilson, too, had second thoughts about granting the Arab peoples self-determination.

Ottoman Empire and the Arab World, 1914 In 1914, the Ottoman Empire, also known as Turkey, controlled much of the Arab world, stretching from the Persian Gulf to the Red Sea.

Secretary of State Lansing worried about the "danger of putting such ideas into the minds of certain races," particularly the "Mohammedans [Muslims] of Syria and Palestine." Wilson reluctantly deleted explicit references to self-determination from the postwar settlements. Rather than grant the Arab peoples independence, Britain and France themselves seized Arab lands that had been ruled by the Turks. This land grab was "legalized" through the device of a mandate to rule the region issued by the League of Nations.

Similarly, Ho Chi Minh, a young Vietnamese nationalist, was embittered by the failure at Versailles to deliver his people from French colonial rule. He decided to become a communist revolutionary. The repercussions of Arab and Vietnamese discontent, though far removed from American interests at the time, would be felt in full force much later.

To those who had taken Wilson's "peace without victory" speech and the Fourteen Points literally, the Versailles Treaty seemed an abomination. The complaints of the critics were individually reasonable, yet their conclusions were not entirely fair. The new map of Europe left fewer people on "foreign" soil than in any earlier period of history. Although the Allies seized the German colonies, they were required, under the mandate system, to render the **League of Nations** annual accounts of their stewardship and to prepare the inhabitants for eventual independence. Above all, Wilson had persuaded the powers to incorporate the League of Nations in the treaty.

Wilson expected the League of Nations to make up for all the inadequacies of the Versailles Treaty. Once the League had begun to function, problems like freedom of the seas and disarmament would solve themselves, he argued, and the relaxation of trade barriers would surely follow. The League would arbitrate international disputes, act as a central body for registering treaties, and employ military and economic sanctions against aggressor nations. Each member promised (Article 10) to protect the "territorial integrity" and "political independence" of all other members. No nation could be made

Dismantling the Ottoman Empire, 1919–1920 The Ottoman Empire was the biggest loser at Versailles: It lost everything apart from Turkey itself; but the Arab nationalists lost as well, because Britain and France, through League-appointed mandates, took control of Syria, Transjordan, Palestine, and Mesopotamia (Iraq).

to go to war against its will, but Wilson emphasized that all were morally obligated to carry out League decisions. By any standard, Wilson had achieved a remarkably moderate peace, one full of hope for the future. Except for the war guilt clause and the heavy reparations imposed on Germany, he could be justly proud of his work.

The Senate Rejects the League of Nations

When Wilson returned from France, he finally directed his attention to the task of winning public approval of his handiwork. A large majority of the people probably favored the League of Nations in principle, though few understood all its implications or were entirely happy with every detail. Wilson had persuaded the Allies to accept certain changes in the original draft to mollify American opposition. No nation could be forced to accept a colonial mandate, and "domestic questions" such as tariffs, the control of immigration, and the Monroe Doctrine were excluded from League control.

Many senators found these modifications insufficient. Even before the peace conference ended, thirty-seven Republican senators signed a manifesto, devised by Henry Cabot Lodge of Massachusetts, opposing Wilson's League and demanding that the question of an international organization be put off until "the urgent business of negotiating peace terms with Germany" had been completed. Wilson rejected this suggestion icily. Further alterations were out of the question. Thus the stage was set for a monumental test of strength between the president and the Republican majority in the Senate.

Partisanship, principle, and prejudice clashed mightily in this contest. A presidential election loomed. Should the League prove a success, the Republicans wanted to be able to claim a share of the credit, but Wilson had refused to allow them to participate

Despite Wilson's serving as mother hen, the
League of Nations never hatched.

Photo Credit: The Granger Collection, New York.

in drafting the document. This predisposed all of them to favor changes.
Politics aside, genuine alarm at the
possible sacrifice of American sovereignty to an international authority
led many Republicans to urge modifi-
cation of the League covenant, or constitution. Yet the noble purpose of
the League made many reluctant to
reject it entirely. The intense desire of
the people to have an end to the long
war made Republican leaders hesitate
before voting down the Versailles
Treaty, and they could not reject the League without rejecting the treaty.

Wilson could count on the Democratic senators almost to a man, but he had to win
over many Republicans to obtain the two-thirds majority necessary for ratification.
Republican opinion divided roughly into three segments. At one extreme were some
dozen "irreconcilables," led by the shaggy-browed William E. Borah of Idaho, an able
and kindly person of progressive leanings but an uncompromising isolationist. Borah
claimed that he would vote against the League even if Jesus Christ returned to earth to
argue in its behalf, and most of his followers were equally inflexible. At the other
extreme stood another dozen "mild" reservationists who were in favor of the League
but who hoped to alter it in minor ways, chiefly for political purposes. In the middle
were the "strong" reservationists, senators willing to go along with the League only if
American sovereignty were fully protected and if it were made clear that their party had
played a major role in fashioning the final document.

Senator Lodge, the leader of the Republican opposition, was an intensely partisan
individual. He possessed a keen intelligence, a mastery of parliamentary procedure, and,
as chairman of the Senate Foreign Relations Committee, a great deal of power. Although
not an isolationist, he had little faith in the League. He also had a profound distrust of
Democrats, especially Wilson, whom he considered a hypocrite and a coward. While
perfectly ready to see the country participate actively in world affairs, Lodge insisted that
its right to determine its own best interests in every situation be preserved. When a
Democratic president tried to ram the Versailles Treaty down the Senate's throat, he
fought him with every weapon he could muster.

Lodge belonged to the strong reservationist faction. His own proposals, known as
the Lodge Reservations, fourteen in number to match Wilson's Fourteen Points, limited
U.S. obligations to the League and stated in unmistakable
terms the right of Congress to decide when to honor these
obligations. Some of the reservations were mere quibbles.
Others, such as the provision that the United States would
not endorse Japan's seizure of Chinese territory, were
included mainly to embarrass Wilson by pointing out compromises he had made at
Versailles. The most important reservation applied to Article Ten of the League

◆●◆ Read the **Document**

*Henry Cabot Lodge's
Objections to the Treaty of
Versailles* at **myhistorylab.com**

covenant, which committed signatories to protect the political independence and territorial integrity of all member nations. Wilson had rightly called Article Ten "the heart of the Covenant." One of Lodge's reservations made it inoperable so far as the United States was concerned "unless in any particular case the Congress . . . shall by act or joint resolution so provide."

Lodge performed brilliantly, if somewhat unscrupulously, in uniting the three Republican factions behind his reservations. He got the irreconcilables to agree to them by conceding their right to vote against the final version in any event, and he held the mild reservationists in line by modifying some of his demands and stressing the importance of party unity. Reservations—as distinct from amendments—would not have to win the formal approval of other League members. In addition, the Lodge proposals dealt forthrightly with the problem of reconciling traditional concepts of national sovereignty with the new idea of world cooperation. Supporters of the League could accept them without sacrifice of principle. Wilson, however, refused to agree.

This foolish intransigence seems almost incomprehensible in a man of Wilson's intelligence and political experience. In part his hatred of Lodge accounts for it, in part his faith in his League. His physical condition in 1919 also played a role. At Paris he had suffered a violent attack of indigestion that was probably a symptom of a minor stroke. Thereafter, many observers noted small changes in his personality, particularly increased stubbornness and a loss of good judgment. Instead of making concessions, the president set out early in September on a nationwide speaking crusade to rally support for the League. In three weeks, Wilson traveled some 10,000 miles by train and gave forty speeches, some of them brilliant. On September 25, after an address in Pueblo, Colorado, he collapsed. A few days later, in Washington, he suffered a severe stroke that partially paralyzed his left side.

For nearly two months the president was almost totally cut off from affairs of state, leaving supporters of the League leaderless while Lodge maneuvered the reservations through the Senate. Gradually, popular attitudes toward the League shifted. The arguments of the irreconcilables persuaded many citizens that Wilson had made too sharp a break with America's isolationist past and that the Lodge Reservations were therefore necessary. Other issues connected with the reconversion of society to a peacetime basis increasingly occupied the public mind.

A coalition of Democratic and moderate Republican senators could easily have carried the treaty. That no such coalition was organized was Wilson's fault. Lodge obtained the simple majority necessary to add his reservations to the treaty merely by keeping his own party united. When the time came for the final roll call on November 19, Wilson, bitter and emotionally distraught, urged the Democrats to vote for rejection. "Better a thousand times to go down fighting than to dip your colors to dishonorable compromise," he explained to his wife. Thus the amended treaty failed, thirty-five to fifty-five, the irreconcilables and the Democrats voting against it. Lodge then allowed the original draft without his reservations to come to a vote. Again the result was defeat, thirty-eight to fifty-three. Only one Republican cast a ballot for ratification.

Dismayed but not yet crushed, friends of the League in both parties forced reconsideration of the treaty early in 1920. Neither Lodge nor Wilson would yield an inch. Lodge, who had little confidence in the effectiveness of any league of nations, was under no compulsion to compromise. Wilson, who believed that the League was the world's best hope, did have such a compulsion. Yet he would not compromise either, and this ensured the treaty's defeat.

Wilson's behavior is further evidence of his physical and mental decline. Had he died or stepped down, the treaty, with reservations, would almost certainly have been ratified. When the Senate balloted again in March, half the Democrats voted for the treaty with the Lodge Reservations. The others, mostly southern party regulars, joined the irreconcilables. Together they mustered thirty-five votes, seven more than the one-third that meant defeat.

The Red Scare

Business boomed in 1919 as consumers spent wartime savings on cars, homes, and other goods that had been in short supply during the conflict. But temporary shortages caused inflation; by 1920 the cost of living stood at more than twice the level of 1913. Workers demanded that their wages be increased as well. The unions, grown strong during the war, struck for wage increases. Over four million workers, one in five in the labor force, were on strike at some time during 1919.

The activities of radicals in the labor movement led millions of citizens to associate unionism and strikes with the new threat of communist world revolution. Although there were only a relative handful of communists in the United States, Russia's experience persuaded many that a tiny minority of ruthless revolutionaries could take over a nation of millions if conditions were right. Communists appointed themselves the champions of workers; labor unrest attracted them magnetically. When strikes broke out, some accompanied by violence, many people interpreted them as communist-inspired preludes to revolution.

But organized labor in America had seldom been truly radical. The Industrial Workers of the World (IWW) had made little impression in most industries. But some labor leaders had been attracted to socialism, and many Americans failed to distinguish between the common ends sought by communists and socialists and the entirely different methods by which they proposed to achieve those ends. When a general strike paralyzed Seattle in February 1919, the fact that a procommunist had helped organize it sent shivers down countless conservative spines. When the radical William Z. Foster began a drive to organize the steel industry at about this time, the fears became more intense. In September 1919 a total of 343,000 steelworkers walked off their jobs, and in the same month the Boston police went on strike. Violence marked the steel strike, and the suspension of police protection in Boston led to looting and fighting that ended only when Governor Calvin Coolidge called out the National Guard.

During the same period a handful of terrorists caused widespread alarm by attempting to murder various prominent persons, including John D. Rockefeller, Justice Oliver Wendell Holmes Jr., and Attorney General A. Mitchell Palmer. Although the terrorists were anarchists and anarchism had little in common with communism, many citizens lumped all extremists together and associated them with a monstrous assault on society.

What aroused the public even more was the fact that most radicals were not American citizens. Wartime fear of alien saboteurs easily transformed itself into peacetime terror of foreign radicals. In place of Germany, the enemy became the lowly immigrant, usually an Italian or a Jew or a Slav and usually an industrial worker. In this muddled way, radicalism, unionism, and questions of racial and national origins combined to make many Americans believe that their way of life was in imminent danger. That few immigrants were radicals, that most workers had no interest in communism, and that the extremists themselves were faction-ridden and irresolute did not affect conservative thinking. From all over the country came demands that radicals be ruthlessly suppressed. Thus the **"red scare"** was born.

Attorney General Palmer was the key figure in the resulting purge. He had been a typical progressive, a supporter of the League of Nations and such reforms as woman suffrage and child labor legislation. But pressure from Congress and his growing conviction that the communists really were a menace led him to join the "red hunt." Soon he was saying of the radicals, "Out of the sly and crafty eyes of many of them leap cupidity, cruelty, insanity, and crime; from their lopsided faces, sloping brows, and misshapen features may be recognized the unmistakable criminal type."

In August 1919, Palmer established within the Department of Justice the General Intelligence Division, headed by J. Edgar Hoover, to collect information about clandestine radical activities. In November, Justice Department agents in a dozen cities swooped down on the meeting places of an anarchist organization known as the Union of Russian Workers. More than 650 persons, many of them unconnected with the union, were arrested but in only forty-three cases could evidence be found to justify deportation.

Nevertheless, the public reacted so favorably that Palmer, thinking now of winning the 1920 Democratic presidential nomination, planned an immense roundup of communists. He obtained 3,000 warrants, and on January 2, 1920, his agents, reinforced by local police and self-appointed vigilantes, struck simultaneously in thirty-three cities.

About 6,000 persons were taken into custody, many of them citizens and therefore not subject to the deportation laws, many others unconnected with any radical cause. Some were held incommunicado for weeks while the authorities searched for evidence against them. In a number of cases, individuals who went to visit prisoners were themselves thrown behind bars on the theory that they too must be communists. Hundreds of suspects were jammed into filthy "bullpens," beaten, and forced to sign "confessions."

The public tolerated these wholesale violations of civil liberties because of the supposed menace of communism. Gradually, however, protests began to be heard, first from lawyers and liberal magazines, then from a wider segment of the population. No revolutionary outbreak had taken place. Of 6,000 seized in the Palmer raids, only 556 proved liable to deportation. The widespread ransacking of communists' homes and meeting places produced mountains of inflammatory literature but only three pistols.

Palmer, attempting to maintain the crusade, announced that the radicals planned a gigantic terrorist demonstration for May Day, 1920. In New York and other cities thousands of police were placed on round-the-clock duty; federal troops stood by anxiously. But the day passed without even a rowdy meeting. Suddenly Palmer appeared ridiculous. The red scare swiftly subsided.

The Election of 1920

Wilson still hoped for vindication at the polls in the presidential election, which he sought to make a "great and solemn referendum" on the League. He would have liked to run for a third term, but in his enfeebled condition he attracted no support among Democratic leaders. The party nominated James M. Cox of Ohio.

Cox favored joining the League, but the election did not produce the referendum on the new organization that Wilson desired. The Republicans, whose candidate was another Ohioan, Senator Warren G. Harding, equivocated shamelessly on the issue.

The election turned on other matters, largely emotional. Disillusioned by the results of the war, many Americans had their fill of idealism. They wanted, apparently, to end the long period of moral uplift and reform agitation that had begun under Theodore Roosevelt and return to what Harding called "normalcy."

To the extent that the voters were expressing opinions on Wilson's League, their response was overwhelmingly negative. Senator Harding, a strong reservationist, swept the country, winning over 16.1 million votes to Cox's 9.1 million. In July 1921, Congress formally ended the war with the Central Powers by passing a joint resolution.

The defeat of the League was a tragedy both for Wilson, whose crusade for a world order based on peace and justice ended in failure, and for the world, which was condemned to endure another, still more horrible and costly war. Perhaps this dreadful outcome could not have been avoided. Had Wilson compromised and Lodge behaved like a statesman instead of a politician, the United States would have joined the League, but it might well have failed to respond when called on to meet its obligations. As events soon demonstrated, the League powers acted timidly and even dishonorably when challenged by aggressor nations.

Yet it might have been different had the Senate ratified the Versailles Treaty. What was lost when the treaty failed was not peace but the possibility of peace, a tragic loss indeed.

Milestones

1914	United States invades Veracruz, Mexico	1918	Sedition Act limits freedom of speech
	Great War begins in Europe		Wilson announces Fourteen Points
1915	German U-boat torpedoes *Lusitania*		Republicans gain control of both houses of Congress
1916	Wilson appoints Louis D. Brandeis to Supreme Court		Armistice ends the Great War
	Adamson Act gives railroad workers eight-hour day	1918–1919	Flu epidemic kills 600,000 Americans
	"Pancho" Villa burns Columbus, New Mexico	1919	Steel workers strike
	Wilson is reelected president		Red scare culminates in Palmer raids
1917	Germany resumes unrestricted submarine warfare		Big Four meet at Paris Peace Conference
	Russian Revolution begins		Senate rejects Versailles Treaty and League of Nations
	United States declares war on Central Powers		Wilson wins Nobel Peace Prize, suffers massive stroke
	Bernard Baruch heads War Industries Board	1920	Senate again rejects Versailles Treaty and League of Nations
	Former President Taft heads War Labor Board		Warren Harding is elected president

✓—Study and Review at www.myhistorylab.com

Review Questions

1. The chapter's introduction draws a parallel between the American efforts to fight terrorism in Afghanistan and Iraq and Woodrow Wilson's crusade to make the world "safe for democracy." Does the history of American involvement in World War I teach any "lessons" about foreign wars?

2. Why did Woodrow Wilson recommend neutrality at the outset of the European war and why did he change his mind?

3. Did progressivism play a role in leading the United States into World War I? Did it shape how the war was waged?

4. What problems did the United States encounter in mobilizing for war? How did the war effort contribute to the growth of the American state?

5. How did the war affect minorities and women? How did it restrict dissent and labor?

6. What were the arguments for and against American ratification of the League of Nations?

Key Terms

Allied Powers
Central Powers
Espionage Act

Fourteen Points
League of Nations
"red scare"

Sedition Act
War Industries Board
   (WIB)

Postwar Society and Culture: Change and Adjustment

((•—[Hear the Audio at myhistorylab.com

Do you drink too much?

MANY COLLEGE STUDENTS DRINK A LOT. IN 2008 THE NATIONAL CENTER on Addiction and Substance Abuse (CASA) at Columbia University found that 44 percent of college students were binge-drinkers and that nearly one in four fulfilled the medical criteria for substance abuse. In 2010 the National Institute on Alcohol Abuse and Alcoholism reported that alcohol annually caused nearly 100,000 sexual assaults and date rapes and 1,700 deaths of college students.

"It's time to get the 'high' out of higher education," declared Joseph A. Califano, president of CASA and former U.S. secretary of health, education, and welfare. He blamed college administrators for condoning a "college culture of abuse." Campaigns to promote responsible drinking accomplished little, he noted. The only effective strategy was campus-wide prohibition.

But such words caused many to bristle. In 2010, after Iowa City banned those under twenty-one from bars, the *Daily Iowan* at the University of Iowa claimed that "harsh restrictions on alcohol drive the behavior underground, pushing young people to use more hard liquor in unsupervised private house parties." "Let's not repackage the Prohibition Era of the 1920s," the article concluded. When the University of Hawaii considered banning alcohol at the football stadium, another professor cited the nation's experience with Prohibition eighty years earlier. "You cannot root out the drinking of alcohol by outlawing it," he added.

The Prohibition Era was in many ways a response to unsettling social changes. The flood of immigration during the early 1900s had strained the nation's social fabric, especially in cities. Young women were challenging traditional gender roles. African Americans were leaving the South in droves and demanding rights that had been long deferred. Gays were becoming visible—at least to each other. Movies and radio, and even artists and writers, stimulated a rebellious youth culture. Advertising encouraged people to lose themselves in the delights of consumption.

These transformations also elicited opposition. The federal government curtailed immigration and cracked down on foreign-born radicals. The Ku Klux Klan reemerged to intimidate immigrants and blacks. Traditionalists inveighed against the enticements of popular culture and decline in faith. Prohibition was only the most visible expression of a reaction against social and cultural change.

Closing the Gates to New Immigrants

In 1921 Congress, reflecting a widespread prejudice against a huge influx of eastern and southern European immigrants, passed an emergency act establishing a quota system. Each year 3 percent of the number of foreign-born residents of the United States in 1910 (about 350,000 persons) might enter the country. Each country's quota was based on the number of its nationals in the United States in 1910. This meant that only a relative handful of the total would be from southern and eastern Europe. In 1924 the quota was reduced to 2 percent and the base year shifted to 1890, thereby lowering further the proportion of southern and eastern Europeans admitted.

In 1929 Congress established a system that allowed only 150,000 immigrants a year to enter the country. Each national quota was based on the supposed origins of the entire white population of the United States in 1920, not merely on the foreign-born.

The system was complicated and unscientific, for no one could determine with accuracy the "origins" of millions of citizens. More seriously, it ignored America's long history of constantly changing ethnic diversity. The motto *E Pluribus Unum*—Out of Many, One—conceived to represent the unity of the original thirteen states, applied even more appropriately to the blending of different cultures into one nationality. The new law sought to freeze the mix.

The law reduced actual immigration to far below 150,000 a year. Between 1931 and 1939, for example, only 23,000 British immigrants came to the United States, far below Britain's annual quota of 65,000. Meanwhile, hundreds of thousands of southern and eastern Europeans waited for admission.

The United States had closed the gates. The **National Origins Act** caused the foreign-born percentage of the population to fall from about 13 percent in 1920 to 4.7 percent in 1970. Instead of an open, cosmopolitan society eager to accept, in Emma Lazarus's stirring line, the "huddled masses yearning to breathe free," America now became committed to preserving a homogeneous, "Anglo-Saxon" population.

Distaste for the "new" immigrants from eastern Europe, many of whom were Jewish, expanded into a more general anti-Semitism in the 1920s. American Jews, whether foreign-born or native, were subjected to increasing discrimination, not because they were slow in adopting

"Give me your tired, your poor, your huddled masses yearning to breathe free, the wretched refuse of your teeming shore"—these words of Emma Lazarus, inscribed at the base of the Statue of Liberty, tell only part of the story. Most immigrants were young and hopeful, like this family at Ellis Island; many were resolute and ambitious. The restriction of immigration during the 1920s, conceived to exclude misfits, also deprived the nation of people such as these.

Photo Credit: Culver Pictures, Inc.

American ways but because many of them were getting ahead in the world somewhat more rapidly than expected. Prestigious colleges like Harvard, Yale, and Columbia that had in the past admitted Jews based on their academic records now imposed unofficial but effective quotas. Medical schools also established quotas, and no matter how talented, most young Jewish lawyers and bankers could find places only in so-called "Jewish" firms.

New Urban Social Patterns

The census of 1920 revealed that for the first time a majority of Americans (54 million in a population of 106 million) lived in "urban" rather than "rural" places. These figures are somewhat misleading because the census classified anyone in a community of 2,500 or more as urban. Of the 54 million "urban" residents in 1920, over 16 million lived in villages and towns of fewer than 25,000 persons and the evidence suggests strongly that a large majority of them held ideas and values more like those of rural citizens than like those of city dwellers. But the truly urban Americans, the one person in four who lived in a city of 100,000 or more, were increasing steadily in number and influence. More than 19 million persons moved from farms to cities in the 1920s, and the population living in centers of 100,000 or more increased by about a third.

The urban environment transformed family structure, educational opportunities, and dozens of other aspects of human existence. Indeed, since most of the changes in the relations of husbands, wives, and children that had occurred in the nineteenth century were related to the fact that people were leaving farms to work in towns and cities, these trends continued and were intensified in the early twentieth century as more and more people settled in urban centers.

Earlier differences between working-class and middle-class family structures persisted. In 1920 about a quarter of the American women who were working were married, but less than 10 percent of all married women were working. Middle-class married women who worked were nearly all either childless or highly paid professionals who were able to employ servants. Most male skilled workers now earned enough to support a family in

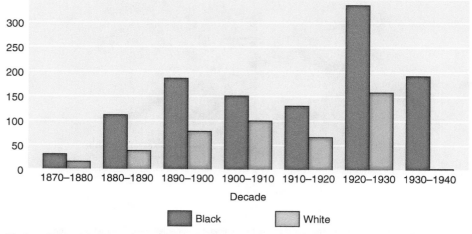

Black and White Out-Migration from Virginia and North and South Carolina, 1870–1940

modest comfort so long as they could work steadily, but an unskilled laborer still could not. Wives in most such families helped out, usually by taking in laundry or sewing.

By the 1920s the idea of intrafamily democracy had emerged. In such families, husbands and wives would deal with each other as equals; given existing conditions, this meant sharing housework and childcare, downplaying male authority, and stressing mutual satisfaction in sexual and other matters. On the one hand, they should be friends and lovers, not merely housekeepers, earners of money, and producers of children. On the other hand, advocates of these companionate relationships believed that there was nothing particularly sacred about marriage; divorce should be made easier for couples that did not get along, provided they did not have children.

Much attention was given to "scientific" child-rearing. Childcare experts agreed that routine medical examinations and good nutrition were of central importance, but they were divided about how the socialization and psychological development of the young should be handled. One school stressed rigid training. Children could be "spoiled" by indulgence; toilet training should begin early in infancy; thumb sucking should be suppressed; too much kissing could turn male youngsters into "mama's boys." Another school favored a more permissive approach. Toilet training could wait; parents should pay attention to their children's expressed needs, not impose a generalized set of rules on them.

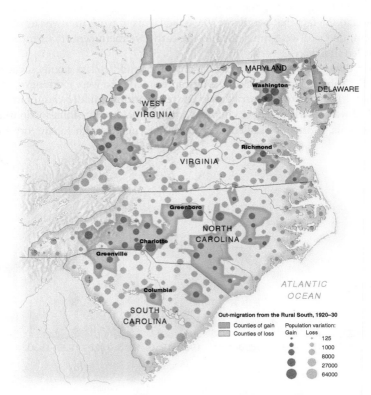

Population Losses in the South The graph shows that whites and especially blacks were leaving the South in large numbers, especially during the 1920s. The map shows that while many urban areas in the South gained population, most rural areas lost population.

The growth of large cities further loosened social constraints on sexuality. Amidst the sea of people that surged down the streets or into the subways, the solitary individual acquired a freedom derived from anonymity. (For further perspective on urban life, see Re-Viewing the Past, *Chicago*.) Homosexuals, in particular, developed a set of identifying signals and fashioned a distinctive culture in parks, cafeterias, nightclubs, and rooming houses of big cities.

The Younger Generation

The 1920s has been described as the Jazz Age, the era of "flaming youth," when young people danced to syncopated "African" rhythms, careened about the countryside in automobiles in search of pleasure and forgetfulness, and made gods of movie stars and professional athletes. This view of the period bears a superficial resemblance to reality. "Younger people," one observer noted in 1922, were attempting "to create a way of life free from the bondage of an authority that has lost all meaning." But if they differed from their parents and grandparents, it was primarily because young people were adjusting to more profound and more rapid changes in their world than their grandparents could have imagined.

Trends that were barely perceptible during the Progressive Era now reached avalanche proportions. This was particularly noticeable in relationships between the sexes. Courtship, for example, was transformed. In the late nineteenth century, a typical young man "paid a call" on a female friend. He met and conversed with her parents, perhaps over coffee and cookies. The couple remained at home, the parents nearby if not actually participating in what was essentially a social event held in a private place.

By the 1920s paying calls was being replaced by *dating*; the young man called only to "pick up" his "date," to go off, free of parental supervision, to whatever diversion they wished. There is no question that for young people of the 1920s, relations between the sexes were becoming more relaxed and uninhibited. Respectable young women smoked cigarettes, something previously done in public only by prostitutes and bohemian types. They cast off heavy corsets, wore lipstick and "exotic" perfumes, and shortened both their hair and their skirts, the latter rising steadily from instep to ankle to calf to knee and beyond as the decade progressed. For decades female dressmakers and beauty salon proprietors had sold their own beauty products. By 1920, however, new cosmetic corporations, managed primarily by men, appropriated the products and marketing strategies of local women entrepreneurs and catered to national mass markets.

Freudian psychology and the more accessible ideas of the British "sexologist" Havelock Ellis reached steadily deeper into the popular psyche. Since sex was "the central function of life," Ellis argued, it must be "simple and natural and pure and good." Bombarded by these exciting ideas, to say nothing of their own inclinations, young people found casting off their inhibitions more and more tempting.

Conservatives bemoaned what they described as the breakdown of moral standards, the fragmentation of the family, and the decline of parental authority—all with some reason. Nevertheless, society was not collapsing. Much of the rebelliousness of the young, like their particular style of dress, was faddish in nature, in a sense a kind of youthful conformity. This was particularly true of college students. Elaborate rituals governed every aspect of their extracurricular life, which was consuming a steadily larger share of most students' time and energy. Fraternity and sorority initiations, "proms," attendance at Saturday afternoon football games, styles of dress, and college slang, seemingly aspects of independence and free choice, were nearly everywhere shaped and controlled by peer pressure.

But young people's new ways of relating to one another, while influenced by the desire to conform, were not mere fads and were not confined to people under thirty. This can be seen most clearly in the birth control movement, the drive to legalize the use of contraceptives.

The "New" Woman

The young people of the 1920s were more open about sex and perhaps more sexually precocious than the young had been before the war. This does not mean that most of them engaged in sexual intercourse before marriage or that they tended to marry earlier. Single young people might "believe in" birth control, but relatively few (at least by modern standards) had occasion to practice it. Contraception was a concern of married people, and particularly of married women.

The leading American proponent of birth control in the 1920s, actually the person who coined the term, was Margaret Sanger. Before the war she was a political radical, a friend of Eugene Debs, "Big Bill" Haywood, and the anarchist Emma Goldman. Gradually, however, her attention focused on the plight of the poor women she encountered while working as a nurse; many of these women, burdened by large numbers of children, knew nothing about contraception. Sanger began to write articles and pamphlets designed to enlighten them, but when she did so she ran afoul of the Comstock Act of 1873, an anti-obscenity law that banned the distribution of information about contraception from the mail. She was frequently in trouble with the law, but she was persistent to the edge of fanaticism. In 1921 she founded the American Birth Control League and two years later a research center. (Not until the 1960s, however, did the Supreme Court determine that the right to use contraceptives was guaranteed by the Constitution.)

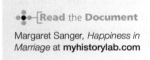
Read the Document
Margaret Sanger, *Happiness in Marriage* at **myhistorylab.com**

Other gender-based restrictions and limitations of particular importance to women also seemed to be breaking down. The divorce laws had been modified in most states. More women were taking jobs, attracted by the expanding demand for clerks, typists, salespeople, receptionists, telephone operators, and similar service-oriented occupations. Over 10.6 million women were working by the end of the decade, in contrast with 8.4 million in 1920. The Department of Labor's Women's Bureau, outgrowth of a wartime agency, was founded in 1920 and was soon conducting investigations of the working conditions women faced in different industries and how various laws affected them.

But most of these gains were illusory. Relaxation of the strict standards of sexual morality did not eliminate the double standard. More women worked, but most of the jobs they held were still menial or of a kind that few men wanted: domestic service, elementary school teaching, clerical work, selling behind a counter. When they competed for jobs with men, women usually received much lower wages. Women's Bureau studies demonstrated this repeatedly; yet when the head of the bureau, Mary Anderson, tried to get employers to raise women's wages, most of them first claimed that the men had families to support, and when she reminded them that many female employees also had family responsibilities, they told her that there was a "tacit understanding" that women were to make less than men.

More women graduated from college, but the colleges placed more emphasis on subjects like home economics that seemed designed to make them better housewives rather than professional nutritionists or business executives. As one Vassar College

This photograph of Margaret Sanger was taken during her trial in January 1917. Having opened the nation's first birth control clinic in Brooklyn, New York, she was convicted of disseminating information on contraception and served thirty days in prison. Friends had advised Sanger to dress conservatively and affect a persona of motherhood. Despite her demure clothing, her eyes express her characteristic assertiveness.

administrator (a woman!) said, colleges should provide "education for women along the lines of their chief interests and responsibilities, motherhood and the home."

The 1920s proved disillusioning to feminists, who now paid a price for their single-minded pursuit of the right to vote in the Progressive Era. After the ratification of the Nineteenth Amendment, many activists, assuming the battle won, lost interest in agitating for change. They believed that the suffrage amendment had given them the one weapon needed to achieve whatever women still lacked. In fact, it soon became apparent that women did not vote as a bloc. Many married women voted for the candidates their husbands supported.

When radical feminists discovered that voting did not automatically bring true equality, they founded the National Woman's Party (NWP) and began campaigning for an equal rights amendment. Their dynamic leader, Alice Paul, disdained specific goals such as disarmament, ending child labor, and liberalized birth control. Total equality for women was the one objective. The party considered protective legislation governing the hours and working conditions of women discriminatory. This caused the so-called social feminists, who believed that children and working women needed the protection provided by such laws, to break away.

The NWP never attracted a wide following, but only partly because of the split with the social feminists. Many of the younger radical women were primarily concerned with their personal freedom to behave as they wished; politics did not interest them. But a more important reason was that nearly all the radicals failed to see that questions of gender—the attitudes that men and women *were taught* to take toward each other—stood in the way of sexual equality. Many more women joined the more moderate League of Women Voters, which attempted to mobilize support for a broad spectrum of reforms, some of which had no specific connection to the interests of women as such. The entire women's movement lost momentum. The battle for the equal rights amendment persisted through the 1930s, but it was lost. By the end of that decade the movement was moribund.

Popular Culture: Movies and Radio

The postwar decade saw immense changes in popular culture. Unlike the literary flowering of the era, these changes seemed in tune with the times, not a reaction against them. This was true in part because they were products as much of technology as of human imagination.

Chicago

Chicago (2003) is a tale of illicit sex, booze, and "all that jazz." The characters played by Renée Zellweger and Catherine Zeta-Jones aspire to cabaret stardom. Each is married, each is jilted, and each shoots her wayward lover because "he had it coming." The newspapers gleefully promote the stories. From prison, while awaiting trial for murder, the women compete to garner the most headlines, courting the fame that will boost their careers. Richard Gere, who plays their celebrity lawyer, "razzle dazzles" all Chicago (including the juries) and gets the women acquitted. *Chicago* is a musical. It does not claim to be history. The movie, however, is based on a true story; and both the movie and the story illuminate important aspects of the Roaring Twenties.

On March 11, 1924, Walter Law, an automobile salesman, was found dead from a gunshot wound to the head. A pistol and an empty bottle of gin were on the floor. The car was registered to Belva Gaertner, a twice-divorced cabaret singer known as Belle Brown. Police hurried to her rooming house and peppered her with questions.

"We went driving, Mr. Law and I," she told them. She explained that they had stopped at the Bingham "café," bought a bottle of gin (illegally, since this was during Prohibition), and drove around town. "I don't know what happened next," she declared. During the interrogation Gaertner paced nervously, perhaps for good reason: Her clothes were soaked with blood. The police charged her with murder.

On April 3, police received a phone call from Beulah Annan, a young married woman who worked in a laundry. She said that a man had attempted to rape her and that she had shot him. Police raced to her apartment, where they found Harry Kalstedt dead from a gunshot wound. Annan insisted that she had acted in self-defense, and her husband supported her story. But police hammered away at the fact that Kalstedt had worked at the same laundry as Annan, and that he had been shot in the back. Annan eventually confessed that the two had been having an affair. When he threatened to dump her, she shot him. For two hours, as he lay dying, she drank cocktails and listened to a recording of "Hula Lou," a foxtrot about a Hawaiian girl "with more sweeties than a dog has fleas."

Maurine Watkins, a young reporter, covered both stories for the Chicago *Tribune*. Murder had long been a staple of local journalism, but Watkins recognized the extraordinary appeal of this story: jazz, booze, and two comely "lady murderesses," as Watkins termed them. While awaiting trial in prison, the women provided Watkins with delicious quotes.

Gaertner told Watkins that she was innocent. "No woman can love a man enough to kill him," she explained. "There are always plenty more. " When the grand jury ruled that she could be tried for murder, Gaertner was irritated. "That was bum," she snapped. She called the jurors "narrow-minded old birds—bet they never heard a jazz band in their lives. Now, if I'm tried, I want worldly men, broad-minded men, men who know what it is to get out a bit. Why, no one like that would convict me!"

Watkins described Gaertner as "stylish" and "classy" but called Annan the "prettiest woman ever accused of murder in Chicago"—"young, slender, with bobbed auburn hair; wide set, appealing blue eyes, upturned nose; translucent skin, faintly, very faintly, rouged, an ingenuous smile. Refined features, intelligent expression—an 'awfully nice girl.'" This account appeared on the front page.

During the trial, Annan's attorney pointed to "this frail little girl, struggling with a drunken brute." On May 25, after deliberating less than two hours, the all-male jury acquitted her of the crime. Two weeks after Annan's trial, Gaertner was also found not

Catherine Zeta-Jones and Renée Zellweger from the movie *Chicago*.

Beulah Annan, "lady murderess."
Source: DN-0076798/*Chicago Daily News*/Chicago Historical Society.

guilty. "Another pretty woman gone free," muttered the prosecutor.

Unlike the movie's "lady murderesses," Annan and Gaertner did not team up in a cabaret act. Annan had a nervous breakdown, was institutionalized, and died in 1928. Of Gaertner's subsequent life, little is known. Watkins abandoned journalism and entered Yale drama school. In 1926 she wrote *Chicago*, a comedy derived from the Gaertner and Annan trials, and it ran on Broadway for 172 performances. The next year Cecil B. De Mille adapted the play as a silent movie. In 1975 director Bob Fosse bought the rights to *Chicago* and created the Broadway musical on which the 2003 movie was based.

The "lady murderesses" became part of the lore of the Roaring Twenties; the story seemed to confirm the fears of traditionalists. One minister warned about jazz's "wriggling movement and sensuous stimulation" of the body's "sensory center." Silk stockings, skirts that exposed knees, and straight dresses that de-emphasized the waist further suggested that women's bodies were not meant solely for childbirth. The movie makes all of these points with suitable salaciousness.

The movie also reiterates widespread concerns about city life. Several months after the acquittal of Gaertner and Annan, *Literary Digest* warned "country girls" of the moral dangers of large cities. Such fears echoed the judgments of sociologists, especially those of "the Chicago school" of urban sociology, headed by Robert Park of the University of Chicago. The Chicago

sociologists contended that large cities disrupted traditional bonds of family and community and fostered crime and deviance. In *The Gold Coast and the Slum* (1929), sociologist Harvey Zorbaugh maintained that life in much of downtown Chicago was "the direct antithesis of all we are accustomed to think of as normal in society." Big-city life was characterized by a "laxity of conventional standards, and of personal and social disorganization."

Scholars now recognize that the portrait of urban city life as propounded by "the Chicago school"—and by movies such as *Chicago*—was overdrawn. Urbanization did not shatter family and ethnic ties. Neighborliness and community persisted even in blighted tenement districts. Few people cast off social conventions, much less succumbed to murderous impulses. In short, Belva Gaertner and Beulah Annan were good copy, and stories such as theirs helped make that celebrated decade roar, but most folks painted the town less vividly, if at all.

Questions for Discussion

- Compare the photograph of Beulah Annan with those of actresses Catherine Zeta-Jones and Renée Zellweger. What are the similarities and differences and what do they suggest about Hollywood's rendering of the past?
- Why would Hollywood take pains to depict the visual aspects of the past accurately?

The first motion pictures were made around 1900, but the medium only came into its own after the Great War. The early films, such as the eight-minute epic *The Great Train Robbery* (1903), were brief, action-packed, and unpretentious. Professional actors and most educated people viewed them with amused contempt. But their success was instantaneous with recent immigrants and many other slum dwellers. In 1912 there were nearly 13,000 movie houses in the United States, more than 500 in New York City alone.

By the mid-1920s the industry, centered in Hollywood, California, was the fourth largest in the nation in capital investment. Movie "palaces" seating several thousand people sprang up in the major cities. Daily ticket sales averaged more than 10 million. With the introduction of talking movies, *The Jazz Singer* (1927) being the first of significance, and color films a few years later, the motion picture reached technological maturity. Costs and profits mounted; by the 1930s million-dollar productions were common.

Many movies were still tasteless trash catering to the prejudices of the multitude. Sex, crime, war, romantic adventure, broad comedy, and luxurious living were the main themes, endlessly repeated in predictable patterns. Critics charged that the movies were destroying the legitimate stage (which underwent a sharp decline), corrupting the morals of youth, and glorifying the materialistic aspects of life.

Nevertheless the motion picture made positive contributions to American culture. Beginning with D. W. Griffith's *Birth of a Nation* (1915), filmmakers created an entirely new theatrical art. Movies enabled dozens of established actors to reach wider audiences and developed many first-rate new ones. As the medium matured, it produced many dramatic works of high quality. At its best the motion picture offered a breadth and power of impact superior to anything on the traditional stage.

Charlie Chaplin was the greatest film star of the era. His characterization of the sad-eyed little tramp with his toothbrush moustache and cane, tight coat, and baggy trousers became famous throughout the world. Chaplin's films were superficially unpretentious. But his work proved both universally popular and enduring; he was perhaps the greatest comic artist of all time. The animated cartoon, perfected by Walt Disney in the 1930s, was a lesser but significant cinematic achievement; Mickey Mouse, Donald Duck, and other Disney cartoon characters gave endless delight to millions of children.

Even more pervasive than the movies in its effects on the American people was radio. Wireless transmission of sound was developed in the late nineteenth century by many scientists in Europe and the United States. During the war radio was put to important military uses and was strictly controlled, but immediately thereafter the airwaves were thrown open.

Radio was briefly the domain of hobbyists, thousands of "hams" broadcasting in indiscriminate fashion. Even under these conditions, the manufacture of radio equipment became a big business. In 1920 the first commercial station (KDKA in Pittsburgh) began broadcasting, and by the end of 1922 over 500 stations were in operation. In 1926 the National Broadcasting Company, the first continent-wide network, was created.

It took little time for broadcasters to discover the power of the new medium. When one pioneer interrupted a music program to ask listeners to phone in requests, the station received 3,000 calls in an hour. The immediacy of radio explained its tremendous impact. As a means of communicating the latest news, it had no peer; beginning with the broadcast of the 1924 presidential nominating conventions, all major public events were covered live. Advertisers seized on radio too; it proved to be as effective a way to sell soap as to transmit news.

In 1927 Congress limited the number of stations and parceled out wavelengths to prevent interference. Further legislation in 1934 established the Federal Communications Commission (FCC), with power to revoke the licenses of stations that failed to operate in the public interest. But the FCC placed no effective controls on programming or on advertising practices.

Read the Document

Advertisements from 1925 and 1927 at **myhistorylab.com**

The Golden Age of Sports

The extraordinary popularity of sports in the postwar period can be explained in a number of ways. People had more money to spend and more free time to fill. Radio was bringing suspenseful, play-by-play accounts of sports contests into millions of homes, thus encouraging tens of thousands to want to see similar events. New means of persuasion developed by advertisers to sell lipstick, breakfast cereal, and refrigerators were applied with equal success to sporting events and to the athletes who participated in them.

There had been great athletes before; indeed probably the greatest all-around athlete of the twentieth century was Jim Thorpe, a Sac and Fox Indian who won both the pentathlon and the decathlon at the 1912 Olympic Games, made Walter Camp's All-American football team in 1912 and 1913, then played major league baseball for several years before becoming a pioneer founder and player in the National Football League. But what truly made the 1920s a golden age was a coincidence—the emergence in a few short years of a remarkable collection of what today would be called superstars.

In football there was the University of Illinois's Harold "Red" Grange, who averaged over ten yards a carry during his college career and who in one incredible quarter during the 1924 game between Illinois and Michigan carried the ball four times and scored a touchdown each time, gaining in the process 263 yards.

During the same years William "Big Bill" Tilden dominated tennis, winning the national singles title every year from 1920 to 1925 along with nearly every other tournament he entered. Beginning in 1923, Robert T. "Bobby" Jones ruled over the world of golf with equal authority, his climactic achievement being his capture of the amateur and open championships of both the United States and Great Britain in 1930.

A few women athletes dominated their sports during this golden age in similar fashion. In tennis Helen Wills was three times United States singles champion and the winner of the women's singles at Wimbledon eight times in the late 1920s and early 1930s. The swimmer Gertrude Ederle, holder of eighteen world records by the time she was seventeen, swam the English Channel on her second attempt, in 1926. She was not only the first woman to do so, but she did it faster than any of the four men who had previously made it across.

However, the sports star among stars was "the Sultan of Swat," baseball's Babe Ruth. Ruth not only dominated baseball, he changed it from a game ruled by pitchers and low scores to one in which hitting was more greatly admired. Originally himself a brilliant pitcher, his incredible hitting ability made him more valuable in the outfield, where he could play every day. Before Ruth, John "Home Run" Baker was the most famous slugger; his greatest annual home run total was 12, achieved shortly before the Great War. Ruth hit twenty-nine in 1919 and fifty-four in 1920, his first year with the New York Yankees. By 1923 he was so feared that pitchers intentionally walked him more than half the times he appeared at the plate.

Newly built Yankee Stadium on opening day of the 1923 baseball season. Babe Ruth hit his first home run and soon Yankee Stadium was dubbed "the House that Ruth Built." That year, perhaps his best, Ruth hit forty-one home runs, batted .393, and drew 170 walks. He got on base more than half the times he appeared at the plate. Ruth's feats matched the colossal appearance of Yankee Stadium, whose arches evoked the imperial grandeur of ancient Rome.

The achievements of these and other outstanding athletes had a cumulative effect. New stadiums were built, and they were filled by "the largest crowds that ever witnessed athletic sports since the fall of Rome."

Urban–Rural Conflicts: Fundamentalism

These were buoyant times for people in tune with the times. However, the tensions and hostilities of the 1920s exaggerated an older rift in American society—the conflict between urban and rural ways of life. To many among the scattered millions who tilled the soil and among the millions who lived in towns and small cities, the new city-oriented culture seemed sinful, overly materialistic, and unhealthy.

Yet there was no denying its fascination. Made even more aware of the appeal of the city by radio and the automobile, farmers and townspeople coveted the comfort and excitement of city life at the same time that they condemned its vices. Rural society proclaimed the superiority of its ways at least in part to protect itself from temptation. Change, omnipresent in the postwar world, must be resisted even at the cost of individualism and freedom.

One expression of this resistance was a resurgence of religious fundamentalism. Although it was especially prevalent among Baptists and Methodists, fundamentalism was primarily an attitude of mind, profoundly conservative, rather than a religious idea. Fundamentalists rejected the theory of evolution as well as advanced hypotheses on the origins of the universe.

What made crusaders of the fundamentalists was their resentment of modern urban culture. The teaching of evolution must be prohibited, they insisted. Throughout the 1920s they campaigned vigorously for laws banning discussion of Darwin's theory in textbooks and classrooms. By 1929 five southern states had passed laws prohibiting the teaching of evolution in the public schools.

Their greatest asset in this crusade was William Jennings Bryan. After leaving Wilson's Cabinet in 1915 he devoted much time to religious and moral issues, but without applying himself conscientiously to the study of these difficult questions. He went about the country charging that "they"—meaning the mass of educated Americans—had "taken the Lord away from the schools." He denounced the use of public money to undermine Christian principles, and he offered $100 to anyone who would admit to being descended from an ape. His immense popularity in rural areas assured him a wide audience, and no one came forward to take his money.

The fundamentalists won a minor victory in 1925, when Tennessee passed a law forbidding instructors in the state's schools and colleges to teach "any theory that denies the story of the Divine Creation of man as taught in the Bible." The bill passed both houses by big majorities; few legislators wished to expose themselves to charges that they did not believe the Bible.

On learning of the passage of this act, the American Civil Liberties Union announced that it would finance a test case challenging its constitutionality if a Tennessee teacher would deliberately violate the statute. Urged on by friends, John T. Scopes, a young biology teacher in Dayton, reluctantly agreed to do so. He was arrested. A battery of nationally known lawyers came forward to defend him, and the state obtained the services of Bryan himself. The **Scopes trial**, also known as the "Monkey Trial," became an overnight sensation.

Clarence Darrow, chief counsel for the defendant, stated the issue clearly. "Scopes isn't on trial," he said, "civilization is on trial. No man's belief will be safe if they win." The comic aspects of the trial obscured this issue. Scopes's conviction was a foregone conclusion; after the jury rendered its verdict, the judge fined him $100.

Nevertheless, the trial exposed the danger of the fundamentalist position. The high point came when Bryan agreed to testify as an expert witness on the Bible. In a sweltering courtroom, the lanky, rough-hewn Darrow cross-examined the aging champion of fundamentalism, exposing his childlike faith and his disdain for the science of the day. "I believe in a God that can make a whale and can make a man and make both do what He pleases," Bryan explained.

The Monkey Trial ended badly for nearly everyone concerned. Scopes moved away from Dayton; the judge,

The Scopes trial was a media sensation; it even gave rise to popular songs, such as this one by Billy Rose.

Photo Credit: Nashville Public Library, Special Collections.

John Raulston, was defeated when he sought reelection; Bryan died in his sleep a few days after the trial. But fundamentalism continued to flourish, not only in the nation's backwaters but also in many cities, brought there by rural people in search of work. In retrospect, even the heroes of the Scopes trial—science and freedom of thought—seem somewhat less stainless than they did to liberals at the time. The account of evolution in the textbook used by Scopes was hopelessly deficient and laced with bigotry, yet it was advanced as unassailable fact. In a section on the "Races of Man," for example, it described Caucasians as "the highest type of all . . . represented by the civilized white inhabitants of Europe and America."

Urban–Rural Conflicts: Prohibition

The conflict between the countryside and the city was fought on many fronts, and in one sector the rural forces achieved a quick victory. This was the Eighteenth Amendment, ratified in 1919, which prohibited the manufacture, transportation, and sale of alcoholic beverages. Although there were some big-city advocates of prohibition, the Eighteenth Amendment, in the words of one historian, marked a triumph of the "Corn Belt over the conveyor belt."

The temperance movement had been important since the age of Jackson; it was a major issue in many states during the Gilded Age, and by the Progressive Era powerful organizations like the Anti-Saloon League and the Women's Christian Temperance Union were seeking to have drinking outlawed entirely. Indeed, prohibition was a typical progressive reform, moralistic, backed by the middle class, and aimed at frustrating "the interests"—in this case the distillers.

World War I aided the prohibitionists by increasing the need for food. The Lever Act of 1917 outlawed the use of grain in the manufacture of alcoholic beverages, primarily as a conservation measure. The prevailing dislike of foreigners helped the dry cause still more: Beer drinking was associated with Germans. State and local laws had made a large part of the country dry by 1917. National prohibition became official in January 1920.

This "experiment noble in purpose," as Herbert Hoover called it, achieved a number of socially desirable results. It reduced the annual national consumption of alcohol from 2.6 gallons per capita in the period just before the war to less than 1 gallon in the early 1930s. Arrests for drunkenness fell off sharply, as did deaths from alcoholism. Fewer workers squandered their wages on drink. If the drys had been willing to legalize beer and wine, the experiment might have worked. Instead, by insisting on total abstinence, they drove thousands of moderates to violate the law. Strict enforcement became impossible, especially in the cities.

In areas where sentiment favored prohibition strongly, liquor remained difficult to find. Elsewhere, anyone with sufficient money could obtain it easily. Smuggling became a major business, *bootlegger* a household word. Private individuals busied themselves learning how to manufacture "bathtub gin." Many druggists issued prescriptions for alcohol with a free hand. The manufacture of wine for religious ceremonies was legal, and consumption of sacramental wine jumped by 800,000 gallons during the first two years of prohibition. The saloon disappeared, replaced by the speakeasy, a supposedly secret bar or club operating under the benevolent eye of the local police.

That the law was often violated does not mean that it was ineffective any more than violations of laws against theft and murder mean that those laws are ineffective.

Although gangsters such as Alphonse "Scarface Al" Capone of Chicago were engaged in the liquor traffic, their "organizations" existed before the passage of the Eighteenth Amendment. But prohibition widened already serious rifts in the social fabric of the country. Organized crime became more powerful. Besides undermining public morality by encouraging hypocrisy, prohibition almost destroyed the Democratic party as a national organization. Democratic immigrants in the cities hated it, but southern Democrats sang its praises, often while continuing to drink (the humorist Will Rogers quipped that Mississippi would vote dry "as long as the voters could stagger to the polls").

The hypocrisy of prohibition had a particularly deleterious effect on politicians, a class seldom famous for candor. Members of Congress catered to the demands of the powerful lobby of the Anti-Saloon League yet failed to grant adequate funds to the Prohibition Bureau. Nearly all the prominent leaders, Democrat and Republican, from Wilson and La Follette to Hoover and Franklin D. Roosevelt, equivocated shamelessly on the liquor

((•─[**Hear** the **Audio**
Prohibition is a Failure at
myhistorylab.com

question. By the end of the decade almost every competent observer recognized that prohibition at least needed to be overhauled, but the well-organized and powerful dry forces rejected all proposals for modifying it.

The Ku Klux Klan

The most horrible manifestation of the social malaise of the 1920s was the revival of the Ku Klux Klan. This new Klan, founded in 1915 by William J. Simmons, a former preacher, admitted only native-born white Protestants. The distrust of foreigners, blacks, Catholics, and Jews implicit in this regulation explains why it flourished in the social climate that spawned religious fundamentalism, immigration restriction, and prohibition. In a little over a year the Klan enrolled 100,000 recruits, and by 1923 they claimed the astonishing total of 5 million.

A Ku Klux Klan initiation ceremony photographed in Kansas in the 1920s. During its peak influence at mid-decade, Klan endorsement was essential to political candidates in many areas of the West and Midwest. Campaigning for reelection in 1934, an Indiana congressman testified, "I was told to join the Klan, or else."
Source: Kansas State Historical Society.

Simmons gave his society trappings and mystery calculated to attract gullible and bigoted people who yearned to express their frustrations and hostilities without personal risk. Klansmen masked themselves in white robes and hoods and enjoyed a childish mumbo jumbo of magnificent-sounding titles and dogmas. They burned crosses in the night, organized mass demonstrations to intimidate people they disliked, and put pressure on businessmen to fire black workers from better-paying jobs.

The Klan had relatively little appeal in the Northeast or in metropolitan centers in other parts of the country, but it found many members in mid-sized cities and in the small towns and villages of midwestern and western states. The rationale was an urge to return to an older, supposedly finer America and to stamp out all varieties of nonconformity. Klansmen persecuted gamblers, "loose" women, violators of the prohibition laws, and anyone who happened to differ from them on religious questions or who belonged to a "foreign race."

The very success of the Klan led to its undoing. Factionalism sprang up, and rival leaders squabbled over the large sums that had been collected from the membership. The cruel and outrageous behavior of the organization roused both liberals and conservatives in every part of the country. And of course its victims joined forces against their tormentors. When the powerful leader of the Indiana Klan, a middle-aged reprobate named David C. Stephenson, was convicted of assaulting and causing the death of a young woman, the rank and file abandoned the organization in droves. The Klan remained influential for a number of years, but it ceased to be a dynamic force after 1924. By 1930 it had only some 9,000 members.

Read the Document

Creed of Klanswomen at **myhistorylab.com**

Literary Trends

The literature of the 1920s reflects the disillusionment of the intellectuals. The wasteful horrors of the Great War and then the antics of the fundamentalists and the cruelty of the red-baiters and the Klan turned them into critics of society. Many intellectuals deplored the 1927 execution of Nicola Sacco and Bartolomeo Vanzetti, Italian immigrants (and anarchists) who were deprived of a fair trial in a murder case. They included the poet Edna St. Vincent Millay, the playwright Maxwell Anderson, and the novelists Upton Sinclair and John Dos Passos. After the war the poet Ezra Pound dropped his talk of an American Renaissance and wrote instead of a "botched civilization."

Read the Document

Bartolomeo Vanzetti, Court Statement at **myhistorylab.com**

The symbol of what some called the "lost generation," in his own mind as well as to his contemporaries and to later critics, was F. Scott Fitzgerald. Born to modest wealth in St. Paul, Minnesota, in 1896, Fitzgerald attended Princeton and served in the army during the Great War. He rose to sudden fame in 1920 when he published *This Side of Paradise*, a somewhat sophomoric novel that appealed powerfully to college students and captured the fears and confusions of the lost generation. In *The Great Gatsby* (1925), a more mature work, Fitzgerald depicted a modern millionaire—coarse, unscrupulous, jaded, in love with another man's wife. Gatsby's tragedy lay in his dedication to a woman who, Fitzgerald made clear, did not merit his passion.

The tragedy of *The Great Gatsby* was related to Fitzgerald's own. Pleasure-loving and extravagant, he squandered the money earned by *This Side of Paradise*. When *The Great Gatsby* failed to sell as well, he turned to writing potboilers. "I really worked hard as hell last winter," he told the critic Edmund Wilson, "but it was all trash and it nearly broke my heart." While some of his later work, particularly *Tender Is the Night* (1934), is first-class, he descended into the despair of alcoholism and ended his days as a Hollywood scriptwriter.

Many young American writers and artists became expatriates in the 1920s. They flocked to Rome, Berlin, and especially Paris, where they could live cheaply and escape what seemed to them the "conspiracy against the individual" prevalent in their own country. Some made meager livings as journalists, translators, and editors, perhaps turning an extra dollar from time to time by selling a story or a poem to an American magazine or a painting to a tourist.

Ernest Hemingway was the most talented of the expatriates. He had served in the Italian army during the war and been grievously wounded (in spirit as well as in body). He settled in Paris in 1922 to write. His first novel, *The Sun Also Rises* (1926), portrayed the café world of the expatriate and the rootless desperation, amorality, and sense of outrage at life's meaninglessness that obsessed so many in those years. In *A Farewell to Arms* (1929) he drew on his military experiences to describe the confusion and horror of war.

Hemingway's books were best-sellers and he became a legend in his own time. Few novelists have been as capable of suggesting powerful emotions and action in so few words. Mark Twain and Stephen Crane were his models; Gertrude Stein, a writer and revolutionary genius, his teacher. But his style was his own—direct, simple, taut, sparse:

> I went out the door and down the hall to the room where Catherine was to be after the baby came. I sat in a chair there and looked at the room. I had the paper in my coat that I had bought when I went out for lunch and I read it. . . . After a while I stopped reading and turned off the light and watched it get dark outside. *(A Farewell to Arms)*

Source: Reprinted with the permission of Scribner, a Division of Simon & Schuster, Inc., from *A Farewell to Arms* by Ernest Hemingway. Copyright © 1929 by Charles Scribner's Son's; copyright renewed 1956 by Ernest Hemingway. All rights reserved.

This kind of writing, evoking rather than describing emotion, fascinated readers and inspired hundreds of imitators; it made a permanent mark on world literature. What Hemingway had to say was of less universal interest. He wrote about bullfights, hunting and fishing, and violence; while he did so with masterful penetration, these themes placed limits on his work that he never transcended. The critic Alfred Kazin summed up Hemingway in a sentence: "He brought a major art to a minor vision of life."

Edith Wharton was of the New York aristocracy. She was educated by tutors and governesses and never went to college. She traveled frequently to Europe, eventually chose to live there, and took up writing. After co-authoring a book on home decoration, she wrote novels on marriage and manners in some ways reminiscent of Henry James. In Paris at the outset of the Great War, she threw herself into war-related charities. But while the shock of the war jolted Fitzgerald and Hemingway into the vanguard of innovation, she retreated from the jangling energy of postwar life and culture. The product of her retreat, *The Age of Innocence* (1920), offered a penetrating portrait of an unsettlingly serene if vanished world. The Nation remarked that Wharton had described the wealthy of old New York "as familiarly as if she loved them and as lucidly as if she hated them."

Although neither was the equal of Hemingway, Fitzgerald, or Wharton, two other writers of the 1920s deserve mention: H. L. Mencken and Sinclair Lewis. Each reflected the distaste of intellectuals for the climate of the times. Mencken, a Baltimore newspaperman and founder of one of the great magazines of the era, the *American Mercury*, was a thoroughgoing cynic. He coined the word *booboisie* to define the complacent, middle-class majority, and he fired superbly witty broadsides at fundamentalists, prohibitionists, and "Puritans." "Puritanism," he once said, "is the haunting fear that someone, somewhere, may be happy."

But Mencken was never indifferent to the many aspects of American life that roused his contempt. Politics at once fascinated and repelled him, and he assailed the statesmen of his generation with magnificent impartiality:

> [On Coolidge]: "A cheap and trashy fellow, deficient in sense and almost devoid of any notion of honor—in brief, a dreadful little cad."

> [On Hoover]: "Lord Hoover is no more than a pious old woman, a fat Coolidge."

> Source: H. L. Mencken

Mencken's diatribes, while amusing, were not profound. In perspective he seems more a professional iconoclast than a constructive critic; like both Fitzgerald and Hemingway, he was something of a perennial adolescent. However, he consistently supported freedom of expression of every sort.

Sinclair Lewis was probably the most popular American novelist of the 1920s. Like Fitzgerald, his first major work brought him instant fame and notoriety—and for the same reason. *Main Street* (1920) portrayed the smug ignorance and bigotry of the American small town so accurately that even Lewis's victims recognized themselves; his title became a symbol for provinciality and middle-class meanness of spirit. In *Babbitt* (1922), he created what many people considered the typical businessman of the 1920s, gregarious, a "booster," blindly orthodox in his political and social opinions, a slave to every cliché, and full of loud self-confidence, but under the surface a bumbling, rather timid fellow who would have liked to be better than he was but dared not try. Lewis went on to dissect the medical profession in *Arrowsmith* (1925), religion in *Elmer Gantry* (1927), and fascism in *It Can't Happen Here* (1935).

The "New Negro"

The postwar reaction brought despair for many blacks. Aside from the barbarities of the Klan, they suffered from the postwar middle-class hostility to labor. The increasing presence of southern blacks in northern cities also caused conflict. Some 393,000 settled in New York, Pennsylvania, and Illinois in the 1920s, most of them in New York City, Philadelphia, and Chicago. The black population of New York City more than doubled between 1920 and 1930.

In earlier periods blacks in northern cities had tended to live together, but in small neighborhoods scattered over large areas. Now the tendency was toward concentration in what came to be called ghettos.

Even in small northern cities where they made up only a tiny proportion of the population, blacks were badly treated. When Robert S. and Helen M. Lynd made their classic sociological analysis of "Middletown" (Muncie, Indiana), they discovered that although black and white children attended the same schools, the churches, the larger movie houses, and other places of public accommodation were segregated. The local YMCA had a gymnasium where high school basketball was played, but the secretary refused to allow any team with a black player to use it. Even the news in Muncie was segregated. Local papers chronicled the affairs of the black community—roughly 5 percent of the population—under the heading "In Colored Circles."

Coming after the hopes inspired by wartime gains, the disappointments of the 1920s produced a new militancy among many blacks. In 1919 W. E. B. Du Bois wrote in *The Crisis*, "We are cowards and jackasses if . . . we do not marshal every ounce of our brain and brawn to fight . . . against the forces of hell in our own land." He increased his commitment to black nationalism, organizing a series of Pan African Conferences in an effort—futile, as it turned out—to create an international black movement.

Du Bois never made up his mind whether to work for integration or black separatism. Such ambivalence never troubled Marcus Garvey, a West Indian whose Universal Negro Improvement Association attracted hundreds of thousands of followers in the early 1920s. Garvey had nothing but contempt for whites, for light-skinned blacks like Du Bois, and for organizations such as the NAACP, which sought to bring whites and blacks together to fight segregation and other forms of prejudice. "Back to Africa" was his slogan; the black man must "work out his salvation in his motherland."

Garvey's message was naive, but it served to build racial pride among the masses of poor and unschooled blacks. He organized black businesses of many sorts, including a company that manufactured black dolls. He established a corps of Black Cross nurses and a Black Star Line Steamship Company to transport blacks back to Africa.

More sophisticated black leaders like Du Bois detested Garvey, whom they thought something of a charlatan. In 1923 Garvey's steamship line went into bankruptcy. He was convicted of defrauding the thousands of his supporters who had invested in its stock and was sent to prison. Nevertheless, his message, if not his methods, helped to create the "New Negro," proud of being black and prepared to resist both mistreatment and white ideas. The ghettos produced compensating advantages for blacks. One effect, not fully utilized until later, was to increase their political power by enabling them to elect representatives to state legislatures and

A painting from Jacob Lawrence's Migration Series (1940–1941).
Source: Gift of Mrs. David M. Levy. (28.1942.20). ©The Museum of Modern Art/Artists Rights Society/Art Resource, NY.

The Making of Black Harlem In 1911, African Americans lived mostly in a dozen-block region of Harlem; by 1930, they had created a predominantly black city of well over 100 city blocks.

Congress, and to exert considerable influence in closely contested elections. More immediately, city life stimulated self-confidence; despite their horrors, the ghettos offered economic opportunity, political rights, and freedom from the everyday debasements of life in the South. The ghetto was a black world where black men and women could be themselves.

Black writers, musicians, and artists found in the ghettos both an audience and the "spiritual emancipation" that unleashed their capacities. Jazz, the great popular music of the age, was largely the creation of black musicians working in New Orleans before the turn of the century. By the 1920s it had spread throughout the country and to most of the rest of the world. White musicians and white audiences took it up—in a way it became a force for racial tolerance and understanding.

Harlem, the largest black community in the world, became in the 1920s a cultural capital, center of the **Harlem Renaissance**. Black newspapers and magazines flourished along with theatrical companies and libraries. Du Bois opened *The Crisis* to

Watch the Video

The Harlem Renaissance at **myhistorylab.com**

young writers and artists, and a dozen "little" magazines sprang up. Langston Hughes, one of the most talented poets of the era, described the exhilaration of his first arrival in this city within a city, a magnet for every black intellectual and artist: "Harlem! I . . . dropped my bags, took a deep breath, and felt happy again." In 1925 Zora Neale Hurston joined with Hughes to create a literary magazine, and celebrated the lives of ordinary black workers.

With some exceptions, African American writers like Hughes and Hurston did not share in the disillusionment that afflicted so many white intellectuals. The persistence of prejudice angered them and made them militant. But to be militant, one must be at some

Zora Neale Hurston, a major figure of the Harlem Renaissance, wrote eighteen novels—many of which were made into movies.

Photo Credit: © Estate of Carl Van Vechten, Bruce Kellner.

level hopeful. Sociologists and psychologists (for whom the ghettos were indispensable social laboratories) were demonstrating that environment rather than heredity was preventing black economic progress. Together with the achievements of creative blacks, which for the first time were being appreciated by large numbers of white intellectuals, these discoveries seemed to herald the eventual disappearance of racial prejudice. The black, Alain Locke wrote in *The New Negro* (1925), "lays aside the status of beneficiary and ward for that of a collaborator and participant in American civilization." Alas, as Locke and other black intellectuals were soon to discover, this prediction, like so many made in the 1920s, did not come to pass.

Economic Expansion

Despite the turmoil of the times and the dissatisfactions expressed by some of the nation's best minds, the 1920s was an exceptionally prosperous decade. Business boomed, real wages rose, unemployment declined. The United States was as rich as all Europe; perhaps 40 percent of the world's total wealth lay in American hands. Little wonder that business leaders and other conservatives described the period as a "new era."

The prosperity rested on many bases, one of which was the friendly, hands-off attitude of the federal government, which bolstered the confidence of the business community. The Federal Reserve Board kept interest rates low, a further stimulus to economic growth. The continuing mechanization and rationalization of industry provided a more fundamental stimulus to the economy. From heavy road-grading equipment and concrete mixers to devices for making cigars and glass tubes, from pneumatic tools to the dial telephone, machinery was replacing human hands at an ever more rapid rate. Industrial output almost doubled between 1921 and 1929 without any substantial increase in the industrial labor force.

Most important, American manufacturing was experiencing a remarkable improvement in efficiency. The method of breaking down the complex processes of production into many simple operations and the use of interchangeable parts were nineteenth-century innovations; in the 1920s they were adopted on an almost universal scale. The moving assembly line which carried the product to the worker, first devised by Henry Ford in his automobile plant in the decade before World War I, speeded production and reduced costs. In ten years the hourly output of Ford workers quadrupled.

The Age of the Consumer

The growing ability of manufacturers to produce goods meant that great effort had to be made to create new consumer demands. Advertising and salesmanship were raised almost to the status of fine arts. Bruce Barton, one of the advertising "geniuses" of the era, wrote a best-selling book, *The Man Nobody Knows* (1925), in which he described Jesus as the "founder of modern business," the man who "picked up twelve men from the bottom ranks . . . and forged them into an organization that conquered the world."

Producers concentrated on making their goods more attractive and on changing models frequently to entice buyers into the market. The practice of selling goods on the installment plan helped bring expensive items within the reach of the masses. Inventions and technological advances created new or improved products: radios, automobiles, electric appliances such as vacuum cleaners and refrigerators, gadgets like cigarette lighters, and new forms of entertainment like motion pictures.

Undoubtedly the automobile had the single most important impact on the nation's economy in the 1920s. Although well over a million cars a year were being regularly produced by 1916, the real expansion of the industry came after 1921. Output reached 3.6 million in 1923 and fell below that figure only twice during the remainder of the decade. By 1929, 23 million private cars clogged the highways, an average of nearly one per family.

Watch the Video

The rise and fall of the automobile economy at **myhistorylab.com**

The auto industry created companies that manufactured tires and spark plugs and other products. It triggered a gigantic road-building program: There were 387,000 miles of paved roads in the United States in 1921, and 662,000 miles in 1929. Thousands of persons found employment in filling stations, roadside stands, and other businesses catering to the motoring public. The tourism industry profited, and the shift of population from the cities to the suburbs accelerated.

The automobile made life more mobile yet also more encapsulated. It changed recreational patterns and family life. In addition, it profoundly affected the way Americans thought. It gave them a freedom never before imagined. The owner of the most rickety jalopy could travel farther, faster, and far more comfortably than a monarch of old with his pureblooded steeds and gilded coaches.

These benefits were real and priceless. Cars also became important

Would women believe the claims of cosmetics advertisements? "Kissproof" promised to make a woman's lips "pulsate with the very spirit of reckless, irrepressible youth." In a 1927 survey of housewives in Columbus, Ohio, Pond's Company found that two-thirds of the women could not even recall the company's advertisements. Younger women, however, were more impressionable. When the J. Walter Thompson advertising agency asked Vassar students to describe cosmetics, they unconsciously used the exact phrases from advertising copy—proof of its power.

Photo Credit: Culver Pictures, Inc.

symbols. They gave their owners the feeling of power and status that a horse gave to a medieval knight. According to some authorities the typical American cared more about owning an automobile than a house.

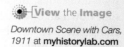

Downtown Scene with Cars, 1911 at **myhistorylab.com**

In time there were undesirable, even dangerous results of the automotive revolution: roadside scenery disfigured by billboards, gas stations, and other enterprises aimed at satisfying the traveler's needs; horrendous traffic jams; soaring accident rates; air pollution; and the neglect of public transportation, which was an important cause of the deterioration of inner cities. All these disadvantages were noticed during the 1920s, but in the springtime of the new industry they were discounted. The automobile seemed an unalloyed blessing—part toy, part tool, part symbol of American freedom, prosperity, and individualism.

Henry Ford

The person most responsible for the growth of the automobile industry was Henry Ford, a self-taught mechanic from Greenfield, Michigan. Ford was neither a great inventor nor one of the true automobile pioneers. Ford's first brilliant insight was to "get the prices down to the buying power." Through mass production, cars could be made cheaply enough to put them within reach of the ordinary citizen. In 1908 he designed the Model T Ford, a simple, tough box on wheels. In a year he proved his point by selling 11,000 Model Ts. Relentlessly cutting costs and increasing efficiency with the assembly line system, he expanded production at an unbelievable rate. By 1925 he was turning out more than 9,000 cars a day, one approximately every ten seconds, and the price of the Model T had been reduced below $300.

Ford's second insight was the importance of high wages in stimulating output (and selling more automobiles). The assembly line simplified the laborer's task and increased the pace of work; at the same time it made each worker much more productive. Jobs became boring and fatiguing, and absenteeism and labor turnover became serious problems. To combat this difficulty, in 1914 Ford established the $5 day, an increase of about $2 over prevailing wages. The rate of turnover in his plant fell 90 percent, and although critics charged that he recaptured his additional labor costs by speeding up the line, his policy had a revolutionary effect on wage rates. Later he raised the minimum to $6 and then to $7 a day.

Ford's profits soared along with sales; since he owned the entire company, he became a billionaire. He also became an authentic folk hero: his homespun style, his dislike of bankers and sophisticated society, and his intense individualism endeared him to millions. He stood as a symbol of the wonders of the American system—he had given the nation a marvelous convenience at a low price, at the same time enriching himself and raising the living standards of his thousands of employees.

Unfortunately, Ford had the defects of his virtues in full measure. He paid high wages but refused to deal with any union and he employed spies to investigate the private lives of his workers, and gangsters and thugs to enforce plant discipline. When he discovered a worker driving any car but a Ford, he had him dismissed. So close was the supervision in the factory that workers devised the "Ford whisper," a means of talking without moving one's lips.

Success made Ford stubborn. The Model T remained essentially unchanged for nearly twenty years. Other companies, notably General Motors, were soon turning out better vehicles for very little more money. Customers, increasingly affluent and style-conscious, began to shift to Chevrolets and Chryslers. Finally, in 1927, Ford shut down all operations for eighteen months in order to retool for the Model A. His competitors rushed in during this period to fill the vacuum. Although his company continued to make a great deal of money, Ford never regained the dominant position he had held for so long.

Ford was enormously uninformed, yet—because of his success and the praise the world heaped on him—he did not hesitate to speak out on subjects far outside his area of competence, from the evils of drink and tobacco to medicine and international affairs. He developed political ambitions and published virulent anti-Semitic propaganda. He said he would not give five cents for all the art in the world.

While praising his talents as a manufacturer, historians have not dealt kindly with Ford the man, in part no doubt because he once said, "History is more or less the bunk."

The Airplane

Henry Ford was also an early manufacturer of airplanes, and while the airplane industry was not economically important in the 1920s, its development in that decade laid the basis for changes in lifestyles and attitudes at least as momentous as those produced by the automobile. The invention of the internal combustion gasoline engine, with its extremely high ratio of power to weight, made the airplane possible, which explains why the early experiments with "flying machines" took place at about the same time that the prototypes of the modern automobile were being manufactured. Wilbur and Orville Wright made their famous flight at Kitty Hawk, North Carolina, in 1903, five years before Ford produced his Model T. Another pair of brothers, Malcolm and Haimes Lockheed, built their Model G, one of the earliest commercial planes in 1913.

The great event of the decade for aviation, still an achievement that must strike awe in the hearts of reflective persons, was Charles A. Lindbergh's nonstop flight from New York to Paris in May 1927. It took more than thirty-three hours for Lindbergh's single-engine *Spirit of St. Louis* to cross the Atlantic, a formidable physical achievement for the pilot as well as an example of skill and courage. When the public learned that the intrepid "Lucky Lindy" was handsome, modest, uninterested in converting his new fame into cash, and a model of propriety (he neither drank nor smoked), his role as American hero was ensured. It was a role Lindbergh detested—one biographer has described him as "by nature solitary"—but could not avoid.

Lindbergh's flight enormously increased public interest in flying, but it was a landmark in aviation technology as well. The day of routine passenger flights was at last about to dawn. In July 1927, a mere two months after the *Spirit of St. Louis* touched down at Le Bourget Field in France, William E. Boeing of Boeing Air Transport began flying passengers and mail between San Francisco and Chicago, using the M–40, a plane of his own design and manufacture. Early in 1928 he changed the company name to United Aircraft and Transport. Two years later Boeing produced the first all-metal low-wing plane and, in 1933, the twin-engine 247, a prototype for many others.

In retrospect the postwar era seems even more a period of transition than it appeared to most people at the time. Rarely had change come so swiftly, and rarely had old and new existed side by side in such profusion. Creativity and reaction, hope and despair, freedom and repression—the modern world in all its unfathomable complexity was emerging.

Milestones

1903	Wright brothers fly at Kitty Hawk, NC	1926	Gertrude Ederle swims English Channel
1908	Henry Ford designs Model T automobile		Ernest Hemingway publishes *The Sun Also Rises*
1914	Ford establishes $5 day for autoworkers		
1919	Eighteenth Amendment outlaws alcoholic beverages (Prohibition)	1927	Charles Lindbergh flies solo across Atlantic
	Nineteenth Amendment gives women right to vote		Sacco and Vanzetti are executed
1920	Sinclair Lewis publishes *Main Street*		*The Jazz Singer*, first motion picture with sound, is released
	First commercial radio station, KDKA, Pittsburgh, begins broadcasting		Jack Dempsey loses heavyweight boxing title to Gene Tunney
1920s	Black culture flourishes in Harlem Renaissance		Babe Ruth hits sixty home runs
1921	Margaret Sanger founds American Birth Control League	1928	John B. Watson publishes *The Psychological Care of Infant and Child*
1924	Ku Klux Klan membership peaks		
1925	Scopes is convicted for teaching evolution	1929	Capone's gang kills Moran's in Valentine's Day Massacre
	F. Scott Fitzgerald publishes *The Great Gatsby*		

✓—[Study and Review at www.myhistorylab.com

Review Questions

1. The introduction suggests that the prohibition of alcohol encouraged people to flaunt other conventions. To what extent were the cultural shifts of the 1920s a rebellion against tradition?

2. How did traditionalists respond to these social and cultural transformations? Was the fundamental tension, as the chapter suggests, between rural and urban cultures? Or was it between classes or ethnic groups?

3. How did technological changes such as radio, the automobile, and the airplane influence culture? How did "mass culture" touch the lives of Americans? Did it improve life or diminish it?

4. How did the 1920s liberate women, African Americans, and minorities?

Key Terms

Harlem Renaissance   National Origins Act   Scopes trial

From "Normalcy" to Economic Collapse: 1921–1933

From Chapter 25 of *American Destiny: Narrative of a Nation*, Combined Volume, Fourth Edition.
Mark C. Carnes and John A. Garraty. Copyright © 2012 by Pearson Education, Inc. Published by
Pearson Prentice Hall. All rights reserved.

From "Normalcy" to Economic Collapse: 1921–1933

((•—[Hear the Audio at myhistorylab.com

Will you get a job?

IN JUNE, 2009 KYLE DALEY GRADUATED FROM UCLA WITH A 3.5 AVERAGE.
He applied for 600 jobs, mostly entry-level positions in large corporations. He got two interviews but no job. He was not alone. In 2010 the Labor Department reported that nearly 11 percent of recent college graduates were without jobs, the highest rate on record. Because two-thirds had taken out student loans averaging $23,200, many considered bankruptcy.

Daley and his age cohort had grown up during the most prosperous decades the American nation had ever witnessed. But it all came crashing down in 2008. The enormous hot-air balloon that was the U.S. housing market burst. Worldwide financial markets, tethered to U.S. mortgages, fell precipitously. Major investment firms declared bankruptcy. Massive layoffs ensued. "I don't remember any time, maybe even the Great Depression, when things went down so fast," observed Paul Volker, the eighty-one-year-old former chairman of the Federal Reserve.

The Great Depression had similarly been preceded by an era of economic prosperity. In 1924 Commerce Secretary Herbert Hoover had proclaimed "a new era" in which cutthroat competition was being superseded by cooperative associations of producers. This heralded "infinite possibilities of moral progress." Such words perhaps sounded hollow, coming in the wake of a Harding administration disgraced by scandal. By 1924 Calvin Coolidge was president, to be succeeded by Hoover in 1929; both presided over a nation that basked in the dawn of a prosperous new era, though a few dark war clouds could be seen in the distance. Many Americans, giddy over their stock market winnings, placed more and more bets on Wall Street. When it all went bust in 1929, many found themselves mired in the depths of the Great Depression.

Harding and "Normalcy"

Warren G. Harding was a newspaperman by trade, publisher of the *Marion Star*, with previous political experience as a legislator and lieutenant governor in his home state, Ohio, and as a U.S. senator. No president, before or since, looked more like a statesman; few were less suited for running the country.

Harding's genial nature and lack of strong convictions made him attractive to many of the politicos after eight years of the headstrong Wilson. During the campaign he exasperated sophisticates by his ignorance and imprecision. He coined the famous vulgarism *normalcy* as a substitute for the word *normality*, and committed numerous other blunders. Senator Lodge, ordinarily a stickler for linguistic exactitude, replied acidly that he found Harding a paragon by comparison with Wilson, "a man who wrote English very well without ever saying anything." A large majority of the voters, untroubled by the candidate's lack of erudition, shared Lodge's confidence that Harding would be a vast improvement over Wilson.

Harding has often been characterized as lazy and incompetent. In fact, he was hardworking and politically shrewd; his major weaknesses were indecisiveness and an unwillingness to offend. He turned the most important government departments over to efficient administrators of impeccable reputation: Charles Evans Hughes, the secretary of state; Herbert Hoover in the Commerce Department; Andrew Mellon in the Treasury; and Henry C. Wallace in Agriculture. He kept track of what these men did but seldom initiated policy in their areas. However, Harding gave many lesser offices, and a few of major importance, to the unsavory "Ohio Gang" headed by Harry M. Daugherty, whom he made attorney general.

The president was too kindly, too well-intentioned, and too unambitious to be dishonest. He appointed corrupt officials like Daugherty, Secretary of the Interior Albert B. Fall, Director of the Mint "Ed" Scobey, and Charles R. Forbes, head of the new Veterans Bureau, out of a sense of personal obligation or because they were old friends who shared his taste for poker and liquor. Before 1921 he had enjoyed holding office. In the lonely eminence of the White House, however, he found only misery. "The White House is a prison," he complained. "I can't get away from the men who dog my footsteps. I am in jail."

"The Business of the United States is Business"

Secretary of the Treasury Mellon, multimillionaire banker and master of the aluminum industry, dominated the administration's domestic policy. Mellon set out to lower the taxes of the rich, reverse the low-tariff policies of the Wilson period, return to the laissez-faire philosophy of McKinley, and reduce the national debt by cutting expenses and administrating the government more efficiently.

In principle his program had considerable merit. Tax rates designed to check consumer spending in time of war and to raise the huge sum needed to defeat the Central Powers were undoubtedly hampering economic expansion in the early 1920s. Certain industries that had sprung up in the United States during the Great War were suffering from German and Japanese competition now that the fighting had ended. Rigid regulation necessary during a national crisis could well be dispensed with in peacetime. And efficiency and economy in government are always desirable.

Yet Mellon carried his policies to unreasonable extremes. He proposed eliminating inheritance taxes and reducing the tax on high incomes by two-thirds, but he opposed lower rates for taxpayers earning less than $66,000 a year, apparently not realizing that economic expansion required greater mass consumption as well. Freeing the rich from "oppressive" taxation, he argued, would enable them to invest

Big oil's plans to drill in the Teapot Dome oil reserves led to a major scandal in the Harding administration. (See also Re-Viewing the Past, *There Will Be Blood*.)

more in potentially productive enterprises, the success of which would create jobs for ordinary people. Mellon succeeded in balancing the budget and reducing the national debt by an average of over $500 million a year. So committed were the Republican leaders to retrenchment that they even resisted the demands of veterans, organized in the politically potent American Legion, for an "adjusted compensation" bonus.

That the business community heartily approved the policies of Harding and Coolidge is not surprising. Both presidents were uncritical advocates of the business point of view. "We want less government in business and more business in government," Harding pontificated, to which Coolidge added, "The business of the United States is business." Harding and Coolidge used their power of appointment to convert regulatory bodies like the Interstate Commerce Commission (ICC) and the Federal Reserve Board into pro-business agencies that ceased almost entirely to restrict the activities of the industries they were

••••Read the Document

Purinton, *Big Ideas from Big Business* at myhistorylab.com

122

supposed to be controlling. The ICC became almost the reverse of what it had been in the Progressive Era.

The Harding Scandals

At least Mellon was honest. The Ohio gang used its power in the most corrupt way imaginable. Jesse Smith, a crony of Attorney General Daugherty, was what today would be called an influence peddler. When he was exposed in 1923, he committed suicide. Charles R. Forbes of the Veterans Bureau siphoned millions of dollars appropriated for the construction of hospitals into his own pocket. When he was found out, he fled to Europe. Later he returned, stood trial, and was sentenced to two years in prison. His assistant, Charles F. Cramer, committed suicide. Daugherty himself was implicated in the fraudulent return of German assets seized by the alien property custodian to their original owners. He escaped imprisonment only by refusing to testify on the ground that he might incriminate himself.

The worst scandal involved Secretary of the Interior Albert B. Fall, a former senator. In 1921 Fall arranged with the complaisant Secretary of the Navy Edwin Denby for the transfer to the Interior Department of government oil reserves being held for the future use of the navy. He then leased these properties to private oil companies. Edward L. Doheny's Pan-American Petroleum Company got the Elk Hills reserve in California; the Teapot Dome reserve in Wyoming was turned over to Harry F. Sinclair's Mammoth Oil Company. When critics protested, Fall explained that it was necessary to develop the Elk Hills and Teapot Dome properties because adjoining private drillers were draining off the navy's oil. Nevertheless, in 1923 the Senate ordered a full-scale investigation, conducted by Senator Thomas J. Walsh of Montana. It soon came out that Doheny had "lent" Fall $100,000 in hard cash, handed over secretly in a "little black bag." Sinclair had given Fall over $300,000 in cash and negotiable securities. (For more on Doheny and Fall, see Re-Viewing the Past, *There Will Be Blood.*)

Although the three culprits in the **Teapot Dome scandal** escaped conviction on the charge of conspiring to defraud the government, Sinclair was sentenced to nine months in jail for contempt of the Senate and for tampering with a jury, and Fall was fined $100,000 and given a year in prison for accepting a bribe. In 1927 the Supreme Court revoked the leases and the two reserves were returned to the government.

> **Read the Document**
>
> *Executive Orders and Senate Resolutions on Teapot Dome* at **myhistorylab.com**

The public still knew little of the scandals when, in June 1923, Harding left Washington on a speaking tour that included a visit to Alaska. His health was poor and his spirits low, for he had begun to understand how his "Goddamn friends" had betrayed him. On the return trip from Alaska, he suffered a heart attack. He died in San Francisco on August 2.

Few presidents have been more deeply mourned by the people at the moment of their passing. Harding's kindly nature, his very ordinariness, increased his human appeal. Three million people viewed his coffin as it passed across the country. When the scandals came to light, sadness turned to scorn and contempt.

There Will Be Blood

In 2008 Daniel Day-Lewis won the Academy Award for his portrayal of Daniel Plainview in *There Will Be Blood,* a movie about wildcatting oil exploration in California in the early 1900s. Day-Lewis portrayed Plainview as a remorseless predator who lied with fluency and cheated with sincerity. He coaxed and coerced property owners into granting him oil leases on his own terms. When he didn't get what he wanted, he lashed out in violence.

Day-Lewis's Plainview fixed his coal-black eyes onto people like a fighter-pilot locking onto a target. A reviewer for the *New York Times* called Day-Lewis's performance "among the greatest I've ever seen." Day-Lewis filled Plainview "with so much rage and purpose you wait for him to blow," the reviewer added.

By the usual conventions of Hollywood, the evil Plainview would be vanquished by a white-hatted hero. But in *There Will Be Blood* no good guys ride to the rescue because there were no good guys: *Everyone* is after money.

In the absence of a conflict between good and evil, the movie turns on the question: What made Plainview so bad? Certainly, he was long-suffering. The movie begins with him in a mine shaft, hacking away at rock with a pick and scrabbling through the shards on his hands and knees, looking without success for a glint of gold or silver. When he fell down the shaft and broke his leg, he climbed out by himself. These powerfully

discouraging scenes, which take up the first twenty minutes of the movie, include no dialogue whatsoever: Plainview's struggle was a solitary one.

This provides a motivational clue. Plainview hated everyone—with the exception of his son. "I see the worst in people," he declared. "I've built my hatreds up over the years, little by little." He crushed enemies not because he craved wealth but because he could not abide anyone getting the better of him. Which raises the larger question: Were the obsessions of Daniel Plainview characteristic of the industrial and financial magnates of the age?

Plainview, "born in Fond du Lac, Wisconsin," was based on California oil magnate, Edward L. Doheny, himself born in Fond du Lac. The son of a poor Irish immigrant, Doheny left home at a young age and prospected for gold and silver in New Mexico. He had little luck. His wife and children went hungry; she became an alcoholic and committed suicide. In 1891 Doheny gave up prospecting and went to Los Angeles to find a job. One day he spotted a man with a cart whose wheels were coated in tar. Doheny asked what had happened, and the man mentioned a tar pit at the corner of Patton and State Streets, near what is now Dodger Stadium.

Doheny acquired the oil rights to the area and began digging, shoveling dirt and tar into buckets and hauling it to the surface. At the depth of 155 feet, he was nearly killed by toxic fumes; then he studied a diagram of an oil rig and built a crude derrick. He used a sharpened eucalyptus tree as the drill. At 460 feet, he struck oil. Within a few years, he had built scores of derricks throughout Los Angeles. The growth of the city that became synonymous with the automobile was literally fueled by the oil that lay beneath it.

Photo Credit: Private Collection.

Doheny's first oil strike at Signal Hill near Los Angeles.

Photo Credit: Courtesy of the Library of Congress.

Edward L. Doheny, California oil magnate.

Photo Credit: Marcel Thomas/ Getty Images - WireImage.com.

Daniel Day-Lewis as Daniel Plainview.

By 1920 southern California had become the world's leading oil-producer, and Doheny had become rich.

There Will Be Blood omitted the next stage in Doheny's life. In 1900 he went to Mexico and worked out a deal with the dictator Profirio Diaz for the oil rights to some promising regions of the undeveloped country. In 1910, Doheny hit several enormous gushers; soon his company was the largest oil producer in the world. His chief competitor in Mexico was Weetman Pearson, an English engineer and builder who had also wangled a lucrative deal out of Diaz.

Doheny was a tough and even ruthless businessman; he made many enemies. But it was not until the 1920s that he attained notoriety. He was among the oilmen who secured from Albert B. Fall, Harding's interior secretary, the right to drill in oil fields that were kept as an emergency reserve for the navy. On learning that Fall was in financial difficulties, Doheny sent his son Ned to Fall's apartment with $100,000 in cash. Fall accepted the money.

Several years later Doheny and his son were among those indicted for bribing Fall. In a Senate hearing Doheny professed his innocence. He had not bribed a government official; he had helped a friend. The amount of the gift—$100,000—was "a bagatelle to me," the equivalent of "the ordinary individual" giving $25 to a down-and-out neighbor. The statement drew gasps from the audience. Doheny, though acquitted, became the era's exemplar of greed and corruption.

There Will Be Blood ends with Plainview living alone in an enormous mansion. When an old antagonist stops by, seeking a handout, Plainview, drunk and enraged, murders

him. The scene was filmed in the actual Beverly Hills mansion that Doheny had built for his son. In 1929 a deranged family friend who lived in the mansion shot and killed Ned before turning the gun on himself. It was some measure of Doheny's shattered reputation that rumors long circulated that Doheny had himself murdered both men. One recent historian has argued that Doheny was responsible for the deaths if only because his greed poisoned everything around him.

There Will Be Blood came out just before the great financial collapse of 2008–2009, when wildcatting financiers inflicted several trillion dollars' damage upon the global economy. It is tempting to see in such behavior a heart of darkness, such as the film imputed to Doheny. But we must remember that while Doheny was no paragon of propriety, he was no murderer. In painting him with the oily hues of a Daniel Plainview, Hollywood transformed the oil magnate into caricature. Indeed, Hollywood's search for box-office gushers is itself reminiscent of Day-Lewis's character. And if, like Plainview, it plays fast and loose with the literal truth, can it really be blamed?

Questions for Discussion

- Doheny pursued wealth with obsessive determination. In *Wall Street* (1987), the character Gordon Gekko declares that "Greed is good." How does greed promote economic growth? How does it become a destructive force?
- Did Doheny benefit society and, if so, how? How did he harm it?

Coolidge Prosperity

Had he lived, Harding might well have been defeated in 1924 because of the scandals. Vice President Coolidge, unconnected with the troubles and not the type to surround himself with cronies of any kind, seemed the ideal person to clean out the corrupt officials. Coolidge was a taciturn, extremely conservative New Englander with a long record in Massachusetts. He preferred to follow public opinion and hope for the best.

Coolidge defused his predecessor's scandals by replacing Harding's Attorney General Daugherty with Harlan Fiske Stone, dean of the Columbia University Law School. Soon Coolidge became the darling of the conservatives. His admiration for businessmen and his devotion to laissez-faire knew no limit. Andrew Mellon, whom he kept on as secretary of the Treasury, became his mentor in economic affairs.

Coolidge won the 1924 Republican nomination easily. The Democrats, badly split, required 103 ballots to choose a candidate. The southern wing, dry, anti-immigrant, pro-Klan, had fixed on William G. McAdoo, Wilson's secretary of the Treasury. The eastern, urban, wet element supported Governor Alfred E. Smith of New York, child of the slums, a Catholic who had compiled a distinguished record in social welfare legislation. After days of futile politicking, the party compromised on John W. Davis, a conservative corporation lawyer closely allied with the Morgan banking interests.

Dismayed by the conservatism of Coolidge and Davis, Robert M. La Follette, backed by the farm bloc, the Socialist party, the American Federation of Labor, and numbers of intellectuals, entered the race as the candidate of a new Progressive party. The Progressives adopted a neopopulist platform calling for the nationalization of railroads, the direct election of the president, the protection of labor's right to bargain collectively, and other reforms.

The situation was the opposite of 1912, when one conservative had run against two liberals and had been swamped. Coolidge received 15.7 million votes, Davis 8.4 million, La Follette 4.8 million. Conservatism was clearly the dominant mood of the country.

While Coolidge reigned, complacency was the order of the day. "Mr. Coolidge's genius for inactivity is developed to a very high point," the correspondent Walter Lippmann wrote. "It is a grim, determined, alert inactivity, which keeps Mr. Coolidge occupied constantly."[1] "The country," the president reported to Congress in 1928, "can regard the present with satisfaction, and anticipate the future with optimism."

Peace without a Sword

Presidents Harding and Coolidge handled foreign relations in much the same way they managed domestic affairs. Harding deferred to senatorial prejudice against executive domination in the area and let Secretary of State Charles Evans Hughes make policy. Coolidge adopted a similar course. In directing foreign relations, they faced the obstacle of a resurgent isolationism. The bloodiness of the Great War convinced millions that the only way to be sure it would not happen again was to "steer clear" of "entanglements." That these famous words had been used by Washington and Jefferson in vastly different contexts did not deter the isolationists of the 1920s from

---

[1]Coolidge was physically delicate, plagued by chronic stomach trouble. He required ten or eleven hours of sleep a day.

attributing to them the same authority they gave to Scripture. On the other hand, far-flung American economic interests, as well as the need for both raw materials for industry and foreign markets for America's growing surpluses of agricultural and manufactured goods, made close attention to and involvement in developments all over the world unavoidable.

Isolationist sentiments, therefore, did not deter the government from seeking to advance American interests abroad. The Open Door concept remained predominant; the State Department worked to obtain opportunities in underdeveloped countries for exporters and investors, hoping both to stimulate the American economy and to bring stability to "backward" nations. Although this policy sometimes roused local resentments because of the tendency of the United States to support entrenched elites while the mass of peasants and city workers lived in poverty, it also resulted in a further retreat from active interventionism.

The first important diplomatic event of the period revealed a great deal about American foreign policy after the Great War. During the war, Japan had greatly increased its influence in East Asia, especially in Manchuria, the northeastern province of warlord-dominated China. To maintain the Open Door in China, it would be necessary to check Japanese expansion. But there was little hope of restoring the old spheres of influence, which the mass of Chinese people bitterly resented. In addition, Japan, the United States, and Great Britain were engaged in expensive naval building programs, a competition none of them really wanted but from which all dared not withdraw unilaterally.

In November 1921, hoping to reach a general agreement with China, Japan, and the Europeans that would keep China open to the commerce of all and slow the armaments race, Secretary of State Hughes convened a conference in Washington. By the following February the Washington Conference had drafted three major treaties and a number of lesser agreements.

In the Five-Power Treaty, the United States, Great Britain, France, Japan, and Italy agreed to stop building battleships for ten years and to reduce their fleets of battleships to a fixed ratio, with Great Britain and the United States limited to 525,000 tons, Japan to 315,000 tons, and France and Italy to 175,000 tons. The new ratio was expected to produce a balance of forces in the Pacific.

The Four-Power Treaty, signed by the United States, Great Britain, Japan, and France, committed these nations to respect one another's interests in the islands of the Pacific and to confer in the event that any other country launched an attack in the area.

All the conferees signed the Nine-Power Treaty, agreeing to respect China's independence and to maintain the Open Door. On the surface, this was of monumental importance to the United States since it seemed to mean that Japan had given up its territorial ambitions on the Asian mainland and that both the Japanese and the Europeans had formally endorsed the Open Door concept.

The treaties, however, were uniformly toothless. The signers of the Four-Power Treaty agreed only to consult in case of aggression in the Pacific; they made no promises to help one another or to restrict their own freedom of action. As President Harding assured the Senate, "there [was] no commitment to armed force, no alliance, no written or moral obligation to join in defense."

The naval disarmament treaty said nothing about the number of other warships that the powers might build, about the far more important question of land and air forces, or about the underlying industrial and financial structures that controlled the ability of the nations to make war. In addition, the 5:5:3 ratio actually enabled the Japanese to dominate the western Pacific. It made the Philippine Islands indefensible and exposed Hawaii to possible attack. In a sense these American bases became hostages of Japan. Yet Congress was so unconcerned about Japanese sensibilities that it refused to grant any immigration quota to Japan under the National Origins Act of 1924, even though the formula applied to other nations would have allowed only 100 Japanese a year to enter the country. The law, Secretary Hughes warned, produced in Japan "a sense of injury and antagonism instead of friendship and cooperation."

Hughes did not think war a likely result, but Japanese resentment of "white imperialism" played into the hands of the military party in that nation. Many Japanese army and navy officers considered war with the United States inevitable.

As for the key Nine-Power Treaty, Japan did not abandon its territorial ambitions in China, and China remained so riven by conflict among the warlords and so resentful of the "imperialists" that the economic advantages of the Open Door turned out to be small indeed.

The United States entered into all these agreements without realizing their full implications and not really prepared to play an active part in East Asian affairs. The Japanese soon realized that the United States would not do much to defend its interests in China.

The Peace Movement

The Americans of the 1920s wanted peace but would neither surrender their prejudices nor build the defenses necessary to make it safe to indulge these passions.

Peace societies flourished, among them the Carnegie Endowment for International Peace, designed "to hasten the abolition of war, the foulest blot upon our civilization," and the Woodrow Wilson Foundation, aimed at helping "the liberal forces of mankind throughout the world . . . who intend to promote peace by the means of justice."

So great was the opposition to international cooperation that the United States refused to accept membership on the World Court, although this tribunal could settle disputes only when the nations involved agreed. Too many peace lovers believed that their goal could be attained simply by pointing out the moral and practical disadvantages of war.

The culmination of this illusory faith in preventing war by criticizing it came with the signing of the Kellogg-Briand Pact in 1928. The treaty was born in the fertile brain of French Foreign Minister Aristide Briand, who was eager to collect allies against possible attack by a resurgent Germany. In 1927 Briand proposed to Secretary of State Frank B. Kellogg that their countries agree never to go to war with each other. Kellogg found the idea as repugnant as any conventional alliance, but American isolationists and pacifists found the suggestion fascinating. To extricate himself from this situation, Kellogg suggested that the pact be broadened to include all nations. Now Briand was angry. Like Kellogg, he saw how meaningless such a treaty would be, especially when Kellogg insisted that it be hedged with a proviso that "every nation is free at all times . . . to defend its territory from attack and it alone is competent to decide when circumstances require war in self-defense." Nevertheless, Briand too found public pressures irresistible. In August 1928, at Paris, diplomats from fifteen nations bestowed upon one another an "international kiss," condemning "recourse to war for the solution of international controversies" and renouncing war "as an instrument of national policy." Seldom has so unrealistic a promise been made by so many intelligent people. Yet most Americans considered the Kellogg-Briand Pact a milestone in the history of civilization: The Senate, habitually so suspicious of international commitments, ratified it eighty-five to one.

The Good Neighbor Policy

The conflict between the desire to avoid foreign entanglements and the desire to advance American economic interests is well-illustrated by events in Latin America. In dealing with this part of the world, Harding and Coolidge performed neither better nor worse than Wilson had. In the face of continued radicalism and instability in Mexico, which caused Americans with interests in land and oil rights to suffer heavy losses, President Coolidge acted with forbearance. The Mexicans were able to complete their social and economic revolution in the 1920s without significant interference by the United States.

Under Coolidge's successor, Herbert Hoover, the United States began at last to treat Latin American nations as equals. Hoover reversed Wilson's policy of trying to teach them "to elect good men." The Clark Memorandum (1930), written by Undersecretary of State J. Reuben Clark, disassociated the right of intervention in Latin America from the Roosevelt Corollary. The corollary had been an improper extension of the Monroe Doctrine, Clark declared. The right of the United States to intervene depended rather on "the doctrine of self-preservation."

The distinction seemed slight to Latin Americans, but since it seemed unlikely that the existence of the United States could be threatened in the area, it was important. By 1934 the marines who had been occupying Nicaragua, Haiti, and the Dominican Republic had all been withdrawn and the United States had renounced the right to intervene in Cuban affairs. Instead of functioning as the policeman for the region, the United States would be its "**good neighbor**." Unfortunately, the United States did little to try to improve social and economic conditions in the Caribbean region, so the underlying envy and resentment of "rich Uncle Sam" did not disappear.

The Totalitarian Challenge

The futility and danger of isolationism were exposed in September 1931 when the Japanese, long dominant in Chinese Manchuria, marched their army in and converted the province into a puppet state named Manchukuo. This violated both the Kellogg-Briand and Nine-Power pacts. China, now controlled by General Chiang Kai-shek, appealed to the League of Nations and to the United States for help. Neither would intervene. When League officials asked about the possibility of American cooperation in some kind of police action, President Hoover refused to consider either economic or military reprisals.

The League sent a commission to Manchuria to investigate. Henry L. Stimson, Hoover's secretary of state, announced (the Stimson Doctrine) that the United States would never recognize the legality of seizures made in violation of American treaty rights. This served only to irritate the Japanese.

In January 1932 Japan attacked Shanghai. When the League at last officially condemned their aggressions, the Japanese withdrew from the organization and extended their control of northern China. The lesson of Manchuria was not lost on Adolf Hitler, who became chancellor of Germany on January 30, 1933.

In surveying the diplomatic events of 1920–1929, it is easy to condemn the United States and the European democracies for their unwillingness to stand up for principles, their refusal to resist when Japan and later Germany and Italy embarked

Photo Credit: The Granger Collection, New York.

The League of Nations covenant, the Kellogg Pact, the Nine-Power Treaty—all were mere scraps of paper. They did nothing to prevent Japan's invasion of Manchuria in 1931.

on the aggressions that led to World War II. It is also proper to place some of the blame for the troubles of the era on the United States and the European democracies, which controlled much of the world's resources and were primarily interested in holding on to what they had.

War Debts and Reparations

The democracies did not take a strong stand against Japan in part because they were quarreling about other matters. Particularly divisive was the controversy over war debts—those of Germany to the Allies and those of the Allies to the United States. The United States had lent more than $10 billion to its comrades-in-arms. Since most of this money had been spent on weapons and other supplies in the United States, it might well have been considered part of America's contribution to the war effort. The public, however, demanded full repayment—with interest. "These were loans, not contributions," Secretary of the Treasury Mellon firmly declared. The total, to be repaid over a period of sixty-two years, amounted to more than $22 billion.

The Allies tried to load their obligations to the United States, along with the other costs of the war, on the backs of the Germans. They demanded that the Germans pay reparations amounting to $33 billion. If this sum were collected, they declared, they could rebuild their economies and obtain the international exchange needed to pay their debts to the United States. But Germany was reluctant even to try to pay such huge reparations, and when Germany defaulted, so did the Allies.

Everyone shared the blame: the Germans because they resorted to a runaway inflation that reduced the mark to less than one trillionth of its prewar value, at least in part in hopes of avoiding their international obligations; the Americans because they refused to recognize the connection between the tariff and the debt question; and the Allies because they made little effort to pay even a reasonable proportion of their obligations.

In 1924 an international agreement, the Dawes Plan, provided Germany with a $200 million loan designed to stabilize its currency. Germany agreed to pay about $250 million a year in reparations. In 1929 the Young Plan further scaled down the reparations bill. In practice, the Allies paid the United States about what they collected from Germany. Since Germany got the money largely from private American loans, the United States would have served itself and the rest of the world far better had it written off the war debts at the start. In any case, in the late 1920s Americans stopped lending money to Germany, the Great Depression struck, Germany defaulted on its reparations payments, and the Allies then gave up all pretense of meeting their obligations to the United States. The last token payments were made in 1933. All that remained was a heritage of mistrust and hostility.

The Election of 1928

Meanwhile, dramatic changes had occurred in the United States. The climax of Coolidge prosperity came in 1928. The president decided not to run again, and Secretary of Commerce Hoover, whom he detested, easily won the Republican nomination. Hoover was the intellectual leader, almost the philosopher, of the New Era. American capitalists, he believed, had learned to curb their selfish instincts.

Although stiff, uncommunicative, and entirely without experience in elective office, Hoover made an admirable candidate in 1928. His roots in the Midwest and West (Iowa-born, he was raised in Oregon and educated at Stanford University in California) neatly balanced his outstanding reputation among eastern business tycoons. He took a "modern" approach to both capital and labor; businessmen should cooperate with one another and with their workers too. He opposed both unionbusting and trustbusting. His

Herbert Hoover relaxes during the 1928 presidential campaign. "That man has been offering me advice for the last five years," President Coolidge said of his secretary of commerce, "all of it bad."

career as a mining engineer had given him a wide knowledge of the world, yet he had become highly critical of Europe.

The Democrats, having had their fill of factionalism in 1924, could no longer deny the nomination to Governor Al Smith. Superficially, Smith was Hoover's antithesis. Born and raised in New York's Lower East Side slums, he had been schooled in machine politics by Tammany Hall. He was a Catholic, Hoover a Quaker, a wet where Hoover supported prohibition; he dealt easily with people of every race and nationality, while Hoover had little interest in and less knowledge of African Americans and immigrants. However, like Hoover, Smith managed to combine a basic conservatism with humanitarian concern for the underprivileged. As adept in administration as Hoover, he was equally uncritical of the American capitalist system.

View the Image

A Heavy Load for Al (1928) at **myhistorylab.com**

In the election Hoover triumphed, 444 to 87 in the Electoral College, 21.4 million to 14 million in the popular vote. All the usually Democratic border states and even North Carolina, Florida, and Texas went to the Republicans, along with the entire West and the Northeast save for Massachusetts and Rhode Island.

After this defeat the Democratic party appeared on the verge of extinction. Nothing could have been further from the truth. The religious question and his big-city roots had hurt Smith, but the chief reason he lost was prosperity—and the good times were soon to end. Hoover's overwhelming victory also concealed a political realignment that was taking place. Working-class voters in the cities, largely Catholic and unimpressed by Coolidge prosperity, had swung heavily to the Democrats. In 1924 the twelve largest cities had been solidly Republican; in 1928 all went Democratic. In agricultural states like Iowa, Smith ran far better than Davis had in 1924, for Coolidge's vetoes of bills designed to raise farm prices had caused considerable resentment. A new coalition of urban workers and dissatisfied farmers was in the making.

Economic Problems

The American economic system of the 1920s had grave flaws. Certain industries did not share in the good times. The coal business, suffering from the competition of petroleum, entered a period of decline. Cotton and woolen textiles also lagged because of the competition of new synthetics, principally rayon. Industry began to be plagued by falling profit margins and chronic unemployment.

The movement toward consolidation in industry, somewhat checked during the latter part of the Progressive Era, resumed; by 1929, 200 corporations controlled nearly half the nation's corporate assets. General Motors, Ford, and Chrysler turned out nearly 90 percent of all American cars and trucks. Four tobacco companies produced over 90 percent of the cigarettes. One percent of all financial institutions controlled 46 percent of the nation's banking business. Most large manufacturers, aware that bad public relations resulting from the unbridled use of monopolistic power outweighed any immediate economic gain, sought stability and "fair" prices rather than the maximum profit possible at the moment. "Regulated" competition was the order of the day, oligopoly the typical situation. The trade association movement flourished; producers formed voluntary organizations to exchange information, discuss policies toward government and the public, and "administer" prices in their industry. Usually the largest corporation, such as U.S. Steel in the iron and steel business, became the "price leader," its competitors, some themselves giants, following slavishly.

The success of the trade associations depended in part on the attitude of the federal government, for such organizations might well have been attacked under the antitrust laws. Their defenders, including President Harding, argued that the associations made business more efficient and prevented violent gyrations of prices and production. Secretary of Commerce Hoover put the facilities of his department at the disposal of the associations. After Coolidge became president, the antitrust division of the Justice Department itself encouraged the trade associations to cooperate in ways that had previously been considered violations of the Sherman Act.

Even more important to the trade associations were the good times. With profits high and markets expanding, the most powerful producers could afford to share the bounty with smaller, less efficient competitors.

The weakest element in the economy was agriculture. Farm prices slumped and farmers' costs mounted. Besides having to purchase expensive machinery in order to compete, farmers were confronted by high foreign tariffs and in some cases quotas on the importation of foodstuffs. As crop yields per acre rose, chiefly because of the increased use of chemical fertilizers, agricultural prices fell further.

Despite the efforts of the farm bloc, the government did little to improve the situation. President Harding opposed direct aid to agriculture as a matter of principle. During his administration Congress strengthened the laws regulating railroad rates and grain exchanges and made it easier for farmers to borrow money, but it did nothing directly to increase agricultural income. Nor did the high tariffs on agricultural produce have much effect. Being forced to sell their surpluses abroad, farmers found that world prices depressed domestic prices despite the tariff wall.

Thus the unprecedented prosperity rested on unstable foundations. The problem was mainly one of maldistribution of resources. Productive capacity raced ahead of buying power. Too large a share of the profits was going into too few pockets. The 27,000 families with the highest annual incomes in 1929 received as much money as the 11 million with annual incomes of under $1,500, the minimum sum required at that time to maintain a family decently. High earnings and low taxes permitted huge sums to pile up in the hands of individuals who did not invest the money productively. A good deal of it went into stock market speculation, which led to the "big bull market" and eventually to the Great Depression.

The Stock Market Crash of 1929

In the spring of 1928, prices on the New York Stock Exchange, already at a historic high, began to surge. As the presidential campaign gathered momentum, the market increased its upward pace, stimulated by the candidates' efforts to outdo each other in praising the marvels of the American economic system. A few conservative brokers expressed alarm, warning that most stocks were grossly overpriced. The majority scoffed at such talk.

During the first half of 1929 stock prices climbed still higher. A mania for speculation swept the country, thousands of small investors putting their savings in common stocks. Then, in September the market wavered. Amid volatile fluctuations stock averages eased downward. Most analysts contended that the stock exchange was "digesting" previous

Walter Thompson saw his assets evaporate during the stock market collapse in 1929. Desperate for cash (like nearly everyone else) he offered his snappy roadster for $100.

gains. A Harvard economist expressed the prevailing view when he said that stock prices had reached a "permanently high plateau" and would soon resume their advance.

On October 24 a wave of selling sent prices spinning. Nearly 13 million shares changed hands—a record. Bankers and politicians rallied to check the decline, as they had during the Panic of 1907. But on October 29, the bottom seemed to drop out. More than 16 million shares were sold, prices plummeting. The boom was over.

Hoover and the Depression

The collapse of the stock market did not cause the Depression; stocks rallied late in the year, and business activity did not begin to decline significantly until the spring of 1930. The Great Depression was a worldwide phenomenon caused chiefly by economic imbalances resulting from the chaos of the Great War. In the United States too much wealth had fallen into too few hands, with the result that consumers were unable to buy all the goods produced. The trouble came to a head mainly because of the easy-credit policies of the Federal Reserve Board and the Mellon tax structure, which favored the rich. Its effects were so profound and prolonged because the politicians (and for that matter the professional economists) did not fully understand what was happening or what to do about it.

The chronic problem of underconsumption operated to speed the downward spiral. Unable to rid themselves of mounting inventories, manufacturers closed plants and laid off workers, thereby causing demand to shrink further. Automobile output fell from 4.5 million units in 1929 to 1.1 million in 1932. When Ford closed his Detroit plants in 1931, some 75,000 workers lost their jobs, and the decline in auto production affected a host of suppliers and middlemen as well.

The financial system cracked under the strain. More than 1,300 banks closed their doors in 1930, 3,700 more during the next two years. Each failure deprived thousands of persons of funds that might have been used to buy goods; when the Bank of the United States in New York City became insolvent in December 1930, 400,000 depositors found their savings immobilized. And of course the industrial depression worsened the depression in agriculture by further reducing the demand for American foodstuffs. Every economic indicator reflected the collapse. New investments declined from $10 billion in 1929 to $1 billion in 1932, and the national income fell from over $80 billion to under $50 billion in the same brief period. Unemployment, under 1 million at the height of the boom, rose to at least 13 million.

President Hoover was an intelligent man, experienced in business matters and knowledgeable in economics. Secretary of the Treasury Mellon believed that the economy should be allowed to slide unchecked until the cycle had found its bottom. "Let the slump liquidate itself," Mellon urged. "Liquidate labor, liquidate stocks, liquidate the farmers. . . . People will work harder, live a more moral life. Values will be adjusted, and enterprising people will pick up the wrecks from less competent people." Hoover realized that such a policy would cause unbearable hardship for millions. He rejected Mellon's advice to let the Depression run its course.

Hoover's program for ending the Depression evolved gradually. At first he called on businessmen to maintain prices and wages. The government should cut taxes in order to increase consumers' spendable income, institute public works programs to stimulate production and create jobs for the unemployed, lower interest rates to make it easier for businesses to borrow in order to expand, and make loans to banks and industrial corporations threatened with collapse and to homeowners unable to meet mortgage payments. The president also proposed measures making it easier for farmers to borrow money, and he suggested that the government should support cooperative farm marketing schemes designed to solve the problem of overproduction. He called for an expansion of state and local relief programs and urged all who could afford it to give more to charity. Above all he tried to restore public confidence: The economy was basically healthy; the Depression was only a minor downturn; prosperity was "just around the corner."

Although Hoover's plans were theoretically sound, they failed to check the economic slide, in part because of curious limitations in his conception of how they should be implemented. He placed far too much reliance on his powers of persuasion and the willingness of citizens to act in the public interest without legal compulsion. He urged manufacturers to maintain wages and keep their factories in operation, but the manufacturers soon slashed wages and curtailed output sharply. He permitted the Federal Farm Board to establish semipublic stabilization corporations with authority to buy up surplus wheat and cotton, but he refused to consider crop or acreage controls. The stabilization corporations poured out hundreds of millions of dollars without checking falling agricultural prices because farmers increased production faster than the corporations could buy up the excess for disposal abroad.

Hoover resisted proposals to shift responsibility from state and local agencies to the federal government, despite the fact—soon obvious—that they lacked the resources to cope with the emergency. By 1932 the federal government, with Hoover's approval, was spending $500 million a year on public works projects, but because of the decline in state and municipal construction, the total public outlay fell nearly $1 billion below what it had been in 1930. More serious was his refusal, on constitutional grounds, to allow federal funds to be used for the relief of individuals.

Unfortunately the Depression was drying up the sources of private charities just as the demands on these organizations were expanding. State and municipal agencies were swamped just when their capacities to tax and borrow were shrinking. By 1932 more than 40,600 Boston families were on relief (compared with 7,400 families in 1929); in Chicago 700,000 persons—40 percent of the workforce—were unemployed. Only the national government possessed the power and the credit to deal adequately with the crisis.

Yet Hoover would not act. He set up a committee to coordinate local relief activities but insisted on preserving what he called "the principles of individual and local responsibility." For the federal government to take over relief would "lead to the super-state where every man becomes the servant of the state and real liberty is lost."

Federal loans to commercial enterprises were constitutional, he believed, because the money could be put to productive use and eventually repaid. When drought destroyed the crops of farmers in the South and Southwest in 1930, the government lent them money to buy seed and even food for their livestock, but Hoover would permit no direct relief for the farmers themselves. In 1932 he approved the creation of the Reconstruction Finance Corporation (RFC) to lend money to banks, railroads, and insurance companies. The RFC represented an important extension of national authority, yet it was thoroughly in line with Hoover's philosophy. Its loans, secured by solid collateral, were commercial transactions, not gifts; the agency did almost nothing for individuals in need of relief. The same could be said of the Glass-Steagall Banking Act of 1932, which eased the tight credit situation by permitting Federal Reserve banks to accept corporate stocks and bonds as security for loans. The public grew increasingly resentful of the president's doctrinaire adherence to principle while breadlines lengthened and millions of willing workers searched fruitlessly for jobs.

As time passed and the Depression worsened, Hoover put more stress on the importance of balancing the federal budget, reasoning that since citizens had to live within their limited means in hard times, the government should set a good example. This policy was counterproductive; by reducing its expenditures the government made the Depression worse, which reduced federal revenue further. By June 1931 the budget was nearly $500 million in the red.

Hoover understood the value of pumping money into a stagnant economy. He might have made a virtue of necessity. The difficulty lay in the fact that nearly all "informed" opinion believed that a balanced budget was essential to recovery. The most prestigious economists insisted on it, and so did business leaders, labor leaders, and even most socialists.

Much of the contemporary criticism of Hoover and a good deal of that heaped on him by later historians was unfair. Yet his record as president shows that he was too rigidly wedded to a particular theory of government to cope effectively with the problems of the day. Since these problems were in a sense insoluble, flexibility and a willingness to experiment were essential to any program aimed at restoring prosperity. Hoover lacked these qualities. He was

Watch the Video

Prosperity of the 1920s and the Great Depression at **myhistorylab.com**

his own worst enemy, being too uncompromising to get on well with the politicians and too aloof to win the confidence and affection of ordinary people. He had too much faith in himself and his plans. When he failed to achieve the results he anticipated, he attracted, despite his devotion to duty and his concern for the welfare of the country, not sympathy but scorn.

The Economy Hits Bottom

During the spring of 1932, as the economy sounded the depths, thousands of Americans faced starvation. In Philadelphia during an eleven-day period when no relief funds were available, hundreds of families existed on stale bread, thin soup, and garbage. In the nation as a whole, only about one-quarter of the unemployed were receiving any public aid. Many people were evicted, and they often gathered in ramshackle communities constructed of packing boxes, rusty sheet metal, and similar refuse on swamps, garbage dumps, and other wasteland. People began to call these places "Hoovervilles."

View the Image

Depression Breadlines in New York City at **myhistorylab.com**

Thousands roamed the countryside begging and scavenging for food. At the same time, food prices fell so low that farmers burned corn for fuel. Iowa and Nebraska farmers organized "farm holiday" movements, refusing to ship their crops to market in protest against the thirty-one-cent-a-bushel corn and thirty-eight-cent wheat. They blocked roads and rail lines, dumped milk, overturned trucks, and established picket lines to enforce their boycott.

The national mood ranged from apathy to resentment. In 1931 federal immigration agents and local groups in the Southwest began rounding up Mexican-Americans and deporting them. Some of those returned to Mexico had entered the United States illegally; others had come in properly. Unemployed Mexicans were ejected because they might become public charges, those with jobs because they were presumably taking bread from the mouths of citizens.

In June and July 1932, 20,000 Great War veterans marched on Washington to demand immediate payment of their "adjusted compensation" bonuses. When Congress rejected their appeal, some 2,000 refused to leave, settling in a jerrybuilt camp of shacks and tents at Anacostia Flats, a swamp bordering the Potomac. President Hoover, alarmed, charged incorrectly that the **Bonus Army** was largely composed of criminals and radicals and sent troops into the Flats to disperse it with bayonets, tear gas, and tanks. The

View the Image

Burning Bonus Army Shacks, 1932 at **myhistorylab.com**

task was accomplished amid much confusion; fortunately no one was killed. The protest had been aimless and not entirely justified, yet the spectacle of the U.S. government chasing unarmed veterans with tanks appalled the nation.

The unprecedented severity of the Depression led some persons to favor radical economic and political changes. The disparity between the lots of the rich and the poor, always a challenge to democracy, became more striking and engendered considerable bitterness. "Unless something is done to provide employment," two labor leaders warned Hoover, "disorder . . . is sure to arise. . . . There is a growing demand that the entire business and social structure be changed because of the general dissatisfaction with the present system."

Photo Credit: University of Washington Libraries, Special Collections, Lee 20102.

Evicted from their homes, many unemployed people gravitated to vacant industrial property, where they erected hovels from scraps of lumber, tarpaper, and cardboard. This shantytown is outside of Seattle.

The communist party gained few converts among farmers and industrial workers, but a considerable number of intellectuals, alienated by the trends of the 1920s, responded positively to the communists' emphasis on economic planning and the total mobilization of the state to achieve social goals. Even the cracker-barrel humorist Will Rogers was impressed by reports of the absence of serious unemployment in Russia. "All roads lead to Moscow," the former muckraker Lincoln Steffens wrote.

The Depression and Its Victims

Depression is a word used by economists but also by psychologists, and the depression of the 1930s had profound psychological effects on its victims as well as the obvious economic ones. Almost without exception people who lost their jobs first searched energetically for new ones, but when they remained unemployed for more than a few months they sank gradually into despair. E. Wight Bakke, a Yale sociologist who interviewed hundreds of unemployed men in the United States and England during the Depression, described the final stage of decline as "permanent readjustment," by which he meant that the long-term jobless simply gave up. The settlement house worker Lillian Wald came to a similar conclusion. Unemployed people at her famous Henry Street settlement, she noticed, had lost both "ambition and pride."

Simple discouragement alone does not explain why so many of the jobless reacted this way. People who had worked all their adult lives often became ashamed of themselves when they could not find a job. Professor Bakke reported that half the unemployed people in New Haven that he interviewed never applied for public assistance no matter how desperate their circumstances. The Depression affected the families of the jobless in many ways. It caused a dramatic drop in the birthrate, from 27.7 per thousand population in 1920 to 18.4 per thousand in the early 1930s, the lowest in American history. Sometimes it strengthened family ties. Some unemployed men spent more time with their children and helped their wives with cooking and housework. Others, however, became impatient when their children demanded attention, refused to help around the house, sulked, or took to drink.

The influence of wives in families struck by unemployment tended to increase, and in this respect women suffered less psychologically from the Depression. They were usually too busy trying to make ends meet to become apathetic. But the way they used this influence varied. Some wives were sympathetic, others scornful, when the "breadwinner" came home with empty hands. If there is any generalization about the effects of the Depression on family relations it is probably an obvious one—where relationships were close and loving they became stronger, where they were not, the results could be disastrous.

The Election of 1932

As the end of his term approached, President Hoover seemed to grow daily more petulant and pessimistic. The Depression, coming after twelve years of Republican rule, probably ensured a Democratic victory in any case, but his attitude as the election neared alienated many voters and turned defeat into rout.

Confident of victory, the Democrats chose Governor Franklin Delano Roosevelt of New York as their presidential candidate. Roosevelt owed his nomination chiefly to his success as governor. Under his administration, New York had led the nation in providing relief for the needy and had enacted an impressive program of old-age pensions, unemployment insurance, and conservation and public power projects. In 1928, while Hoover was carrying New York against Smith by a wide margin, Roosevelt won election by 25,000 votes. In 1930 he swept the state by a 700,000-vote majority, double the previous record. He also had the advantage of the Roosevelt name (he was a distant cousin of the inimitable TR), and his sunny, magnetic personality contrasted favorably with that of the glum and colorless Hoover.

Roosevelt was far from being a radical. Although he had supported the League of Nations while campaigning for the vice presidency in 1920, during the 1920s he had not seriously challenged the basic tenets of Coolidge prosperity. He never had much difficulty adjusting his views to prevailing attitudes. His life before the Depression gave little indication that he understood the aspirations of ordinary people or had any deep commitment to social reform.

Roosevelt was born to wealth and social status in Dutchess County, New York, in 1882. He was educated at the exclusive Groton School and then at Harvard. Ambition as much as the desire to render public service motivated his career in politics; even after an attack of polio in 1921 had badly crippled both his legs, he refused to abandon his

A vigorous-looking Franklin D. Roosevelt campaigns for the presidency in 1932. His vice-presidential running mate, John N. Garner, and the conveniently placed post allowed the handicapped candidate to stand when greeting voters along the way.

hopes for high office. During the 1920s he was a hardworking member of the liberal wing of his party. He supported Smith for president in 1924 and 1928.

Roosevelt was a marvelous campaigner. Like every great political leader, he took as much from the people as he gave them, understanding the causes of their confusion and sensing their needs. "I have looked into the faces of thousands of Americans," he told a friend. "They have the frightened look of lost children. . . . They are saying: 'We're caught in something we don't understand; perhaps this fellow can help us out.'"

On matters such as farm policy, the tariff, and government spending, Roosevelt equivocated, contradicted himself, or remained silent. Nevertheless Roosevelt's basic position was unmistakable. There must be a "re-appraisal of values," a "New Deal." Instead of adhering to conventional limits on the extent of federal power, the government should do whatever was necessary to protect the unfortunate and advance the public good. Lacking concrete answers, Roosevelt advocated a point of view rather than a plan: "The country needs bold, persistent experimentation. It is common sense to take a method and try it. If it fails, admit it frankly and try another. But above all, try something."

The popularity of this approach was demonstrated in November. Hoover, who had lost only eight states in 1928, won only six, all in the Northeast, in 1932. Roosevelt amassed 22.8 million votes to Hoover's 15.8 million and carried the Electoral College, 472 to 59.

◀ ◀ Read the Document

Hoover, New York Campaign Speech at **myhistorylab.com**

During the interval between the election and Roosevelt's inauguration in March 1933, the Great Depression reached its nadir. The holdover "lame duck" Congress, last of its kind, proved incapable of effective action.[2] President Hoover, perhaps understandably, hesitated to institute changes without the cooperation of his successor. Roosevelt, for equally plausible reasons, refused to accept responsibility before assuming power officially. The nation, curiously apathetic in the face of so much suffering, drifted aimlessly, like a sailboat in a flat calm.

---

[2]The Twentieth Amendment (1933) provided for convening new Congresses in January instead of the following December. It also advanced the date of the president's inauguration from March 4 to January 20.

Milestones

1921–1922	Washington Conference tries to slow arms race	1930	Clark Memorandum renounces Roosevelt Corollary to Monroe Doctrine
1923	President Harding dies; Coolidge becomes president		Hawley-Smoot tariff raises duties on foreign manufactures
	Teapot Dome and other Harding scandals are exposed		Ten-year Dust Bowl begins in South and Midwest
1924	Dawes Plan restructures German reparations payments	1931	Japan invades Manchuria
	National Origins Act establishes immigration quotas		Hoover imposes moratorium on war debts
	Coolidge is elected president	1932	Federal troops disperse Bonus Army marchers in Washington, DC
1928	Fifteen nations sign Kellogg-Briand Pact to "outlaw" war		Reconstruction Finance Corporation (RFC) lends to banks, railroads, insurance companies
	Herbert Hoover is elected president		
1929	New York Stock Exchange crash ends big bull market; Great Depression begins		Franklin Delano Roosevelt is elected president
	Young Plan further reduces German reparations	1933	Japan withdraws from League of Nations

✓● ⌐Study and Review at **www.myhistorylab.com**

Review Questions

1. The introduction draws a parallel between the crash of the stock market in 1929 and the U.S. mortgage market in 2008–2009 as explanations of subsequent economic crises. What were the main differences?
2. What were the similarities in the policies of Harding, Coolidge, and Hoover? The differences?
3. What factors explained the prosperity of the 1920s? In what ways was that prosperity shaky?
4. During the 1920s and early 1930s, what role did the United States play in Latin America? In the worsening situations in Europe and Asia?
5. How did the election of 1932 constitute a political "revolution"?

Key Terms

Bonus Army

"good neighbor"

Teapot Dome scandal

The New Deal: 1933–1941

From Chapter 26 of *American Destiny: Narrative of a Nation*, Combined Volume, Fourth Edition.
Mark C. Carnes and John A. Garraty. Copyright © 2012 by Pearson Education, Inc. Published by
Pearson Prentice Hall.

The New Deal: 1933–1941

((•─[Hear the Audio at myhistorylab.com

Do you have health insurance?

IN MARCH 2010, CONGRESS NARROWLY PASSED A MAJOR HEALTH reform law. It requires most employers to provide employees with health insurance and allows parents to extend coverage of their children to age twenty-six. It also creates a fund of nearly a trillion dollars to pay for health insurance for many people not covered by employer-paid policies until 2020.

President Barack Obama compared the battle to the one waged by Franklin D. Roosevelt sixty-five years earlier over guaranteed incomes for the elderly. "When FDR proposed Social Security, he was accused of being a Socialist," Obama observed. Michelle Bachmann, a Republican congresswoman from Minnesota, opposed the health insurance proposal for that very reason: "If you look at FDR and Barack Obama, this is really the final leap to socialism."

President Franklin D. Roosevelt signed the Social Security Act in 1935, the cornerstone of his New Deal to counteract the Great Depression. Other New Deal initiatives sought to put the unemployed to work on government projects; to use federal funds to help farmers by raising the price of agricultural products; to reorganize banks, and to alter federal regulation of corporations.

These measures generated opposition. Conservatives regarded much of the New Deal as an unconstitutional infringement of private rights; populists and Marxists denounced the New Deal as a band-aid that failed to address the root causes of poverty. But times were bad. The nation was in desperate trouble. Through it all, Roosevelt won the allegiance of voters who regarded him almost as an economic savior and the New Deal as gospel.

The Hundred Days

As the date of Franklin Roosevelt's inauguration approached, the banking system completely disintegrated and a financial panic swept the land. Depositors lined up before the doors of even the soundest institutions, desperate to withdraw their savings. Hundreds of banks were forced to close. In February, to check the panic, the governor of Michigan declared a "bank holiday," shutting every bank in the state for eight days.

Maryland, Kentucky, California, and a number of other states followed suit; by inauguration day four-fifths of the states had suspended all banking operations. Other issues loomed, especially war clouds over Europe and east Asia, but few Americans could look much beyond their own immediate, and increasingly dire, economic prospects.

Watch the Video

FDR's Inauguration at **myhistorylab.com**

Something drastic had to be done. The most conservative business leaders were as ready for government intervention as the most advanced radicals. Partisanship, while not disappearing, was for once subordinated to broad national needs. A sign of this change came in February, even before Roosevelt took office, when Congress submitted to the states the Twenty-First Amendment, putting an end to prohibition. Before the end of the year the necessary three-quarters of the states had ratified it, and the prohibition era was over.

It was unquestionably Franklin D. Roosevelt who provided the spark that reenergized the American people. His inaugural address reassured the country and at the same time stirred it to action. "The only thing we have to fear is fear itself. . . . This Nation asks for action, and action now. . . . I assume unhesitatingly the leadership of this great army of our people. . . ." Many such lines punctuated the brief address, which captured the heart of the country; almost half a million letters of congratulation poured into the White House. When Roosevelt summoned Congress into a special session on March 9, the legislators outdid one another to enact his proposals into law. In the following "hundred days" serious opposition, in the sense of an organized group committed to resisting the administration, simply did not exist.

Roosevelt had the power and the will to act but no comprehensive plan of action. He and his eager congressional collaborators proceeded in a dozen directions at once, often at cross-purposes with themselves and one another. One of the first administration measures was the Economy Act, which reduced the salaries of federal employees by 15 percent and cut various veterans' benefits. Such belt-tightening measures could only make the Depression worse. But most **New Deal** programs were designed to stimulate the economy. All in all, an impressive body of new legislation was placed on the statute books.

On March 5 Roosevelt declared a nationwide bank holiday and placed an embargo on the exportation of gold. To explain the complexities of the banking problem to the public, Roosevelt delivered the first of his "fireside chats" over a national radio network. "I want to talk for a few minutes with the people of the United States about banking," he explained. His warmth and steadiness reassured millions. A plan for

A 1933 banner celebrates the repeal of prohibition.

Photo Credit: The Granger Collection, New York.

reopening the banks under Treasury Department licenses was devised, and soon most of them were functioning again, public confidence in their solvency restored.

In April Roosevelt took the country off the gold standard, hoping thereby to cause prices to rise. Before the session ended, Congress established the Federal Deposit Insurance Corporation (FDIC) to guarantee bank deposits. It also forced the separation of investment banking and commercial banking concerns while extending the power of the Federal Reserve Board over both types of institutions, and it created the Home Owners Loan Corporation (HOLC) to refinance mortgages and prevent foreclosures. It passed the Federal Securities Act requiring promoters to make public full financial information about new stock issues and giving the Federal Trade Commission the right to regulate such transactions.

The National Recovery Administration (NRA)

Problems of unemployment and industrial stagnation had high priority during the hundred days. Congress appropriated $500 million for relief of the needy, and it created the **Civilian Conservation Corps (CCC)** to provide jobs for men between the ages of eighteen and twenty-five in reforestation and other conservation projects. To stimulate industry, Congress passed one of its most controversial measures, the National Industrial Recovery Act (NIRA). Besides establishing the Public Works Administration with authority to spend $3.3 billion, this law permitted manufacturers to draw up industry-wide codes of "fair business practices." Under the law producers could agree to raise prices and limit production without violating the antitrust laws. The law gave workers the protection of minimum wage and maximum hours regulations and guaranteed them the right "to organize and bargain collectively through representatives of their own choosing," an immense stimulus to the union movement.

The NIRA was a variant on the idea of the corporate state. This concept envisaged a system of industry-wide organizations of Capitalists and workers (supervised by the government) that would resolve conflicts internally, thereby avoiding wasteful economic competition and dangerous social clashes. It was an outgrowth of the trade association idea, although Hoover, who had supported voluntary associations, denounced it because of its compulsory aspects. It was also similar to experiments being carried out by the fascist dictator Benito Mussolini in Italy and by the Nazis in Adolf Hitler's Germany. It did not, of course, turn America into a fascist state, but it did herald an increasing concentration of economic power in the hands of interest groups, both industrialists' organizations and labor unions.

The act created a government agency, the **National Recovery Administration (NRA)**, to supervise the drafting and operation of the business codes. Drafting posed difficult problems, first because each industry insisted on tailoring the agreements to its special needs and second because most manufacturers were unwilling to accept all the provisions of Section 7a of the law, which guaranteed workers the right to unionize and bargain collectively. Many employers were more interested in the monopolistic aspects of the act than in boosting wages and encouraging unionization. In practice, the largest manufacturers in each industry drew up the codes.

The NRA did not end the Depression. There was a brief upturn in the spring of 1933, but the expected revival of industry did not take place; in nearly every case the dominant producers in each industry used their power to raise prices and limit production rather than to hire more workers and increase output.

Beginning with the cotton textile code, however, the agreements succeeded in doing away with the centuries-old problem of child labor in industry. They established the principle of federal regulation of wages and hours and led to the organization of thousands of workers, even in industries where unions had seldom been significant. Within a year John L. Lewis's United Mine Workers expanded from 150,000 members to half a million. About 100,000 automobile workers joined unions, as did a comparable number of steelworkers.

Labor leaders used the NIRA to persuade workers that Roosevelt wanted them to join unions—which was something of an overstatement. In 1935, because the craft-oriented AFL had displayed little enthusiasm for enrolling unskilled workers on an industry-wide basis, John L. Lewis, together with officials of the garment trade unions, formed the Committee for Industrial Organization (CIO) and set out to rally workers in each of these mass-production industries into one union without regard for craft lines. Since a union containing all the workers in a factory was easier to organize and direct than separate craft unions, this was a far more effective way of unionizing factory labor. The AFL expelled these unions, however, and in 1938 the CIO became the Congress of Industrial Organizations. Soon it rivaled the AFL in size and importance.

View the Image
PWA in Action Poster at **myhistorylab.com**

The Agricultural Adjustment Administration (AAA)

Roosevelt was more concerned about the plight of the farmers than that of any other group because he believed that the nation was becoming overcommitted to industry. The Agricultural Adjustment Act of May 1933 combined compulsory restrictions on production with government payments to growers of wheat, cotton, tobacco, pork, and a few other staple crops. The object was to lift agricultural prices to "parity" with industrial prices, the ratio in most cases being based on the levels of 1909–1914, when farmers had been reasonably prosperous. In return for withdrawing part of their land from cultivation, farmers received "rental" payments from the **Agricultural Adjustment Act (AAA)**.

Since the 1933 crops were growing when the law was passed, Secretary of Agriculture Henry A. Wallace, son of Harding's secretary of agriculture and himself an experienced farmer and plant geneticist, decided to pay farmers to destroy the crops in the field. Cotton planters plowed up 10 million acres, receiving $100 million in return. Thereafter, limitation of acreage proved sufficient to raise some agricultural prices. Tobacco growers benefited, and so did those who raised corn and hogs. The price of wheat also rose, though more because of bad harvests than because of the AAA program. But dairy farmers and cattlemen were hurt by the law, as were the railroads (which had less freight to haul) and, of course, consumers. Many farmers insisted that the NRA was raising the cost of manufactured goods more than the AAA was raising the prices they received for their crops.

A far more serious weakness of the program was its effect on tenant farmers and sharecroppers, many of whom lost their livelihoods when owners took land out of production to obtain AAA payments. In addition many landowners substituted machinery for labor. In the Cotton Belt

Read the Document
An Attack on New Deal Farm Policies at **myhistorylab.com**

farmers purchased more than 100,000 tractors during the 1930s. Each could do the work of several tenant or sharecropping families. Yet acreage restrictions and mortgage relief helped thousands of others. The AAA was a drastic change of American policy, but foreign producers of coffee, sugar, tea, rubber, and other staples had adopted the same techniques of restricting output and subsidizing growers well before the United States did.

The Dust Bowl

A protracted drought compounded the plight of the farmers, especially in dry sections of the Midwest. During the first third of the twentieth century, midwestern farmers perfected dryland techniques. This entailed "dragging" the fields after rainfall to improve absorption, raking them repeatedly to eliminate water-devouring weeds, and plowing the soil deeply and frequently to allow rain to sink in quickly. The use of tractors, combines, plows, and trucks during the 1920s made possible this intensive working of the fields. Farmers planted the driest areas in winter wheat, which required little moisture; in Nebraska and Iowa, most farmers planted corn.

Then came the dust storms. During the winter of 1933–1934, bitter cold killed off the winter wheat and heavy storms pulverized the soil. By March 1934 driving winds whipped across the Great Plains. In April storms from the Dakotas belched great clouds of dust through Nebraska and Kansas. In May, after the fields had been plowed, more windstorms scattered the seeds and topsoil.

The summer of 1934 was dry, especially in the Dakotas and western Kansas. These farmers were accustomed to dry weather, but the topsoil had been loosened through dryland farming. Strong winds scooped up the dried-out dirt and blew it in

A huge dust cloud engulfs Dodge City, Kansas in 1935.
Source: Kansas State Historical Society.

148

heaving clouds throughout the plains. Dust, forced into people's lungs, induced "dust pneumonia," a respiratory ailment that sometimes proved fatal.

The winds devastated wheat and corn. Over 30 percent of the crops in much of North Dakota, South Dakota, Nebraska, Kansas, and the Oklahoma panhandle failed. Two years later, another drought produced similar results. Coming in the midst of the Great Depression, this second calamity proved more than many farmers could bear. Tens of thousands abandoned their farms.

The Tennessee Valley Authority (TVA)

Although Roosevelt could do little about the midwestern droughts, he did propose a major initiative to alter the economic infrastructure of the upper South. During the Great War the government had constructed a hydroelectric plant at Muscle Shoals, Alabama, to provide power for factories manufacturing synthetic nitrate explosives. After 1920 farm groups and public power enthusiasts, led by Senator George W. Norris of Nebraska, had blocked administration plans to turn these facilities over to private Capitalists, but their efforts to have the site operated by the government had been defeated by presidential vetoes.

During his first hundred days, Roosevelt proposed a **Tennessee Valley Authority (TVA)** to implement a broad experiment in social planning. Besides expanding the hydroelectric plants at Muscle Shoals and developing nitrate man-

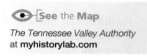

See the **Map**

The Tennessee Valley Authority at **myhistorylab.com**

ufacturing in order to produce cheap fertilizers, he envisioned a coordinated program of soil conservation, reforestation, and industrialization.

Over the objections of private power companies, Congress passed the TVA Act in May 1933. This law created a board authorized to build dams, power plants, and transmission lines and to sell fertilizers and electricity to individuals and local communities. The board could undertake flood control, soil conservation, and reforestation projects and improve the navigation of the river. Although the TVA never became the comprehensive regional planning organization some of its sponsors had anticipated, it improved the standard of living of millions of inhabitants of the valley.

The Tennessee Valley Authority Although the Tennessee Valley Authority (TVA) never fully became the regional planning organization its sponsors had anticipated, the TVA nevertheless was able to expand the hydroelectric plants at Muscle Shoals, Alabama, and build dams, power plants, and transmission lines to service the surrounding area.

Table 1 First New Deal and First Hundred Days (March–June, 1933)

Legislation	Purpose
Banking Act	Provided federal loans to private bankers
Beer-Wine Revenue Act	Repealed Prohibition
Civilian Conservation Corps (CCC)	Created jobs for unemployed young men
Federal Emergency Relief Act (FERA)	Gave federal money to states and localities to provide relief of poor
Agricultural Adjustment Act (AAA)	Raised farm prices by restricting production
Tennessee Valley Authority (TVA)	Massive construction project that generated employment—and electricity—in Tennessee Valley
National Industrial Recovery Act (NIRA)	Created structure for business and labor to cooperate to make particular industries more profitable

The New Deal Spirit

By the end of the hundred days a large majority of the country labeled the New Deal a solid success. Considerable recovery had taken place, but more basic was the fact that Roosevelt had infused his administration with a spirit of bustle and optimism.

Although Roosevelt was not much of an intellectual, his openness to suggestion made him eager to draw on the ideas and energies of experts of all sorts. New Deal agencies soon teemed with college professors and young lawyers without political experience.

The New Deal lacked any consistent ideological base. Theorists never impressed Roosevelt much. His New Deal drew on the old populist tradition, as seen in its antipathy to bankers and its willingness to adopt schemes for inflating the currency; on the New Nationalism of Theodore Roosevelt, in its dislike of competition and its de-emphasis of the antitrust laws; and on the ideas of social workers trained in the Progressive Era. Techniques developed by the Wilsonians also found a place in the system: Louis D. Brandeis had considerable influence on Roosevelt's financial reforms, and New Deal labor policy was an outgrowth of the experience of the War Labor Board of 1917–1918.

Within the administrative maze that Roosevelt created, rival bureaucrats battled to enforce their views. The "spenders," led by Tugwell, clashed with those favoring strict economy, who gathered around Lewis Douglas, director of the budget. Roosevelt mediated between the factions. Washington became a battleground for dozens of special interest groups: the Farm Bureau Federation, the unions, the trade associations, and the silver miners. While the system was superior to that of Roosevelt's predecessors—who had allowed one interest, big business, to predominate—it slighted the unorganized majority. The NRA aimed frankly at raising the prices paid by consumers of manufactured goods; the AAA processing tax came ultimately from the pocketbooks of ordinary citizens.

The Unemployed

At least 9 million persons were still without work in 1934. Yet the Democrats confounded the political experts, including their own, by increasing their already large majorities in both houses of Congress in the 1934 elections. All the evidence indicates

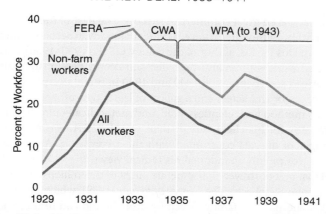

THE NEW DEAL: 1933-1941

Unemployment and Federal Action, 1929–1941 Unemployment of non-farm workers reached nearly 40 percent by early 1933. The Federal Emergency Relief Act (FERA) and Civil Works Administration (CWA) (both in 1933) and the Works Progress Administration (WPA) (1935) put millions back to work.

that most of the jobless continued to support the administration. Their loyalty can best be explained by Roosevelt's unemployment policies.

In May 1933 Congress had established the Federal Emergency Relief Administration (FERA) and given it $500 million to be dispensed through state relief organizations. Roosevelt appointed Harry L. Hopkins, an eccentric but brilliant and dedicated social worker, to direct the FERA. Hopkins insisted that the unemployed needed jobs, not handouts. In November he persuaded Roosevelt to create the Civil Works Administration (CWA) and swiftly put 4 million people to work building and repairing roads and public buildings, teaching, decorating the walls of post offices with murals, and utilizing their special skills in dozens of other ways.

In May 1935 Roosevelt put Hopkins in charge of the **Works Progress Administration (WPA)**. By the time this agency was disbanded in 1943 it had found employment for 8.5 million people. Besides building public works, the WPA made important cultural contributions. It developed the Federal Theatre Project, which put actors, directors, and stagehands to work; the Federal Writers' Project, which turned out valuable guidebooks, collected local lore, and published about 1,000 books and pamphlets; and the Federal Art Project, which employed painters and sculptors. In addition, the National Youth Administration created part-time jobs for more than 2 million high school and college students.

At no time during the New Deal years did unemployment fall below 10 percent of the workforce, and in some places it was much higher. WPA did not go far enough, chiefly because Roosevelt could not escape his fear of drastically unbalancing the budget. The president also hesitated to undertake projects that might compete with private enterprises. Yet his caution did him no good politically; the business interests he sought to placate were becoming increasingly hostile to the New Deal.

Literature during the Depression

Some American novelists found Soviet communism attractive and wrote "proletarian" novels in which ordinary workers were the heroes, and stylistic niceties gave way to the rough language of the street and the factory. Most of these books are of little artistic merit, and none achieved great commercial success. The best of the Depression writers avoided the party line, although they were critical of many aspects of American life.

One was John Dos Passos, author of the trilogy *U.S.A.* (1930–1936), a massive, intricately constructed work with an anti-capitalist and deeply pessimistic point of view. It portrayed American society between 1900 and 1930 in broad perspective, interweaving the stories of five major characters and a galaxy of lesser figures.

Dos Passos's method was relentless, cold, and methodical—utterly realistic. He displayed no sympathy for his characters or their world. *U.S.A.* was a monument to the despair and anger of liberals confronted with the Depression. After the Depression, however, Dos Passos rapidly abandoned his radical views.

The novel that best portrayed the desperate plight of the millions impoverished by the Depression was John Steinbeck's *The Grapes of Wrath* (1939), which described the fate of the Joads, an Oklahoma farm family driven by drought and bad times to abandon their land and become migratory laborers in California. Steinbeck captured the patient bewilderment of the downtrodden, the brutality bred of fear that characterized their exploiters, and the furious resentments of the radicals of the 1930s. He depicted the parching blackness of the Oklahoma dust bowl, the grandeur of California, the backbreaking toil of the migrant fruit pickers, and the ultimate indignation of a people repeatedly degraded.

William Faulkner, probably the finest American novelist of the era, responded in still another way. Between 1929 and 1932, he burst into prominence with four major novels: *The Sound and the Fury*, *As I Lay Dying*, *Sanctuary*, and *Light in August*.

Faulkner was essentially a pessimist. His characters continually experience emotions too intense to be bearable, often too profound and too subtle for the natures he had given them. Nevertheless his stature was beyond question, and unlike so many other novelists of the period he maintained a high level in his later years.

Three Extremists: Long, Coughlin, and Townsend

Roosevelt's moderation and the desperation of the poor roused extremists both on the left and on the right. The most formidable was Louisiana's Senator Huey Long, the "Kingfish." Raised on a farm in northern Louisiana, Long was successively a traveling salesman, a lawyer, state railroad commissioner, governor, and, after 1930, U.S. senator. By 1933 his rule in Louisiana was absolute. Long was certainly a demagogue—yet the plight of all poor people concerned him deeply. More important, he tried to do something about it.

As a reformer, Long stood in the populist tradition; he hated bankers and "the interests." He believed that poor people, regardless of color, should have a chance to earn a decent living and get an education. His arguments were simplistic, patronizing, possibly insincere, but effective. "Don't say I'm working for niggers," he told one northern journalist. "I'm for the poor man—all poor men. Black and white, they all gotta have a chance. . . . 'Every Man a King'—that's my slogan."

Long had supported the New Deal at the start. But partly because he thought Roosevelt too conservative and partly because of his own ambition, he soon broke with the administration. While Roosevelt was probably more hostile to the big financiers than to any other interest, Long denounced him as "a phoney" and a stooge of Wall Street.

By 1935 Long's "Share Our Wealth" movement had a membership of over 4.6 million. His program called for the confiscation of family fortunes of more than $5 million and a tax of 100 percent on incomes over $1 million a year, the money to be used to buy every family a "homestead" (a house, a car, and other necessities) and provide an annual family income of $2,000 to $3,000, plus old-age pensions, educational benefits, and veterans' pensions. As the 1936 election approached, he planned to organize a third party to split the liberal vote. He assumed that the Republicans would win the election and so botch the job of fighting the Depression that he could sweep the country in 1940.

Less powerful than Long but more widely influential was Father Charles E. Coughlin, the "Radio Priest." A genial Canadian of Irish lineage, Coughlin in 1926 began broadcasting a weekly religious message over station WJR in Detroit. His mellifluous voice attracted a huge national audience, and the Depression gave him a secular cause. In 1933 he had been an eager New Dealer, but his dislike of New Deal financial policies—he believed that inflating the currency would end

•●•[Read the Document
Coughlin, *A Third Party (1936)*
at **myhistorylab.com**

the Depression—and his need for ever more sensational ideas to hold his radio audience led him to turn against the New Deal. By 1935 he was calling Roosevelt a "great betrayer and liar."

Although Coughlin's National Union for Social Justice was especially appealing to Catholics, it attracted people of every faith, particularly in the lower-middle-class districts of the big cities. He attacked bankers, New Deal planners, Roosevelt's farm program, and the alleged sympathy of the administration for Communists and Jews, both of which Coughlin denounced in his weekly talks. His program resembled fascism more than any leftist philosophy, but he posed a threat, especially in combination with Long, to the continuation of Democratic rule.

Charles E. Coughlin, the "Radio Priest," was the father of conservative "talk radio."

Photo Credit: Courtesy of the Library of Congress.

Another rapidly growing movement alarmed the Democrats in 1934–1935: Dr. Francis E. Townsend's campaign for "old-age revolving pensions." Townsend, a retired California physician, had an oversimplified and therefore appealing "solution" to the nation's troubles. He advocated paying every person aged sixty years and over a pension of $200 a month, the only conditions being that the pensioners not hold jobs and that they spend the entire sum within thirty days. Their purchases, he argued, would stimulate production, thereby creating new jobs and revitalizing the economy. A stiff transactions tax, collected whenever any commodity changed hands, would pay for the program.

Economists quickly pointed out that with about 10 million persons eligible for the Townsend pensions, the cost would amount to $24 billion a year—roughly half the national income. But among the elderly the scheme proved extremely popular. Although most Townsendites were anything but radical politically, their plan, like Long's "Share Our Wealth" scheme, would have revolutionized the distribution of wealth in the country. The movement marked the emergence of a new force in American society. With medical advances lengthening the average life span, the percentage of old people in the population was rising. The breakdown of close family ties in an increasingly mobile society now caused many of these citizens to be cast adrift to live out their last years poor, sick, idle, and alone.

With the possible exception of Long, the extremists had little understanding of practical affairs. Collectively, however, they represented a threat to Roosevelt; their success helped to make the president see that he must move boldly to restore good times or face serious political trouble in 1936.

Political imperatives had much to do with Roosevelt's decisions, and the influence of Justice Brandeis and his disciples, notably Felix Frankfurter, was great. They urged Roosevelt to abandon his probusiness programs, especially the NRA, and stress restoring competition and taxing corporations more heavily. The fact that most businessmen were turning away from him encouraged the president to accept this advice; so did the Supreme Court's decision in *Schecter v. United States* (May 1935), which declared the National Industrial Recovery Act unconstitutional. (The case involved the provisions of the NRA Live Poultry Code; the Court voided the act on the grounds that Congress had delegated too much legislative power to the code authorities and that the defendants, four brothers engaged in slaughtering chickens in New York City, were not engaged in interstate commerce.)

The Second New Deal

Existing laws had failed to end the Depression. Conservatives roundly denounced Roosevelt, and extremists were luring away some of his supporters. Voters, heartened by the partial success of early New Deal measures, were clamoring for further reforms. But the Supreme Court had declared many key New Deal measures unconstitutional. For these many reasons, Roosevelt, in June 1935, launched what historians call the Second New Deal.

There followed the "second hundred days," one of the most productive periods in the history of American legislation. The National Labor Relations Act—commonly known as the **Wagner Act**—gave workers the right to bargain collectively and prohibited employers from interfering with union organizational activities in their factories. A National Labor Relations Board (NLRB) was established to supervise plant elections and designate successful unions as official bargaining agents when a majority of the workers approved.

Photo Credit: Courtesy Strong National Museum of Play,® Rochester, NY.

Monopoly, patented in 1935, was an instant best-seller: Players risk all their assets in an attempt to secure a real estate monopoly—and thus great wealth.

It was difficult to force some big corporations to bargain "in good faith," as the law required, but the NLRB could conduct investigations of employer practices and issue cease and desist orders when "unfair" activities came to light.

The **Social Security Act** of August 1935 set up a system of old-age insurance, financed partly by a tax on wages (paid by workers) and partly by a tax on payrolls (paid by employers). It created a state-federal system of unemployment insurance, similarly financed. Liberal critics considered this Social Security system inadequate because it did not cover agricultural workers, domestics, self-employed persons, and some other groups particularly in need of its benefits. Health insurance was not included, and because the size of pensions depended on the amount earned, the lowest-paid workers could not count on much support after reaching sixty-five. Yet the law was of major significance. Over the years the pension payments were increased and the classes of workers covered expanded.

The Rural Electrification Administration (REA), created by executive order, also began to function during this remarkable period. The REA lent money at low interest rates to utility companies and to farmer cooperatives interested in bringing electricity to rural areas. When the REA went into operation, only one farm in ten had electricity; by 1950 only one in ten did not.

Another important measure was the Wealth Tax Act of August 1935, which raised taxes on large incomes considerably. Estate and gift taxes were also increased. Stiffer

Table 2 Second New Deal (1935–1938)

Legislation	Purpose
Emergency Relief Appropriations Act (1935)	Created Works Progress Administration (WPA) to give jobs to blacks, white-collar workers, and even artists and writers
Rural Electrification Administration (1935)	Extended electric power lines to rural areas
Social Security Act (1935)	Devised system to provide unemployment insurance and pensions for elderly
Wagner Act (1935)	Guaranteed the rights of unions to organize and negotiate for members
Fair Labor Standards Act (1938)	Set minimum hourly wages and maximum hours of work

taxes on corporate profits reflected the Brandeis group's desire to penalize corporate giantism. Much of the opposition to other New Deal legislation arose from the fact that after these changes in the tax laws were made, the well-to-do had to bear a larger share of the cost of *all* government activities.

Herbert Hoover epitomized the attitude of conservatives when he called the New Deal "the most stupendous invasion of the whole spirit of Liberty that the nation has witnessed." Undoubtedly many opponents of the New Deal sincerely believed that it was undermining the foundations of American freedom. The cost of the New Deal also alarmed them. By 1936 some members of the administration had fallen under the influence of the British economist John Maynard Keynes, who argued that the world Depression could be conquered if governments would deliberately unbalance their budgets by reducing interest rates and taxes and by increasing expenditures to stimulate consumption and investment.

Roosevelt never accepted Keynes's theories; he conferred with the economist in 1934 but could not grasp the "rigmarole of figures" with which Keynes deluged him. Nevertheless the imperatives of the Depression forced him to spend more than the government was collecting in taxes; thus he adopted in part the Keynesian approach. Conservative businessmen considered him financially irresponsible, and the fact that deficit spending seemed to be good politics made them seethe with rage.

The Election of 1936

The election of 1936 loomed as a showdown. The GOP candidate, Governor Alfred M. Landon of Kansas, was a former follower of Theodore Roosevelt, a foe of the Ku Klux Klan in the 1920s, and a believer in government regulation of business. But he was a poor speaker and against the charm and political astuteness of Roosevelt, Landon's arguments—chiefly that he could administer the government more efficiently than the president—made little impression.

On election day the country gave the president a tremendous vote of confidence. He carried every state but Maine and Vermont. The Republicans elected only eighty-nine members of the House of Representatives and their strength in the Senate fell to sixteen, an all-time low. In dozens of city and state elections, Democratic candidates also made large gains. Both Roosevelt's personality and his program had captivated the land. He seemed irresistible, the most powerfully entrenched president in the history of the United States.

Read the **Document**

FDR, *Fireside Chat* at **myhistorylab.com**

Roosevelt did not win in 1936 because of the inadequacies of his foes. Having abandoned his efforts to hold the businessmen, whom he now denounced as "economic royalists," he appealed for the votes of workers and the underprivileged. The new labor unions gratefully poured thousands of dollars into the campaign to reelect him. Black voters switched to the Democrats in record numbers. Farmers liked Roosevelt because of his evident concern for their welfare. Countless elderly persons backed Roosevelt out of gratitude for the Social Security Act.

Roosevelt Tries to Undermine the Supreme Court

On January 20, in his second inaugural address, Roosevelt spoke of the plight of millions of citizens "denied the greater part of what the very lowest standards of today call the necessities of life." A third of the nation, he added without exaggeration, was "ill-housed, ill-clad, ill-nourished." He interpreted his landslide victory as a mandate for further reforms, and with his prestige and his immense congressional majorities, nothing appeared to stand in his way. Nothing, that is, except the Supreme Court.

Throughout Roosevelt's first term the Court had stood almost immovable against increasing the scope of federal authority and broadening the general power of government, state as well as national, to cope with the exigencies of the Depression. Of the nine justices, only Louis Brandeis, Benjamin N. Cardozo, and Harlan Fiske Stone viewed the New Deal sympathetically. Four others—James C. McReynolds, Willis Van Devanter, Pierce Butler, and George Sutherland—were intransigent conservatives. Chief Justice Charles Evans Hughes and Justice Owen J. Roberts, while more open-minded, tended to side with the conservatives on many questions.

Much of the early New Deal legislation, pushed through Congress at top speed during the hundred days, had been drafted without proper regard for the Constitution. Even the liberal justices considered the National Industrial Recovery Act unconstitutional.

In 1937 all the major measures of the second hundred days appeared doomed. The Wagner Act had little chance of winning approval, experts predicted. Lawyers were advising employers to ignore the Social Security Act, so confident that the Court would declare it unconstitutional.

Faced with this situation, Roosevelt decided to ask Congress to shift the balance on the Court by increasing the number of justices, thinly disguising the purpose of his plan by making it part of a general reorganization of the judiciary. A member of the Court who reached the age of seventy would have the option of retiring at full pay. Should such a justice choose not to retire, the president was to appoint an additional justice, up to a maximum of six, to ease the burden of work for the aged jurists who remained on the bench.

Roosevelt knew that this measure would run into resistance, but he expected that the huge Democratic majorities in Congress could override any opposition and that the public would back him solidly. No astute politician had erred so badly in estimating the effects of an action since Stephen A. Douglas introduced the Kansas-Nebraska bill in 1854.

Although polls showed the public fairly evenly divided on the "court-packing" bill, the opposition was vocal and influential. To the expected denunciations of conservatives were added the complaints of liberals fearful that the principle of court packing might in the future be used to subvert civil liberties. Opposition in Congress was immediate and intense; many who had cheerfully supported every New Deal bill came out against the plan. Chief Justice Hughes released a devastating critique; even the liberal Brandeis—the oldest judge on the court—rejected the bill out of hand.

For months Roosevelt stubbornly refused to concede defeat, but in July 1937 he had to yield. Minor administrative reforms of the judiciary were enacted, but the size of the Court remained unchanged.

The struggle did result in saving the legislation of the Second New Deal. Alarmed by the threat to the Court, Justices Hughes and Roberts beat a strategic retreat on a series of specific issues. While the debate was raging in Congress, they sided with the liberals in upholding first a minimum wage law of the state of Washington that was little different from a New York act the Court had recently rejected, then the Wagner Act, and then the Social Security Act. In May Justice Van Devanter retired and Roosevelt replaced him with Senator Hugo Black of Alabama, a New Dealer. The conservative justices thereupon gave up the fight, and soon Roosevelt was able to appoint enough new judges to give the Court a large pro-New Deal majority. No further measure of significance was declared unconstitutional during his presidency. The Court fight hurt Roosevelt severely. When the president summoned a special session of Congress in November 1937 and submitted a program of "must" legislation, not one of his bills was passed.

The New Deal Winds Down

With unemployment high, wages low, and workers relatively powerless against their employers, most Americans had liked New Deal labor legislation and sympathized with the industrial unions whose growth it stimulated. The NRA, the Wagner Act, and the CIO's organization of industries like steel and automobiles changed the power structure within the economy. What amounted to a revolution in the lives of wage earners had occurred. Unionization had meant fair methods of settling disputes about work practices and a measure of job security based on seniority for tens of thousands of workers. The CIO in particular had done much to increase the influence of labor in politics and to bring blacks and other minorities into the labor movement.

In 1937 a series of "sit-down strikes" broke out, beginning at the General Motors plant in Flint, Michigan. The tolerant attitude of the Roosevelt administration ensured the strikers against government intervention. Fearful that all-out efforts to clear their plants would result in the destruction of expensive machinery, most employers capitulated to the workers' demands. All the automobile manufacturers but Henry Ford quickly came to terms with the United Automobile Workers.

The major steel companies, led by U.S. Steel, recognized the CIO and granted higher wages and a forty-hour week. The auto and steel unions alone boasted more than 725,000 members by late 1937; other CIO units conquered the rubber industry, the electrical industry, the textile industry, and many more.

These gains and the aggressive way in which the unions pursued their objectives gave many members of the middle class second thoughts concerning the justice of labor's demands. Sit-down strikes, the disregard of unions for the "rights" of nonunion workers, and the violence that accompanied some strikes seemed to many not merely unreasonable but also a threat to social order. The enthusiasm of such people for all reform cooled rapidly.

While the sit-down strikes and the Court fight were going on, the New Deal suffered another heavy blow. Business conditions had been gradually improving since 1933. Heartened by the trend, Roosevelt cut back sharply on the relief program in June 1937, with disastrous results. Between August and October the economy slipped downward like sand through a chute. Stock prices plummeted; unemployment rose by 2 million; industrial production slumped. This "Roosevelt recession" further damaged the president's reputation.

In April 1938 Roosevelt again committed himself to heavy deficit spending. At his urging Congress passed a $3.75 billion public works bill. Two major pieces of legislation were also enacted at about this time. A new AAA program set marketing quotas and acreage limitations for growers of staples like wheat, cotton, and tobacco and authorized the Commodity Credit Corporation to lend money to farmers on their surplus crops.

The second measure, the Fair Labor Standards Act, abolished child labor and established a national minimum wage of 40 cents an hour and a maximum workweek of 40 hours, with time and a half for overtime. Although the law failed to cover many of the poorest-paid types of labor, its passage meant wage increases for 750,000 workers. In later years many more classes of workers were brought within its protection, and the minimum wage was repeatedly increased.

These measures further alienated conservatives without dramatically improving economic conditions. The resistance of many Democratic members of Congress to additional economic and social "experiments" hardened. As the 1938 elections approached, Roosevelt decided to go to the voters in an effort to strengthen party discipline and reenergize the New Deal. He singled out a number of conservative Democratic senators, notably Walter F. George of Georgia, Millard F. Tydings of Maryland, and "Cotton Ed" Smith of South Carolina, and tried to "purge" them by backing other Democrats in the primaries.

The purge failed. Southern voters liked Roosevelt but resented his interference in local politics. Smith dodged the issue of liberalism by stressing the question of white supremacy. Tydings emphasized Roosevelt's "invasion" of Maryland. All three senators were easily renominated and then reelected in November. In the nation at large the Republicans made important gains for the first time since Roosevelt had taken office. The Democrats maintained nominal control of both houses of Congress, but the conservative coalition, while unable to muster the votes to do away with accomplished reforms, succeeded in blocking additional legislation.

Significance of the New Deal

After World War II broke out in 1939, the Great Depression was swept away on a wave of orders from the beleaguered European democracies. For this prosperity, Roosevelt received much undeserved credit. Despite the aid given to the jobless, the generation of workers born between 1900 and 1910 who entered the 1930s as unskilled laborers had their careers permanently stunted by the Depression. Far fewer rose to middle-class status than at any time since the 1830s and 1840s.

Roosevelt's willingness to experiment with different means of combating the Depression made sense because no one really knew what to do; however, his uncertainty about the ultimate objectives of the New Deal was counterproductive. He vacillated

To hold back immense volumes of water, the Hoover Dam, seen from above, consisted of 2.5 million cubic yards of concrete which, at the base, was thicker than two football fields set end-to-end. It was built through the New Deal.

between seeking to stimulate the economy by deficit spending and trying to balance the budget, between a narrow "America first" economic nationalism and a broad-gauged international approach, between regulating monopolies and trust-busting, and between helping the underprivileged and bolstering those already strong.

Roosevelt's fondness for establishing new agencies to deal with specific problems vastly increased the federal bureaucracy, indirectly added to the influence of lobbyists, and made it more difficult to monitor government activities. His cavalier attitude toward constitutional limitations on executive power, which he justified as being necessary in a national emergency, set in motion trends that so increased the prestige and authority of the presidency that the balance among the executive, legislative, and judicial branches was threatened.

Yet these are criticisms after the fact. Because of New Deal decisions, many formerly unregulated areas of American life became subject to federal authority: the stock exchange, agricultural prices and production, labor relations, old-age pensions, relief of the needy. By encouraging the growth of unions, the New Deal probably helped workers obtain a larger share of the profits of industry. By putting a floor under the income of many farmers, it checked the decline of agricultural living standards, though not that of the agricultural population. The Social Security program, with all its inadequacies, lessened the impact of bad times on an increasingly large proportion of the population and provided immense psychological benefits to all.

Watch the Video

Responding to the Great Depression: Whose New Deal? at **myhistorylab.com**

Women as New Dealers: The Network

Largely because of the influence of Eleanor Roosevelt and Molly Dewson, head of the Women's Division of the Democratic National Committee, the Roosevelt administration employed far more women in positions of importance than any earlier one. Secretary of Labor Frances Perkins, the first woman appointed to a Cabinet post, had been active in labor relations for more than twenty years, as secretary of the Consumers' League during the progressive period, as a factory inspector immediately after the war, and as chair of the New York State Industrial Commission. As secretary of labor she helped draft

New Deal labor legislation and kept Roosevelt informed on various labor problems outside the government.

Through her newspaper column "My Day" and as a speaker on public issues, Eleanor Roosevelt became a major political force, especially in the area of civil rights, where the administration needed constant prodding.

She particularly identified with efforts to obtain better treatment for blacks, in and out of government. Her best-known action occurred in 1939 after the Daughters of the American Revolution (DAR) refused to permit the use of their Washington auditorium for a concert by the black contralto Marian Anderson. Eleanor Roosevelt resigned from the DAR in protest, and after the president arranged for Anderson to sing at the Lincoln Memorial, she persuaded a small army of dignitaries to sponsor the concert. An interracial crowd of 75,000 people attended the performance. The *Chicago Defender*, an influential black newspaper, noted that the First Lady "stood like the Rock of Gibraltar against pernicious encroachments on the rights of minorities."

Blacks during the New Deal

The shift of black voters from the Republican to the Democratic party during the New Deal years was one of the most significant political turnarounds in American history. In 1932 when things were at their worst, fewer African Americans defected from the Republican party than the members of any other traditionally Republican group. Four years later, however, blacks voted for Roosevelt in overwhelming numbers.

Blacks supported the New Deal for the same reasons that whites did, but how the New Deal affected blacks in general and racial attitudes specifically are more complicated questions. Claiming that he dared not antagonize southern congressmen, whose votes he needed for his recovery programs, Roosevelt did nothing about civil rights before 1941 and relatively little thereafter. For the same reason, many southern white liberals hesitated to support racial integration for fear that other liberal causes could be injured as a result.

Many of the early New Deal programs treated blacks as second-class citizens. They were often paid at lower rates than whites under NRA codes and the early farm programs shortchanged black tenants and sharecroppers. TVA developments were rigidly segregated, and almost no blacks got jobs in TVA offices. Because the Social Security Act excluded agricultural laborers and domestic servants, it did nothing for hundreds of thousands of poor black workers or for Mexican American farmhands in the Southwest. In 1939 unemployment was twice as high among blacks as among whites, and whites' wages were double the level of blacks' wages.

The fact that members of racial minorities got less than they deserved did not keep most of them from becoming New Dealers: Half a loaf was more than any American government had given blacks since the time of Ulysses S. Grant.

In the labor movement the new CIO unions accepted black members, and this was particularly significant because these unions were organizing industries—steel, automobiles, and mining among others—that employed large numbers of blacks. Thus, while black Americans suffered horribly during the Depression, New Deal efforts to counteract its effects brought them some relief and a measure of hope. And this became

Photo Credit: Courtesy of the Library of Congress.

Black sharecroppers evicted from their tenant farms were photographed by Arthur Rothstein along a Missouri road in 1939. Rothstein was one of a group of outstanding photographers who created a unique "sociological and economic survey" of the nation between 1936 and 1942 under the aegis of the Farm Security Administration.

increasingly true with the passage of time. During Roosevelt's second term, blacks found far less to criticize than had been the case earlier.

A New Deal for Indians

New Deal policy toward American Indians built on earlier trends but carried them further. During the Harding and Coolidge administrations more Indian land had passed into the hands of whites, and agents of the Bureau of Indian Affairs had tried to suppress elements of Indian culture that they considered "pagan" or "lascivious." In 1924 Congress finally granted citizenship to all Indians, but it was still generally agreed by whites that Indians should be treated as wards of the state. Assimilation had failed; Indian languages and religious practices, patterns of family life, Indian arts and crafts had all resisted generations of efforts to "civilize" the tribes.

Government policy took a new direction in 1933 when President Roosevelt named John Collier commissioner of Indian affairs. In the 1920s Collier had studied the Indians of the Southwest and been appalled by what he learned. He became executive secretary of the American Indian Defense Association and, in 1925, editor of a reform-oriented magazine, *American Indian Life*. By the time he was appointed commissioner, the Depression had reduced perhaps a third of the 320,000 Indians living on reservations to penury.

Collier tried to revive the spirits of these people. He was particularly eager to encourage the revival of tribal governments that could represent the Indians in dealings with the United States government and function as community service centers.

In part because of Collier's urging, Congress passed the Indian Reorganization Act of 1934. This law did away with the Dawes Act allotment system and enabled Indians to establish tribal governments with powers like those of cities, and it encouraged Indians to return individually owned lands to tribal control. About 4 million of the 90 million acres of Indian land lost under the allotment system were returned to the tribes.

In truth the problem was more complicated than Collier had imagined. Indians who owned profitable allotments, such as those in Oklahoma who held oil and mineral rights, did not relish turning over their land to tribal control. All told, 77 of 269 tribes voted against communal holdings.

Collier resigned in 1945, and in the 1950s Congress "terminated" most government efforts aimed at preserving Indian cultures. Nevertheless, like so many of its programs, the New Deal's Indian policy was a bold effort to deal constructively with a long-standing national problem.

The Role of Roosevelt

How much of the credit for New Deal policies belongs personally to Franklin D. Roosevelt is debatable. He had little to do with many of the details and some of the broad principles behind the New Deal. His knowledge of economics was skimpy, his understanding of many social problems superficial, and his political philosophy distressingly vague. The British leader Anthony Eden described him as "a conjurer, skillfully juggling with balls of dynamite, whose nature he failed to understand."

Nevertheless, every aspect of the New Deal bears the brand of Roosevelt's remarkable personality. Roosevelt constructed the coalition that made the program possible; his humanitarianism made it a reform movement of major significance. Although

A miner greets the president. Franklin's "first-class temperament" compensated for his "second-class intellect," Justice Oliver Wendell Holmes famously observed.

Photo Credit: UPI/CORBIS-NY.

considered by many a terrible administrator because he encouraged rivalry among his subordinates, assigned different agencies overlapping responsibilities, failed to discharge many incompetents, and frequently put off making difficult decisions, he was in fact one of the most effective chief executives in the nation's history.

Like Andrew Jackson, Roosevelt maximized his role as leader of all the people. His informal biweekly press conferences kept the public in touch with developments and himself in tune with popular thinking. His "fireside chats" convinced millions that he was personally interested in each citizen's life and welfare, as in a way he was. At a time when the size and complexity of the government made it impossible for any one person to direct the nation's destiny, Roosevelt managed the minor miracle of personifying that government to 130 million people.

While the New Deal was still evolving, contemporaries recognized Roosevelt's right to a place beside Washington, Jefferson, and Lincoln among the great presidents. Yet as his second term drew toward its close, some of his most important work still lay in the future.

The Triumph of Isolationism

Franklin Roosevelt was at heart an internationalist, but like most world leaders in the 1930s, he placed revival of his own country's limping economy ahead of general world recovery. In April 1933 he took the United States off the gold standard, hoping that devaluing the dollar would make it easier to sell American goods abroad. The following month the World Economic Conference met in London. Delegates from sixty-four nations sought ways to increase world trade, perhaps by a general reduction of tariffs and the stabilization of currencies. After flirting with the idea of currency stabilization, Roosevelt threw a bombshell into the conference by announcing that the United States would not return to the gold standard. His decision increased international ill feeling, and the conference collapsed.

Against this background, vital changes in American foreign policy took place. Unable to persuade the country to take positive action against aggressors, internationalists like Secretary of State Stimson had begun in 1931 to work for a discretionary arms embargo law to be applied by the president in time of war against whichever side had broken the peace. By early 1933 Stimson had obtained Hoover's backing for an embargo bill, as well as the support of President-elect Roosevelt. First the munitions manufacturers and then the isolationists pounced on it, and in the resulting debate it was amended to make the embargo apply to *all* belligerents.

Stimson's policy would have permitted arms shipments to China but not to Japan, which might have discouraged the Japanese from attacking. As amended, the embargo would have automatically applied to both sides, thus removing the United States as an influence in the conflict. Although Roosevelt accepted the change, the internationalists in Congress did not, and when they withdrew their support the measure died.

The danger of another world war mounted steadily as Germany, Italy, and Japan repeatedly resorted to force to achieve their expansionist aims. In March 1935 Hitler instituted universal military training and denounced the settlement at Versailles. In May Mussolini massed troops in Italian Somaliland, using a trivial border clash as a pretext for threatening the ancient kingdom of Ethiopia.

Congress responded by passing a series of **neutrality acts** to prevent the United States from being drawn into a wider war. The Neutrality Act of 1935 forbade the sale of munitions to all belligerents whenever the president should proclaim that a state of war existed. Americans who took passage on belligerent ships after such a proclamation had been issued would do so at their own risk. Roosevelt would have preferred a discretionary embargo or no new legislation at all, but he dared not rouse the ire of the isolationists by vetoing the bill.

In October 1935 Italy invaded Ethiopia and Roosevelt invoked the new neutrality law. Secretary of State Cordell Hull asked American exporters to support a "moral embargo" on the sale of oil and other products not covered by the act. His plea was ignored; oil shipments to Italy tripled between October and January. Italy quickly overran and annexed Ethiopia. In February 1936 Congress passed a second neutrality act forbidding all loans to belligerents.

Then, in the summer of 1936, civil war broke out in Spain. The rebels, led by the reactionary General Francisco Franco and strongly backed by Italy and Germany, sought to overthrow the somewhat leftist Spanish Republic. Here, clearly, was a clash between democracy and fascism, and the neutrality laws did not apply to civil wars. However, Roosevelt now became more fearful of involvement than some isolationists. The president believed that American interference might cause the conflict in Spain to become a global war, and he was wary of antagonizing the substantial number of American Catholics who were sympathetic to the Franco regime. At his urging Congress passed another neutrality act broadening the arms embargo to cover civil wars.

Isolationism now reached its peak. A public opinion poll revealed in March 1937 that 94 percent of the people thought American policy should be directed at keeping out of all foreign wars rather than trying to prevent wars from breaking out. In April Congress passed still another neutrality law. It continued the embargo on munitions and loans, forbade Americans to travel on belligerent ships, and gave the president discretionary authority to place the sale of other goods to belligerents on a cash-and-carry basis. This played into the hands of the aggressors. While German planes and cannons were turning the tide in Spain, the United States was denying the hard-pressed Spanish loyalists even a case of cartridges.

In January 1938 the House narrowly defeated the Ludlow amendment, which would have prohibited Congress from declaring war without the prior approval of the nation's voters.

President Roosevelt, in part because of domestic problems such as the Supreme Court packing struggle and the wave of sit-down strikes, and in part because of his own vacillation, seemed to have lost control over the formulation of American foreign policy. The American people, like wild creatures before a forest fire, were rushing in blind panic from the conflagration.

War Again in Asia and Europe

There were limits beyond which Americans would not go. In July 1937 the Japanese resumed their conquest of China, pressing ahead on a broad front. Roosevelt believed that invoking the neutrality law would only help the well-armed Japanese. Taking advantage of the fact that neither side had formally declared war, he allowed the shipment of arms and supplies to both sides.

Roosevelt came gradually to the conclusion that resisting aggression was more important than keeping out of war, but when he did, the need to keep the country united

In 1939 Hitler reviews goose-stepping troops during a celebration of his 50th birthday.

Photo Credit: Hugo Jaeger/Timepix/Time Life Pictures/Getty Images.

led him at times to be less than candid in his public statements. Hitler's annexation of Austria in March 1938 caused him deep concern. The Nazis' vicious anti-Semitism had caused many of Germany's 500,000 Jewish citizens to seek refuge abroad. Now 190,000 Austrian Jews were under Nazi control. When Roosevelt learned that the Germans were burning synagogues, expelling Jewish children from schools, and otherwise mistreating innocent people, he said that he "could scarcely believe that such things could occur." But public opinion opposed changing the immigration law so that more refugees could be admitted, and the president did nothing.

In September 1938 Hitler demanded that Czechoslovakia cede the German-speaking Sudetenland to the Reich. British Prime Minister Neville Chamberlain and French Premier Edouard Daladier, in a conference with Hitler at Munich, yielded to Hitler's threats and promises and persuaded the Czechs to surrender the region. Roosevelt failed again to speak out. But when the Nazis seized the rest of Czechoslovakia in March 1939, Roosevelt called for "methods short of war" to demonstrate America's determination to check the fascists.

When Hitler threatened Poland in the spring of 1939, demanding the free city of Danzig and the Polish Corridor separating East Prussia from the rest of Germany, and when Mussolini invaded Albania, Roosevelt urged Congress to repeal the 1937 neutrality act so that the United States could sell arms to Britain and France in the event of war. Congress refused.

In August 1939 Germany and the Soviet Union signed a nonaggression pact, prelude to their joint assault on Poland. On September 1 Hitler's troops invaded Poland, at last provoking Great Britain and France to declare war. Roosevelt immediately asked Congress to repeal the arms embargo. In November, in a vote that followed party lines closely, the Democratic majority pushed through a law permitting the sale of arms and other contraband on a cash-and-carry basis. Short-term loans were authorized, but American vessels were forbidden to carry any products to the belligerents. Since the Allies controlled the seas, cash-and-carry gave them a tremendous advantage.

The German attack on Poland effected a basic change in American thinking. Keeping out of the war remained an almost universal hope, but preventing a Nazi victory became the ultimate, if not always conscious, objective of many citizens. In Roosevelt's case it was perfectly conscious, although he dared not express his feelings candidly because of isolationist strength in Congress and the country. He moved slowly, responding to rather than directing the course of events.

Poland fell in less than a month; then, Hitler loosed his armored divisions. Between April 9 and June 22 he taught the world the awful meaning of ***Blitzkrieg***— lightning war, spearheaded by tanks and supporting aircraft. Denmark, Norway, the Netherlands, Belgium, and France were successively overwhelmed. The British army, pinned against the sea at Dunkirk, saved itself from annihilation only by fleeing across the English Channel. After the French submitted to his harsh terms on June 22, Hitler controlled nearly all of western Europe.

Roosevelt responded to these disasters in a number of ways. In the fall of 1939, reacting to warnings from Albert Einstein and other scientists that the Germans were trying to develop an atomic bomb, he committed federal funds to a top-secret atomic bomb program, which came to be known as the **Manhattan Project**. Even as the British and French were falling back, he sold them, without legal authority, surplus government arms. When Italy entered the war against France, the president called the invasion a stab in the back. During the first five months of 1940 he asked Congress to appropriate over $4 billion for national defense. To strengthen national unity he named Henry L. Stimson secretary of war[1] and another Republican, Frank Knox, secretary of the navy.

After the fall of France, Hitler attempted to bomb and starve the British into submission. The epic air battles over England during the summer of 1940 ended in a decisive defeat for the Nazis, but the Royal Navy, which had only about 100 destroyers, could not control German submarine attacks on shipping. In this desperate hour, Prime Minister Winston Churchill, who had replaced Chamberlain in May 1940, asked Roosevelt for fifty old American destroyers to fill the gap.

Japanese Expansion, 1920–1941 The Japanese empire, which conquered Korea early in the twentieth century, seized Manchuria in 1931; Jehol, north of Beijing, in 1933; and the rest of China after 1937.

German Expansion, 1936–1939 In March 1936, Hitler's forces reoccupied the Rhineland. In 1938 Germany annexed Austria and wrested the Sudetenland from Czechoslovakia, and in 1939 occupied the remaining Czech lands.

---

[1]Stimson had held this post from 1911 to 1913 in the Taft Cabinet!

The navy had 240 destroyers in commission and more than fifty under construction. But direct loan or sale of the vessels would have violated both international and American laws. Any attempt to obtain new legislation would have roused fears that the United States was going down the path that had led it into World War I. Long delay if not outright defeat would have resulted. Roosevelt therefore arranged to "trade" the destroyers for six British naval bases in the Caribbean. In addition, Great Britain leased bases in Bermuda and Newfoundland to the United States.

The destroyers-for-bases deal was a masterful achievement. It helped save Great Britain, and at the same time it circumvented isolationist prejudices since the president could present it as a shrewd bargain that bolstered America's defenses. A string of island bastions in the Atlantic was more valuable than fifty old destroyers.

Lines were hardening throughout the world. In September 1940, despite last-ditch isolationist resistance, Congress enacted the first peacetime draft in American history. Some 1.2 million draftees were summoned for one year of service, and 800,000 reservists were called to active duty. That same month Japan signed a mutual-assistance pact with Germany and Italy. This Rome-Berlin-Tokyo coalition—the **Axis Powers**—fused the conflicts in Europe and Asia, turning the struggle into a global war.

A Third Term for FDR

In the midst of these events the 1940 presidential election took place. Roosevelt was easily renominated. Vice President Garner, who had become disenchanted with Roosevelt and the New Deal, did not seek a third term; at Roosevelt's dictation, the party chose Secretary of Agriculture Henry A. Wallace to replace him.

By using concern about the European war to justify running for a tradition-breaking third term, Roosevelt brought down on his head the hatred of conservative Republicans and the isolationists of both major parties, just when they thought they would be rid of him. The Republicans nominated the darkest of dark horses, Wendell L. Willkie of Indiana, the utility magnate who had led the fight against the TVA in 1933.

Despite his political inexperience and Wall Street connections, Willkie made an appealing candidate. He was an energetic, charming, openhearted man. His rough-hewn, rural manner (one Democrat called him "a simple, barefoot Wall Street lawyer") won him wide support in farm districts. Willkie had difficulty, however, finding issues on which to oppose Roosevelt. The New Deal reforms were too popular and too much in line with his own thinking to invite attack. He believed as strongly as the president that America could no longer ignore the Nazi threat.

In the end Willkie focused his campaign on Roosevelt's conduct of foreign relations. While rejecting the isolationist position, Willkie charged that Roosevelt intended to make the United States a participant in the war. Roosevelt retorted (disingenuously, since he knew he was not a free agent in the situation), "I have said this before, but I shall say it again and again and again: Your boys are not going to be sent into any foreign wars." In November Roosevelt carried the country handily, though by a smaller majority than in 1932 or 1936. The popular vote was 27 million to 22 million, the electoral count 449 to 82.

The Undeclared War

The election encouraged Roosevelt to act more boldly. When Prime Minister Churchill informed him that the cash-and-carry system would no longer suffice because Great Britain was rapidly exhausting its financial resources, he decided at once to provide the British with whatever they needed. Instead of proposing to lend them money, a step certain to rouse memories of the vexatious war debt controversies, he devised the lend-lease program, one of his most ingenious and imaginative creations.

First he delivered a "fireside chat" that stressed the evil intentions of the Nazis and the dangers that a German victory would create for America. Aiding Britain should be looked at simply as a form of self-defense. When the radio talk provoked a favorable public response, Roosevelt went to Congress in January 1941 with a plan calling for the expenditure of $7 billion for war materials that the president could sell, lend, lease, exchange, or transfer to any country whose defense he deemed vital to that of the United States. After two months of debate, Congress gave him what he had asked for.

Although the wording of the **Lend-Lease Act** obscured its immediate purpose, the saving of Great Britain, the president was frank in explaining his plan. He did not minimize the dangers involved, yet his mastery of practical politics was never more in evidence. To counter Irish American prejudices against the English, he pointed out that the Irish Republic would surely fall under Nazi domination if Hitler won the war. He coupled his demand for heavy military expenditures with his enunciation of the idealistic "Four Freedoms"—freedom of speech, freedom of religion, freedom from want, and freedom from fear—for which, he said, the war was being fought.

After the enactment of lend-lease, aid short of war was no longer seriously debated. The American navy began to patrol the North Atlantic, shadowing German submarines and radioing their locations to British warships and planes. In April 1941 U.S. forces occupied Greenland; in May the president declared a state of unlimited national emergency. After Hitler invaded the Soviet Union in June, Roosevelt moved slowly, for anti-Soviet feeling in the United States was intense.[2] But it was obviously to the nation's advantage to help any country that was resisting Hitler's armies. In November, $1 billion in lend-lease aid was put at the disposal of the Soviet Union.

Meanwhile, Iceland was occupied in July 1941, and the draft law was extended in August—by the margin of a single vote in the House of Representatives. In September the German submarine *U–652* fired a torpedo at the destroyer *Greer* in the North Atlantic. The *Greer*, which had provoked the attack by tracking *U–652* and flashing its position to a British plane, avoided the torpedo and dropped nineteen depth charges in an effort to sink the submarine.

Roosevelt announced that the *Greer* had been innocently "carrying mail to Iceland." He called the U-boats "the rattlesnakes of the Atlantic" and ordered the navy to "shoot on sight" any German craft in the waters south and west of Iceland and to convoy merchant vessels as far as that island. After the sinking of the destroyer *Reuben James* on October 30, Congress voted to allow the arming of American merchant ships and to permit them to carry cargoes to Allied ports. For all practical purposes, though not yet officially, the United States had gone to war.

---

[2]During the 1930s the Soviet Union took a far firmer stand against the fascists than any other power, but after joining Hitler in swallowing up Poland, it attacked and defeated Finland during the winter of 1939–1940 and annexed the Baltic states. These acts virtually destroyed the small communist movement in the United States.

Cinderella Man

As *Cinderella Man* (2005) opens, boxer James J. Braddock (Russell Crowe) lands a right-hook that sends his opponent sprawling to the canvas—a knockout. Braddock raises his hands in triumph. The crowd roars and a jazz band blares.

When Braddock arrives at his home in New Jersey, his wife, Mae (Renée Zellweger) leaps into his arms. "I'm so proud of you," she says. Three children mob their father. Later, as Braddock prepares for bed, he sets his gold watch and thick wallet onto a polished wood dresser. The year is 1928.

Abruptly, the scene dissolves. A cheap, unfinished dresser comes into focus. The watch and wallet are gone. Braddock, unshaven, looks wearily around a squalid hovel. The children, on mattresses in shadows, cough and wheeze. The year is 1933.

Braddock, like much of the nation, has fallen on hard times, his savings wiped out by the Depression. Worse, he has broken his powerful right hand and, desperate for money, resumed boxing before it healed. He tries to work at the dockyards but often there is no work to be had. The grocer refuses credit. The milkman stops deliveries. The power company shuts off the gas and electricity. His children, underfed and chilled, become sick. Braddock returns to Madison Square Garden, hat in hand, and begs for money. He also applies and receives federal assistance—welfare—at $6.40 a week. Compared to Braddock, Cinderella had it easy.

Then Braddock's agent, an unlikely fairy godmother, shows up with an extraordinary proposition. A huge, young bruiser and leading contender for the heavyweight title—"Corn" Griffin—had been scheduled to fight the next evening at Madison Square Garden. But Griffin's opponent has backed out at the last minute. Rather than cancel the fight, Madison Square Garden has offered Braddock $250 to serve as Griffin's punching bag. Desperate, Braddock accepts.

What happens the next day—June 14, 1934—is the stuff of fairy tales. Braddock borrows boxing boots and heads to Madison Square Garden. When Braddock enters the ring, his robe bears another boxer's name.

After the opening bell, Griffin, a thick-necked bull of a man, charges Braddock and pounds him mercilessly. Braddock, sustained only by raw courage—and a tough chin, survives the first two rounds. Then, in the third, he surprises Griffin with a thunderous hook, knocking the giant out cold.

Because Griffin was the top contender, Braddock himself is placed on the list of contenders. He proceeds to score one upset after another until he's next in line to face Max Baer (Craig Bierko), the heavyweight champion whose fearsome right has killed two boxers. The manager of Madison Square Garden requires Braddock to sign a waiver absolving it of responsibility should Braddock also perish at Baer's hands.

On June 13, 1935, the night of the fight, as Mae goes to church to pray, reporters speculate on whether Braddock can last a single round. The betting odds against Braddock are the worst in memory. But a movie named after a fairy tale must have a happy ending, and *Cinderella Man* comes through. After fifteen harrowing rounds, Braddock wins a unanimous decision. In 364 days, he has gone from impoverished "bum" to heavyweight champion of the world.

"This is a true story," declared director Ron Howard. Yet fairy tales, by definition, are make-believe; and Hollywood, by reputation, believes in nothing as fervently as the dollar. Thus viewers are entitled to ask: Does *Cinderella Man* tell the actual story of James J. Braddock?

The surprising answer, given the implausibility of the plot, is yes, up to a point. And that point begins with the Baer-Braddock fight: Madison Square Garden did not warn Braddock of the danger of fighting Baer or oblige him to sign a waiver. Also, the fight was no slugfest. The *New York Times* dubbed

Russell Crowe and Renée Zellweger embrace in *Cinderella Man*.

it "one of the worst heavyweight championship contests" in boxing history. Reporters assumed that Baer failed to take the early rounds seriously, lost others on foolish fouls, and realized too late that he was behind. Baer, too, was no unfeeling monster. Most interesting is the movie's error of omission, or, more precisely, of suppression. It makes no mention of the fact that Baer proudly trumpeted his Jewish ancestry. Baer had a large Star of David stitched onto his trunks, an image that appears in the movie once, briefly and from a distance.

Why did director Howard evade the truth about Baer? The likely answer is that Howard knew that fairy tales require villains as well as heroes. *Cinderella Man's* Braddock looms larger for slaying the Big Bad Baer.

In fact, the real enemy was the Great Depression. Braddock understood this. When asked how he managed to turn his career around, he explained, "I was fighting for milk." Damon Runyon, the writer who first called Braddock "Cinderella Man," recognized that the boxer's story took on mythic proportions because it encapsulated the aspirations of an entire nation.

But the movie misses the point that many ethnic groups had their own boxing champions. After Braddock had upset Griffin, he fought Joe Louis, the Brown Bomber. While the movie rightly shows Irish Americans praying for Braddock, it neglects the millions of African Americans who also gathered around radios, praying for Louis. Jewish fans, similarly, identified with Baer, cherishing his 1933 defeat of the German boxer, Max Schmeling, Hitler's favorite. When Braddock defeated Baer, many Jews were devastated.

Madison Square Garden, keenly aware of the ethnic appeal of boxing, worked hard to ensure that nearly every major immigrant group had someone to cheer for on fight night. Boxing promoters were among the first to learn that in sports, as in entertainment more generally, segregation did not pay.

Cinderella Man depicts, with considerable accuracy, a simple and good man's triumph over adversity. His story was, indeed, the stuff of myth. But in its earnest attempt to universalize Braddock's appeal, the movie obscures the ethnic divisions that characterized so much of American life during the first half of the twentieth century.

Question for Discussion
- Do you think the Depression encouraged solidarity among Americans of different races and ethnicities, because everyone could empathize with each other's suffering? Or did it exacerbate tensions by pitting different groups against each other in search of scarce jobs?

Milestones

1933	FDR becomes president
	Hitler is elected German chancellor
	FDR proclaims Good Neighbor Policy
	Banking Act gives FDR broad powers
	Civilian Conservation Corps (CCC) employs 250,000 young men
	Federal Emergency Relief Act (FERA) funds relief programs
	Agricultural Adjustment Act (AAA) seeks relief for farmers
	Tennessee Valley Authority (TVA) plans dams and power plants
	National Industrial Recovery Act (NIRA) establishes Public Works Administration (PWA) and National Recovery Administration (NRA)
	Banking Act establishes Federal Deposit Insurance Corporation (FDIC)
	Civil Works Administration puts 4 million to work
	Twenty-First Amendment ends prohibition
1934	Indian Reorganization Act gives tribes more autonomy
	Securities and Exchange Commission (SEC) regulates stocks and bonds
	Federal Communications Commission (FCC) regulates interstate and foreign communication
	Federal Housing Administration (FHA) gives housing loans
1935	Emergency Relief Appropriation Act creates Works Project Administration (WPA)
	Rural Electrification Administration brings electricity to farms

1935	Supreme Court rules NIRA unconstitutional in *Schechter v. United States*
	National Labor Relations Act (Wagner-Connery) encourages unionization
	Social Security Act guarantees pensions and other benefits
	Neutrality Act forbids wartime arms sales to belligerents
	Italy invades and annexes Ethiopia
	Walter Millis publishes isolationist *The Road to War: America, 1914–1917*
1936	FDR is reelected president in record landslide
	Supreme Court declares AAA unconstitutional
1937	Roosevelt tries to pack Supreme Court
	Japanese in China seize Beijing, Shanghai, Nanking
1938	Fair Labor Standards Act abolishes child labor, sets minimum wage
	House of Representatives defeats Ludlow (isolationist) Amendment
	Britain and France appease Hitler at Munich
1939	Germany invades Poland; World War II begins
1940	Hitler conquers Denmark, Norway, the Netherlands, Belgium, France
	FDR is reelected to third term
	Axis Powers sign Rome-Berlin-Tokyo pact
	Isolationists form America First Committee
1941	Lend-Lease Act helps Britain

✓ ● Study and Review at www.myhistorylab.com

Review Questions

1. The introduction of this chapter compares the 2010 health insurance law with that establishing Social Security in 1935. In what ways is the comparison an apt one? How did the measures and times differ? Was Social Security a form of socialism?

2. Compare the First and Second New Deals. What were the similarities and differences?

3. What was the impact of the Great Depression on art, literature, and popular culture? How did it affect women and minority groups? Labor?

4. How did the New Deal expand the role of the federal government?

5. Why did Asia and Europe slip into war in the 1930s? How did the United States respond during that decade and why?

Key Terms

Agricultural Adjustment
  Act (AAA)
Axis Powers
Blitzkrieg
Civilian Conservation
  Corps (CCC)
Lend-Lease Act

Manhattan Project
National Recovery
  Administration
  (NRA)
neutrality acts
New Deal
Social Security Act

Tennessee Valley
  Authority (TVA)
Wagner Act
Works Progress
  Administration
  (WPA)

War and Peace: 1941–1945

From Chapter 27 of *American Destiny: Narrative of a Nation*, Combined Volume, Fourth Edition.
Mark C. Carnes and John A. Garraty. Copyright © 2012 by Pearson Education, Inc. Published by
Pearson Prentice Hall. All rights reserved.

War and Peace: 1941–1945

((•—Hear the Audio at myhistorylab.com

Does the war in Afghanistan touch your life?

ALTHOUGH ALL YOUNG AMERICAN MEN ARE REQUIRED TO REGISTER for the military draft, none has actually been drafted since the 1970s. (Registration exists in the event of a national military emergency.) In place of conscription, the Department of Defense has recruited all-volunteer military services. In times of peace, most generals prefer a volunteer army: Professional soldiers are better trained and often more attentive to orders; but in times of war, when recruiting officers struggle to fill quotas and tours-of-duty are extended, many generals call for a return to the draft.

By 2010, a heated debate among officers surfaced in the *Armed Forces Journal*. Most defended the professional army, noting that the quality of recruits was higher than in two decades. But other officers called for a return to the "citizen soldiers" envisioned by Washington and Jefferson. One reason was that wars fought by conscripts ensured that the nation as a whole engaged in the war effort. The *Seattle Times* observed that although the Iraq war had gone on far longer than World War II, "life for most Americans has clicked along without personal loss or even higher federal taxes." "Marines are at war," one general complained, "America is at the mall."

Such remarks underscored how different the current conflicts in Iraq and Afghanistan are from World War II, a monstrous global war among advanced industrial nations. Of every five American males between the ages of twenty and twenty-five, four served in World War II. At the beginning of World War II, 4 million Americans paid income tax; by its end, 43 million did so. Over 85 million Americans—half the nation's population—spent $185 billion to buy war bonds. Food and gasoline were rationed. World War II required the mobilization of the entire nation.

World War II transformed society, too. In the absence of so many young men, women assumed new roles and worked at different types of jobs. African Americans, Hispanics, American Indians, and other minorities found new opportunities even as they encountered persistent discrimination. Americans of Japanese extraction were relocated against their will to isolated camps. Technological change—culminating in the atom bomb—transformed everyone's lives. It was a war unlike any other.

The Road to Pearl Harbor

Neither the United States nor Japan wanted war. Roosevelt considered Germany by far the more dangerous enemy and was alarmed by the possibility of simultaneously fighting German armies in Europe and Japanese forces in the Pacific. In the spring of 1941 Secretary of State Cordell Hull conferred in Washington with the Japanese ambassador, Kichisaburo Nomura, in an effort to resolve their differences. Hull showed little appreciation of the political and military situation in East Asia. He demanded that Japan withdraw from China.

Japan might well have accepted limited annexations in the area in return for the removal of American trade restrictions, but Hull insisted on total withdrawal, to which even the moderates in Japan would not agree. When Hitler invaded the Soviet Union, thereby removing the threat of Russian intervention in East Asia, Japan decided to complete its conquest of China and occupy French Indochina even at the risk of war with the United States. Roosevelt retaliated in July 1941 by freezing Japanese assets in the United States and clamping an embargo on oil.

Now the ultranationalist war party in Japan assumed control. Nomura was instructed to tell Hull that Japan would refrain from further expansion if the United States and Great Britain would cut off all aid to China and lift the economic blockade. Japan promised to pull out of Indochina once "a just peace" had been established with China. When the United States rejected these demands, the Japanese prepared to attack the Dutch East Indies, British Malaya, and the Philippines. To immobilize the U.S. Pacific fleet, they planned a surprise air assault on the Hawaiian naval base at Pearl Harbor.

Photo Credit: Superstock/Art Life Images.

Japan's surprise attack on Pearl Harbor on December 7, 1941, killed more than 2,400 American sailors and soldiers and thrust the United States into World War II. President Roosevelt asked Congress for a declaration of war the next day, calling the attack "a date that will live in infamy."

An American cryptanalyst, Colonel William F. Friedman, had cracked the Japanese diplomatic code: The Japanese were making plans to attack in early December. But in the hectic rush of events, both military and civilian authorities failed to make effective use of the information collected. They expected the blow to fall somewhere in East Asia, possibly the Philippines.

The garrison at Pearl Harbor was alerted against "a surprise aggressive move in any direction." The commanders there, Admiral Husband E. Kimmel and General Walter C. Short, believing an attack impossible, took precautions only against Japanese sabotage. Thus when planes from Japanese aircraft carriers swooped down upon Pearl Harbor on the morning of December 7, they found easy targets. In less than two hours they reduced the Pacific fleet to a smoking ruin: two battleships destroyed, six others heavily battered, nearly a dozen lesser vessels put out of action. More than 150 planes were wrecked; over 2,400 soldiers and sailors were killed and 1,100 wounded.

Never had American armed forces suffered a more devastating or shameful defeat. Although the official blame was placed chiefly on Admiral Kimmel and General Short, responsibility for the disaster was widespread. Military and civilian officials in Washington had failed to pass on all that they knew to Hawaii or even to one another.

On December 8 Congress declared war on Japan. Formal war with Germany and Italy was still not inevitable—isolationists were far more ready to resist the "yellow peril" in Asia than to fight in Europe. The Axis Powers, however, honored their treaty obligations to Japan and on December 11 declared war on the United States. America was now fully engaged in another great war, World War II.

Mobilizing the Home Front

World War II placed immense strains on the American economy and produced immense results. About 15 million men and women entered the armed services; they, and in part the millions more in Allied uniforms, had to be fed, clothed, housed, and supplied with equipment ranging from typewriters and paper clips to rifles, grenades, tanks, and airplanes. Congress granted wide emergency powers to the president. However, while the Democrats retained control of both houses throughout the war, their margins were relatively narrow. A coalition of conservatives in both parties frequently prevented the president from having his way and exercised close control over expenditures.

Roosevelt was an inspiring war leader but not a very good administrator. The squabbling and waste characteristic of the early New Deal period made relatively little difference—what mattered then was raising the nation's spirits and keeping people occupied; efficiency was less than essential, however desirable. But in wartime, the nation's fate, perhaps that of the entire free world, depended on delivering weapons and supplies to the battlefronts.

Roosevelt's greatest accomplishment was his inspiring of industrialists, workers, and farmers with a sense of national purpose. In this respect his function duplicated his earlier role in fighting the Depression, and he performed it with even greater success.

The tremendous economic expansion can be seen in the official production statistics. In 1939 the United States was still mired in the Great Depression. The gross national product amounted to about $91.3 billion. In 1945, after allowing for changes in the price level, it was $166.6 billion. Manufacturing output nearly doubled and agricultural output rose

22 percent. In 1939 the United States turned out fewer than 6,000 airplanes, in 1944 more than 96,000. Shipyards produced 237,000 tons of vessels in 1939, 10 million tons in 1943.

This growth was especially notable in the South and Southwest. This region got a preponderance of the new army camps built for the war as well as a large share of the new defense plants. Southern productive capacity increased by about 50 percent, and southern per capita output, while still low, crept closer to the national average.

Wartime experience proved that the Keynesian economists were correct in saying that government spending would spark economic growth. About 8 million people were unemployed in June 1940. After Pearl Harbor, unemployment virtually disappeared, and by 1945 the civilian workforce had increased by nearly 7 million. Military mobi-

A poster encourages women to work in munitions to support the war effort.

lization had begun well before December 1941, by which time 1.6 million men were already under arms. Economic mobilization proceeded much more slowly, mainly because the president refused to centralize authority. For months after Pearl Harbor various civilian agencies squabbled with the military over everything from the allocation of scarce raw materials to the technical specifications of weapons. Roosevelt refused to settle these conflicts.

The War Economy

Yet by early 1943 the nation's economic machinery had been converted to a wartime footing and was functioning effectively. Supreme Court Justice James F. Byrnes resigned from the Court to become a sort of "economic czar." His Office of War Mobilization had complete control over priorities and prices. Rents, food prices, and wages were strictly regulated, and items in short supply were rationed to consumers. While wages and prices had soared during 1942, after April 1943 they leveled off. Thereafter the cost of living scarcely changed until controls were lifted after the war.

Wages and prices remained in fair balance. Overtime work fattened paychecks, and a new stress in labor contracts on paid vacations, premium pay for night work, and various forms of employer-subsidized health insurance were added benefits. The war effort had almost no adverse effect on the standard of living of

View the Image

Ration Stamps WWII at
myhistorylab.com

the average citizen, a vivid demonstration of the productivity of the American economy. The manufacture of automobiles ceased and pleasure driving became next to impossible because of gasoline rationing, but most civilian activities went on much as they had before Pearl Harbor. While items such as meat, sugar, and shoes were rationed, they were doled out in amounts adequate for the needs of most persons.

The federal government spent twice as much money between 1941 and 1945 as in its entire previous history. This made heavy borrowing necessary. The national debt, which stood at less than $49 billion in 1941, increased by more than that amount each year between 1942 and 1945 and totaled nearly $260 billion when the war ended. However, more than 40 percent of the total was met by taxation, a far larger proportion than in any earlier war.

This policy helped to check inflation by siphoning off money that would otherwise have competed for scarce consumer goods. Heavy excise taxes on amusements and luxuries further discouraged spending, as did the government's war bond campaigns, which persuaded patriotic citizens to lend part of their income to Uncle Sam. High taxes on incomes (up to 94 percent) and on excess profits (95 percent) convinced people that no one was profiting inordinately from the war effort.

The income tax, which had never before touched the mass of white-collar and industrial workers, was extended downward until nearly everyone had to pay it. To collect efficiently the relatively small sums paid by most persons, Congress adopted the payroll-deduction system proposed by Beardsley Ruml, chairman of the Federal Reserve Bank of New York. Employers withheld the taxes owed by workers from their paychecks and turned the money over to the government.

The steeply graduated tax rates, combined with a general increase in the income of workers and farmers, effected a substantial shift in the distribution of wealth in the United States. The poor became richer, while the rich, if not actually poorer, collected a smaller proportion of the national income. The wealthiest 1 percent of the population had received 13.4 percent of the national income in 1935 and 11.5 percent in 1941. In 1944 this group received 6.7 percent.

War and Social Change

World War II altered the patterns of American life in many ways. Never was the population more fluid. The millions who put on uniforms found themselves transported first to training camps in every section of the country and then to battlefields scattered from Europe and Africa to the far reaches of the Pacific. Burgeoning new defense plants, influenced by a government policy of locating them in "uncongested areas," drew other millions to places like Hanford, Washington, and Oak Ridge, Tennessee, where great atomic energy installations were constructed, and to the aircraft factories of California and other states. As in earlier periods the trend was from east to west and from the rural south to northern cities.

During the war the marriage rate rose steeply, from 75 per thousand adult women in 1939 to 118 in 1946. Many young couples felt the need to put down roots before the husbands went off to risk death in distant lands. The population of the United States had increased by only 3 million during the Depression decade of the 1930s; during the next *five* years it rose by 6.5 million.

Minorities in Time of War: Blacks, Hispanics, and Indians

The war affected black Americans in many ways. Several factors helped improve their lives. One was their own growing tendency to demand fair treatment. Another was the reaction of Americans to Hitler's barbaric treatment of millions of Jews, an outgrowth of his doctrine of "Aryan" superiority. These barbarities compelled millions of white citizens to reexamine their views about race. If the nation expected African Americans to risk their lives for the common good, how could it continue to treat them as second-class citizens? Black leaders pointed out the inconsistency between fighting for democracy abroad and ignoring it at home.

Blacks in the armed forces were treated more fairly than they had been in World War I. They were enlisted for the first time in the air force and the marines, and they were given more responsible positions in the army and navy. Altogether about a million served, about half of them overseas. The extensive and honorable performance of these units could not be ignored by the white majority.

However, segregation in the armed services was maintained. The navy continued to confine black and Hispanic sailors to demeaning, noncombat tasks, and black soldiers were often provided with inferior recreational facilities and otherwise mistreated in and around army camps, especially those in the South. However, economic realities operated significantly to the advantage of black civilians. More of them had been unemployed in proportion to their numbers than any other group; now the labor shortage brought employment for all. More than 5 million blacks moved from rural areas to cities between 1940 and 1945 in search of work. At least a million of them found defense jobs in the North and on the West Coast, often developing valuable skills that had been difficult for blacks to acquire before the war because of the discriminatory policies of trade unions and many employers. The black population of Los Angeles, San Francisco, Denver, Buffalo, Milwaukee, and half a dozen other large industrial cities more than doubled in that brief period. The migrants were

"above and beyond the call of duty"

DORIE MILLER
Received the Navy Cross
at Pearl Harbor, May 27, 1942

A poster commemorates Doris "Dorie" Miller, a mess attendant aboard the USS *West Virginia* at Pearl Harbor. Before the ship sank, Miller manned an antiaircraft machine gun and shot down several Japanese planes. He won the Navy Cross for courage, the first awarded to an African American.

Photo Credit: Courtesy of the Library of Congress.

mostly forced to live in urban ghettoes, but their very concentration (and the fact that outside the South blacks could vote freely) made them important politically.

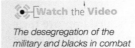

Watch the Video

The desegregation of the military and blacks in combat at **myhistorylab.com**

However, prejudice and mistreatment of blacks did not cease. In areas around defense plants white resentment of the black "invasion" mounted. By 1943, 50,000 new blacks had crowded into Detroit. A wave of strikes disrupted production at U.S. Rubber and several former automobile plants where white workers laid down their tools to protest the hiring of blacks. In June a race riot marked by looting and bloody fighting raged for three days. By the time federal troops restored order, twenty-five blacks and nine whites had been killed. Rioting also erupted in New York and many other cities.

In Los Angeles the attacks were upon Hispanic residents. Wartime employment needs resulted in a reversal of the Depression policy of forcing Mexicans out of the Southwest, and many thousands flocked north in search of work. Most had to accept menial jobs. But work was plentiful, and they, as well as resident Spanish-speaking Americans, experienced rising living standards.

Blacks became increasingly embittered. Roy Wilkins, head of the NAACP, put it this way in 1942: "No Negro leader with a constituency can face his members today and ask full

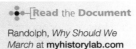

Read the Document

Randolph, *Why Should We March* at **myhistorylab.com**

support for the war in the light of the atmosphere the government has created." Many black newspaper editors were so critical of the administration that conservatives demanded they be indicted for sedition.

Roosevelt would have none of that, but the militants annoyed him; he felt that they should hold their demands in abeyance until the war had been won. Apparently he failed to realize the depth of black anger, and in this he was no different from the majority of whites. A revolution was in the making, yet in 1942 a poll revealed that a solid majority of whites still believed that black Americans were satisfied with their place in society. The riots of 1943 undoubtedly disabused some of them of this illusion.

Concern about national unity did lead to a reaction against the New Deal policy of encouraging Indians to preserve their ancient cultures and develop self-governing communities. There was even talk of going back to the allotment system and trying to assimilate Indians into the larger society. In fact, the war encouraged assimilation in several ways. More than 24,000 Indians served in the armed forces, an experience that brought them into contact with new people, new places, and new ideas. Many thousands more left the reservations to work in defense industries in cities all over the country.

The Treatment of German and Italian Americans

Although World War II affected the American people far more drastically than had World War I, it produced much less intolerance and fewer examples of the repression of individual freedom of opinion. People seemed able to distinguish between Italian fascism and Italian Americans and between the government of Nazi Germany and Americans of German descent in a way that had escaped their parents. The fact that few Italian Americans admired Mussolini and that nearly all German Americans were vigorously anti-Nazi helps explain this. So does the fact that both groups were well-organized and prepared to use their considerable political power if necessary to protect themselves from abuse. Nevertheless, U.S. military authorities arrested some 14,000 Germans and Italians as security risks.

Americans went to war in 1941 without illusions and without enthusiasm, determined to win but expecting only to preserve what they had. They therefore found it easier to tolerate dissent, to view the dangers they faced realistically, and to concentrate on the real foreign enemy without venting their feelings on domestic scapegoats. The nation's 100,000 conscientious objectors met with little hostility.

Internment of Japanese Americans

The relatively tolerant treatment of most Americans of German and Italian descent makes the nation's policies toward American citizens of Japanese extraction all the more difficult to comprehend. Generals on the West Coast were understandably unnerved by the Japanese attack on Pearl Harbor and warned that people of Japanese descent might engage in sabotage or espionage for Japan. "The Japanese race is an enemy race," General John L. Dewitt claimed. The 112,000 Americans of Japanese ancestry, the majority of them native-born citizens, were "potential enemies." "The very fact that no sabotage has taken place to date," Dewitt observed, "is a disturbing and confirming indication that such action will be taken." Secretary of War Stimson proposed the relocation of the West Coast people of Japanese extraction, including American citizens, to **internment camps** in Wyoming, Arizona, and other interior states.

The Japanese were properly indignant but also baffled, in some cases hurt more than angry. "We didn't feel Japanese. We felt American," one woman, the mother of three small children, recalled many years later. Some Japanese Americans challenged military authorities. Gordon Hirabayashi, an American citizen and senior at the University of Washington, refused to report for transportation to an internment camp. After being convicted and sentenced to prison, he decided to appeal. Previous Supreme Courts had ruled that the government could deprive Americans of their freedoms during war only when the "military necessity" was compelling. By the time the Supreme Court ruled on his and similar cases, the Japanese military had been thrown back in the Pacific; no

A Japanese girl in California, tagged for relocation to an internment camp, clutches her doll.

Photo Credit: Anthony Potter Collection/Getty Images Inc. - Hulton Archive Photos.

Japanese Relocation from the West Coast, 1942–1945 Japanese and Japanese Americans who lived in the West Coast Military Area were ordered to report to various "assembly centers," from which they were then deported to inland internment or isolation camps.

invasion was even conceivable. Yet the justices worried that if they declared the internment policy to be unconstitutional, they would appear, "out of step" with the nation, as Justice Felix Frankfurter put it. In June 1943, the Court upheld the conviction of Hirabayashi. Finally, in *Ex parte Endo*, it forbade the internment of loyal Japanese American citizens. Unfortunately the latter decision was not handed down until December 1944.

Women's Contributions to the War Effort

With economic activity on the rise and millions of men going off to war, a sudden need for more women workers developed. The trends of the 1920s—more women workers and more of them married—soon accelerated. By 1944, 6.5 million additional women had entered the workforce, and at the peak of war production in 1945, more than 19 million women were employed, many of them in well-paying industrial jobs. Additional thousands were serving in the armed forces: 100,000 in the Women's Auxiliary Army Corps, others in navy, marine, and air corps auxiliaries.

◉ View the Image

Rosie the Riveter at **myhistorylab.com**

At first there was considerable resistance to what was happening. About one husband in three objected in principle to his wife taking a job. Many employers in so-called heavy industry and in other fields traditionally dominated by men doubted that women could handle such tasks. Unions frequently made the same point, usually without much evidence.

These male attitudes lost force in the face of the escalating demand for labor. That employers usually did not have to pay women as much as men made them attractive, as did the fact that they were not subject to the draft. A breakthrough occurred when the big Detroit automobile manufacturers agreed to employ women on their wartime production lines. Soon women were working not only as riveters and cab drivers but also as welders, as machine tool operators, and in dozens of other occupations formerly the exclusive domain of men.

Women took wartime jobs for many reasons other than the obvious economic ones. Patriotism, of course, was important, but so were the excitement of entering an entirely new world, the desire for independence, even loneliness. "It's thrilling work, and exciting, and something women have never done before," one woman reported. She was talking about driving a taxi.

Black women workers had a particularly difficult time: employers often hesitating to hire them because they were black, and black men looking down on them because they were women. But the need for willing hands was infinite. Sybil Lewis of Sapula, Oklahoma, went to Los Angeles and found a job as a waitress in a black restaurant. Then she responded to a notice of a training program at Lockheed Aircraft, took the course, and became a riveter making airplane gas tanks. When an unfriendly foreman gave her a less attractive assignment, she moved on to Douglas Aircraft. By 1943 she was working as a welder in a shipyard.

Few wartime jobs were easy, and for women there were special burdens, not the least of which was the prejudice of many of the men they worked with. For married women there was housework to do after a long day. One War Manpower Commission bureaucrat figured out that Detroit defense plants were losing 100,000 woman-hours a month because of employees taking a day off to do the family laundry. Although the government made some effort to provide day-care facilities, there were never nearly enough; this was one reason why relatively few women with small children entered the labor market during the war.

Newly married wives of soldiers and sailors (known generally as "war brides") often followed their husbands to training camps, where life was often as difficult as it was around defense plants. Whatever their own behavior, war brides quickly learned that society applied a double standard to infidelity, especially when it involved a man presumably risking his life in some far-off land. There was a general relaxation of sexual inhibitions, part of a decades-long trend but accelerated by the war. So many hasty marriages, followed by long periods of separation, also brought a rise in divorces, from about 170 per thousand marriages in 1941 to 310 per thousand in 1945.

Of course "ordinary" housewives also had to deal with shortages, ration books, and other inconveniences during the war. In addition most took on other duties and bore other burdens, such as tending "victory gardens" and preserving their harvests, using crowded public transportation when there was no gas for the family car, mending and patching old clothes when new ones were unavailable, participating in salvage drives, and doing volunteer work for hospitals, the Red Cross, or various civil defense and servicemen's centers.

Allied Strategy: Europe First

Only days after Pearl Harbor, Prime Minister Churchill and his military chiefs met in Washington with Roosevelt and his advisers. In every quarter of the globe, disaster threatened. The Japanese were gobbling up East Asia. Hitler's armies, checked outside Leningrad and Moscow, were preparing for a massive attack in the direction of Stalingrad, on the

⊙ See the **Map**

World War II in Europe
at **myhistorylab.com**

Volga River. German divisions under General Erwin Rommel were beginning a drive across North Africa toward the Suez Canal. U-boats were taking a heavy toll in the North Atlantic. British and American leaders believed that eventually they could muster enough force to smash their enemies, but whether or not the troops already in action could hold out until this force arrived was an open question.

The decision of the strategists was to concentrate first against the Germans. Japan's conquests were in remote and, from the point of view of the **Allies**, relatively unimportant regions. If the Soviet Union surrendered, Hitler's position in Europe might prove impregnable.

American leaders wanted to attack German positions in France, at least by 1943. The Soviets, with their backs to the wall and bearing the full weight of the German war machine, heartily agreed. Churchill, however, was more concerned with protecting Britain's overseas possessions than with easing the pressure on the Soviet Union. He advocated instead air bombardment of German industry combined with an attempt to drive the Germans out of North Africa, and his argument carried the day.

During the summer of 1942 Allied planes began to bomb German cities. In a crescendo through 1943 and 1944, British and American bombers pulverized the centers of Nazi might. While air attacks did not destroy the German army's capacity to fight, they hampered war production, tangled communications, and brought the war home to

The firebombing of Hamburg (painted here by Floyd Davis, who flew with the Anglo American mission in 1943) killed 50,000 and destroyed Hamburg.

Photo Credit: U.S. Army Center of Military History, ATTN: AAMH-MDC (Sarah Forgey), 103 Third Avenue, Bldg. 35, Fort Lesley J. McNair, Washington, DC 20319-5058; sarah.forgey1@us.army.mil; 202-761-4022.

the German people. Humanitarians deplored the heavy loss of life among the civilian population, but the response of the realists was that Hitler had begun indiscriminate bombing, and victory depended on smashing the German war machine.

In November 1942 an Allied army commanded by General Dwight D. Eisenhower struck at French North Africa. After the fall of France, the Nazis had set up a puppet regime in those parts of France not occupied by their troops, with headquarters at Vichy in central France. This collaborationist Vichy government controlled French North Africa. But the North African commandant, Admiral Jean Darlan, agreed to switch sides when Eisenhower's forces landed. After a brief show of resistance, the French surrendered.

Eisenhower now pressed forward quickly against the Germans in North Africa. In February 1943 at Kasserine Pass in the desert south of Tunis, American tanks met Rommel's Afrika Korps. The battle ended in a standoff, but with British troops closing in from their Egyptian bases to the East, the Germans were soon trapped and crushed. In May, after Rommel had been recalled to Germany, his army surrendered.

In July 1943, while air attacks on Germany continued and the Russians slowly pushed the Germans back from the gates of Stalingrad, the Allies invaded Sicily from

The Liberation of Europe After November, 1942, Allied armies pushed the German-Italian armies back on three fronts: the Soviets, from the East; and American-British armies from North Africa and then, after the Normandy invasion, from France.

Africa. In September they advanced to the Italian mainland. Mussolini had already fallen from power and his successor, Marshal Pietro Badoglio, surrendered. However, the German troops in Italy threw up an almost impregnable defense across the rugged Italian peninsula. The Anglo American army inched forward, paying heavily for every advance. Monte Cassino, halfway between Naples and Rome, did not fall until May 1944, the capital itself not until June; months of hard fighting remained before the country was cleared of Germans. The Italian campaign was an Allied disappointment even though it weakened the enemy.

Germany Overwhelmed

By the time the Allies had taken Rome, the mighty army needed to invade France had been collected in England under Eisenhower's command. On **D-Day**, June 6, 1944, the assault forces stormed ashore at five points along the coast of Normandy, supported by a great armada and thousands of planes and paratroops. Against fierce but ill-coordinated German resistance, they established a beachhead: Within a few weeks a million troops were on French soil. (See Re-Viewing the Past, *Saving Private Ryan.*)

Thereafter victory was assured, though nearly a year of hard fighting lay ahead. In August the American Third Army under General George S. Patton erupted southward into Brittany and then veered east toward Paris. Another Allied army invaded France from the Mediterranean in mid-August and advanced rapidly north. Free French troops were given the honor of liberating Paris on August 25. Belgium was cleared by British and Canadian units a few days later. By mid-September the Allies were fighting on the edge of Germany itself.

The front now stretched from the Netherlands along the borders of Belgium, Luxembourg, and France all the way to Switzerland. If the Allies had mounted a massive assault at any one point, the struggle might have been brought to a quick conclusion. Although the two armies were roughly equal in size, the Allies had complete control of the air and twenty times as many tanks as the foe. The pressure of the advancing Russians on the eastern front made it difficult for the Germans to reinforce their troops in the west. But General Eisenhower believed a concentrated attack was too risky. He prepared instead for a general advance.

While he was regrouping, the Germans on December 16 launched a counterattack, planned by Hitler himself, against the Allied center in the Ardennes Forest. The Germans hoped to break through to the Belgian port of Antwerp, thereby splitting the Allied armies in two. The plan was foolhardy and therefore unexpected, and it almost succeeded. The Germans drove a salient ("the bulge") about fifty miles into Belgium. But once the element of surprise had been overcome, their chance of breaking through to the sea was lost. Eisenhower concentrated first on preventing them from broadening the break in his lines and then on blunting the point of their advance. By late January 1945 the old line had been reestablished.

The Battle of the Bulge cost the United States 77,000 casualties and delayed Eisenhower's offensive, but it exhausted the Germans' last reserves. The Allies then pressed forward to the Rhine, winning a bridgehead on the far bank of the river on March 7. Thereafter, one German city fell almost daily. With the Soviets racing westward against crumbling resistance, the end could not be long delayed. In April, American and Soviet

Table 1 Turning Points of the War in Europe

Summer 1942	British bombing of German cities brings war home to Germany
November 1942	U.S./British invasion of North Africa, defeat of Rommel
February 1943	Germans turned back at Stalingrad, beginning of German retreat from Soviet Union
July 1943	U.S./British invasion of Sicily
June 1944	D-Day: U.S./British invasion of northern France
January 1945	Battle of the Bulge: Last-ditch German offensive defeated
May 8, 1945	Germany surrenders

forces made contact at the Elbe River. A few days later, with Soviet shells reducing his capital to rubble, Hitler, by then probably insane, took his own life in his Berlin air raid shelter. On May 8 Germany surrendered.

As the Americans drove swiftly forward in the late stages of the war, they began to overrun Nazi concentration camps where millions of Jews and others had been murdered. The Americans were horrified by what they discovered, but they should not have been surprised. Word of this holocaust, in which 12 million people (half of them Jews) were slaughtered, had reached the United States much earlier. At first the news had been dismissed as propaganda, then discounted as grossly exaggerated. Hitler was known to hate Jews and to have persecuted them, but that he could order the murder of millions of innocent people, even children, seemed beyond belief. By 1943, however, the truth could not be denied.

Watch the Video

Nazi Murder Mills at **myhistorylab.com.** WARNING: This clip is very graphic.

Little could be done about those already in the camps, but there were thousands of refugees in occupied Europe who might have been spirited to safety. President Roosevelt declined to make the effort; he refused to bomb the Auschwitz death camp in Poland or the rail lines used to bring victims to its gas chambers on the grounds that the destruction of German soldiers and military equipment took precedence over any other objective. Thus, when American journalists entered the camps with the advancing troops, saw the heaps of still-unburied corpses, and talked with the emaciated survivors, their reports caused a storm of protest in America.

The Naval War in the Pacific

Defeating Germany first had not meant abandoning the Pacific region entirely to the Japanese. While armies were being trained and matériel accumulated for the European struggle, much of the available American strength was diverted to maintaining vital communications in East Asia and preventing further Japanese expansion.

See the Map

World War II in the Pacific at **myhistorylab.com**

Saving Private Ryan

Steven Spielberg's *Saving Private Ryan* (1998), starring Tom Hanks, has been widely praised as the most realistic combat movie ever made. This judgment is based chiefly on its re-creation of the June 6, 1944, Allied assault on Omaha Beach during the invasion of Normandy. The camera focuses on Hanks, rain dripping from his helmet, huddled in a crowded landing vessel. Explosions rumble in the distance. The ship plows through heavy seas toward a blackened brow of land. Around him, men vomit. Explosions become louder and sharper. Nearby ships strike mines and blow up; others are obliterated by shell-fire. Hanks's landing craft lurches to avoid the mayhem. Like hail against a tin roof, gunfire riddles the landing craft. Some of the men are hit, and the others hunch lower, still vomiting. A deafening din envelops the ship as its bow opens. A curtain of bullets cuts down the men in front. Hanks and several others leap into the sea, but the ship has stopped far short of the beach. They sink. As bullets tear through the water, ripping into those still submerged, Hanks struggles to the surface. He swims, weaponless, toward the beach.

He has crossed the threshold of hell, and over the next fifteen minutes viewers descend with him the rest of the way.

Saving Private Ryan differs from other combat films not in the graphic horror of the bloodshed, but in its randomness. The audience expects Hanks to survive the opening scenes of the movie in which he stars, and he does. But all other bets are off: a valiant exploit, a kind gesture, a handsome face—none of these influences the grim lottery of battle. A medic frenziedly works on a severely wounded man, injecting morphine, compressing arteries, and binding wounds. Then more bullets splatter his patient beyond recognition. "Why can't you bastards give us a chance?" the medic screams. That is the point: When huge armies converge, hurling high explosives and steel at each other, one's chances of survival are unaffected by ethics or aesthetics.

But having made this point with heart-pounding emphasis, the movie subverts it. Hanks, unnerved and dispirited, initially hunkers down in the relative safety of the seawall. But then he does his job, rallying his men. They blast a hole through obstacles, crawl toward the concrete fortifications above, penetrate trench defenses, blow up bunkers, and seize the hill. Many perish in the effort; Hanks, an infantry captain, is among the survivors.

Then comes a new mission that occupies the remainder of the movie. George C. Marshall, U.S. Army Chief of Staff, has learned of a Mrs. Ryan who has been notified on a single day that three of her sons were killed in action. Her fourth son, James, a private in the 101st Airborne, has just parachuted into Normandy behind German lines. Marshall orders that Private Ryan be returned to safety. This mission is given to Hanks and his platoon. They march inland, encounter snipers, ambushes, and, in the final scenes, a large detachment of German armored vehicles. But they also find Ryan (played by Matt Damon).

Along the way, the movie asks many provocative questions, such as whether war improves those who fight. "I think this is all good for me, sir," one earnest soldier confides to Hanks. "Really," Hanks says with a faint smile, "how is that?" The soldier cites Ralph Waldo Emerson: "War educates the senses. Calls into action the will. Perfects the physical constitution." "Emerson had a way of finding the bright side," Hanks deadpans. Hanks's hand twitches uncontrollably, a physical manifestation of a disordered soul. War, demonstrably, has not made men better.

Except in one way: Hanks and his men have repeatedly demonstrated a willingness to give up their lives for others. Indeed, the movie's central dilemma concerns the moral arithmetic of sacrifice. Is it right to risk eight men to save one? To send a thousand men to near certain death in an initial assault at Omaha Beach to improve the chances of

Actual photograph of American troops approach code-named Omaha Beach at Normandy.

Tom Hanks, Matt Damon, and Edward Burns in *Saving Private Ryan*.

those that follow? To make one generation endure hell so that another may have freedom? The movie provides no ready answers. But in nearly the final scene it does issue a challenge. Hanks, mortally wounded, is lying amidst the corpses of his platoon, and he beckons to Ryan, who is unhurt. "Earn this," Hanks says, vaguely gesturing to the others.

Saving Private Ryan was part of a wave of nostalgic appreciation during the 1990s for the generation that had won World War II. A spate of books, movies, and TV documentaries were other expressions of this phenomenon. On accepting the Oscar for his film, Spielberg thanked his father, a World War II vet, "for showing me that there is honor in looking back and respecting the past."

But respect for the past entails getting it right, and the movie makes some significant errors and omissions. For one, it suggests that the men huddled at the base of the seawall blew up the concrete bunkers on their own. This was not possible. In fact, commanders of destroyers took their ships close to the beaches and fired countless heavy shells into the fortifications, allowing the infantry to move up the hills.

The movie also shows the German soldiers as uniformly expert and professional. But the German army had been decimated by losses in the Soviet Union. The army manning the Normandy defenses included many units composed mostly of old men, boys, or conscripted soldiers from Poland or the Soviet Union. Many surrendered as soon as they encountered American soldiers.

Of the movie's implausible elements, the premise that the U.S. Army high command

ordered a special mission to pluck a grieving mother's son from danger was based on fact. A real Mrs. Niland received telegrams on the same day informing her that three of her sons had been killed in action. Her fourth son, "Fritz," had parachuted into Normandy with the 101st Airborne. The army did in fact snatch him from the front line and return him to safety.

The movie provides a fair rendering of many other elements of the battle: the inaccuracy of aerial bombing, which missed most of the beach fortifications; the confusion caused when hundreds of landing craft failed to reach their destination; the destruction of scores of gliders, which crashed into high hedgerows while attempting to land behind German lines.

Yet through it all, some men, like the captain portrayed by Hanks, drew heroism from some unfathomed depths of the soul. One real soldier at Omaha Beach remembered "a captain and two lieutenants who demonstrated courage beyond belief as they struggled to bring order to the chaos around them."

Saving Private Ryan is not a fully accurate representation of the attack on Omaha Beach, but it depicts—realistically and memorably— how soldiers conferred meaning on the heedless calculus of modern warfare.

Questions for Discussion

- Do generals have the right to order some men to near certain death in order to save others? To save a nation?
- Do soldiers have the right to disobey such orders? Why or why not?

Photo Credit: AP Wide World Photos.

Midway, a tiny Pacific island, mattered only because of its airfield. The Japanese sent a naval task force to invade the island, but in June 1942 U.S. warplanes sank several of the Japanese aircraft carriers accompanying the invasion force. With air cover gone, Japan called off the invasion. Midway marked a turning point in the war in the Pacific.

The navy's aircraft carriers had escaped destruction at Pearl Harbor, a stroke of immense good fortune because the airplane had revolutionized naval warfare. Commanders discovered that carrier-based planes were far more effective against warships than the heaviest naval artillery because of their greater range and more concentrated firepower.

This was demonstrated in May 1942 in the Battle of the Coral Sea. Having captured an empire in a few months without the loss of any warship larger than a destroyer, the Japanese believed the war already won. This led them to overextend themselves.

The Coral Sea lies northeast of Australia and south of New Guinea and the Solomon Islands. Japanese mastery of these waters would cut Australia off from Hawaii and thus from American aid. Admiral Isoroku Yamamoto had dispatched a large fleet of troopships screened by many warships to attack Port Moresby, on the southern New Guinea coast. On May 7–8 planes from the American carriers *Lexington* and *Yorktown* struck the convoy's screen, sinking a small carrier and damaging a large one. Superficially, the battle seemed a victory for the Japanese, for their planes mortally wounded the *Lexington* and sank two other ships, but the troop transports had been forced to turn back—Port Moresby was saved. Although large numbers of cruisers and destroyers took part in the action, none came within sight or gun range of an enemy ship. All the destruction was wrought by carrier aircraft.

Encouraged by the Coral Sea "victory," Yamamoto decided to force the American fleet into a showdown battle by assaulting the Midway Islands, west of Hawaii. His armada never reached its destination. Between June 4 and 7 control of the central Pacific was decided entirely by airpower. American dive bombers sent four large Japanese carriers to the bottom. About 300 Japanese planes were destroyed. The United States lost only the *Yorktown* and a destroyer. Thereafter the initiative in the Pacific war shifted to the Americans, but victory came slowly and at painful cost.

American land forces were under the command of Douglas MacArthur, a brilliant but egocentric general whose judgment was sometimes distorted by his intense concern for his own reputation. MacArthur was in command of American troops in the Philippine Islands when the Japanese struck in December 1941. After his heroic but hopeless defense of Manila and the Bataan peninsula, President Roosevelt had him evacuated by PT boat to escape capture; those under MacArthur's command endured horrific conditions as prisoners of Japan.

Thereafter MacArthur was obsessed with the idea of personally leading an American army back to the Philippines. Although many strategists believed that the islands should be bypassed in the drive on the Japanese homeland, in the end MacArthur convinced the Joint Chiefs of Staff, who determined strategy. Two separate drives were undertaken, one from New Guinea toward the Philippines under MacArthur, the other through the central Pacific toward Tokyo under Admiral Chester W. Nimitz.

Island Hopping

Before commencing this two-pronged advance, the Americans had to eject the Japanese from the Solomon Islands in order to protect Australia from a flank attack. Beginning in August 1942, a series of land, sea, and air battles raged around Guadalcanal Island in this archipelago. Once again American airpower was decisive, although the bravery and skill of the ground forces that actually won the island must not be underemphasized. American pilots, better trained and with tougher planes than the Japanese, had a relatively easier task. They inflicted losses five to six times heavier on the enemy than they sustained themselves. Japanese airpower disintegrated during the long battle, and this in turn helped the fleet to take a heavy toll on the Japanese navy. By February 1943 Guadalcanal had been secured.

In the autumn of 1943 the American drives toward Japan and the Philippines got under way at last. In the central Pacific campaign the Guadalcanal action was repeated on a smaller but equally bloody scale from Tarawa in the Gilbert Islands to

Table 2 Turning Points of World War II in the Pacific

December 7, 1941	Japanese sneak-attack on Pearl Harbor; United States declares war
May 1942	Japanese win Battle of the Coral Sea, but invasion of Australia foiled
June 1942	United States wins Battle of Midway; Japanese advance toward Hawaii turned back
February 1943	United States takes Guadalcanal, along the southernmost periphery of Japanese power
February 1945	United States retakes Philippines
June 1945	United States takes Okinawa, near Japanese islands
August 1945	United States drops atomic bombs on Hiroshima and Nagasaki; Japan surrenders

Kwajelein and Eniwetok in the Marshalls. The Japanese soldiers on these islands fought for every foot of ground. They almost never surrendered. But Admiral Nimitz's forces were in every case victorious. By midsummer of 1944 this arm of the American advance had taken Saipan and Guam in the Marianas. Now land-based bombers were within range of Tokyo.

Meanwhile, MacArthur was leapfrogging along the New Guinea coast toward the Philippines. In October 1944 he landed on Leyte, south of Luzon. Two great naval clashes in Philippine waters, the Battle of the Philippine Sea (June 1944) and the Battle for Leyte Gulf (October 1944), completed the destruction of Japan's sea power and reduced its air force to a band of fanatical suicide pilots called *kamikazes*, who tried to crash bomb-laden planes into American warships and airstrips. The *kamikazes* caused much damage but could not turn the tide. In February 1945 MacArthur liberated Manila.

The end was now inevitable. B-29 Superfortress bombers from the Marianas rained high explosives and firebombs on Japan. The islands of Iwo Jima and Okinawa, only a few hundred miles from Tokyo, fell to the Americans in March and June 1945. But such was the tenacity of the Japanese soldiers that it seemed possible that it would take another year of fighting and perhaps a million more American casualties to subdue the home Japanese islands.

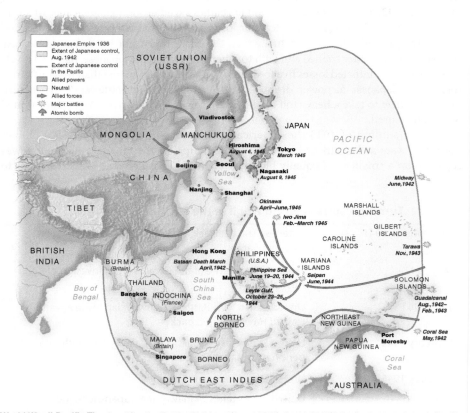

World War II Pacific Theatre After the Battle of Midway (June, 1942), the United States began to seize one Pacific island after another, with one task force pushing west from Pearl Harbor, and another moving north from Australia.

Building the Atom Bomb

At this point came the most controversial decision of the entire war, and it was made by a newcomer on the world scene. In November 1944 Roosevelt had been elected to a fourth term, easily defeating Thomas E. Dewey. Instead of renominating Henry A. Wallace for vice president, whom conservatives considered too radical, the Democratic convention had nominated Senator Harry S Truman of Missouri, a reliable party man well-liked by professional politicians. Then, in April 1945, President Roosevelt died of a cerebral hemorrhage. Thus it was Truman who had to decide what to do when, in July 1945, American scientists placed in his hands a new and awful weapon, the atomic bomb.

After Roosevelt had responded to Albert Einstein's warning in 1939, government-sponsored atomic research had proceeded rapidly, especially after the establishment of the so-called Manhattan Project in May 1943. The manufacture of the element plutonium at Hanford, Washington, and of uranium 235 at Oak Ridge, Tennessee, continued, along with the design and construction of a transportable atomic bomb at Los Alamos, New Mexico, under the direction of J. Robert Oppenheimer. Almost $2 billion was spent before a successful bomb was exploded at Alamogordo, in the New Mexican desert, on July 16, 1945. As that first mushroom cloud formed over the desert, Oppenheimer recalled the prophetic words of the *Bhagavad Gita*: "I am become death, the shatterer of worlds."

●●●┤**Read** the **Document**

Einstein, *Letter to President Roosevelt* at **myhistorylab.com**

Should a bomb with the destructive force of 20,000 tons of TNT be employed against Japan? By striking a major city, its dreadful power could be demonstrated convincingly, yet doing so would bring death to tens of thousands of Japanese civilians. Many of the scientists who had made the bomb now argued against its use. Others suggested alerting the Japanese and then staging a demonstration explosion at sea, but that idea was discarded because of concern that the bomb might fail to explode.

Truman was torn between his awareness that the bomb was "the most terrible thing ever discovered" and his hope that using it "would bring the war to an end." The bomb might cause a revolution in Japan, might lead the emperor to intervene, might even persuade the military to give up. Considering the thousands of Americans who would surely die in any conventional invasion of Japan and, on a less humane level,

Hiroshima lies in ruins, destroyed by an atomic bomb.

influenced by a desire to end the Pacific war before the Soviet Union could intervene effectively and thus claim a role in the peacemaking, the president chose to go ahead. The moral soundness of Truman's decision has been debated ever since. On August 6 the Superfortress *Enola Gay* dropped an atomic bomb on Hiroshima, killing about 78,000 persons (including twenty American prisoners of war) and injuring nearly 100,000 more out of a population of 344,000. Over 96 percent of the buildings in the city were destroyed or damaged. Three days later, while the stunned Japanese still hesitated, a second atomic bomb blasted Nagasaki. On August 15 Japan surrendered.

Thus ended the greatest war in history. Its cost was beyond calculation. No accurate count could be made even of the dead; we know only that the total was in the neighborhood of 20 million. As in World War I, American casualties— 291,000 battle deaths and 671,000 wounded—were smaller than those of the other major belligerents. About 7.5 million Soviets died in battle, 3.5 million Germans, 1.2 million Japanese, and 2.2 million Chinese; Britain and France, despite much smaller populations, suffered losses almost as large as did the United States. And far more than in World War I, American resources, human and matérial, had made victory possible.

No one could account the war a benefit to humanity, but in the late summer of 1945 the future looked bright. Fascism was dead. The successful wartime diplomatic dealings of Roosevelt, Churchill, and the Soviet dictator, Joseph Stalin, encouraged many to hope that the communists were ready to cooperate in rebuilding Europe. Out of the death and destruction had come technological developments that seemed to herald a better world as well as a peaceful one. Enormous advances in the design of airplanes and the development of radar (which some authorities think was more important than any weapons system in winning the war) were about to revolutionize travel and the transportation of goods. Improvements in surgery and other medical advances gave promise of saving millions of lives, and the development of penicillin and other antibiotics, which had greatly reduced the death rate among troops, would perhaps banish all infectious diseases.

Above all, there was the power of the atom. The force that seared Hiroshima and Nagasaki could be harnessed to serve peaceful needs, the scientists promised, with results that might free humanity forever from poverty and toil. The period of reconstruction would be prolonged, but with all the great powers adhering to the new United Nations charter, drafted at San Francisco in June 1945, international cooperation could be counted on to ease the burdens of the victims of war and help the poor and underdeveloped parts of the world toward economic and political independence. Such at least was the hope of millions in the victorious summer of 1945.

Wartime Diplomacy

During the course of World War II every instrument of mass persuasion in the country had been directed toward convincing the people that the Soviets were fighting America's battle as well as their own. Even before Pearl Harbor, former Ambassador Joseph E. Davies wrote in his best-selling *Mission to Moscow* (1941) that Joseph Stalin and other communist leaders were "devoted to the cause of peace for both ideological and practical reasons."

Such views of Joseph Stalin were naive, to say the least, but the United States and the Soviet Union agreed emphatically on the need to defeat Hitler. The Soviets repeatedly expressed a willingness to cooperate with the Allies in dealing with postwar problems. The Soviet Union was one of the twenty-six signers of the Declaration of the United Nations (January 1942), in which the Allies promised to eschew territorial aggrandizement after the war, to respect the right of all peoples to determine their own form of government, to work for freer trade and international economic cooperation, and to force the disarmament of the aggressor nations.[1]

In May 1943 the Soviet Union dissolved the Comintern, its official agency for the promulgation of world revolution. The following October, during a conference in Moscow with the Allies, Soviet Foreign Minister V. M. Molotov joined in setting up a European Advisory Commission to divide Germany into occupation zones after the war. That December, at a conference held in Tehran, Iran, Roosevelt, Churchill, and Stalin discussed plans for a new league of nations. When Roosevelt described the kind of world organization he envisaged, the Soviet dictator offered a number of constructive suggestions.

Between August and October 1944, Allied representatives met at Dumbarton Oaks, outside Washington. The chief Soviet delegate, Andrei A. Gromyko, opposed limiting the use of the veto by the great powers on the future **United Nations (UN)** Security Council, but he did not take a deliberately obstructionist position. At a conference held at Yalta in the Crimea in February 1945 Stalin joined Roosevelt and Churchill in the call for a meeting in April at San Francisco to draft a charter for the UN. "We argued freely and frankly across the table," Roosevelt reported later. "But at the end, on every point, unanimous agreement was reached. I may say we achieved a unity of thought and a way of getting along together."

The UN charter drafted at the 50-nation San Francisco Conference gave each UN member a seat in the General Assembly. The locus of authority in the new organization resided in the Security Council, "the castle of the great powers." This consisted of five permanent members (the United States, the Soviet Union, Great Britain, France, and China) and six others elected for two-year terms.

The Security Council was charged with responsibility for maintaining world peace, but any great power could block UN action whenever it wished to do so. The United States insisted on this veto power as strongly as the Soviet Union did. In effect the charter paid lip service to the Wilsonian ideal of a powerful international police force, but it incorporated the limitations that Henry Cabot Lodge had proposed in his 1919 reservation to Article X of the League Covenant, which relieved the United States from the obligation of enforcing collective security without the approval of Congress.

Allied Suspicion of Stalin

Long before the war in Europe ended, however, the Allies had clashed over important policy matters. Since later world tensions developed from decisions made at this time, an understanding of the disagreements is essential for evaluating several subsequent decades.

---

[1] These were the principles first laid down in the so-called Atlantic Charter, drafted by Roosevelt and Churchill at a meeting on the USS *Augusta* off Newfoundland in August 1941.

Much depends on one's view of the postwar Soviet system. If the Soviet government under Stalin was bent on world domination, events fall readily into one pattern of interpretation. If, having endured an unprovoked assault by the Nazis, it was seeking only to protect itself against the possibility of another invasion, these events are best explained differently. Because the United States has opened nearly all its diplomatic records, we know a great deal about how American foreign policy was formulated and about the mixed motives and mistaken judgments of American leaders. This helps explain why many scholars have been critical of American policy and the "cold warriors" who made and directed it. The Soviet Union, for many years, did not let even its own historians into its archives.

It is clear, however, that the Soviets resented the British-American delay in opening up a second front. They were fighting for survival against the full power of the German armies; any American invasion of northern France, even an unsuccessful one, would have relieved some of the pressure. Roosevelt and Churchill would not move until they were ready, and Stalin had to accept their decision. At the same time, Stalin never concealed his determination to protect his country from future attack by extending its frontier after the war. He warned the Allies repeatedly that he would not tolerate any unfriendly government along the western boundary of the Soviet Union.

Most Allied leaders, including Roosevelt, admitted privately during the war that the Soviet Union would annex territory and possess preponderant power in Eastern Europe after the defeat of Germany, but they never said this publicly. They believed that the Soviets would allow free governments to be created in countries like Poland and Bulgaria.

The Polish question was a terribly difficult one. The war, after all, had been triggered by the German attack on Poland; the British in particular felt a moral obligation to restore that nation to its prewar independence. During the war a Polish government in exile was set up in London, and its leaders were determined—especially after the discovery in 1943 of the murder of some 5,000 Polish officers several years earlier at Katyn, in Russia, presumably by the Soviet secret police—to make no concessions to Soviet territorial demands. Public opinion in Poland (and indeed in all the states along Russia's western frontier) was not so much anti-Soviet as anti-Russian. Yet the Soviet Union's legitimate interests could not be ignored.

Yalta and Potsdam

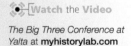

The Big Three Conference at Yalta at **myhistorylab.com**

At the **Yalta Conference**, Roosevelt and Churchill agreed to Soviet annexation of large sections of eastern Poland. In return they demanded that free elections be held in Poland itself. Stalin agreed, almost certainly without intending to keep his promise. The elections were never held; Poland was run by a pro-Soviet puppet regime.

Stalin apparently could not understand why the Allies were so concerned about the fate of a small country remote from their strategic spheres. That they professed to be concerned seemed to him an indication that they had some secret, devious purpose. Roosevelt, however, was worried about the political effects that Soviet control of Poland might have in the United States. Polish Americans would be furious if the United States allowed the Soviets to control their homeland.

But had Roosevelt described the difficulties to the Polish Americans and the rest of the American people more frankly, their

Churchill, Roosevelt, and Stalin meet at the Yalta, U.S.S.R., conference in February 1945. By April 1945, Roosevelt was dead.

reaction might have been less angry. In any case, when he realized that Stalin was going to act as he pleased, Roosevelt was furious. In July 1945, following the surrender of Germany, the new president, Harry Truman, met with Stalin and Churchill at Potsdam, outside Berlin.[2] At the **Potsdam Conference** they agreed to try the Nazi leaders as war criminals, made plans for exacting reparations from Germany, and confirmed the division of the country into four zones to be occupied separately by American, Soviet, British, and French troops. Berlin, deep in the Soviet zone, had itself been split into four sectors. Stalin rejected all arguments that he loosen his hold on Eastern Europe, and Truman made no concessions. But he was impressed by Stalin.

On both sides suspicions were mounting, positions hardening. Yet all the advantages seemed to be with the United States. Was this not, as Henry Luce, the publisher of *Time* had declared, "the American century," an era when American power and American ideals would shape the course of events the world over? Besides its army, navy, and air force and its immense industrial potential, alone among the nations the United States possessed the atomic bomb. When Stalin's actions made it clear that he intended to control Eastern Europe and to exert influence elsewhere in the world, most Americans expressed resentment tempered by amazement. It took time for them to realize that the war had caused a fundamental change in international politics. The United States might be the strongest country in the world, but the western European nations, victor and vanquished alike, were reduced to their own and America's surprise to the status of second-class powers. The Soviet Union, on the other hand, had gained more influence than it had held under the czars and regained the territory it had lost as a result of World War I and the communist revolution.

---

[2]Clement R. Attlee replaced Churchill during the conference after his Labour party won the British elections.

Milestones

1941	Roosevelt prohibits discrimination in defense plants (Fair Employment Practices Committee)	1943	Roosevelt, Churchill, Stalin meet at Tehran, Iran
	Japan attacks Pearl Harbor	1944	Allies invade Normandy, France (D-Day)
	Roosevelt and Churchill draft Atlantic Charter		Battle of the Bulge exhausts German reserves
1942	Executive Order 9066 sends Japanese Americans to relocation camps	1945	Big Three meet at Yalta Conference
	Japanese take Philippines		Fifty nations draft UN Charter at San Francisco
	Carrier-based planes dominate Battle of Coral Sea		Roosevelt dies; Truman becomes president
	U.S. airpower takes control of central Pacific at Battle of Midway		Germany surrenders (V-E Day)
	U.S. troops invade North Africa		United States tests atom bomb at Alamogordo, New Mexico
1943	Oppenheimer directs Manhattan Project to make atom bomb		Truman, Churchill, Stalin meet at Potsdam
	Race riots rage in Detroit and Los Angeles		United States drops atom bombs on Hiroshima and Nagasaki, Japan
	Allies invade Italy		Japan surrenders (V-J Day)

✓● Study and Review at www.myhistorylab.com

Review Questions

1. What did the U.S. government do to mobilize for war? How did the war affect women and minority groups?
2. Why did FDR order that American citizens of Japanese ancestry be placed in internment camps? What was the Supreme Court's response to the constitutionality of this decision?
3. Why, since Japan attacked first, did FDR decide to commit most American resources to defeating the Germans in Europe? What were the key phases of the war in Europe? Of the war in the Pacific?
4. What role did science and technology play in the war?
5. Should Truman have used atomic bombs against Japan? Why had American relations with the Soviet Union deteriorated by 1945?

Key Terms

Allies
D-Day

internment camps
Potsdam Conference

United Nations (UN)
Yalta Conference

Collision Courses, Abroad and at Home: 1946–1960

Do you ever drive too fast?

IN 2009 OVER 10,000 PEOPLE BETWEEN THE AGES OF SIXTEEN AND twenty-four were killed in motor vehicle accidents—the leading cause of death among young people. Each month nearly as many Americans died in car crashes as perished at the World Trade Center on September 11, 2001. American traffic fatalities totaled 34,000.

But it could have been worse—and once was. During the decade of the 1970s, a half million Americans died in traffic accidents—over 50,000 each year. Since Henry Ford first rolled out the Model-T, over three and a half million Americans have died on the nation's roads and highways. Despite the carnage, automobiles have become so much a part of American life that few can imagine living without them.

The ascendancy of the automobile over mass transit was well-established during the 1930s. But World War II put more Americans in motion than ever before. Afterwards, car ownership soared. Designers produced faster and heavier cars for "a wartime generation" that was far "bigger, taller and more active" than its predecessors. Americans hurtled along the new superhighways that the federal government built in part for military purposes.

The American nation, too, was rushing into a new era of Cold War confrontation with the Soviet Union. In both countries new weapons loomed larger, each more menacing than the last. By 1960, hundreds of millions of people could be wiped out in an instant. The Cold War between the superpowers turned hot in Korea, the Middle East, and Latin America. Real foreign spies exacerbated fears of domestic subversion.

Postwar complacency soon gave way to racial confrontation at home. African Americans who had helped defeat Nazi racism accelerated demands for fair treatment. First they challenged Jim Crow segregation in the courts. When these initiatives encountered segregationist roadblocks, they turned to nonviolent protests that they knew would likely trigger violent responses.

From 1946 through 1960, Americans lived dangerously in a postwar era of menacing uncertainty.

From Chapter 28 of *American Destiny: Narrative of a Nation*, Combined Volume, Fourth Edition. Mark C. Carnes and John A. Garraty. Copyright © 2012 by Pearson Education, Inc. Published by Pearson Prentice Hall. All rights reserved.

The Postwar Economy

Economists had feared that the flood of millions of veterans into the job market would cause serious unemployment. But the widespread craving for cars—bigger, faster, and "loaded" with features such as radios and air-conditioners—fueled the postwar economic boom. During the decade of the 1920s American factories had produced 31 million cars. In the 1950s, 58 million rolled off the assembly lines; during the 1960s, 77 million were made. The proliferation of cars contributed to the expansion of related industries, especially oil. Gasoline consumption first touched 15 billion gallons in 1931; it soared to 35 billion gallons in 1950 and to 92 billion in 1970.

Although the car industry was the leading postwar economic sector, war-weary Americans also bought new houses, washing machines, and countless other products. Unable to buy such goods during the war, they used their war-enforced savings to go on a shopping spree that kept factories operating at capacity.

In addition, the government made an unprecedented educational opportunity available to veterans. Instead of a general bonus, which would have stimulated consumption and inflation, in 1944 Congress passed the *GI Bill of Rights*, which made subsidies available to veterans so they could continue their educations, learn new trades, or start new businesses. After the war nearly 8 million veterans took advantage of the education and training grants.

Economic prosperity in the decades after World War II allowed the federal government to increase its military and economic commitments abroad without raising taxes.

Truman Becomes President

When Harry S Truman received the news of Roosevelt's death in 1945, he claimed that he felt as though "the moon, the stars, and all the planets" had suddenly fallen upon him. Although he could not have been quite as surprised as he indicated (Roosevelt was known to have been in extremely poor health), he was acutely conscious of his own limitations.

Truman was born in Missouri in 1884. He served in a World War I artillery unit, and later became a minor cog in the political machine of Democratic boss Tom Pendergast. In 1934 Truman was elected to the U.S. Senate, where he proved to be a loyal but obscure New Dealer. He first attracted national attention during World War II when his "watchdog" committee on defense spending, working with devotion and efficiency, saved the government immense sums. This led to his nomination and election as vice president.

Levittown, New York, in 1949 epitomizes the postwar housing boom.

As president, Truman sought to carry on in the Roosevelt tradition. Curiously, he was at the same time humble and cocky, even brash—both idealistic and cold-bloodedly political. He adopted liberal objectives only to pursue them sometimes by rash, even repressive means. On balance, however, he was a strong and, in many ways, successful president.

But he lost a major battle early on. In June 1947, the new Congress passed the **Taft-Hartley Act**. It outlawed the closed shop (a provision written into many labor contracts requiring new workers to join the union before they could be employed). Most important, it authorized the president to seek court injunctions to prevent strikes that, in his opinion, endangered the national interest.

Truman vetoed the bill, but Congress overrode it. The Taft-Hartley Act made the task of unionizing industries more difficult, but it did not seriously hamper existing unions.

The Containment Policy

Although he was vice president during much of World War II, Truman had been excluded from all foreign policy discussions. He was not granted full security clearance and thus knew little about the Manhattan Project. While FDR had concluded at Yalta that he could charm or otherwise personally cope with the Soviet dictator, Truman resolved to deal with Stalin firmly.

Repeatedly Stalin made it clear that he had no intention of even consulting with Western leaders about his domination of Eastern Europe, and he seemed intent on extending his power deep into war-devastated central Europe. By January 1946 Truman had decided to stop "babying" the Russians.

Truman's problem was that Stalin had far more military divisions than anyone else. Truman had swiftly responded to the postwar clamor to "bring the boys home." In the two years following the surrender of Japan, the armed forces of the United States had dwindled from 6 million to 1.5 million. Stalin, who kept domestic foes out of office by shooting them, ignored domestic pressure to demobilize the Red Army, estimated by U.S. intelligence at twice the size of the American army.

Stalin and the mighty Red Army evoked the image of Hitler's troops pouring across the north European plains. Like Hitler, Stalin was a cruel dictator who championed an ideology of world conquest. George Kennan, a scholarly foreign officer who also had served in Moscow, thought that ideology was more symptom than cause. Marxism, he wrote, provided the intellectual "fig-leaf of morality and respectability" for naked Soviet aggression. In an influential article, "The Sources of Soviet Conduct," published anonymously in the July 1947 issue of *Foreign Affairs*, Kennan argued that the instability and illegitimacy of the Soviet regime generated explosive internal pressures. These forces, vented outward, would cause the Soviet Union to

A propaganda poster enshrining Stalin proclaims that he has led his people "Forward to Communism!"

Photo Credit: Hoover Institution Archives, Stanford, CA.

expand "constantly, wherever it is permitted to move" until it filled "every nook and cranny available to it in the basin of world power." A policy of "long-term, patient but firm and vigilant containment" was the best means of dealing with the Soviet Union.

The Atom Bomb: A "Winning" Weapon?

Although Truman authorized use of the atom bomb to force the surrender of Japan, he had hoped that a demonstration of the weapon's power also would inhibit Stalin and serve as a counterweight to the Red Army. Stalin, however, refused to be intimidated. He knew that the American atomic arsenal—slightly more than a dozen bombs in 1947—was insufficient to destroy the Soviet Union's military machine.

The atomic bomb was a doubtful deterrent for another reason. Sobering accounts of the devastation of Hiroshima and Nagasaki and the suffering of the victims of radiation poisoning left many Americans uneasy. Even Truman doubted whether the American people would again "permit" their president to use atomic weapons for aggressive purposes.

In November 1945 the United States suggested that the UN supervise all nuclear energy production, and the General Assembly created an Atomic Energy Commission to study the question. In June 1946 Commissioner Bernard Baruch offered a plan for the eventual outlawing of atomic weapons. Under this proposal UN inspectors operating without restriction anywhere in the world would ensure that no country made bombs clandestinely. When, at an unspecified date, the system was established successfully, the United States would destroy its stockpile of bombs.

Most Americans thought the Baruch plan magnanimous, and some considered it positively foolhardy, but the Soviets rejected it. They would neither permit UN inspectors in the Soviet Union nor surrender the Soviet Union's veto power over Security Council actions dealing with atomic energy. They demanded that the United States destroy its bombs at once. American leaders did not comply; they believed that the atom bomb would be, in Baruch's words, their "winning weapon" for years to come.

A Turning Point in Greece

The strategy of containment began to take shape early in 1947 as a result of a crisis in Greece. Greek communists, waging a guerrilla war against the monarchy, were receiving aid from communist Yugoslavia and Bulgaria. Great Britain had been assisting the monarchists but could no longer afford this drain on its resources. In February 1947 the British informed President Truman that they would cut off aid to Greece.

The British predicament forced American policymakers to confront the fact that their European allies had not been able to rebuild their war-weakened economies. That the Soviet Union was actually discouraging the Greek rebels out of fear of American intervention in the area the policymakers ignored.

Truman asked Congress to approve what became known as the **Truman Doctrine**. If Greece or Turkey fell to the communists, he said, all of the Middle East might be lost. To prevent this "unspeakable tragedy," he asked for $400 million in military and economic aid to Greece and Turkey. "It must be the policy of the United States to support free peoples who are resisting attempted subjugation by armed minorities or by outside pressures," he said.

⊶ Read the Document

Truman Doctrine, 1947
at **myhistorylab.com**

By exaggerating the consequences of inaction and by justifying his request on ideological grounds, Truman obtained his objective. The result was the establishment of a right-wing, military-dominated government in Greece. In addition, by not limiting his request to the specific problem posed by the situation in Greece, Truman caused considerable concern in many countries.

The threat to Western Europe certainly loomed large in 1947. The entire continent seemed in danger of falling into communist hands without the Soviet Union raising a finger.

The Marshall Plan and the Lesson of History

In a 1946 speech entitled "The Lesson of History," George C. Marshall, army chief of staff during World War II, reminded Americans that their isolationism had contributed to Hitler's unchecked early aggression. This time, Marshall noted, the people of the United States must be prepared to act against foreign aggressors. In 1947 Marshall was named secretary of state. He outlined an extraordinary plan by which the United States would finance the reconstruction of the European economy. "Hunger, poverty, desperation, and chaos" were the real enemies of freedom and democracy, Marshall said. The need was to restore "the confidence of the European people in the economic future of their own countries." Even the Soviet Union and Soviet-bloc nations would be eligible for American aid.

The European powers eagerly seized upon what became known as the **Marshall Plan**, a massive infusion of American aid to rebuild Europe after World War II. European leaders set up a sixteen-nation Committee for European Economic Cooperation, which soon submitted plans calling for up to $22.4 billion in American assistance.

The Soviet Union and its European satellites were tempted by the offer and sent representatives to the initial planning meetings. But Stalin grew anxious that his satellite states would be drawn into the orbit of the United States. He recalled his delegates and demanded that Soviet bloc nations do likewise. Those who hesitated were ordered to report to the Kremlin. "I went to Moscow as the Foreign Minister of an independent sovereign state," Jan Masaryk of Czechoslovakia commented bitterly. "I returned as a lackey of the Soviet government."

In February 1948 a communist coup took over the Czechoslovak government; Masaryk fell (or more likely was pushed) out a window to his death. These strong-arm tactics brought to mind the Nazi takeover of Czechoslovakia a decade earlier and helped persuade Congress to appropriate over $13 billion for the Marshall aid program. Results exceeded all expectations. By 1951 Western Europe was booming.

But Europe was now divided in two. In the West, where American-influenced governments were elected, private property was respected if often taxed heavily, and corporations gained influence and power. In the East, where the Soviet Union imposed its will and political system on client states, deep-seated resentment festered among subject peoples.

In March 1948 Great Britain, France, Belgium, the Netherlands, and Luxembourg signed an alliance aimed at social, cultural, and economic collaboration. The Western nations abandoned their understandable but counterproductive policy of crushing Germany economically. They announced plans for creating a single West German Republic with a large degree of autonomy.

In June 1948 the Soviet Union retaliated by closing off surface access to Berlin from the west. For a time it seemed that the Allies must either fight their way into the city or abandon it to the communists. Unwilling to adopt either alternative, Truman decided to fly

Recipients of Marshall Plan Aid, 1948–1952 Marshall Plan aid was originally offered to the Soviet Union and communist bloc states. Stalin, however, refused to accept American aid and ordered Soviet satellites to refuse, too. All did, except Yugoslavia, whose disobedience infuriated Stalin.

supplies to the capital from Frankfurt, Hannover, and Hamburg. American C-47 and C-54 transports delivered enough food, fuel, and other goods necessary to maintain more than 2 million West Berliners. The **Berlin airlift** put the Soviets in an uncomfortable position; if they were determined to keep supplies from West Berlin, they would have to start the fighting. They were not prepared to do so. In May 1949 they lifted the blockade.

American generals intensified preparation of contingency plans in the event of a Soviet attack.

The Election of 1948

In the spring of 1948 President Truman's fortunes were at low ebb. Public opinion polls suggested that a majority of the people considered him incompetent or worse. The Republicans seemed so sure to win the 1948 presidential election that many prominent

Democrats began to talk of denying Truman the nomination. Two of FDR's sons came out for General Eisenhower as the Democratic candidate. Governor Dewey, who again won the Republican nomination, ran confidently (even complacently), certain that he would carry the country.

Truman's position seemed hopeless because he had alienated both southern conservatives and northern liberals. The Southerners were particularly distressed because in 1946 the president had established a Committee on Civil Rights, which had recommended antilynching and antipoll tax legislation and the creation of a permanent Fair Employment Practices Commission. When the Democratic convention adopted a civil rights plank, the southern delegates walked out. Southern conservatives then founded the States' Rights ("Dixiecrat") party and nominated J. Strom Thurmond of South Carolina for president.

In 1948 the strongly Republican *Chicago Daily Tribune* printed its post-election headlines before all the returns were in. For Truman, it was the perfect climax to his hard-won victory.

As for the liberals, in 1947 a group that believed Truman's containment policy a threat to world peace organized a new Progressive party and nominated former Vice President Henry A. Wallace. With two minor candidates sure to cut into the Democratic vote, the president's chances seemed minuscule.

Truman launched an aggressive whistle-stop campaign. He excoriated the "do-nothing" Republican Congress, which had rejected his program and passed the Taft-Hartley Act, and he warned labor, farmers, and consumers that if Dewey won, Republican "gluttons of privilege" would do away with all the gains of the New Deal years.

Millions were moved by Truman's arguments and by his courageous fight against great odds. The success of the Berlin airlift during the presidential campaign helped him considerably, as did disaffection among normally Republican midwestern farmers. The Progressive party fell increasingly into the hands of communist sympathizers, driving away many liberals who might otherwise have supported Wallace.

The president reinvigorated the New Deal coalition and won an amazing upset victory on election day. He collected 24.1 million votes to Dewey's 21.9 million, the two minor candidates being held to about 2.3 million. In the Electoral College his margin was a thumping 303 to 189.

Truman's victory encouraged him to press forward with what he called his **Fair Deal** program. He urged Congress to raise the minimum wage, fund an ambitious public housing program, develop a national health insurance system, and repeal the Taft-Hartley Act. However, relatively little of Truman's Fair Deal was enacted into law. Congress approved a federal housing program and measures increasing the minimum wage and Social Security benefits, but these were merely extensions of New Deal legislation.

Containing Communism Abroad

During Truman's second term the confrontation between the United States and the Soviet Union dominated the headlines. To strengthen ties with the European democracies, in April 1949 the North Atlantic Treaty was signed in Washington. The United States, Great Britain, France, Italy, Belgium, the Netherlands, Luxembourg, Denmark, Norway, Portugal, Iceland, and Canada[1] agreed "that an armed attack against one or more of them in Europe or North America shall be considered an attack against them all" and that in the event of such an attack each would take "individually and in concert with the other Parties, such action as it deems necessary, including the use of armed force." The pact established the **North Atlantic Treaty Organization (NATO)**.

In September 1949 the Soviet Union detonated an atomic bomb. When the explosion was confirmed, Truman called for rapid expansion of the American nuclear arsenal. He also asked his advisers to determine whether the United States should develop a new weapon thousands of times more destructive than atomic bombs. The "super" or hydrogen bomb would replicate the fusion process on the surface of the sun. The Atomic Energy Commission argued that there was no military use for hydrogen bombs, which would destroy hundreds of square miles as well as precipitate a dangerous arms race with the Soviet Union. The Joint Chiefs of Staff disagreed. Even if the hydrogen bomb could not be used in battle, they argued, its mere existence would intimidate enemies; and, the military men added, the Soviets would themselves build a hydrogen bomb whether or not the United States did so. (Unbeknownst to American leaders, Stalin had already ordered development of the hydrogen bomb.) On January 31, 1950, Truman publicly announced that "though none wants to use it" he had no choice but to proceed with a hydrogen bomb.

In Asia the effort to contain communism in China had failed utterly. After World War II, Nationalists under Chiang Kai-shek (sometimes spelled Jiang Jieshi) dominated the south; communists under Mao Zedong controlled much of the north. Truman tried to bring Chiang's Nationalists and Mao's communists together. He sent General Marshall to China to seek a settlement, but neither Chiang nor Mao would make significant concessions. In January 1947 Truman recalled Marshall and named him secretary of state. Soon thereafter civil war, suspended during the Japanese occupation, erupted in China.

By the end of 1949 communist armies had administered a crushing defeat to the nationalists. The remnants of Chiang Kai-shek's forces fled to the island of Formosa, now called Taiwan. Mao ruled China. The "loss" of China to communism strengthened right-wing elements in the Republican party. They charged that Truman had not backed the Nationalists strongly enough and that he had stupidly underestimated Mao's dedication to the cause of world revolution.

Containment had relied on American money, materials, and know-how, but not on American soldiers. In early 1950, Truman proposed to pare the budget by further reducing the nation's armed forces. Truman also called for a thorough review of the concept of containment. Dean Acheson, who recently had succeeded George Marshall as secretary of state, supervised the study. In March, it was submitted to the National Security Council, assigned a numerical designation (NSC-68), classified top secret, and sent to the nation's military and diplomatic leaders for review.

---

[1] In 1952, Greece and Turkey joined the alliance, and in 1954 so did West Germany.

NSC-68 called for an enormous military expansion. The Soviet Union, it declared, was engaged in a worldwide assault on freedom. Instead of relying on other nations, the United States itself must develop sufficient military forces to stop communism from spreading *anywhere in the world*. Military spending therefore had to be increased from $14 billion to nearly $50 billion. If the Soviet Union failed to keep up with the American expenditures, it would no longer pose a military threat, and if it attempted to match the high levels of American military spending, its less efficient economic system would collapse from the strain.

The document was submitted to Truman on April 7, 1950. He had planned significant cuts to the defense budget; the prospect of increasing it by 350 percent appalled him. Within a few months, however, events in Korea changed his mind.

Hot War in Korea

After World War II the province of Korea was taken from Japan and divided at 38° north latitude into the Democratic People's Republic in the north, backed by the Soviet Union, and the Republic of Korea in the south, backed by the United States and

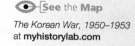

See the Map

The Korean War, 1950–1953
at **myhistorylab.com**

the UN. Both powers withdrew their troops from the peninsula. The Soviets left behind a well-armed local force, but the Republic of Korea's army was small and ill-trained.

America's first line of defense against communism in East Asia was to be its island bases in Japan and the Philippines. In a speech in January 1950 Acheson deliberately excluded Korea from what he described as the "defensive perimeter" of the United States in Asia. It was up to the South Koreans, backed by the UN, to protect themselves, Acheson said. This encouraged the North Koreans to attack. In June 1950, when their armored divisions, led by 150 Soviet-made tanks, rumbled across the thirty-eighth parallel, the South Koreans failed to stop them.

Truman was at his family home in Independence, Missouri, when Acheson telephoned with the news of the North Korean attack. On the flight to Washington, Truman recalled how the communists in Korea were acting "just as Hitler, Mussolini, and the Japanese had acted ten, fifteen, and twenty years earlier." "If this were allowed to go unchallenged," he concluded, "it would mean a third world war, just as similar incidents had brought on the Second World War." With the backing of the UN Security Council (but without asking Congress to declare war), he sent American planes into battle.[2] Ground troops soon followed. Truman also ordered the adoption of NSC-68 "as soon as feasible."

Nominally the Korean War was a struggle between the invaders and the United Nations. General MacArthur, placed in command, flew the blue UN flag over his headquarters, and sixteen nations supplied troops for his army. However, more than 90 percent of the forces were American. At first the North Koreans pushed them back rapidly, but in September a front was stabilized around the port of Pusan, at the southern tip of Korea. Then MacArthur executed a brilliant amphibious invasion, landing at the west coast city of Inchon, fifty miles south of the thirty-eighth parallel. Their lines of supply destroyed, the North Koreans retreated in disorder. By October the battlefront had moved north of the 1945 boundary.

---

[2]The Soviet Union, which could have vetoed this action, was at the moment boycotting the Security Council because the UN had refused to give the Mao Zedong regime China's seat on that body.

General MacArthur now proposed the conquest of North Korea, even if it meant bombing "privileged sanctuaries" on the Chinese side of the Korean border. A few of Truman's civilian advisers, the most important being George Kennan, opposed advancing into North Korea, fearing intervention not only by the Red Chinese but also by the Soviets.

Truman authorized MacArthur to advance as far as the Yalu River, the boundary between North Korea and China. It was an unfortunate decision. As the advance progressed, ominous reports came from north of the Yalu. Mao's Foreign Minister warned that the Chinese would not tolerate seeing their neighbors being "savagely invaded by imperialists." Alarmed, Truman flew to Wake Island, in the Pacific, to confer with MacArthur. The general, who had a low opinion of Asian soldiers, assured him that the Chinese would not dare to intervene. If they did, he added, his army would crush them easily; the war would be over by Christmas.

The Chinese counteroffensive of November 1950 caught the Americans by surprise and cut off many units. Here, a U.S. Marine rests during the retreat that winter.

Photo Credit: CORBIS-NY.

Seldom has a general miscalculated so badly. Ignoring intelligence reports and dividing his advancing units, he drove toward the Yalu recklessly. Suddenly, on November 26, thirty-three Chinese divisions, hidden along the interior mountains of Korea, smashed through the center of MacArthur's lines. Overnight a triumphant advance became a bloody, disorganized retreat. MacArthur now spoke of the "bottomless well of Chinese manpower" and justified his earlier confidence by claiming that he was fighting "an entirely new war."

The UN army rallied south of the thirty-eighth parallel, and MacArthur then urged that he be permitted to bomb Chinese installations north of the Yalu. He also suggested a naval blockade of the coast of China and the use of Chinese Nationalist troops. Truman rejected these proposals on the ground that they would lead to a third world war. MacArthur, who tended to ignore the larger political aspects of the conflict, attempted to rouse Congress and the public against the president by openly criticizing administration policy. Truman ordered him to be silent. When the general persisted in his criticisms, Truman fired him.

As the months passed and the casualties mounted, many citizens became disillusioned and angry. Military men backed the president almost unanimously. General Omar N. Bradley, chairman of the Joint Chiefs of Staff, said that a showdown with communist China "would involve us in the wrong war, at the wrong place, at the wrong time and with the wrong enemy." In June 1951 the communists agreed to discuss an armistice in Korea, although the negotiations dragged on interminably. The war was unresolved when Truman left office: by the time it was over, it had produced 157,000 American casualties, including 54,200 dead.

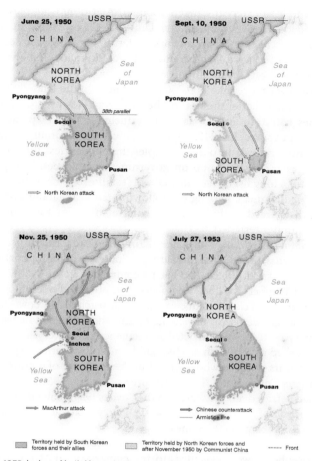

Korean War, 1950–1953 In June, North Korea nearly overran South Korea (top maps). But in September MacArthur counterattacked at Inchon and advanced far into North Korea (bottom left). The intervention of the Chinese in November led to a stalemate (bottom right).

If the Korean War persuaded Truman to adopt NSC-68, it also exposed the failings of the policy. By conceiving of communism as a monolithic force it tended to make it so, driving Red China and the Soviet Union into each other's arms. By committing American military forces to potential trouble spots throughout the world, it increased the likelihood they would prevail in none.

The Communist Issue at Home

The Korean War highlighted the paradox that, at the pinnacle of its power, the influence of the United States in world affairs was declining. Its monopoly on nuclear weapons had been lost. China had passed into the communist orbit. Elsewhere in Asia and throughout Africa, new nations, formerly colonial possessions of the Western powers, were adopting a "neutralist" position in the Cold War. Despite the billions poured into armaments and foreign aid, national security seemed far from ensured.

Internal as well as external dangers loomed. Alarming examples of communist espionage in Canada, Great Britain, and the United States convinced many citizens that clever conspirators were everywhere at work undermining American security. Both the Republicans and conservative Democratic critics of Truman's domestic policies were charging that he was "soft" on communists.

There were never more than 100,000 communists in the United States, and party membership plummeted after the start of the Cold War. However, the possibility that a handful of spies could do enormous damage fueled a kind of panic that could be used for partisan purposes. In 1947, hoping to defuse the communists-in-government issue by being more zealous in pursuit of spies than his critics, Truman established a Loyalty Review Board to check up on government employees. The program made even sympathy for a long list of vaguely defined "totalitarian" or "subversive" organizations grounds for dismissal. During the following ten years about 2,700 government workers were discharged, only a relative handful of them for legitimate reasons. A much larger number resigned.

In 1948 Whittaker Chambers, an editor of *Time* who had formerly been a communist, charged that Alger Hiss, president of the Carnegie Endowment for International Peace and a former State Department official, had been a communist in the 1930s. Hiss denied the charge and sued Chambers for libel. Chambers then produced microfilms purporting to show that Hiss had copied classified documents for dispatch to Moscow. Hiss could not be indicted for espionage because of the statute of limitations; instead he was charged with perjury. In January 1950, he was convicted and sentenced to a five-year jail term.

If a distinguished official such as Hiss had been disloyal, anything seemed possible. The case fed the fears of those who believed in the existence of a powerful communist underground in the United States. The disclosure in February 1950 that a British scientist, Klaus Fuchs, had betrayed atomic secrets to the Soviets heightened these fears, as did the arrest and conviction of his American associate, Harry Gold, and two other Americans, Julius and Ethel Rosenberg, on the same charge.

Although they were not major spies and the information they revealed was not crucial, the Rosenbergs were executed, to the consternation of many liberals in the United States and elsewhere. However, information gathered by other spies had speeded the Soviet development of nuclear weapons. This fact encouraged some Republicans to press the communists-in-government issue hard.

McCarthyism

In February 1950 an obscure senator, Joseph R. McCarthy of Wisconsin, introduced this theme in a speech to the even less well-known Ohio County Republican Women's Club of Wheeling, West Virginia. "The reason we find ourselves in a position of impotency," he stated, "is not because our only powerful potential enemy has sent men to invade our shores, but rather because of the traitorous actions of those who have been treated so well by this nation." The State Department, he added, was "infested" with communists.

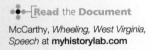

Read the Document

McCarthy, *Wheeling, West Virginia, Speech* at **myhistorylab.com**

McCarthy had no shred of evidence to back up these statements, as a Senate committee headed by the conservative Democrat Millard Tydings of Maryland soon demonstrated. He never exposed a single spy or secret American communist.

But because of the government loyalty program, the Hiss case, and other recent events, thousands of people were too eager to believe McCarthy to listen to reason. Within a few weeks he was the most talked of person in Congress. When McCarthy's victims indignantly denied his charges, he distracted the public with still more sensational accusations directed at other innocents. Even General Marshall, whose patriotism was beyond question, was subjected to McCarthy's abuse. The general, he said, was "steeped in falsehood," part of a "conspiracy so immense and an infamy so black as to dwarf any previous venture in the history of man."

McCarthy was totally unscrupulous and his crude tactics would have failed if the public had not been so worried about communism. The worries were caused by the reality of Soviet military power, the attack on Korea, the loss of the nuclear monopoly, and the stories about spies, some of them true.

Dwight D. Eisenhower

As the 1952 presidential election approached, Truman's popularity was again at low ebb; he chose not to seek reelection. In choosing their candidate, the Republicans passed over the twice-defeated Dewey and their most prominent leader, Senator Robert A. Taft of Ohio, an outspoken conservative, and nominated General Dwight D. Eisenhower.

Eisenhower's popularity did not grow merely out of his achievements in World War II. His genial personality and evident desire to avoid controversy proved widely appealing. In his reluctance to seek political office, Eisenhower reminded the country of George Washington, whereas his seeming ignorance of current political issues was no more a handicap to his campaign than the similar ignorance of Jackson and Grant in their times. People "liked Ike" because his management of the Allied armies suggested that he would be equally competent as head of the complex federal government. Eisenhower's campaign was also the first to use television effectively. It featured what came to be known as "spots," twenty-second tapes of candidate Eisenhower responding to questions about his opinions on issues, important and trivial. Eisenhower's promise during the campaign to go to Korea if elected to try to bring the war to an end was a political masterstroke.

Many critics lampooned Eisenhower for his banal amusements. A popular bumper sticker read: "BEN HOGAN [a famous golfer] FOR PRESIDENT. IF WE'RE GOING TO HAVE A GOLFER FOR PRESIDENT, LET'S HAVE A GOOD ONE." Others have viewed Eisenhower's passion for golf as characteristic of his presidential style: methodical, prudent, and, when in the rough, disarmingly shrewd.

The Democrats nominated Governor Adlai E. Stevenson of Illinois, whose grandfather had been vice president under Grover Cleveland. Stevenson's unpretentiousness was appealing, and his witty, urbane speeches captivated intellectuals. In retrospect, however, it is clear that he had not the remotest chance of defeating the popular Eisenhower.

The result was a Republican landslide: Eisenhower received almost 34 million votes to Stevenson's 27 million, and in the Electoral College his margin was 442 to 89.

On the surface, Eisenhower seemed the antithesis of Truman. The Republicans had charged the Democratic administration with being wasteful and extravagant, and Eisenhower planned to run his administration on sound business principles. He spoke scornfully of "creeping socialism," called for more local control of government affairs, and promised to reduce federal spending to balance the budget and cut taxes. He believed that by battling with Congress and pressure groups over the details of legislation, his immediate predecessors had sacrificed part of their status as chief representative of the American people.

Eisenhower proved to be an excellent politician. He knew how to be flexible without compromising his basic values. His "conservatism" became first "dynamic conservatism" and then "progressive moderation."

Yet his policies toward illegal Mexican immigrants and native Americans proved less than humane. In 1954 he authorized Operation Wetback, which rounded up and deported nearly a million illegal Mexican immigrants. He also sought to weaken New Deal policies that strengthened Native American tribes as political entities. Indian leaders resisted this change, and the policy ended in 1961.

The Eisenhower-Dulles Foreign Policy

The American people, troubled and uncertain over the stalemate in Korea, counted on Eisenhower to find a way to employ the nation's immense strength constructively. The new president shared the general feeling that a change of tactics in foreign affairs was needed. He counted on his secretary of state to solve the practical problems.

His choice, John Foster Dulles, was a lawyer with considerable diplomatic experience. He had been an outspoken critic of Truman's policy of containment. In a May 1952 article in *Life* entitled "A Policy of Boldness," he argued that global military containment was both expensive and ineffective. Instead of waiting for the communist powers to make a move and then "containing" them, the United States would build so many powerful nuclear weapons that the Soviet Union or communist China wouldn't dare take provocative actions. An

An eleven-megaton hyrdrogen bomb is detonated over Bikini Atoll in March 1954. One megaton had the explosive power of 1 million tons of TNT. (The bomb that had destroyed Hiroshima had the equivalent of 12,500 tons of TNT.) An earlier atom bomb test at Bikini Island prompted a French fashion designer to give the name "bikini" to his explosively provocative bathing suit.

immense arsenal of nuclear bombs, loaded on the nation's formidable fleet of bombers, would ensure a **massive retaliation** against any aggressor. Such a "new look" military would be cheaper to maintain than a large standing army, and it would prevent the United States from being caught up in "local" conflicts like the Korean War.

Korea offered the first test of his views. After Eisenhower's post-election trip to Korea failed to bring an end to the war, Dulles signaled his willingness to use tactical nuclear weapons in Korea by showily transferring nuclear warheads from the United States mainland to bomber units stationed in East Asia. Several weeks later, in July 1953, the Chinese signed an armistice that ended hostilities but left Korea divided. The administration interpreted the softening of the Chinese position as proof that the nuclear threat had worked.

Emboldened by his apparent triumph, Dulles again brandished the nation's nuclear arsenal. Chiang Kai-shek had stationed 90,000 soldiers—one-third of his army—in Quemoy and Matsu, two small islands located a few miles from mainland China. In 1954 the Chinese communists began shelling the islands, presumably in preparation to invade them. Chiang appealed for American protection, warning that loss of the islands would bring about the collapse of Nationalist China. At a press conference in 1955 Eisenhower announced his willingness to use nuclear weapons to defend the islands. The Chinese communists backed down.

Massive retaliation succeeded in reducing the defense budget by allowing Eisenhower to pare a half million men from the armed forces. On balance, however, Dulles's strategy was flawed, and many of his schemes were preposterous. Above all, massive retaliation was an extremely dangerous policy when the Soviet Union possessed nuclear weapons as powerful as those of the United States.

McCarthy Self-Destructs

Although the State Department was now controlled by Dulles, a Republican and hard-line anticommunist, Senator McCarthy refused to moderate his attacks on the department. In 1953 television newscaster Edwin R. Murrow cast doubt on McCarthy's methods; soon he and McCarthy were pummeling each other on television.

((•—[Hear the **Audio**

Joseph P. McCarthy Speech
at **myhistorylab.com**

But McCarthy finally overreached himself. Early in 1954 he turned his guns on the army, accusing Pentagon officials of trying to blackmail his committee. The resulting Army-McCarthy hearings, televised before the country, and Murrow's increasingly sharp criticisms, proved the senator's undoing. When the hearings ended in June 1954 after some million words of testimony, his spell had been broken.

The Senate, with President Eisenhower (who despised McCarthy but who considered it beneath his dignity as president to "get into the gutter with that guy") applying pressure behind the scenes, at last moved to censure him in December 1954. Although he continued to issue statements and wild charges, the country no longer listened. In 1957 he died of cirrhosis of the liver.

Asian Policy after Korea

Shortly after an armistice was finally arranged in Korea in July 1953, new trouble erupted far to the south in the former French colony of Indochina. Nationalist rebels led by the communist Ho Chi Minh had been harassing the French in Vietnam, one of the three puppet kingdoms (the others were Laos and Cambodia) fashioned by France in Indochina after the defeat of the Japanese. When China recognized the rebels, who were known as the Vietminh, and supplied them with arms, President Truman countered with economic and military assistance to the French, and President Eisenhower continued and expanded this assistance.

Early in 1954 Ho Chi Minh's troops trapped and besieged a French army in the remote stronghold of Dien Bien Phu. In May the garrison surrendered. Several months later France, Great Britain, the Soviet Union, and China signed an agreement dividing Vietnam along the seventeenth parallel. France withdrew from the area. The northern sector became the Democratic Republic of Vietnam, controlled by Ho Chi Minh; the southern sector remained in the hands of the emperor, Bao Dai. An election to settle the future of all Vietnam was scheduled for 1956.

When it seemed likely that the communists would win that election, Ngo Dinh Diem, a conservative anticommunist, overthrew Bao Dai and became president of South Vietnam. The United States supplied his government liberally with aid. The planned election was never held, and Vietnam remained divided.

Dulles responded to the diplomatic setback in Vietnam by establishing the Southeast Asia Treaty Organization (SEATO), but only three Asian nations—the Philippine Republic (which was granted independence in 1947), Thailand, and Pakistan—joined this alliance.[3]

Israel and the Middle East

Truman and Eisenhower had intervened in the Far East because of a direct communist threat. But as the American love affair with cars turned into an obsession, United States policymakers became increasingly attentive to the Middle East, where seas of oil had been recently discovered. Iran, Iraq, Kuwait, and Saudi Arabia sat upon nearly 60 percent of the world's known reserves.

After World War II, Zionists, who had long sought to promote Jewish immigration to Palestine, intensified their efforts. The slaughter of six million European Jews by the Nazis strengthened Jewish claims to a homeland and intensified pressure to allow hundreds of thousands of Jewish refugees to immigrate to Palestine, which was governed by Great Britain according to a League of Nations mandate. But the influx of Jewish settlers, and their calls for creation of a Jewish state (Israel), provoked Palestinian and Arab leaders. Fighting broke out. President Truman angered Arab leaders by endorsing the partition of the region into an Israeli and a Palestinian state. In 1947, the United Nations voted for partition and on May 14, 1948, the State of Israel was established. Within hours, Truman recognized its sovereignty.

Then Arab armies from Egypt, Jordan, Iraq, Syria, and Lebanon attacked Israel. Although badly outnumbered, the Israelis were better organized and better armed than the Arabs and drove them off with relative ease. Nearly a million local Arabs were displaced, causing a desperate refugee problem in nearby countries.

President Truman had consistently placed support for Israel before other considerations in the Middle East, partly because of the conviction that survivors of the Nazi holocaust were entitled to a country of their own and partly because of the political importance of the Jewish vote in the United States. Dulles and Eisenhower tried to restore

---

[3]The other signatories were Great Britain, France, the United States, Australia, and New Zealand.

balance and mollify the Arabs by deemphasizing American support of Israel. Gas-hungry Americans could ill afford to alienate the Arab world.

In 1952 Colonel Gamal Abdel Nasser emerged as the strongman of Egypt. The United States was prepared to lend Nasser money to build a huge dam on the Nile at Aswan that would provide irrigation and electric power for much of the region. However, Eisenhower would not sell Egypt arms, but the communists would.

For this reason Nasser drifted toward the communist orbit. When Eisenhower then decided not to finance the Aswan Dam, Nasser responded by nationalizing the Suez Canal. This move galvanized the British and French. In conjunction with the French, and without consulting the United States, the British in 1956 decided to take back the canal by force. The Israelis, alarmed by repeated Arab hit-and-run raids, also attacked Egypt.

Events moved swiftly. Israeli armored columns crushed the Egyptian army in the Sinai Peninsula in a matter of days. France and Britain occupied Port Said at the northern end of the canal. Nasser sank ships to block the channel. In the UN the Soviet Union and the United States introduced resolutions calling for a cease-fire. Both were vetoed by Britain and France.

Then the Soviet Union threatened to send "volunteers" to help defend Egypt and launch atomic missiles against France and Great Britain if they did not withdraw. Eisenhower also demanded that the invaders pull out of Egypt. On November 6, only nine days after the first Israeli units had invaded Egypt, British Prime Minister Anthony Eden announced a cease-fire. Israel withdrew its troops.

The United States had won a measure of respect in the Arab countries, but at what cost? Its major allies had been humiliated. Their ill-timed attack had enabled the Soviet Union to recover much of the prestige it had lost as a result of its brutal suppression of a Hungarian revolt that had broken out a week before the Suez fiasco.

When the Soviet Union seemed likely to profit from its "defense" of Egypt in the crisis, the president announced the Eisenhower Doctrine (January 1957), which stated that the United States was "prepared to use armed force" anywhere in the Middle East against "aggression from any country controlled by international communism." In practice, the Eisenhower Doctrine amounted to little more than a restatement of the containment policy.

Eisenhower and Khrushchev

In 1956 Eisenhower was reelected, defeating Adlai Stevenson even more decisively than he had in 1952. Despite evident satisfaction with their leader, however, the American people were in a sober mood. Hopes of pushing back the Soviet Union with clever stratagems and moral fervor were fading. Although the United States detonated the first hydrogen bomb in November 1952, the Soviets followed suit within six months. The Cold War between the superpowers had become yet more chilling.

Stalin died in March 1953, and after a period of internal conflict within the Kremlin, Nikita Khrushchev emerged as the new master of the Soviet Union. Prone to violent tantrums and tearful histrionics, Khrushchev delighted in shocking people with words and gestures. In the most famous of these, he pounded his shoe on the table during a debate at the United Nations. Although a product of the Soviet system, Khrushchev recognized its deep failings and resolved to purge it of Stalinism. He released political prisoners from Stalin's gulags, or political prison camps, and told wide-eyed party functionaries that Stalin had committed monstrous crimes.

Vice President Richard M. Nixon and Soviet leader Nikita Khrushchev engage in a "kitchen debate" over the future of capitalism at a Moscow trade fair in 1959. Although the encounter did little to advance United States-Soviet relations, it established Nixon's credentials as a tough negotiator.

Photo Credit: Elliot Erwitt/Magnum Photos, Inc.

Eisenhower, a seasoned analyst of military capabilities, understood that Khrushchev's antics were meant to conceal the Soviet Union's many weaknesses: the bitter opposition to Soviet rule among peoples of Eastern Europe; the deficiencies of the overcentralized Soviet economy, especially in agriculture; and the bureaucratic stultification of its armed forces. Thousands of American airplanes were based in Europe, northern Africa, and Turkey, placing most Soviet targets within easy range. The United States would win (whatever that meant) any nuclear war.

But this advantage disappeared in the exhaust trail of a Soviet rocket, launched on October 4, 1957, that carried a 184-pound capsule named *Sputnik* far above the atmosphere into earth orbit. Soon, American policymakers knew, Soviet missiles capable of reaching

Table 1 The Cold War Escalates

Year	Event	Significance
1947	George Kennan's "Sources of Soviet Conduct"	Outlines rationale for "containment" of Soviet Union
1947	Truman Doctrine	United States supports Greece and Turkey against communist threats
1948	Marshall Plan	United States provides economic aid to Western Europe
1949	Soviet Union detonates atom bomb	Truman calls for development of hydrogen bomb
1950	North Korea invades South Korea	Truman intervenes, as does communist China
1950	NSC-68 adopted	Truman authorizes worldwide expansion of U.S. military to stop Soviet aggression anywhere
1952	United States detonates hydrogen bomb	Soviet Union follows suit, 1953
1953	NSC-68 replaced with "massive retaliation"	Dulles-Eisenhower signal willingness to start a nuclear war to defend American interests
1957	Soviet Union launches *Sputnik*	Shows Soviet capacity to hit American targets with nuclear weapons

American soil would be tipped with nuclear warheads. The nation's far-flung network of bomber defenses had become obsolete, and with it the strategy of massive retaliation.

Eisenhower refused to take chances. He secretly authorized high-altitude American planes to spy on key Soviet military installations. On May 1, 1960, high over Sverdlovsk, an industrial center deep in the Soviet Union, an American U–2 spy plane was shot down by antiaircraft fire. The pilot of the plane survived the crash, and he confessed to being a spy. His cameras contained aerial photographs of Soviet military installations. When Eisenhower assumed full responsibility for the mission, Khrushchev accused the United States of "piratical" and "cowardly" acts of aggression.

Latin America Aroused

Events in Latin America compounded Eisenhower's difficulties. During World War II the United States, needing Latin American raw materials, had supplied its southern neighbors liberally with economic aid.

But as the Cold War progressed, the United States neglected Latin America. Economic problems plagued the region, and in most nations reactionary governments reigned. Radical Latin Americans accused the United States of supporting cliques of wealthy tyrants, whereas conservatives blamed insufficient American economic aid for the plight of the poor.

Eisenhower, eager to improve relations, stepped up economic assistance. Resistance to communism nonetheless continued to receive first priority. In 1954 the government of Jacobo Arbenz Guzman in Guatemala began to import Soviet weapons. The United States promptly dispatched arms to neighboring Honduras. Within a month an army led by an exiled Guatemalan officer marched into the country from Honduras and overthrew Arbenz. Elsewhere in Latin America, Eisenhower, as Truman had before him, continued to support regimes that were kept in power by the local military.

Events in Cuba demonstrated that there was no easy solution to Latin American problems. In 1959 a revolutionary movement headed by Fidel Castro overthrew Fulgencio Batista, one of the most noxious of the Latin American dictators. Eisenhower recognized the Castro government at once, but the Cuban leader soon began to criticize the United States in highly colored speeches. Castro confiscated American property without providing adequate compensation, suppressed civil liberties, and entered into close relations with the Soviet Union. After he negotiated a trade agreement with the Soviet Union in February 1960, which enabled the Russians to obtain Cuban sugar at bargain rates, the United States retaliated by prohibiting the importation of Cuban sugar into America.

Khrushchev then announced that if the United States intervened in Cuba, he would defend the country with atomic weapons. "The Monroe Doctrine has outlived its time," Khrushchev warned. Shortly before the end of his second term, Eisenhower broke off diplomatic relations with Cuba.

Fighting the Cold War at Home

The looming Soviet threat brought the Cold War closer to the American people than ever before. Such fears provided public support for increased spending on defense. In 1955 Eisenhower worried that a Soviet nuclear attack would plunge American cities into chaos. The roads out of threatened cities "would be the breeder of a deadly congestion within hours of an attack," he noted. He therefore backed a federally-funded highway system; this would not only facilitate the evacuation of cities but would also allow the army to mobilize more rapidly. The National Interstate and Defense Highway Act of 1956 became the largest public works project in the nation's history.

The Soviet Union's success in building atomic and hydrogen bombs, and especially in launching an orbiting satellite before the United States, also prompted Eisenhower to initiate a sweeping reform of the nation's schools. "The defense of the nation depends upon the mastery of modern techniques

This interchange near Seattle was part of the interstate highway system advanced by Eisenhower to facilitate both military transports and civilian evacuations.

developed from complex scientific principles," he declared. In 1958 he signed the National Defense Education Act. It provided federal aid to promote study of science, mathematics and foreign languages in large, comprehensive (and sometimes anonymous) high schools.

"Godless" communism posed an ideological as well as military threat. In 1954 the Reverend George Docherty warned his Presbyterian congregation in Washington, DC, that "little Muscovites" in the Soviet Union were pledging allegiance to "hammer and sickle" atheism. But an "atheistic American," he intoned, was "a contradiction in terms." Later that day Eisenhower, commenting on the sermon, told a radio audience that whatever their "personal creed," Americans still "believed in a higher power." A few months later he signed a law that added the phrase "one nation under God" to the Pledge of Allegiance. The next year, Congress added "In God We Trust" to the nation's currency.

◉ Watch the Video

Duck and Cover at myhistorylab.com

Blacks Challenge Segregation

Another front in the Cold War concerned race relations. How could African and Asian leaders be persuaded to reject communism and follow the example of the United States when American blacks were treated so poorly? American diplomats winced when the finance minister of Ghana was refused a meal at the Howard Johnson's, a chain restaurant, in Dover, Delaware. "Colored people are not allowed to eat in here," the manager explained to the African leader. Vice President Nixon declared, "In the world-wide struggle in which we are engaged, racial prejudice is a gun we point at ourselves."

But racial confrontations remained in the news. During and after World War II a demand for change had developed in the South. Its roots lay in southern industrialization, in the shift from small sharecropping holdings to large commercial farms, in the vast wartime expenditures of the federal government on aircraft factories and army bases in the region; in the impact of the GI Bill on southern colleges and universities, and in the gradual development of a southern black middle class.

Black soldiers who had served abroad demanded that they be treated with respect when they returned home. In 1947 Jackie Robinson, a black officer who had been court-martialed—and acquitted—for refusing to move to the back of a segregated military bus during World War II, was ready to integrate major league baseball. When his team—the Brooklyn Dodgers—checked into the Ben Franklin Hotel in Philadelphia, he was refused a room. A week later the Dodgers went to Pittsburgh. When he took his position at second base, the Pirates refused to come onto the field. Only under threat of forfeiting the game would they play against Robinson.

More blacks insisted on their right to vote—and many got it. In 1940 only 2 percent of African Americans in the south were registered to vote; by 1947, that had increased to 12 percent. But white resistance remained formidable. In 1946 Eugene Talmadge, behind in the polls, won his race for governor by promising that if he were elected "no Negro will vote in Georgia for four years."

In this photo opportunity, Phillies manager Ben Chapman refused to shake Jackie Robinson's hand. Instead, he leaned toward Robinson and said quietly, "Jackie, you know, you're a good ballplayer, but you're still a nigger to me." Robinson replied by leading the Dodgers to the pennant and winning Rookie of the Year honors.

The NAACP (the National Association for the Advancement of Colored People) decided that the time had come to challenge segregation in the courts. Thurgood Marshall, the organization's chief staff lawyer, went from state to state filing legal challenges to the "separate but equal" principle laid down in *Plessy v. Ferguson* in 1896. In 1938 the Supreme Court had ordered the University of Missouri law school to admit a black student because no law school for blacks existed in the state. This decision gradually forced some southern states to admit blacks to advanced programs.

In 1953 President Eisenhower appointed California's Governor Earl Warren chief justice of the U.S. Supreme Court. Convinced that the Court must take the offensive in the cause of civil rights, Warren succeeded in welding his associates into a unit on this question. In 1954 an NAACP-sponsored case, **Brown v. Board of Education of Topeka**, came up for decision. Marshall submitted a mass of sociological evidence to show that the mere fact of segregation made equal education impossible and did serious psychological damage to both black and white children. Speaking for a unanimous Court, Warren reversed the *Plessy* decision. "In the field of public education, the doctrine of 'separate but equal' has no place," he declared. "Separate educational facilities are inherently unequal." The next year the Court ordered the states to end segregation "with all deliberate speed."

Read the Document

Brown v. Board of Education of Topeka, Kansas at **myhistorylab.com**

Flouting the Court's decision, few districts in the southern and border states integrated their schools. As late as September 1956, barely 700 of the South's 10,000 school districts had been desegregated.

Angry jeers from whites rain down on Elizabeth Eckford, one of the first black students to arrive for registration at Little Rock's Central High School in 1957. State troops turned black students away from the school until President Eisenhower overruled the state decision and called in the National Guard to enforce integration.

President Eisenhower thought equality for blacks could not be obtained by government edict. He said that the Court's ruling must be obeyed, but he did little to discourage southern resistance to desegregation.

However, in 1957 events compelled him to act. When the school board of Little Rock, Arkansas, opened Central High School to a handful of black students, the governor of the state, Orval M. Faubus, called out the National Guard to prevent them from entering the school. Unruly crowds taunted the students and their parents. Eisenhower could not ignore the direct flouting of federal authority. After the mayor of Little Rock sent him a telegram saying, in part, "situation is out of control and police cannot disperse the mob," Eisenhower dispatched 1,000 paratroopers to Little Rock and summoned 10,000 National Guardsmen to federal duty, thus removing them from Faubus's control. The black students then began to attend class. A token force of soldiers was stationed at Central High for the entire school year to protect them.

Watch the Video

How did the Civil Rights Movement change American schools? at myhistorylab.com

Direct Action Protests: The Montgomery Bus Boycott

While Marshall and the NAACP were dismantling the legal superstructure of segregation, its institutional foundations remained. Blacks increasingly took action on their own.

This change first came to national attention during the Eisenhower administration in the rigidly segregated city of Montgomery, Alabama. On Friday, December 1, 1955, Rosa Parks, a seamstress at the Montgomery Fair department store, boarded a bus on her way home from her job. She dutifully took a seat toward the rear as custom and law required. As white workers and shoppers filled the forward section, the driver ordered her to give up her place to a white passenger. Parks, who was also secretary of the Montgomery NAACP chapter, refused. She had decided, she later recalled, that "I would have to know once and for all what rights I had as a human being and a citizen."

She was arrested. Over the weekend, Montgomery's black leaders organized a boycott. "Don't ride the bus . . . Monday," their mimeographed notice ran. "If you work, take a cab, or share a ride, or walk." Monday dawned bitterly cold, but the boycott was a total success.

Most Montgomery blacks could not afford to miss a single day's wages, so the protracted struggle to get to work was difficult to maintain. Black-owned taxis reduced their rates sharply, and when the city declared this illegal, car pools were quickly organized. Few African Americans owned cars. Although nearly everyone who did volunteered, there were never more than 350 cars available to the more than 10,000 people who needed rides to their jobs and back every day. Nevertheless, the boycott went on.

Late in February the Montgomery authorities obtained indictments of 115 leaders of the boycott, but this move backfired because it focused national attention on the situation. A young clergyman, the Reverend Martin Luther King, Jr., was emerging as the leader of the boycott. A gifted speaker, he became an overnight celebrity. (See American Lives, "Martin Luther King, Jr.") Money poured in from all over the country to support the movement. The boycott lasted for over a year. Finally the Supreme Court declared the local law enforcing racial separation unconstitutional: Montgomery had to desegregate its public transportation system.

This success encouraged blacks elsewhere in the South to band together against segregation. A new organization founded in 1957, the **Southern Christian Leadership Conference (SCLC)**, headed by King, moved to the forefront of the civil rights movement. Other organizations joined the struggle, notably the Congress of Racial Equality (CORE), which had been founded in 1942. The direct action movement was becoming a broad-based nationwide civil rights movement.

The Election of 1960

As the end of his momentous second term approached, Eisenhower somewhat reluctantly endorsed Vice President Richard Nixon as the Republican candidate to succeed him. Nixon had originally skyrocketed to national prominence by exploiting the public fear of communist subversion. In 1947 he was an obscure young congressman from California; in 1950 he won a seat in the Senate; two years later Eisenhower chose him as his running mate.

The Democrats nominated Senator John F. Kennedy of Massachusetts. His chief rival for the nomination, Lyndon B. Johnson of Texas, the Senate majority leader, became his running mate. Kennedy was the son of Joseph P. Kennedy, a wealthy businessman who had served as ambassador to Great Britain under Franklin Roosevelt. During World War II, Kennedy served in the Pacific, captaining a torpedo boat. When the boat was sliced in two by a Japanese destroyer, Kennedy showed personal courage in rescuing his men. Besides wealth, intelligence, good looks, and charm, Kennedy had the advantage of his Irish-Catholic ancestry, a valuable asset in heavily Catholic Massachusetts. After three terms in the House, he moved on to the Senate in 1952.

Watch the Video
Kennedy-Nixon Debate at **myhistorylab.com**

After his landslide reelection in 1958, only Kennedy's religion seemed to limit his political future. No Catholic had ever been elected president. Nevertheless, influenced by Kennedy's victories in the Wisconsin and West Virginia primaries—the latter establishing him as an effective campaigner in a predominantly Protestant region—the Democratic convention nominated him.

Kennedy had not been a particularly liberal congressman. He was not involved in the civil rights movement. He enthusiastically endorsed the Cold War and indicted the Eisenhower administration for falling behind the Soviet Union in the race to build missiles. He admitted frankly that he liked Senator Joseph McCarthy and thought that "he may have something" in his campaign against supposed communists in government. However, as a presidential candidate, he sought to appear more forward-looking. He stressed his youth and "vigor" (a favorite word) and promised to open a **New Frontier** for the country. Nixon ran on the Eisenhower record, which he promised to extend in liberal directions.

MARTIN LUTHER KING, JR.

On December 1, 1955, Rosa Parks was arrested for violating Montgomery's segregation laws. Black leaders immediately made plans to boycott the city buses the following Monday.

On Monday morning, the buses were nearly empty. That afternoon black leaders met to discuss strategy for a public meeting that evening. One minister urged that they keep their plans secret. E. D. Nixon, a railroad porter and president of the local NAACP, jumped to his feet: "How do you think you can run a bus boycott in secret?" Then he lost his temper. "You ministers have lived off these wash-women for the last hundred years and ain't never done nothing for them."

As Nixon was finishing his diatribe, the new minister in town strode into the room. Young, well-dressed Martin Luther King, Jr. was regarded as something of a dandy. Now, all eyes turned to the dapper latecomer. He called on the ministers to act in open and use their names. Someone proposed that King be named president of the protest movement. Nearly everyone agreed.

That evening, hundreds filled the largest Baptist church, with many more spilling onto the lawn and streets. A loudspeaker was set up. Inside, King outlined the situation, and then, slipping into a preaching mode, began to roll off one booming phrase after another. "And you know, my friends, there comes a time when people get tired of being trampled over by the iron feet of oppression," he said in a deep voice. By the time he finished, his words were drowned out by the stomping of feet and the roars of the crowd outside.

King's rhetorical mastery stunned nearly everyone. He was only twenty-six, and had served as a pastor for only a year.

His father had been minister of the largest Baptist church in Atlanta, and Martin's circumstances as a child had been comfortable. He briefly attended a special school run by Atlanta University, then the local public high school before going to Morehouse College in Atlanta. He eventually followed in his father's footsteps.

He attended Crozer seminary in Pennsylvania. After finishing at the top of his class, he went to Boston University, where he earned a doctorate in philosophy. He resolved to become a successful preacher in a big-city church.

In 1953 King married Coretta Scott; the next year he was appointed pastor at Dexter Avenue Baptist Church in Montgomery.

But in the first week of December, 1955, his life had taken an unexpected turn. He would be given the task of forging into a single movement the disparate elements of the black community. He would adapt the passive nonviolence tactics used by Indian nationalist Mohandas Gandhi to gain independence from Britain, and apply them to the American South. He would use the language of Christian brotherhood to reach out to whites. He would lead the movement that would change the nation.

But that was in the future. In December 1955, a convergence of fateful circumstances had pushed him into leadership of a bus boycott. Twelve years later, he would be dead, victim of an assassin's bullet.

The Rev. Martin Luther King, Jr., Coretta Scott King, and their children share a moment of calm in Montgomery, 1956. That year, while King was addressing a mass meeting, his house was bombed; Coretta and the children were unhurt.

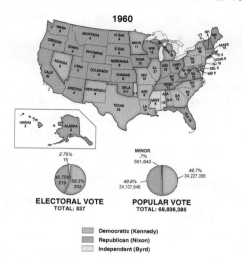

1960

ELECTORAL VOTE
TOTAL: 537

2.75%
15

40.75%
219

56.5%
303

POPULAR VOTE
TOTAL: 68,836,385

MINOR
.7%
501,643

49.6%
34,107,646

49.7%
34,227,096

Democratic (Kennedy)
Republican (Nixon)
Independent (Byrd)

Election of 1960 Like nearly all Democrats since the Compromise of 1877, Kennedy carried most of the South. White Southerners opposed the party of Lincoln, and few black Southerners had been registered to vote.

A series of television debates between the candidates helped Kennedy by enabling him to demonstrate his maturity and mastery of the issues. Although both candidates laudably avoided it, the religious issue was important. His Catholicism helped Kennedy in eastern urban areas but injured him in many farm districts and throughout the West. Kennedy's victory, 303 to 219 in the Electoral College, was paper-thin in the popular vote, 34,227,000 to 34,109,000.

The years since the end of World War II had been dominated by the prospect of war more terrible than anyone could imagine. By the end of 1960 Eisenhower was less concerned about a communist victory than the impact of the arms race on America itself. By then defense expenditures devoured one-tenth of the nation's GNP. In his final speech as president, Eisenhower warned of the "grave implications" resulting from "the conjunction of an immense military establishment and a large arms industry." What Eisenhower called the **military-industrial complex** potentially endangered "the very structure of our society." Could the nation mount a worldwide defense of democracy without endangering that democracy at home?

Milestones

1944	Congress provides subsidies to veterans in GI Bill of Rights	1950	UN counterattack in Korea is driven back by Red Chinese army
1946	UN creates Atomic Energy Commission	1952	Dwight D. Eisenhower is elected president
1947	Taft-Hartley Act regulates unions and labor disputes	1953	John Foster Dulles institutes "New Look" nuclear-based foreign policy
	Truman announces Truman Doctrine to stop communism's spread		Korean War ends with armistice
	George Kennan ("X") urges containment policy in *Sources of Soviet Conduct*	1954	Senate holds Army–McCarthy hearings
1948	Marshall Plan provides funds to rebuild Europe		United States helps overthrow Arbenz in Guatemala
	Harry S Truman is elected president		French are defeated in Indochina after siege of Dien Bien Phu
	State of Israel is created as Jewish homeland; Arabs declare war		Supreme Court orders school desegregation in *Brown v. Board of Education of Topeka*
1948–1949	United States supplies West Berlin during Berlin airlift		Egypt nationalizes Suez Canal in Suez Crisis
1949	United States and eleven other nations form North Atlantic Treaty Organization (NATO)	1955	The Rev. Martin Luther King, Jr., leads Montgomery Bus Boycotts
	Soviet Union detonates atom bomb	1956	Eisenhower is reelected president
1950	North Korea invades South Korea	1957	M. L. King, Jr., and followers form Southern Christian Leadership Conference
	NSC-68 calls for massive military buildup		National Guard enforces desegregation of Central High School in Little Rock, Arkansas
	Alger Hiss is convicted of perjury		
	McCarran Act restricts "subversive" activity	1959	Fidel Castro overthrows Fulgencio Batista, takes power in Cuba
	Senator Joseph McCarthy charges that the State Department is riddled with communists	1960	John F. Kennedy is first Roman Catholic to be elected president

✓•⌐Study and Review at www.myhistorylab.com

Review Questions

1. The late 1940s and 1950s are often characterized as a period of complacency and consensus. Yet this chapter holds that, in foreign and domestic affairs, it was a period of "menacing uncertainty." What constituted the chief elements of menace?

2. Throughout the period from 1946 to 1960, American presidents sought to "contain" communism. How did Eisenhower's "massive retaliation" differ from Truman's worldwide "NSC-68" containment? How did *Sputnik* influence the Cold War?

3. Why did Truman intervene in Korea, and why did the war end in stalemate?

4. What was the impact of the Cold War on American society?

5. Why did the civil rights movement gain momentum after 1945? On what grounds did the Supreme Court overturn the "separate but equal" ruling in *Brown v. Board of Education* (1954)? Why did African Americans subsequently resort to "direct action" protests?

Key Terms

Berlin airlift
Brown v. Board of Education of Topeka
Fair Deal
Marshall Plan
massive retaliation

military-industrial complex
New Frontier
North Atlantic Treaty Organization (NATO)
NSC-68

Southern Christian Leadership Conference (SCLC)
Taft-Hartley Act
Truman Doctrine

228

From Camelot to
Watergate: 1961–1975

From Chapter 29 of *American Destiny: Narrative of a Nation*, Combined Volume, Fourth Edition.
Mark C. Carnes and John A. Garraty. Copyright © 2012 by Pearson Education, Inc. Published by
Pearson Prentice Hall. All rights reserved.

From Camelot to Watergate: 1961–1975

How do you get out of a deep hole?

ON DECEMBER 2, 2009, AS POLLS REVEALED GROWING DISSATISFACTION with the wars in Iraq and Afghanistan, President Barack Obama promised to withdraw all U.S. troops from Iraq within two years. But he announced that he would send an additional 30,000 troops to Afghanistan, where the situation had deteriorated.

"I do not make this decision lightly," he said, noting that he had opposed the war in Iraq. But Afghanistan, he insisted, was different. It had been the home of the Al Qaeda terrorists who attacked on September 11, 2001. By sending more troops to Afghanistan now, Obama believed the military would defeat Al Qaeda more quickly. "There are those who suggest that Afghanistan is another Vietnam," he conceded. "I believe this argument depends on a false reading of history."

Because nothing in the past is exactly like anything else, all historical analogies are flawed. But the history of Vietnam suggests that once soldiers have fought and died for a cause, the task of getting out of a war—short of victory—is not an easy one.

Just before President John F. Kennedy sent the first American troops to Vietnam in 1961, he confided doubts to an aide: "The troops will march in; the bands will play; the crowds will cheer. . . Then we will be told we have to send more troops. It's like taking a drink. The effect wears off, and you have to take another."

By 1963, despite the infusion of some 16,000 U.S. soldiers, South Vietnam was crumbling. In 1965, with a communist takeover imminent, Lyndon Johnson, Kennedy's successor, increased U.S. troop levels to nearly a half million. Yet victory remained elusive. In 1969, his successor, Richard M. Nixon, promised to bring an honorable peace to Vietnam; but American troops remained for another four years.

The long war in Vietnam exposed deep fissures within the nation. Racial divisions widened into gaping holes. Student protests drew violent responses. Nixon's heated rhetoric and illegal campaign tactics heightened tensions. And less than a year after he resigned, communist North Vietnam completed its conquest of South Vietnam. For the United States, the war ended in failure.

Kennedy in Camelot

Having lampooned the Eisenhower administration as stodgy and unimaginative, President Kennedy made a show of his style and wit. He quoted Robert Frost and Dante. He played and replayed recordings of Winston Churchill, hoping to imprint the great orator's sonorous cadences on his own broad Bostonian vowels. At the instigation of his elegant wife, Jacqueline, Kennedy surrounded himself with the finest intellects at glittering White House galas to honor Nobel Prize winners and celebrated artists.

Kennedy's youthful senior staff boasted impressive scholarly credentials. His national security adviser, McGeorge Bundy, had been dean of the faculty at Harvard. Secretary of Defense Robert McNamara also had taught at Harvard before becoming the first nonfamily member to head the Ford Motor Company.

Kennedy's campaign slogan—"Let's get this country moving again"—was embodied in his own active life. He played rugged games of touch football with the press corps and romped with his young children in the Oval Office. In an article for *Sports Illustrated* entitled "The Soft American" published just after the election, Kennedy complained that television, movies, and a comfortable lifestyle had made too many young people flabby. His earliest presidential initiative was a physical fitness campaign in the schools.

Kennedy's image of youthful vigor was enhanced by the beauty and presence of Jacqueline, whose wide-eyed diffidence was universally admired as regal bearing. The image was enhanced by Lerner and Loewe's musical *Camelot*, which opened a few weeks before the inauguration. Its evocation of King Arthur, who sought to lead his virile young knights in challenges great and good, suggested the Kennedy White House. All Washington seemed aglow with excitement and energy.

Never, too, had the substance of an administration been so closely identified with the style of its president. But the dazzle was misleading. Although quick-witted and intelligent, Kennedy was no intellectual. Nor did the president embody physical fitness. Congenital back problems, aggravated by war injuries, forced Kennedy to use crutches or a cane in private and to take heavy doses of painkillers and amphetamines. The president's permanent "tan" did not result from outdoor exercise, as the public assumed, but from Addison's disease, an often fatal failure of the adrenal glands for which Kennedy gave himself daily injections of cortisone. Though he publicly denied it, Kennedy was chronically ill throughout his presidency.

The Cuban Crises

"The torch has been passed to a new generation of Americans," Kennedy declared in his inaugural address. Its chief task was to stop the spread of communism. While Eisenhower had relied on the nation's nuclear arsenal to intimidate the Kremlin, Kennedy proposed to challenge communist aggression whenever and wherever it occurred. A new breed of cold warrior, Kennedy called on young men and women to serve in the Peace Corps, an organization that he created to mobilize American idealism and technical skills to help developing nations. His was a call for commitment—and action.

Perhaps seduced by his own rhetoric, Kennedy blundered almost immediately. Anti-Castro exiles were eager to organize an invasion of their homeland, reasoning that the Cuban people would rise up against Castro and communism as soon as "democratic" forces provided the necessary leadership. Under Eisenhower the CIA had begun training some

2,000 Cuban exiles in Nicaragua. Kennedy was of two minds about the proposed invasion. Some in his administration opposed it strongly, but his closest advisers, including his brother Robert, urged him to give his approval. In the end he did.

The invaders, 1,400 strong, struck in April 1961. They landed at the Bay of Pigs, on Cuba's southern coast. But the Cuban people failed to flock to their lines, and soon Castro's army pinned the invaders down and forced them to surrender. Because American involvement could not be disguised, the affair exposed the United States to all the criticism that a straight-forward assault would have produced, without accomplishing the overthrow of Castro. Worse, it made Kennedy appear impulsive as well as unprincipled. Castro tightened his connections with the Soviet Union.

In June, Kennedy met with Soviet Premier Khrushchev in Vienna. Furious over the invasion of Cuba, Khrushchev blustered about grabbing West Berlin. In August, he abruptly closed the border between East and West Berlin and erected the **Berlin wall**—a barrier of concrete blocks and barbed wire across the city to stop the flow of East Germans into the noncommunist zone. At the same time, the Soviets resumed nuclear testing. Khrushchev ordered detonation of a series of gigantic hydrogen bombs, including one with a power 3,000 times that of the bomb that had devastated Hiroshima.

Photo Credit: AKG-Images.

"Ich bin ein Berliner" (I am a Berliner), Kennedy declared from a balcony in West Berlin in June, 1961, and his words brought a roar of approval from the West Berliners. Gesturing toward the Berlin wall, he called it "the most obvious and vivid demonstration of the failures of the communist system."

Kennedy followed suit: He announced plans to build thousands of nuclear missiles, known as Minutemen, capable of hitting targets on the other side of the world. He expanded the space program, vowing that an American would land on the moon within ten years. The president called on Congress to pass a large increase in military spending.

In secret, Kennedy also resolved to destroy Castro. He ordered military leaders to plan for a full-scale invasion of Cuba. He also instructed the CIA to undertake "massive activity" against Castro's regime. The CIA devised Operation Mongoose, a plan to slip spies, saboteurs, and assassins into Cuba. Although never officially endorsed by the president, Mongoose operated under the oversight of Robert Kennedy.

In 1962 Khrushchev precipitated the most dangerous confrontation of the Cold War. To forestall the anticipated American invasion of Cuba, he moved tanks, heavy bombers, and 42,000 Soviet troops and technicians to the island. His most fateful step was to sneak several dozen guided nuclear missiles into the country and prepare them for launching. The missiles could have hit most of the eastern United States with nuclear warheads.

On October 14 American spy planes spotted the launching pads and missiles. The president faced a dreadful decision. After the **Bay of Pigs fiasco**, he could not again appear to back down to the communists. But if he invaded Cuba or bombed the Soviet bases and missile sites, Khrushchev would likely seize West Berlin or bomb U.S. missile sites in Turkey. Either action might lead to a full-scale nuclear war and millions of deaths.

On October 22 Kennedy addressed the nation on television. The Soviet buildup was "a deliberately provocative and unjustified change in the status quo." He ordered the American navy to stop and search all vessels headed for Cuba and to turn back any containing "offensive" weapons. Kennedy called on Khrushchev to dismantle the missile bases and remove from the island all weapons capable of striking the United States. Any Cuban-based nuclear attack would result, he warned, in "a full retaliatory response upon the Soviet Union."

For days, Soviet ships steamed toward Cuba and work on the missile launching pads continued. An American spy plane was shot down over Cuba. Khrushchev sent a desperate telegram, suggesting that he was near the breaking point. Robert Kennedy and others engaged in frantic negotiations through intermediaries. Then Khrushchev backed down. He recalled the ships, withdrew the missiles, and reduced his military establishment in Cuba to modest proportions. In response, Kennedy lifted the blockade. He also promised not to invade Cuba, thus ensuring Castro's survival; Kennedy further agreed to withdraw U.S. missiles from Turkey, though this latter concession was not made public at the time.

Immediately the president was hailed for his steady nerve and consummate statesmanship; the Cuban missile crisis was widely regarded as his finest hour. Yet in retrospect it appears that he may have overreacted. The Soviet nuclear threat had been exaggerated. After *Sputnik*, the Soviet long-range missile program flopped, though this was not known at the time. By the summer of 1962 a "missile gap" existed, but it was overwhelmingly in favor of the United States, whose nuclear forces outnumbered those of the Soviet Union by a ratio of seventeen to one. Khrushchev's decision to put medium-range missiles in Cuba signified Soviet weakness rather than impending aggression. Both Kennedy and Khrushchev were sobered by the **Cuban missile crisis**. They signed a treaty outlawing nuclear testing in the atmosphere. But Khrushchev's bluff had been called—a public humiliation from which he never recovered. Within two years, hard-liners in the Kremlin forced him out of office. He was replaced by Leonid Brezhnev, an old-style Stalinist who inaugurated an intensive program of long-range missile development. The nuclear arms race moved to new terrain, uncertain and unimaginably dangerous.

JFK's Vietnam War

Truman's attempt to prevent Ho Chi Minh's communist insurgents from seizing Vietnam failed when the French army surrendered to Ho's troops at Dien Bien Phu in 1954. Eisenhower, equally unwilling to accept a communist victory, then supported creation of an anticommunist South Vietnam, headed by Ngo Dinh Diem, a Vietnamese nationalist who hated the communists. While the United States poured millions of dollars into strengthening Diem's South Vietnam, and especially its army, Ho Chi Minh consolidated his rule in North Vietnam. Those Viet Minh units that remained in the South—they came to be known as Vietcong—were instructed to form secret cells and bide their time. During the late 1950s they gained in strength and militancy.

In May 1959 Ho decided that the time had come to overthrow Diem. Vietcong guerrillas infiltrated thousands of villages, ambushed South Vietnamese convoys, and assassinated government officials. Soon the Vietcong controlled large sections of the countryside, some almost within sight of the capital city of Saigon.

Kennedy sharply increased the American military and economic commitment to South Vietnam. At the end of 1961 there were 3,200 American military personnel in the country; within two years, there were more than 16,000, and 120 American soldiers had been killed. Despite the expanded effort, by the summer of 1963 Diem's regime was in ruins. Unable to persuade Diem to moderate his policies, Kennedy sent word to dissident Vietnamese generals of his willingness to support them if they ousted Diem. On November 1 several of these generals surrounded the presidential palace with troops and tanks, seized Diem, and killed him. Kennedy, though appalled by Diem's death, recognized the new junta. The decision to overthrow Diem was fateful; it committed the United States to finding a solution to a worsening situation in Vietnam.

In the summer of 1963, Buddhist monks protested against the rule of Diem (and his brother, the Catholic archbishop of Vietnam) by setting themselves on fire.

"We Shall Overcome": The Civil Rights Movement

In February 1960 four African American college students in Greensboro, North Carolina, sat down at a lunch counter at a Woolworth's store. "We do not serve Negroes," they were told. They returned with more and more demonstrators. By the end of the week over a thousand protesters descended on Woolworth's, led by a phalanx of football players from the nearby black college who cleared the way through a throng of Confederate flag-wavers.

This "sit-in" tactic was not new. But the Greensboro students sparked a national movement; students in dozens of other southern towns and cities copied their example.

Soon more than fifty sit-ins were in progress in southern cities. By the end of 1961 over 70,000 people had participated in such demonstrations. Still another new organization, the **Student Nonviolent Coordinating Committee (SNCC)**, was founded by black college students in 1960 to provide a focus for the sit-in movement and to conduct voter registration drives in the South, actions that more than any other roused the fury of southern segregationists.

●◆●—[Read the Document

Charles Sherrod, *SNCC Memorandum (1961)* at **myhistorylab.com**

This protracted struggle eventually yielded practical and moral benefits for southern whites as well as blacks. Gradually all but the most unwavering defenders of segregation changed their attitudes. But this took time, and many blacks were unwilling to wait.

Some blacks, contemptuous of white prejudices, were urging their fellows to reject "American" society and all it stood for. In the North, black nationalism became a potent force. Elijah Muhammad, leader of the Black Muslim movement, loathed whites so intensely that he demanded that a part of the United States be set aside exclusively for blacks. He urged his followers to be industrious, thrifty, and abstemious—and to view all whites with suspicion and hatred.

"This white government has ruled us and given us plenty hell, but the time has arrived that you taste a little of your own hell," Muhammad said. He scorned Martin Luther King, Jr., and others who advocated Christian nonviolence. Another important Black Muslim, Malcolm X, put it this way in a 1960 speech: "For the white man to ask the black man if he hates him is just like the rapist asking the raped, or the wolf asking the sheep, 'Do you hate me?'"

Whites pour mustard and ketchup over black students (and one white) who were integrating a lunch-counter.

Ordinary southern blacks became increasingly impatient. In the face of brutal repression by local police, many began to question Martin Luther King's tactic of nonviolent protest. After leading a series of demonstrations in Birmingham, Alabama, in 1963, King was thrown in jail. When local white clergymen, professing themselves sympathetic to the blacks' objectives, nonetheless urged an end to "untimely" protests, which (they claimed) "incite hatred and violence," King wrote his now-famous "Letter from Birmingham Jail," which contained this moving explanation of why he and his followers were unwilling to wait any longer for justice:

Watch the Video
Civil Rights Movement at **myhistorylab.com**

[W]hen you take a cross-country drive and find it necessary to sleep night after night in the uncomfortable corners of your automobile because no motel will accept you; when you are humiliated day in and day out by nagging signs reading "white" and "colored"; when your first name becomes "nigger" and your middle name becomes "boy" . . . then you will understand why we find it so difficult to wait.

Source: Copyright 1963 Dr. Martin Luther King Jr; copyright renewed 1991 Coretta Scott King.

The brutal repression of the Birmingham demonstrations, captured in newspaper photos and on television broadcasts, brought a flood of recruits and money to the protesters' cause. Pushed by all these developments, President Kennedy reluctantly began to change his policy. His administration had from the start given lip service to desegregation and encouraged activists' efforts to register black voters in the South, but when confrontations arose the president hesitated, arguing that it was up to local officials to enforce the law. After Birmingham, however, Kennedy supported a modest civil rights bill.

When this measure ran into stiff opposition in Congress, blacks organized a demonstration in Washington, attended by 200,000 people. At this gathering, King delivered his "I Have a Dream" address, looking forward to a time when racial prejudice no longer existed and people of all religions and colors could join hands and say, "Free at last!" Kennedy sympathized with the Washington gathering but feared it would make passage of the civil rights bill more difficult. As in other areas, he was not a forceful advocate of his own proposals.

Watch the Video
Civil Rights March on Washington at **myhistorylab.com**

Tragedy in Dallas: JFK Assassinated

Through it all, Kennedy retained his hold on public opinion. In the fall of 1963 most observers believed he would win a second term. Then, while visiting Dallas, Texas, on November 22, he was shot in the head by an assassin, Lee Harvey Oswald, and died almost instantly.

Kennedy's assassination precipitated an extraordinary series of events. Oswald had fired on the president with a rifle from an upper story of a warehouse. No one saw him pull the trigger. He was apprehended largely because he panicked and killed a policeman across town later in the day. He denied his guilt, but a mass of evidence connected him with the assassination of the president. Before he could be brought to trial, however, he was himself murdered by Jack Ruby, the owner of a Dallas nightclub. The incident took place in full view of television cameras, while Oswald was being transferred from one place of detention to another.

Each day brought new revelations. Oswald had defected briefly to the Soviet Union in 1959, then had returned to the United States and formed a pro-Castro organization in New Orleans. Many concluded that some nefarious conspiracy lay at the root of the tragedy. Oswald, the argument ran, was a pawn—either of communists or anticommunists—whose murder was designed to shield from exposure the masterminds who had engineered the assassination. A special commission headed by Chief Justice Earl Warren was convened to analyze the evidence. After a lengthy investigation, it concluded that Oswald had acted alone.

Instead of dampening charges of conspiracy, the report of the Warren Commission provoked new doubts. As word leaked out about the earlier CIA assassination attempts against Castro, the failure of the Warren Report even to mention Operation Mongoose made the commission suspect, all the more so since several members, including Allen Dulles, former director of the CIA, had known of the operation. While, there is little solid evidence to suggest that Oswald was part of a wider conspiracy, the decision of Dulles and other commissioners to protect CIA secrets engendered skepticism.

One measure of Kennedy's hold on the public imagination was the outpouring of grief that attended his death. Kennedy had given hope to people who had none. Young black civil rights activist Anne Moody, who later wrote *Coming of Age in Mississippi*, was working as a waitress in a segregated restaurant. "Tears were burning my cheeks," she recalled. Her boss, a Greek immigrant, gently suggested she take the rest of the day off. When she looked up, there were tears in his eyes too.

JFK and Jacqueline Kennedy ride in a motorcade with Texas Governor John Connolly and his wife in Dallas, November 22, 1963. Several minutes later, Kennedy was shot and killed; Connolly was wounded.

Photo Credit: CORBIS-NY.

Lyndon Baines Johnson: The Great Society

John F. Kennedy's death made Lyndon B. Johnson president. From 1949 until his election as vice president, Johnson had been a senator from Texas and, for most of that time, Senate Democratic leader. Many people swore by him; few had the fortitude to swear at him. Above all he knew what to do with political power.

Johnson, who had consciously modeled his career after that of Franklin D. Roosevelt, considered social welfare legislation his specialty. The contrast with Kennedy could not have been sharper. Kennedy's plans for federal aid for education, urban renewal, a higher minimum wage, and medical care for the aged were blocked in Congress by Republicans and southern Democrats. But Kennedy had reacted to these defeats mildly, almost wistfully. He thought the machinery of the federal government was cumbersome and ineffective.

Johnson knew how to make it work. On becoming president, he pushed hard for Kennedy's programs. Early in his career Johnson had voted against a bill making lynching a federal crime, and he also had opposed bills outlawing state poll taxes and establishing the federal Fair Employment Practices Commission. But after he became an important figure in national affairs, he consistently championed racial equality. Bills long buried in committee sailed through Congress. Early in 1964 Kennedy's tax cut was passed. A few months later, an expanded version of another Kennedy proposal became law as the **Civil Rights Act of 1964.**

The much-strengthened Civil Rights Act outlawed discrimination by employers against blacks and also against women. It broke down legal barriers to black voting in the southern states and outlawed racial segregation of all sorts in places of public accommodation, such as movie theaters, hotels, and restaurants. In addition, unlike presidents Eisenhower and Kennedy, Johnson established agencies to enforce civil rights legislation.

Johnson's success in steering the Civil Rights Act through Congress confirmed his belief that he could be a reformer in the tradition of Franklin Roosevelt. He declared war on poverty and set out to create a **Great Society** in which poverty no longer would exist.

In 1937 Roosevelt had been accused of exaggeration for claiming that one-third of the nation was "ill-housed, ill-clad, ill-nourished." In fact Roosevelt had underestimated the extent of poverty. Wartime economic growth reduced the percentage of poor people in the country substantially, but in 1960 between 20 and 25 percent of all American families—about 40 million people—were living below the poverty line, a government standard of minimum subsistence based on income and family size.

The presence of so many poor people in an affluent society was deplorable but not difficult to explain. In any community a certain number of people cannot support themselves because of physical, mental, or emotional problems. The United States also included entire regions, the best known being Appalachia, that had been bypassed by economic development and no longer provided their inhabitants with adequate economic opportunities.

Moreover, prosperity and advancing technology had changed the definition of poverty. Telephones, radios and electric refrigerators, and other goods unimaginable to the most affluent Americans of the 1860s, were necessities a hundred years later. But as living standards rose, so did job requirements. Technology was changing the labor market. Educated workers with special skills and good verbal abilities easily found well-paid jobs. Those who had no special skills or were poorly educated went without work.

The Economic Opportunity Act of 1964 created a mixture of programs, among them a Job Corps similar to the New Deal Civilian Conservation Corps, a community

LBJ cultivated the masculine image of a Texas cowboy. Biographers have suggested that Johnson was torn between the expectations of his father, a crude local politician who flouted polite society, and those of his mother, a refined woman who insisted that her son read poetry and practice the violin. Johnson later told biographer Doris Kearns Goodwin that he persisted in Vietnam because he worried that critics would accuse him of being "an unmanly man. A man without a spine."

action program to finance local antipoverty efforts, and a system for training the unskilled unemployed and for lending money to small businesses in poor areas. The programs combined the progressive concept of government aid for those in need with the conservative idea of individual responsibility.

Buttressed by his legislative triumphs, Johnson sought election as president in his own right in 1964. He achieved this ambition in unparalleled fashion. His championing of civil rights won him the almost unanimous support of blacks; his tax policy attracted the well-to-do and the business interests; his war on poverty held the allegiance of labor and other traditionally Democratic groups. His down-home southern antecedents counterbalanced his liberalism on the race question in the eyes of many white southerners.

The Republicans played into his hands by nominating the conservative Senator Barry M. Goldwater of Arizona, whose objective in Congress had been "not to pass laws but to repeal them." As a presidential candidate he favored such laissez-faire policies

Table 1 Making a "Great Society"

Assisted Group	Legislation and Provisions
African Americans	Civil Rights Act (1964): Outlawed discrimination in employment, public accommodations, and federally-funded programs
	Voting Rights Act (1965): Federal registrars sent to the South
Elderly	Medicare (1965): Federally-funded medical care for elderly
Low-income people	Economic Opportunity Act (1964): Federally-funded antipoverty programs and agencies
	Medicaid (1965): Federally-funded health care for welfare recipients
	Housing and Urban Development Act: Federally-funded housing projects and rent support
Students	Elementary and Secondary Education Act (1965): Federal support for public and parochial schools for texts and materials, and for Head Start
	Higher Education Act (1965): Federally-funded loans and scholarships for college students

as cutting back on the Social Security system and doing away with the Tennessee Valley Authority. A large majority of voters found Goldwater out-of-date on economic questions and dangerously aggressive on foreign affairs.

In November, Johnson won a sweeping victory, collecting over 61 percent of the popular vote and carrying the whole country except Goldwater's Arizona and five states in the Deep South.

Quickly Johnson pressed ahead with his Great Society program. In January 1965 he proposed a compulsory hospital insurance system, known as **Medicare**, for all persons over the age of sixty-five. As amended by Congress, the Medicare Act consisted of Part A, hospital insurance for the elderly (funded by increased Social Security taxes), and a voluntary plan, Part B, covering doctors' bills (paid for in part by the government). The law also provided for grants to the states to help pay the medical expenses of poor people, even those below the age of sixty-five. This part of the system was called Medicaid. Before the passage of the Medicare Act, about half of Americans over sixty-five years old had no medical insurance.

Next, Congress passed the Elementary and Secondary Education Act in 1965, which supplied federal funds to school districts; the Higher Education Act (1965), which provided financial aid to college students; and Head Start, a program to prepare poor preschoolers for elementary school. It also provided medical examinations and nutritious meals for children.

Still another important reform was the **Voting Rights Act of 1965**, pressed through Congress by President Johnson after more brutal repressions of civil rights demonstrators in the South. This law provided for federal intervention to protect black registration and voting in six southern states. It applied to state and local as well as federal elections.

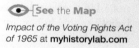

See the **Map**

Impact of the Voting Rights Act of 1965 at **myhistorylab.com**

Other laws passed at Johnson's urging in 1965 and 1966 included the creation of the National Endowment for the Arts and the National Endowment for the Humanities and measures supporting scientific research, highway safety, crime control, slum clearance, clean air, and the preservation of historic sites. Of particular significance was the Immigration Act of 1965, which did away with most provisions of the national-origin system of admitting newcomers. Instead, 290,000 persons a year were to be admitted on the basis of such priorities as job skills and need for political asylum. The law also placed a limit of 120,000 immigrants a year from countries in the Western Hemisphere. Previously, immigration from these countries had been unrestricted.

The Great Society program was one of the most remarkable outpourings of important legislation in American history. On balance, the achievements of the Great Society were far below what President Johnson had promised and his supporters had envisioned. Despite his long political experience, Johnson tried to accomplish too many things too quickly. He relied too heavily on the techniques of political manipulation. Without the crisis atmosphere that had appeared to justify hasty experimentation during the New Deal years, the public judged the results of the Great Society and the president who had shaped it skeptically.

New Racial Turmoil

One reason for skepticism was that the adoption of the Great Society coincided with increasing racial polarization. Black militancy, building steadily during World War II and the

Watch the **Video**

Malcolm X at **myhistorylab.com**

Police watch as the Watts section of Los Angeles burns during riots in August, 1965.

Photo Credit: AP/Wide World Photo.

postwar years, burst forth in the mid-1960s. An important illustration was the response of Black Muslims to Malcolm X's 1964 decision to abandon the organization. A trip to the Middle East had exposed him to Islamic doctrines of racial equality and the brotherhood of man. In response he founded the Organization of Afro-American Unity. In 1965, while making a speech in favor of racial harmony, he was assassinated by Black Muslim fanatics.

Even Martin Luther King, Jr., the herald of nonviolent resistance, became more aggressive. "We are not asking, we are demanding the ballot," he said in January 1965. A few weeks after Malcolm's death, King led a march from Selma, Alabama, to Montgomery as part of a campaign to force Alabama authorities to allow blacks to register to vote. King chose Selma because the county in which it was located had a black majority but only 325 registered black voters. He expected the authorities to react brutally, thus attracting public sympathy for the marchers, and he was not disappointed. His marchers were assaulted by state policemen who wielded clubs and tossed canisters of tear gas.

Many African Americans lost patience with nonviolence. "The time for running has come to an end," declared Stokely Carmichael, chairman of the Student Nonviolent Coordinating Committee (SNCC). "It's time we stand up and take over." He began chanting "Black Power!" and other African-Americans chimed in. Black Power caught on swiftly among militants. This troubled white liberals, who feared that Black Power would antagonize white conservatives. They argued that since blacks made up only about 11 percent of the population, any attempt to obtain racial justice through the use of naked power was sure to fail.

●●─[Read the Document

Black Power 1967 at myhistorylab.com

Meanwhile, black anger erupted in a series of destructive urban riots. The most important occurred in Watts, a ghetto of Los Angeles, in August 1965. A trivial incident brought thousands into the streets. The neighborhood almost literally exploded: For six days Watts was swept by fire, looting, and bloody fighting between local residents and nearly 15,000 National Guardsmen, called up to assist the police. The following two summers saw similar outbursts in scores of cities.

●●─[Read the Document

Watts Riots 1967 at myhistorylab.com

Then, in April 1968, Martin Luther King, Jr., was murdered in Memphis, Tennessee, by a white man, James Earl Ray. Blacks in more than a hundred cities unleashed their anger in outbursts of burning and looting. The death of King appeared to destroy the hope that his peaceful appeal to reason and right could solve the problems of racism.

The most frightening aspect of the riots was their tendency to polarize society on racial lines. Whites fled to the suburbs in droves. Advocates of Black Power became more determined to separate themselves from white influence; they exasperated white supporters of school desegregation by demanding schools of their own. Extremists formed the Black Panther party and collected weapons to resist the police. "Shoot, don't loot," the radical H. Rap Brown advised all who would listen.

From the "Beat Movement" to Student Radicalism

The increased militancy of many American blacks paralleled the emergence of an increasingly strident attitude among many young people as the "conformist" decade of the 1950s gave way to the "activist" 1960s.

This common characterization, however, is overdrawn. The roots of 1960s' dissent were firmly planted in the 1950s. J. D. Salinger, perhaps the most popular writer of the decade and the particular favorite of college students—*The Catcher in the Rye* (1951) sold nearly 2 million copies—wrote about young people whose self-absorption was a product of their alienation from society. Allen Ginsberg's dark, desperate *Howl*, written in 1955, perhaps the most widely read poem of the postwar era, underscored generational differences. "I saw the best minds of my generation destroyed by madness, starving hysterical naked," the poem begins. In *On the Road* (1957), Jack Kerouac, founder of the **beat** (for "beatific") **school**, described a manic, drug-laced flight from traditional values and institutions. In *Catch-22* (1955), Joseph Heller produced a war novel at once farcical and an indignant denunciation of the stupidity and waste of warfare.

But if the "beats" were a fringe group of poets and musicians, their successors in the 1960s—generally known as hippies—could be found in large groups in every big city in the United States and Europe. They were so "turned off" by the modern world that they retreated from it, finding refuge in communes, drugs, and mystical religions. They were disgusted by the dishonesty and sordid antics of so many of the politicians, horrified by the brutality of Vietnam, appalled by racism, and contemptuous of the smugness they encountered in colleges and universities. But they rejected activism. Theirs was a world of folk songs and blaring acid rock music, of "be-ins," "love-ins," casual sex, and drugs. But the 1960s also witnessed the emergence of a new activism. Many students were frustrated by persistent racism and bigotry, but they regarded these as symptoms of a right-wing "power elite" of corporate executives and military and political leaders—a concept outlined in a book of that title by Columbia sociologist C. Wright Mills. In 1962 a small group of students in the **Students for a Democratic Society (SDS)** put together a manifesto for action at a meeting at Port Huron, Michigan: Their main concerns were racial bigotry, the bomb, and the "disturbing paradoxes" associated with these concerns. SDS sought to wrest power from the "military-industrial" complex and institute a radical socialist government. SDS grew, powered by rising college enrollments and a seemingly unending list of local campus issues. The first great student outburst convulsed the University of California at Berkeley in the fall of 1964. Angry students, many veterans of the 1964 fight for black rights in the South, staged sit-down strikes in university buildings to protest the prohibition of political canvassing on the campus. This free speech movement

((•—Hear the Audio

Timothy Leary, *Going Out* *(1966)* at **myhistorylab.com**

A young man perches in a tree with a guitar at Woodstock, a drug- and water-logged music festival that attracted 500,000 to rural New York in 1968.

Photo Credit: John Dominis/Time & Life Pictures/Getty Images.

disrupted the institution over a period of weeks. Hundreds were arrested, the state legislature threatened reprisals, the faculty became involved in the controversy, and the crisis led to the resignation of the president of the University of California, Clark Kerr.

But what transformed student activism from being a local campus irritation to a mass political movement was the decision by Lyndon Johnson to escalate the war in Vietnam.

Johnson Escalates the War

After Diem's assassination in 1963, the situation in South Vietnam worsened. One military coup followed another, and political instability aggravated military incapacity. President Johnson nevertheless felt that he had no choice but to prop up the South Vietnamese regime.

Johnson decided to punish North Vietnam directly for prosecuting the war in the South. In early 1964 he secretly ordered American warships to escort the South Vietnamese navy on commando missions far into the Gulf of Tonkin. After one such mission, American destroyers were fired on by North Vietnamese gunboats. Several nights later during a heavy storm, American ships reported that they were being fired on, though the enemy was never spotted. Using this Tonkin "incident" as pretext, Johnson demanded, and in an air of crisis obtained, an authorization from Congress to "repel any armed attack against the forces of the United States and to prevent further aggression." With this blank check, known as the **Gulf of Tonkin Resolution**, Johnson authorized air attacks in

•●•[Read the Document

The Gulf of Tonkin Resolution Message at **myhistorylab.com**

From 1965 to 1968, American troops in Vietnam conducted "search and destroy" missions to shatter the insurgents. Here a soldier watches as a village is burned.

Photo Credit: © Topham/The Image Works.

The Vietnam War, 1961–1975 As American bombing and "search and destroy" missions spread throughout South Vietnam, North Vietnamese supply lines moved westward, into Laos and Cambodia. U.S. troops and bombers attacked there as well. This destabilized Cambodia, which fell to the brutal Khmer Rouge communists in 1975.

North Vietnam. By the summer of 1965, American bombers were conducting some 5,000 raids each month.

But the hail of bombs on North Vietnam had little effect on the struggle in the South. Worse, the Vietcong expanded the areas under their control. After a fact-finding mission in the war zone, McGeorge Bundy concluded that the prospects were grim for South Vietnam. "The energy and persistence of the Vietcong are astonishing," he reported. "They have accepted extraordinary losses and they come back for more. They show skill in their sneak attacks and ferocity when cornered." If the war was to be won, American soldiers—lots of them—would have to do much of the fighting themselves.

In July 1965 Johnson ordered the first of several huge increases in American ground forces. By the end of 1965, 184,000 Americans were in the field; a year later, 385,000; and after another year, 485,000. By the middle of 1968 the number exceeded 538,000. Each increase was met by corresponding increases from the other side. The Soviet Union and China sent no combat troops, but stepped up their aid, and thousands of North Vietnamese regulars filtered across the seventeenth parallel to fight with the Vietcong guerrillas.

The new American strategy was not to seize any particular battlefield or terrain as in all previous wars, but to kill as many of the enemy as possible through bloody "search and destroy" operations. As the scope of the action broadened, the number of American casualties rose. The United States was engaged in a full-scale war, one that Congress never declared.

The Election of 1968

Gradually the opponents of the war gained numbers and strength. They began to include some of the president's advisers. By late 1967 Secretary of Defense McNamara, who had methodically tracked kill ratios, troop replacement rates, and nearly every other conceivable statistic, concluded that "the figures didn't add up" and the war could not be won. Deeply despondent, he resigned, but did not publicly admit his doubts.

Opposition to the war was especially vehement on college campuses, some students objecting because they thought the United States had no business intervening in the Vietnam conflict, others because they feared being drafted, still others because so many students obtained educational deferments, while young men who were unable to attend college were conscripted.

Then, in November 1967, Eugene McCarthy, a low-keyed, introspective senator from Minnesota, announced his candidacy for the 1968 Democratic presidential nomination. Opposition to the war was his issue.

Preventing Johnson from being renominated seemed impossible. Aside from the difficulty of defeating a "reigning" president, there were the domestic achievements of Johnson's Great Society program: the health insurance program for retired people, greatly expanded federal funding of education and public housing, and the Civil Rights Act. Even Senator McCarthy took his chances of being nominated so lightly that he did not trouble to set up a real organization. He entered the campaign only to "alleviate . . . this sense of political helplessness." Someone, he decided, must step forward to put the Vietnam question before the voters.

Stung by the critics, Johnson ordered General William C. Westmoreland, commander of American forces in Vietnam, to reassure the American people on the course of the war. The general obligingly returned to the United States in late 1967 and told the press that he could see "some light at the end of the tunnel."

Suddenly, early in 1968, on the heels of this announcement, North Vietnamese and Vietcong forces launched a general offensive to correspond with their Lunar New Year (called Tet). Striking thirty-nine of the forty-four provincial capitals, many other towns and cities, and every American base, they caused chaos throughout South Vietnam. They held Hué, the old capital of the country, for weeks. To root insurgents out of Saigon the Americans had to level large sections of the city.

The **Tet offensive** was essentially a series of raids; the communists did not expect to hold the cities indefinitely, and they did not. Their losses were enormous. Nevertheless the psychological impact in South Vietnam and in the United States made Tet a clear victory for the communists. American pollsters reported an enormous shift of public opinion against further escalation of the fighting. When Westmoreland described Tet as a communist defeat and yet requested an additional 206,000 troops, McCarthy, who was

Table 2 Major Events in the Vietnam War, 1961–1968

1961	JFK dispatches thousands of U.S. military "advisers" to South Vietnam
1963	Vietnamese Buddhists rebel; United States supports overthrow of Diem
1964	LBJ obtains Gulf of Tonkin Resolution to expand war
1965	LBJ greatly increases U.S. troop levels
1968	Tet Offensive throughout South Vietnam; LBJ decides not to seek reelection; My Lai Massacre

campaigning in the New Hampshire primary, suddenly became a formidable figure. Thousands of students and other volunteers flocked to the state to ring doorbells on his behalf. On primary election day he polled 42 percent of the Democratic vote. This prompted former attorney general Robert F. Kennedy, brother of the slain president, to declare his candidacy for the Democratic nomination. Like McCarthy, Kennedy opposed Johnson's Vietnam policies but thought his chances of winning were better than McCarthy's.

Confronting this division in the ranks, President Johnson realized he could no longer hope to be an effective president. In a surprising televised announcement, he withdrew from the race. Vice President Hubert H. Humphrey then announced his candidacy, and Johnson threw the weight of his administration behind him.

Kennedy carried several primaries, including California. Immediately after his victory speech in a Los Angeles hotel, however, he was assassinated by Sirhan Sirhan, an Arab nationalist who had been incensed by Kennedy's support of Israel. In effect, Kennedy's death ensured the nomination of Humphrey.

The contest for the Republican nomination was far less dramatic, although its outcome, the nomination of Richard M. Nixon, would have been hard to predict a few years earlier. After his loss to Kennedy in 1960, Nixon ran unsuccessfully for governor of California in 1962, then moved to New York City and joined a prominent law firm. But he remained active in Republican affairs. In 1964 he had campaigned hard for Goldwater. When no other Republican developed extensive support as the 1968 election approached, Nixon entered the race, swept the primaries, and won an easy first-ballot victory at the Republican convention.

Nixon then astounded the country and dismayed liberals by choosing Governor Spiro T. Agnew of Maryland as his running mate. Agnew was a political unknown. Nixon chose him primarily to attract southern votes.

Placating the South seemed necessary because Governor George C. Wallace of Alabama was making a determined bid to win enough electoral votes for his American Independent party to prevent any candidate from obtaining a majority. Wallace was flagrantly anti-black and anti-intellectual. He denounced federal "meddling," the "coddling" of criminals, and the forced integration of schools.

This Republican strategy to win the South heightened the tension surrounding the Democratic convention, which met in Chicago in late August. Humphrey delegates controlled the convention. Several thousand activists, representing a dozen groups and advocating tactics ranging from orderly demonstrations to civil disobedience to indiscriminate violence, descended on Chicago to put pressure on the delegates to repudiate the Johnson Vietnam policy.

In the tense atmosphere that resulted, the party hierarchy overreacted. The mayor of Chicago, Richard J. Daley, whose ability to "influence" election results in a manner favorable to Democrats had often been demonstrated, ringed the convention with policemen to protect it from disruption. This was a reasonable precaution in itself. Inside the building the delegates nominated Humphrey and adopted a war plank satisfactory to Johnson. Outside, however, provoked by the abusive language and violent behavior of radical demonstrators, the police tore into the protesters, in novelist Norman Mailer's graphic phrase, "like a chain saw cutting into wood," while millions watched on television in fascinated horror.

The mayhem in Chicago seemed to benefit Nixon by strengthening the convictions of many voters that the tougher treatment of criminals and dissenters that he and Agnew were calling for was necessary. Those who were critical of the Chicago police tended to blame Humphrey, whom Mayor Daley supported.

Nixon campaigned at a deliberate, dignified pace. He made relatively few public appearances, relying instead on carefully arranged television interviews and taped commercials. He stressed firm enforcement of the law and his desire "to bring us together." As for Vietnam, he would "end the war and win the peace," by just what means he did not say. Agnew, in his blunt, coarse way, assaulted Humphrey, the Democrats, and left-wing dissident groups.

But gradually Humphrey gained ground, and on election day the popular vote was close: Nixon slightly less than 31.8 million, Humphrey nearly 31.3 million. Nixon's Electoral College margin, however, was substantial—301 to 191. The remaining 46 electoral votes went to Wallace, whose 9.9 million votes came to 13.5 percent of the total. Together, Nixon and Wallace received 57 percent of the popular vote.

Nixon as President: "Vietnamizing" the War

When he took office in January 1969, Richard Nixon projected an image of calm and deliberate statesmanship; he introduced no startling changes, proposed no important new legislation. He considered the solution of the Vietnam problem his chief task. Although he insisted during the 1968 campaign that he would end the war on "honorable" terms if elected, he suggested nothing very different from what Johnson was doing.

In office, Nixon first proposed a phased withdrawal of all non-South Vietnamese troops, to be followed by an internationally supervised election in South Vietnam. The North Vietnamese rejected this scheme and insisted that the United States withdraw its forces unconditionally. The intransigence of the North Vietnamese left the president in a difficult position. Nixon could not compel the foe to end a war it had begun against the French nearly a quarter of a century earlier, and every passing day added to the strength of antiwar sentiment, which in turn led to deeper divisions in the country. Yet Nixon could not face up to the consequences of ending the war on the communists' terms.

The president responded to the dilemma by trying to build up the South Vietnamese armed forces so that American troops could pull out without South Vietnam being overrun by the communists. He shipped so many planes to the Vietnamese that within four years they had the fourth-largest air force in the world. He also announced a series of troop cuts.

For a while, events appeared to vindicate Nixon's position. A gradual slowing of military activity in Vietnam had reduced American casualties. Troop withdrawals continued in an orderly fashion. A new lottery system for drafting men for military duty eliminated some of the inequities in the selective service law.

But the war continued. Early in 1970 reports that an American unit had massacred civilians, including dozens of women and children, in a Vietnamese hamlet known as

Photo Credit: Getty Images/Time Life Pictures.

South Vietnamese women and children were among some 300 apparently unarmed civilians killed in the My Lai Massacre in 1968. Lieutenant William Calley was convicted of murder and sentenced to life in prison. After many appeals, he was released in 1974.

My Lai revived the controversy over the purposes of the war and its corrosive effects on those who were fighting it.

Nixon wanted to end the war but he did not want to lose it. The war's human, economic, and social costs could only vex his days and threaten his future reputation. When he reduced the level of the fighting, the communists merely waited for further reductions. When he raised it, many Americans denounced him in increasingly massive antiwar protests. If he pulled out of Vietnam and the communists won, other Americans would be outraged.

Perhaps Nixon's error lay in his unwillingness to admit his own uncertainty, something the greatest presidents—one thinks immediately of Lincoln and Franklin Roosevelt—were never afraid to do. Facing a dilemma, he tried to convince the world that he was firmly in control of events. Thus he heightened the tensions he sought to relax—in America, in Vietnam, and elsewhere.

The Cambodian "Incursion"

Late in April 1970 Nixon announced that Vietnamization was proceeding more rapidly than he had hoped, that communist power was weakening, and that within a year another 150,000 American soldiers would be extracted from Vietnam. A week later he announced that military intelligence had indicated that the enemy was consolidating its "sanctuaries" in neutral Cambodia and that he was therefore dispatching thousands of American troops to destroy these bases.

Nixon's shocking announcement triggered many campus demonstrations. One college where feeling ran high was Kent State University in Ohio. For several days students there clashed with local police; they broke windows and caused other damage to property. When the governor called out the National Guard, angry students showered the soldiers with stones. During a noontime protest on May 4 the guardsmen, who were poorly trained in crowd control, suddenly opened fire. Four students were killed, two of them women who were merely passing by on their way to class.

Watch the Video
Protests Against the Vietnam War at **myhistorylab.com**

While the nation reeled from this shock, two students at Jackson State University were killed by Mississippi state policemen. A wave of student strikes followed, closing down hundreds of colleges, including many that had seen no previous unrest. Moderate students by the tens of thousands joined with the radicals.

The almost universal condemnation of the invasion and of the way it had been planned shook Nixon hard. He backtracked, pulling American ground troops out of Cambodia quickly. But he did not change his Vietnam policy, and in fact Cambodia apparently stiffened his determination. As American ground troops were withdrawn, he stepped up air attacks.

The balance of forces remained in uneasy equilibrium through 1971. But late in March 1972 the North Vietnamese again mounted a series of assaults throughout South Vietnam. Nixon responded with heavier bombing, and he ordered the approaches to Haiphong and other North Vietnamese ports sown with mines to cut off the communists' supplies.

Détente with Communism

But in the midst of these aggressive actions, Nixon and his National Security Adviser Henry Kissinger devised a bold diplomatic offensive, executed in nearly complete secrecy. Nixon and Kissinger made an effective though not always harmonious team. Abandoning a lifetime of treating communism as a single worldwide conspiracy that had to be contained at all costs, Nixon decided to deal with China and the Soviet Union as separate powers and, as he put it, to "live together and work together" with both. Nixon and Kissinger called the new policy **détente**, a French term meaning "the relaxation of tensions between governments." But détente was not an expression of friendship so much as an acknowledgment that for decades the policy of containment had driven China and the Soviet Union closer together.

First Nixon sent Kissinger secretly to China and the Soviet Union to prepare the way for summit meetings with the communist leaders. Both the Chinese and the Soviets agreed to the meetings. Then, in February 1972, Nixon and Kissinger, accompanied by a small army of reporters and television crews, flew to Beijing. After much dining, sightseeing, posing for photographers, and consultation with Chinese officials, Nixon agreed to promote economic and cultural exchanges and supported the admission of communist China to the United Nations. As a result, exports to communist China increased substantially, reaching $4 billion in 1980. Nixon's visit, ending more than twenty years of adamant American refusal to accept the reality of the Chinese revolution, marked a dramatic reversal; as such it was hailed throughout the world.

In May 1972 Nixon and Kissinger flew to Moscow. This trip also produced striking results. The mere fact that it took place while war still raged in Vietnam was remarkable. More important, however, the meeting resulted in a **Strategic Arms Limitation Treaty (SALT)**. The two powers agreed to stop making nuclear ballistic missiles and to reduce the number of antiballistic missiles in their arsenals to 200. Nixon also agreed to permit large sales of American grain to the Soviet Union.

By the summer of 1972, with the presidential election looming in the fall, Kissinger redoubled his efforts to negotiate an end to the Vietnam War. By October he and the North Vietnamese had hammered out a settlement calling for a cease-fire, the return of American prisoners of war, and the withdrawal of United States forces from Vietnam. Shortly before the presidential election Kissinger announced that peace was "at hand."

Nixon in Triumph

A few days later President Nixon was reelected, defeating the Democratic candidate, Senator George McGovern of South Dakota, in a landslide—521 electoral votes to 17. McGovern carried only Massachusetts and the District of Columbia. McGovern's campaign had been hampered by his tendency to advance poorly thought-out proposals, such as his scheme for funneling money directly to the poor, and by his rather bumbling, low-key oratorical style. The campaign marked the historical breakdown of the coalition that Franklin Roosevelt had fashioned and on which he and his Democratic successors, particularly Truman and Johnson, had ridden to power. Of that coalition, only African Americans voted solidly for McGovern.

Nixon had won over hundreds of thousands of voters who had supported Democrats in earlier elections. The "solid South" was again solid, but this time solidly Republican. Nixon's so-called southern strategy of reducing the pressure for school desegregation and otherwise restricting federal efforts on behalf of blacks had a powerful attraction to northern blue-collar workers as well.

Suddenly Nixon loomed as one of the most powerful and successful presidents in American history. His tough-minded but flexible handling of foreign policy questions, even his harsh Vietnamese policy, suggested decisiveness and self-confidence, qualities he had often seemed to lack in his earlier career. His willingness, despite his long history as a militant cold warrior, to negotiate with the communist nations indicated a new flexibility and creativity. His landslide victory appeared to demonstrate that a large majority of the people approved of his way of tackling the major problems of the times.

But Kissinger's agreement with the North Vietnamese came apart when Nguyen Van Thieu, the South Vietnamese president, refused to sign it. Thieu claimed that the agreement, by permitting communist troops to remain in the South, would ensure his ultimate defeat. To Kissinger's chagrin, Nixon sided with Thieu and resumed the bombing of North Vietnam in December 1972, this time sending the mighty B-52s directly over Hanoi and other cities. The destruction they caused was great, but their effectiveness as a means of forcing concessions from the North Vietnamese was at best debatable.

In January 1973 a settlement was finally reached. As with the October "agreement," the North Vietnamese retained control of large sections of the South, and they promised to

President and Mrs. Nixon dine with Chinese communist officials in Beijing in February 1972. Even Nixon's harshest critics conceded that his initiative in reopening United States-China relations was a diplomatic masterstroke.

Photo Credit: Magnum Photos, Inc.

release American prisoners of war within sixty days. Thieu assented this time, largely because Nixon secretly pledged that the United States would "respond with full force" if North Vietnam resumed its offensive. Within several months most prisoners of war were released, and the last American troops were pulled out of Vietnam. More than 57,000 Americans had died in the long war, and over 300,000 more had been wounded. Nearly a million communist soldiers and 185,000 South Vietnamese soldiers were reported killed.

In 1973, too, Kissinger was named secretary of state; he shared the Nobel Prize for Peace with a North Vietnamese diplomat for negotiating an end to the Vietnam War.

Domestic Policy under Nixon

When Nixon became president in 1969, the major economic problem he faced was inflation. This was caused primarily by the heavy military expenditures and easy-money policies of the Johnson administration. Nixon cut federal spending and balanced the 1969 budget, while the Federal Reserve Board forced up interest rates to slow the expansion of the money supply. When prices continued to rise, uneasiness mounted and labor unions demanded large wage increases.

In 1970 Congress passed a law giving the president power to regulate prices and wages. Nixon originally opposed this legislation, but in the summer of 1971 he changed his mind and announced a ninety-day price and wage freeze. Then he set up a pay board and a price commission with authority to limit wage and price increases when the freeze ended. These controls did not check inflation completely—and they angered union leaders, who felt that labor was being shortchanged—but they did slow the upward spiral.

In handling other domestic issues, the president was less firm. Like President Kennedy he was primarily interested in foreign affairs. He supported a bold plan for a "minimum income" for poor families, but dropped it when it alarmed his conservative supporters and got nowhere in Congress. But when a groundswell of public support for conserving natural resources and checking pollution led Congress to pass bills creating the **Environmental Protection Agency (EPA)** and the Clean Air Act of 1970, he signed them cheerfully.

After his triumphant reelection and the withdrawal of the last American troops from Vietnam, Nixon resolved to change the direction in which the nation had been moving

The Clean Air Act of 1970 mandated reductions in air pollution, arguably the most important environmental legislation passed by the United States during the twentieth century.

Photo Credit: Chris Knorr/Corbis RF.

for decades. He announced that he intended to reduce the interference of the federal government in the affairs of individuals. People should be more self-reliant, he said, and he denounced what he called "permissiveness." Excessive concern for the interests of blacks and other minorities must end. Criminals should be punished "without pity." No person or group should be coddled by the state.

These aims brought Nixon into conflict with liberals in both parties, with the leaders of minority groups, and with those alarmed by the increasing power of the executive. The conflict came to a head over the president's anti-inflation policy. After his second inauguration he ended price and wage controls and called for voluntary "restraints." This approach did not work. Prices soared in the most rapid inflation since the Korean War. In an effort to check the rise, Nixon set a rigid limit on federal expenditures. To keep within the limit, he cut back or abolished a large number of social welfare programs and reduced federal grants in support of science and education. He even impounded (refused to spend) funds already appropriated by Congress for purposes of which he disapproved.

The impoundment created a furor on Capitol Hill, but when Congress failed to override his vetoes of bills challenging this policy, it appeared that Nixon was in total command. The White House staff, headed by H. R. Haldeman and John Ehrlichman, dominated the Washington bureaucracy. Critics began to grumble about a new "imperial presidency." No one seemed capable of checking Nixon.

The Watergate Break-In and Cover-Up

On March 19, 1973, James McCord, a former agent of both the Federal Bureau of Investigation and the Central Intelligence Agency accused of burglary, wrote a letter to the judge presiding at his trial. His act precipitated a series of disclosures that first disrupted and then destroyed the Nixon administration.

McCord had been employed during the 1972 presidential campaign as a security officer of the Committee to Re-elect the President (CREEP). At about 1 AM on June 17, 1972, he and four other men had broken into Democratic party headquarters at Watergate, a complex of apartments and offices in Washington. The burglars were members of an unofficial CREEP surveillance group known as "the plumbers." Nixon, who was compelled by a need to conceal information about his administration, had formed the group after the Pentagon Papers, a confidential report on government policy in Vietnam, had been leaked to the press. The "plumbers" had been caught rifling files and installing electronic eavesdropping devices.

Two other Republican campaign officials were soon implicated in the affair. Their arrest aroused suspicions that the Republican party was behind the break-in. Nixon denied it.

Most people evidently took the president at his word. He was far ahead in the polls and seemed so sure to win reelection that it was hard to believe he would stoop to burglary to discover what the Democrats were up to. In any case, the affair did not materially affect the election. When brought to trial early in 1973, most of the Watergate burglars pleaded guilty.

McCord, who did not, was convicted by the jury. Before Judge John J. Sirica imposed sentences on the culprits, however, McCord wrote his letter. High Republican officials had known about the burglary in advance and had paid the defendants "hush money" to keep their connection secret, McCord claimed. Perjury had been committed during the trial.

The truth of McCord's charges swiftly became apparent. The head of CREEP, Jeb Stuart Magruder, and President Nixon's lawyer, John W. Dean III, admitted their involvement. Among the disclosures that emerged over the following months were these:

- Large sums of money had been paid to the burglars at the instigation of the White House to ensure their silence.
- Agents of the Nixon administration had burglarized the office of a psychiatrist, seeking evidence against one of his patients, Daniel Ellsberg, who had been charged with leaking the Pentagon Papers to the *New York Times*. (This disclosure led to the immediate dismissal of the charges against Ellsberg.)
- CREEP officials had attempted to disrupt the campaigns of leading Democratic candidates during the 1972 primaries in a number of illegal ways.
- A number of corporations had made large contributions to the Nixon reelection campaign in violation of federal law.
- The Nixon administration had placed wiretaps on the telephones of some of its own officials as well as on those of journalists critical of its policies without first obtaining authorization from the courts.

These revelations led to the dismissal of John Dean and to the resignations of most of Nixon's closest advisers, including Haldeman, Ehrlichman, and Attorney Generals John Mitchell and Richard Kleindienst. They also raised the question of the president's personal connection with the **Watergate scandal**. This he steadfastly denied. He insisted that he would investigate the Watergate affair thoroughly and see that the guilty were punished. He refused, however, to allow investigators to examine White House documents, on grounds of executive privilege, which he continued to assert in very broad terms.

In the teeth of Nixon's denials, John Dean, testifying under oath, stated flatly and in circumstantial detail that the president had ordered him to pay the Watergate burglars to conceal White House involvement; if true, the president had been guilty of obstructing justice, a serious crime.

Dean had been a persuasive witness, but many people were reluctant to believe that a president could lie so cold-bloodedly to the entire country. Therefore, when it came out during later hearings of the Senate committee investigating the Watergate scandal that the president had systematically made secret tape recordings of White House conversations and telephone calls, the disclosure caused a sensation. It seemed obvious that these tapes would settle the question of Nixon's involvement once and for all. Again Nixon refused to allow access to the evidence.

One result of the scandals and of Nixon's attitude was a precipitous decline in his standing in public opinion polls. Calls for his resignation, even for impeachment, began to be heard. Yielding to pressure, he agreed to the appointment of an "independent" special prosecutor to investigate the Watergate affair, and he promised the appointee, Professor Archibald Cox of Harvard Law School, full cooperation.

Cox swiftly aroused the president's ire by seeking access to White House records, including the tapes. When Nixon refused to turn over the tapes, Cox obtained a subpoena from Judge Sirica ordering him to do so. The administration appealed this decision and lost in the appellate court. Then, while the case was headed for the Supreme Court, Nixon ordered the new attorney general, Elliot Richardson, to dismiss Cox. Both Richardson, who had promised the Senate during his confirmation hearings that the special prosecutor would have a free hand, and his chief assistant resigned rather than do as the president directed. The third-ranking officer of the Justice Department carried out Nixon's order.

These events of Saturday, October 20, promptly dubbed the Saturday Night Massacre, caused an outburst of public indignation. Congress was bombarded by thousands of letters and telegrams demanding the president's impeachment. The House Judiciary Committee began an investigation to see if enough evidence for impeachment existed.

Once again Nixon backed down. He agreed to turn over the tapes to Judge Sirica with the understanding that relevant materials could be presented to the grand jury investigating the Watergate affair but that nothing would be revealed to the public. He then named a new special prosecutor, Leon Jaworski, and promised him access to whatever White House documents he needed. However, it soon came out that several tapes were missing and that an important section of another had been deliberately erased.

Then Vice President Agnew was accused of income tax fraud and of having accepted bribes while serving as Baltimore county executive and governor of Maryland. To escape a jail term Agnew admitted in October that he had been guilty of tax evasion and resigned as vice president.

Acting according to the procedures for presidential and vice-presidential succession of the Twenty-Fifth Amendment, adopted in 1967, President Nixon nominated Representative Gerald R. Ford of Michigan as vice president, and he was confirmed by Congress. Ford had served continuously in Congress since 1949 and as minority leader since 1964. His positions on public issues were close to Nixon's; he was an internationalist in foreign affairs and a conservative and convinced Republican partisan on domestic issues.

The Judgment on Watergate: "Expletive Deleted"

Meanwhile, special prosecutor Jaworski continued his investigation of the Watergate scandals. In March 1974 a grand jury indicted Haldeman; Ehrlichman; former attorney general John Mitchell, who had been head of CREEP at the time of the break-in; and four other White House aides for conspiring to block the Watergate investigation. The jurors also named Nixon an "unindicted co-conspirator," Jaworski having informed them that their power to indict a president was constitutionally questionable. Judge Sirica thereupon turned over the jury's evidence against Nixon to the House Judiciary Committee.

In an effort to check the mounting criticism, late in April Nixon released edited transcripts of the tapes he had turned over to the court the previous November. In addition to much incriminating evidence, the transcripts provided the public with a fascinating and shocking view of how the president conducted himself in private. In conversations he seemed confused, indecisive, and lacking in any concern for the public interest. His repeated use of foul language, so out of keeping with his public image, offended millions. The phrase "expletive deleted," inserted in place of words considered too vulgar for publication in family newspapers, overnight became a catchword.

With the defendants in the Watergate case demanding access to tapes that they claimed would prove their innocence, Jaworski was compelled either to obtain them or to risk having the charges dismissed on the grounds that the government was withholding evidence. He therefore subpoenaed sixty-four additional tapes. Nixon refused to obey the subpoena. Swiftly the case of **United States v. Richard M. Nixon** went to the Supreme Court.

In the summer of 1974—after so many months of alarms and crises—the Watergate drama reached its climax. The Judiciary Committee, following months of study of the evidence behind closed doors, decided to conduct its deliberations in open session. While millions watched on television, thirty-eight members of the House of Representatives debated the charges and finally adopted three articles of impeachment. They charged the president with obstructing justice, misusing the powers of his office, and failing to obey the committee's subpoenas. Except in the case of the last article, many of the Republicans on the committee joined with the Democrats in voting aye, a clear indication that the full House would vote to impeach.

On the eve of the debates, the Supreme Court had ruled unanimously that the president must turn over the sixty-four subpoenaed tapes to the special prosecutor. Executive privilege had its place, the Court stated, but no person, not even a president, could "withhold evidence that is demonstrably relevant in a criminal trial."

When the subpoenaed tapes were released and transcribed, Nixon's fate was sealed. Three recorded conversations between the president and H. R. Haldeman just after the Watergate break-in proved conclusively that Nixon had tried to obstruct justice by engaging the CIA in an effort to persuade the FBI not to follow up leads in the case on the spurious grounds that national security was involved.

Read the Document

House Judiciary Committee's Conclusion on Impeachment at **myhistorylab.com**

When the House Judiciary Committee members read the new transcripts, all the Republican members who had voted against the impeachment articles reversed themselves. Republican leaders told the president categorically that the House would impeach him and that no more than a handful of senators would vote for acquittal.

Nixon Resigns, Ford Becomes President

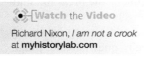

Watch the Video

Richard Nixon, *I am not a crook* at **myhistorylab.com**

On August 8, 1974, Nixon announced his resignation. The resignation took effect at noon on August 9, when Gerald Ford was sworn in as president. "Our long national nightmare is over," Ford declared. Within weeks of taking office, Ford pardoned Nixon for whatever crimes he had committed in office, even any, if such existed, as had yet come to light.

Whether Nixon's resignation marked the end of one era or the beginning of another is a difficult question. Like most critical moments in human history, it seems in retrospect to have been both. Nixon had extricated the United States from Vietnam—though at tremendous cost in lives and money and to little evident purpose. His détente with the Soviet Union and Red China was surely an early sign of the easing of Cold War tensions characteristic of the decades to follow. Moreover, Nixon's assault on liberals, coming just as public disillusionment with the Great Society programs was mounting, put an end to the liberal era that had begun with the reforms of the New Deal.

Milestones

1951	J. D. Salinger publishes *The Catcher in the Rye*	1965	Black Muslim fanatics assassinate Malcolm X
1955	Joseph Heller publishes *Catch-22* Allen Ginsberg publishes *Howl*	1968	Communists strike all over South Vietnam in Tet Offensive
1957	Jack Kerouac publishes *On the Road*		Lyndon Johnson withdraws as candidate for reelection
1960	Black college students found Student Nonviolent Coordinating Committee (SNCC)		Martin Luther King, Jr., is assassinated
	John F. Kennedy elected President		Robert F. Kennedy is assassinated
1961	CIA-trained Cuban exiles launch disastrous Bay of Pigs invasion	1969	Richard Nixon is elected president Nixon announces "Vietnamization" of war
	Soviets build Berlin wall		Apollo 11 lands on the moon
	John F. Kennedy founds Peace Corps	1970	Nixon announces "incursion" into Cambodia
	Freedom riders integrate buses in South		Antiwar student protesters are killed at Kent State University and Jackson State University
1962	Soviet Premier Khrushchev precipitates Cuban missile crisis		
	Students for a Democratic Society (SDS) issues Port Huron Statement		Congress passes Clean Air Act and creates Environmental Protection Agency (EPA)
1963	United States supports coup to oust President Ngo Dinh Diem of South Vietnam	1972	Nixon's "plumbers" burglarize Democratic national headquarters at Watergate complex
	Martin Luther King, Jr., gives "I Have a Dream" speech during March on Washington		Nixon and Kissinger visit China and Soviet Union
	Lee Harvey Oswald assassinates President Kennedy; Lyndon Johnson becomes president		United States and Soviet Union sign Strategic Arms Limitation Treaty (SALT)
1964	Congress endorses escalation of Vietnam War in Gulf of Tonkin Resolution		Nixon is reelected in landslide
	Lyndon Johnson is elected president, begins Great Society program	1973	House Judiciary Committee begins impeachment hearings against Nixon
	Congress passes historic Civil Rights Act		Vice President Spiro Agnew resigns; Gerald Ford is appointed vice president
	Free speech movement disrupts University of California at Berkeley		Last American troops leave Vietnam
1965	Congress passes Immigration Act, ending national quota system		Nixon fires Watergate special prosecutor Archibald Cox (Saturday Night Massacre)
	Medicare Act pays some medical costs for senior citizens and the poor	1974	Supreme Court orders release of Nixon's White House tapes
	Congress funds education with Elementary and Secondary Education Act and Higher Education Act		Nixon resigns; Gerald Ford becomes president and pardons Nixon

√●─⌐Study and Review at www.myhistorylab.com

Review Questions

1. The introduction emphasizes the difficulties JFK, LBJ, and Nixon had in getting out of the "quagmire" that was the Vietnam War. What might they have done differently? Why did they pursue the course they chose?

2. Why did the escalation of the war from 1961 to 1968 fail to produce a victory? How did Nixon change the Vietnam policies of his predecessors? Why didn't they succeed?

3. How did the war affect American society? What effect did student protests have on the war?

4. How did Johnson's Great Society differ from Franklin D. Roosevelt's New Deal? Which aspects of the Great Society proved most successful? Why did others fall short of expectations?

5. What explains the rise of Black Power during the 1960s? Why did the race riots strike just as the federal government was providing tangible assistance on matters of civil rights, racial discrimination, and poverty?

6. Why did Nixon form the "plumbers" and then obstruct justice following the Watergate break-in? Why did Ford pardon Nixon?

Key Terms

Bay of Pigs fiasco
beat school
Berlin wall
Civil Rights Act of 1964
Cuban missile crisis
détente
Environmental Protection Agency (EPA)
Great Society
Gulf of Tonkin Resolution
Medicare
Strategic Arms Limitation Treaty (SALT)
Student Nonviolent Coordinating Committee (SNCC)
Students for a Democratic Society (SDS)
Tet offensive
United States v. Richard M. Nixon
Voting Rights Act of 1965
Watergate scandal

Running on Empty: 1975–1991

((•←[Hear the Audio at myhistorylab.com

Do you pay too much for gas?

DURING THE SUMMER OF 2008, WITH THE PRESIDENTIAL CAMPAIGN in full swing, gas prices topped $4 a gallon. Republican candidate John McCain called for laws allowing oil companies to drill for oil in U.S. coastal waters. Sarah Palin, Governor of oil-rich Alaska and McCain's running mate, put it more succinctly: "Drill, Baby, Drill!"

Senator Barack Obama had opposed offshore drilling. But as gas prices rose, his lead in the polls slipped. With the election less than two months away, Obama reversed course. Now he supported off-shore drilling. Democratic leaders in Congress, scrambling to clamber onto the offshore drilling bandwagon, pushed through a law ending the quarter-century old ban on drilling for oil in federal waters off the Atlantic and Pacific Coasts.

Then, in 2010, a British-owned oil rig forty miles off the coast of Louisiana exploded, killing eleven workers and releasing millions of barrels of crude oil into the Gulf of Mexico. The oil spill was arguably the worst environmental disaster in the nation's history.

For much of the twentieth century, the high cost and environmental risks of offshore oil drilling exceeded the projected profits of such ventures. But that changed in 1970s when the flow of crude oil to the United States and the West was cut off; the price of oil soared. Now offshore drilling made economic sense. Because most of the untapped oil lay beneath the oceans, offshore drilling platforms were built in the North Sea, off the coast of Brazil, and in the Gulf of Mexico.

For a nation dependent on the automobile, the 1970s oil shortage plunged the economy into a deep recession. Factories were closed and workers laid off. A new conservatism prevailed, part of a reaction against the costly measures of LBJ's Great Society. The need for cheap oil, moreover, pushed the United States deeper into the labyrinth of Middle Eastern politics. War would follow.

The Oil Crisis

While most Americans watched, transfixed, as the events of Watergate interred the Nixon presidency, few were aware that a battle on the other side of the world was about to transform their lives. On October 6, 1973, the eve of Yom Kippur, the Jewish Day of Atonement, Egypt and Syria attacked the state of Israel. Six years earlier Israel had trounced the

Egyptians with humiliating ease; it had then seized the Sinai peninsula and the West Bank of the Jordan River, an area including Jerusalem. But now Egypt's armored divisions roared into the Sinai and threatened to slice Israel in half; Syrian troops advanced against Israel farther north.

Israeli Prime Minister Golda Meir pleaded with President Nixon for additional arms and aircraft. The United States immediately airlifted scores of fighter planes and other desperately needed material to Israel. The Israelis recrossed the Suez Canal, cut Egyptian supply

After the Arab oil embargo, gasoline became so scarce that customers were limited to buying ten gallons at a time. This led to long lines at the pumps.

lines, and forced Egypt's president, Anwar Sadat, to capitulate. But the Arab world then aimed its biggest weapon squarely at the United States: It cut off oil shipments to the West.

Deprived of Middle Eastern oil, the American economy sputtered. The price of oil rose to $12 a barrel, up from $3. This sent prices soaring for nearly everything else. Homes were heated with oil, factories were powered by it, utility plants used it to generate electricity, and farm produce was shipped to markets on gas-fueled trucks. The Arab oil embargo pushed up gas prices; service stations intermittently ran out of gasoline; long lines formed at those that remained open.

In the spring of 1974, Henry Kissinger negotiated an agreement that required Israel's withdrawal from some territory occupied since the 1967 war; the Arab nations then lifted the oil embargo. But the principal oil exporting nations—Venezuela, Saudi Arabia, Kuwait, Iraq, and Iran—had learned a valuable lesson: If they limited production, they could drive up the price of oil. After the embargo had ended, their cartel, the **Organization of Petroleum Exporting Countries (OPEC)**, announced another price increase. Gasoline prices doubled overnight.

American automakers who had scoffed at tiny Japanese "boxes" now winced as these foreign competitors claimed the new market for small, fuel-efficient, front-wheel-drive cars. American auto companies were unable to respond to this challenge. As production costs rose, manufacturers needed to sell more of their behemoth models, loaded with expensive options such as air conditioning, power windows, and stereo systems. Because the automobile industry stimulated so many other industries—steel, vinyl, glass, rubber—the nation's manufacturing sector was soon in trouble.

Ford as President

Gerald Ford replaced Nixon as president in the summer of 1974, just as the economy was beginning to deteriorate. At first, the country greeted Ford with a collective sigh of relief. Most observers considered Ford unimaginative, certainly not brilliant. But he was hardworking, and—most important under the circumstances—his record was untouched by scandal.

Ford identified inflation as the chief economic culprit and asked patriotic citizens to signify their willingness to fight it by wearing WIN (Whip Inflation Now) buttons. Almost immediately the economy slumped. Production fell and the unemployment rate rose above 9 percent, about twice the postwar average. The president was forced to ask for tax cuts and other measures aimed at stimulating business activity. This made inflation worse and did little to promote employment.

The Fall of South Vietnam

Depressing news about the economy was compounded by disheartening events in Vietnam. In January 1975, after two years of a bloody "cease-fire", North Vietnam attacked just south of the seventeenth parallel, commencing its two-year plan to conquer South Vietnam. The South Vietnamese army retreated, then fled, and finally dissolved with a rapidity that astonished their attackers.

Ford had always supported the Vietnam War. As the military situation deteriorated, he urged Congress to pour more arms into the South to stem the North Vietnamese advance. The legislators flatly refused to do so, and on May 1, 1975, the Viet Cong and North Vietnamese entered Saigon, which they renamed Ho Chi Minh City. The long Vietnam War was finally over.

Ford versus Carter

Ford's uninspiring record on the economy and foreign policy suggested that he would be vulnerable in 1976. That year the Democrats chose Jimmy Carter, a former governor of Georgia, as their candidate.

Carter had been a naval officer and a substantial peanut farmer and warehouse owner before entering politics. He was elected governor of Georgia in 1970. While governor he won something of a reputation as a southern public official who treated black citizens fairly. Carter's political style was informal. During the campaign for delegates he turned his inexperience in national politics to advantage, emphasizing his lack of connection with the Washington establishment rather than apologizing for it. He repeatedly called attention to his integrity and deep religious faith.

Carter sought to make the election a referendum on morality. After Watergate, an atmosphere of scandal permeated Washington, and aspiring journalists and congressmen trained their sights on Kissinger, who

Georgia governor Jimmy Carter and President Gerald Ford debate in 1976. The campaign featured Carter's candor in a *Playboy* interview: "I've committed adultery in my heart many times." The headline stories often neglected the sentences that followed: "This is something that God recognizes I will do—and I have done it—and God forgives me for it."

remained secretary of state after Nixon's resignation. The most significant of the allegations was his meddling in the affairs of Chile, which in 1970 elected Salvador Allende, a Marxist, as president. After Allende's election, Kissinger called on the CIA to "destabilize" Allende's regime. In 1973, Allende was murdered in a military coup and his government toppled. Carter promised an administration of "constant decency" in contrast to Kissinger's penchant for secret diplomacy and covert skullduggery.

In the Republican primaries, Ford was challenged by Ronald Reagan, ex-governor of California, a movie actor turned politician who was the darling of the Republican right wing. Reagan was an excellent speaker, whereas Ford proved somewhat bumbling on the stump. Reagan, too, hammered away at Kissinger, citing his "immoral" détente with communist China. At Reagan's insistence, the Republican platform denounced "secret agreements, hidden from our people"—another jab at Kissinger.

Both Republican candidates gathered substantial blocs of delegates, but Ford staved off the Reagan challenge. That Ford did not win easily, possessed as he was of the advantage of incumbency, made his chances of election in November appear slim.

When the final contest began, both candidates were vague with respect to issues, a situation that hurt Carter particularly because he had made so much of honesty and straight

Ford Presidential Campaign Ad: Feeling Good About America at **myhistorylab.com**

talk. With both candidates stumbling toward the finish line, pundits predicted an extremely close contest, and they were right: Carter won, 297 electoral votes to 241, having carried most of the South, including Texas, and a few large industrial states. He also ran well in districts dominated by labor union members. The wish of the public to punish the party of Richard Nixon probably was a further reason for his victory.

The Carter Presidency

Carter shone brightly in comparison with Nixon, and he seemed more forward-looking and imaginative than Ford. He tried to give a tone of democratic simplicity and moral fervor to his administration. After delivering his inaugural address he walked with his wife Rosalynn and their daughter Amy in the parade from the Capitol to the White House instead of riding in a limousine. They enrolled Amy, a fourth-grader, in a largely black Washington public school. Soon after taking office he held a "call-in"; for two hours he answered questions phoned in by people from all over the country.

Carter's actual administration of his office did not go nearly so well. He put so many Georgians in important posts that his administration took on a parochial character. The administration developed a reputation for submitting complicated proposals to Congress with great fanfare and then failing to follow up on them. Whatever matter Carter was considering at the moment seemed to absorb him totally—other urgent matters were allowed to drift.

A National Malaise

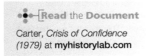

Carter, Crisis of Confidence (1979) at **myhistorylab.com**

To Carter, the nation's economic woes were symptomatic of a more fundamental flaw in the nation's soul. In a heralded television speech he complained that "a moral and spiritual crisis" had sapped people's energies and undermined civic pride. Critics responded that the nation needed a president rather than a preacher, and that sermons on the emptiness of consumption rang hollow to those who had lost their jobs.

The economic downturn, though triggered by the energy shortage, had more fundamental causes. In the prosperous postwar decades, many companies had grown too big and complacent, more attuned to the demands of the corporate bureaucracy than the needs of customers. Workers' boredom lowered productivity. Absenteeism at General Motors and Ford had doubled during the 1960s. On an average day in 1970, 5 percent of GM's workforce was missing without explanation, and on Mondays and Fridays 10 percent failed to show up. Two years later simmering discontents among young workers boiled over at the GM assembly division at Lordstown, Ohio. GM had installed robotic welding machines, streamlined the workforce, and accelerated the assembly line: 100 cars passed through the line each hour—40 more than under the previous system. Without authorization from the national UAW, younger workers refused to work at the faster pace, allowing many chassis to pass through untouched and throwing the factory into chaos.

Union membership slipped badly from the high point of the mid–1950s, when over one in three nonagricultural workers belonged to unions; by 1978, the proportion had declined to one in four, and by 1990, one in six. During the 1940s and 1950s, most workers voted to join a union, pay dues, and have the organization bargain for them. By 1978, however, union organizers were losing three-fourths of their campaigns to represent workers; and many workers who belonged to unions were opting to get out. Every year, 800 more union shops voted to rescind their affiliation.

The economic crisis after 1973 was unsettling because, for the first time in the nation's history, the rising tide of unemployment had failed to extinguish inflation. Millions of workers lost their jobs, yet wages and prices continued to rise. The term **stagflation** (a combination of stagnation and inflation) was coined to describe this anomaly. In 1971 an inflation rate of 5 percent had so alarmed President Nixon that he had imposed a price freeze. By 1975 inflation had soared to 11 percent and by 1979, it peaked at a whopping 13 percent; unemployment ranged from 6 to 10 percent, nearly twice the usual postwar level.

Carter had promised to fight inflation by reducing government spending and balancing the budget and to stimulate the economy by cutting taxes, policies that were very much like those of Nixon and Ford. He advanced an admirable if complicated plan for conserving energy and reducing the dependence of the United States on OPEC oil. This plan would raise the tax on

The skyrocketing price of oil caused many to champion nuclear energy. But on March 28, 1979, the failure of a cooling system caused the Three Mile Island nuclear reactor to overheat and generate radioactivity in the Harrisburg region. The reactor was shut down five days later.

gasoline and impose a new tax on "gas guzzlers," cars that got relatively few miles per gallon. But in his typical fashion he did not press hard for these measures.

The federal government made matters worse in several ways. Wages and salaries rose in response to inflation, but taxes went up more rapidly because larger dollar incomes put people in higher tax brackets. This "bracket creep" caused resentment and frustration among middle-class families. "Taxpayer revolts" erupted as many people turned against expensive government programs for aiding the poor. Federal borrowing to cover the deficit pushed up interest rates and increased the costs of all businesses that had to borrow.

Soaring mortgage rates made it difficult to sell homes. The housing slump meant unemployment for thousands of carpenters, bricklayers, and other construction workers and bankruptcy for many builders. Double-digit interest rates also hurt small businesses seeking to expand. Savings and loan institutions were especially hard-hit because they were saddled with countless mortgages made when rates were as low as 4 and 5 percent. Now they had to pay much more than that to hold deposits and offer even higher rates to attract new money.

Bad as inflation was in the mid-1970s, it got worse in 1979 when further instability in the Middle East nearly tripled the price of oil, which now reached $34 a barrel. This sent gasoline far over the $1 a gallon price barrier many had thought inconceivable. Within months Ford stock, at thirty-two in 1978, plummeted to sixteen; its credit rating with Standard and Poor's fell from AAA to an ignominious BBB. Chrysler, the third largest automaker, tottered near bankruptcy and then fell over the edge, saved in mid-fall only by a $1.2 billion federal loan guarantee. From 1978 to 1982, the jobs of one in three autoworkers were eliminated.

"Constant Decency" in Action

In contrast to the shadowy dealings of the Nixon-Kissinger years, Carter promised to conduct a foreign policy characterized by "constant decency." The defense of "basic human rights" would come before all other concerns. He then cut off aid to Chile and Argentina because of human rights violations. He also negotiated treaties with Panama that provided for the gradual transfer of the Panama Canal to that nation and guaranteed the canal's neutrality. But he said little about what was going on in a long list of other nations whose citizens' rights were being repressed.

The president also intended to carry forward the Nixon-Kissinger policy of détente, and in 1979 another Strategic Arms Limitation Treaty (SALT II) was signed with the Soviet Union. But the following winter the Soviet Union sent troops into Afghanistan to overthrow the government there. Carter denounced the invasion and warned the Soviets that he would use force if they invaded any of the countries bordering the Persian Gulf. He withdrew the SALT treaty, which he had sent to the Senate for ratification. He also refused to allow American athletes to compete in the 1980 Olympic games in Moscow.

Carter's one striking diplomatic achievement was the so-called **Camp David Accords** between Israel and Egypt. In September 1978 President Anwar Sadat of Egypt and Prime Minister Menachem Begin of Israel came to the United States at Carter's invitation to seek a peace treaty ending the state of war that had existed between their two countries for many years.

For two weeks they conferred at Camp David, the presidential retreat outside the capital, and Carter's mediation had much to do with their successful negotiations.

In the treaty Israel promised to withdraw from territory captured from Egypt during the 1967 Israeli-Egypt war. Egypt in turn recognized Israel as a nation, the first Arab country to do so. Peace ensured an uninterrupted supply of Arab oil to the United States. The Camp David Accords were the first and, as it turned out, the last significant agreement between Israel and a major Arab state.

The Iran Crisis: Origins

At this point a dramatic shift in Iran thrust Carter into the spotlight as never before. On November 4, 1979, about 400 armed Muslim militants broke into the American embassy compound in Tehran, Iran, and took everyone within the walls captive.

The seizure had roots that ran far back in Iranian history. During World War II, Great Britain, the Soviet Union, and later the United States occupied Iran and forced its pro-German shah into exile, replacing him with his twenty-two-year-old son, Muhammad Reza Pahlavi. But in the early 1950s power shifted to Prime Minister Muhammad Mossadegh, a leftist who sought to finance social reform by nationalizing the mostly American-owned Anglo-Iranian Oil Company.

In 1953, the Iranian army, backed by the CIA, arrested Mossadegh and put the young Pahlavi in power. The fall of Mossadegh ensured a steady flow of cheap oil, but it turned most Iranians against the United States and Shah Pahlavi. His unpopularity led the shah to purchase enormous amounts of American arms. Over the years Iran became the most powerful military force in the region.

The shah's rule was not one of "constant decency." His secret police, the Savak, brutally suppressed liberal opponents. At the same time, Muslim religious leaders were particularly offended by the shah's attempts to introduce Western ideas and technology into Iran. Because his American-supplied army and his American- and Israeli-trained secret police kept the shah in power, his opponents hated the United States almost as much as they hated their autocratic ruler.

Throughout 1977, riots and demonstrations convulsed Iran. When soldiers fired on protesters, the bloodshed caused more unrest, and that unrest caused even more bloodshed. Over 10,000 civilians were killed; many times that number were wounded. In 1978 the whole country seemed to rise against the shah. Finally, in January 1979, he was forced to flee. A revolutionary government headed by a religious leader, the Ayatollah Ruhollah Khomeini, assumed power. Freedom, he said, was the great enemy of Islam. He also claimed that Islam condoned terror: "Islam says: Whatever good there is exists thanks to the sword and in the shadow of the sword! . . . The sword is the key to paradise, which can be opened only for holy warriors."

Khomeini denounced the United States, the "Great Satan," whose support of the shah, he said, had caused the Iranian people untold suffering. When President Carter allowed the shah to come to the United States for medical treatment, militants in Tehran seized the American embassy.

The Iran Crisis: Carter's Dilemma

The militants announced that the Americans at the embassy would be held hostage until the United States returned the shah to Iran for trial as a traitor. They also demanded that the shah's vast wealth be confiscated and surrendered to the Iranian government. President

Carter rejected these demands. Instead Carter froze Iranian assets in the United States and banned trade with Iran until the hostages were freed.

A stalemate developed. Months passed. Even after the shah, who was terminally ill, left the United States for Panama, the Iranians remained adamant. The **Iranian hostage crisis** produced a remarkable emotional response in the United States. For the first time since the Vietnam War the entire country agreed on something.

In 1979 Islamic militants hold an American embassy worker in Tehran.

Photo Credit: AP Wide World Photos.

Nevertheless the hostages languished in Iran. In April 1980 Carter finally ordered a team of marine commandos flown into Iran in a desperate attempt to free the hostages. The raid was a fiasco. Several helicopters broke down when their rotors sucked desert sand into the engines. Another helicopter crashed and eight commandos were killed. The Iranians made political capital of the incident, gleefully displaying on television the wrecked aircraft and captured American equipment. The stalemate continued. When the shah died in exile in Egypt in July 1980, the Iranians made no move to release the hostages.

The Election of 1980

Despite the failure of the raid and the persistence of stagflation, Carter had more than enough delegates at the Democratic convention to win renomination on the first ballot. His Republican opponent in the campaign that followed was Ronald Reagan.

Reagan had grown up a New Deal Democrat, but during and immediately after World War II he became disillusioned with liberalism. As president of the Screen Actors Guild he attacked the influence of communists in the movie industry. After his movie career ended, Reagan did publicity for General Electric until 1960, then worked for various conservative causes. In 1966 he ran for governor of California, and struck a responsive chord by attacking the counterculture. He won the election and was easily reelected.

Both Carter and Reagan spent much of the 1980 campaign explaining why the other was unsuited to be president. Carter defended his record, though without much conviction. Reagan denounced criminals, drug addicts, and all varieties of immorality and spoke in support of patriotism, religion, family life, and other "old-fashioned" virtues. This won him the enthusiastic backing of fundamentalist religious sects and other conservative groups. He also called for increased spending on defense, and he promised to transfer some functions of the federal government to the states and to cut taxes. He insisted at the same time that the budget could be balanced and inflation sharply reduced.

On election day the voting was light, but Reagan received 8 million more votes than Carter. Dissatisfaction with the economy and the unresolved hostage crisis seem to have determined the result. The Republicans also gained control of the Senate and cut deeply into the Democratic majority in the House of Representatives.

Carter devoted his last weeks in office to the continuing hostage crisis. War had broken out between Iran and Iraq in September. The Iraqi president, Saddam Hussein, had hoped to exploit the chaos following the downfall of the shah to seize oil-rich territory in Iran. Early Iraqi victories prompted the Iranians to free the hostages in return for the release of Iranian assets that had been frozen in the United States. After 444 days in captivity, the fifty-two hostages were set free on January 20, the day Reagan was inaugurated.

Reagan as President

Reagan hoped to change the direction in which the country was moving. He demanded steep reductions in federal spending and the deficit, to be accomplished by cutting social expenditures such as welfare, food stamps and student loans, and by turning many functions of the federal government over to the states. The marketplace, not federal bureaucratic regulations, should govern most economic decisions.

He asked Congress to lower income taxes by 30 percent. When critics objected that this would increase the deficit, the president and his advisers reasoned that the tax cut would leave people with more money, which they would invest in productive ways. The new investment would generate more goods and jobs—and, ultimately, taxes for the federal government. This scheme became known as **Reaganomics**.

Helped by the votes of conservative Democrats, Reagan won congressional approval of the Budget Reconciliation Act, which reduced government expenditures on domestic programs by $39 billion.

Congress enacted most of the tax cuts the president had asked for, lowering individual income taxes by 25 percent over three years, but it resisted reducing the politically popular "entitlement" programs, such as Social Security and Medicare, which accounted for about half of the budget. Reagan himself refused to reduce the military budget to bring the government's income more nearly in line with its outlays. Instead he called for a military buildup

Ronald Reagan rides a horse—a familiar photo opportunity for presidents. But Reagan was an amiable cowboy; his smile and sense of humor were his most disarming weapons. In 1966 just after the election, when reporters asked him what sort of governor he would be, Reagan, a former actor, answered, "I don't know. I've never played a governor." Three months into his presidency, moments after he was seriously wounded in an assassination attempt, he took his wife's hand. "Honey," he said, "I forgot to duck." While being wheeled into the operating room, he quipped to the surgeons, "I hope you are all Republicans."

Photo Credit: Ronald Reagan Presidential Library.

to ensure that the United States would prevail in any war with the Soviet Union, which he called an "evil empire." In particular, he sought to expand and improve the nation's nuclear arsenal. He made no secret of his wish to create so formidable a nuclear force that the Soviets would have to back down in any confrontation. The deficit worsened.

In Central America Reagan sought the overthrow of the left-wing government of Nicaragua and the defeat of communist rebels in El Salvador. He even used American troops to overthrow a Cuban-backed regime on the tiny Caribbean island of Grenada. When criticized for opposing leftist regimes while backing rightist dictators, Jeane Kirkpatrick, U.S. ambassador to the United Nations, explained that "rightist authoritarian regimes can be transformed peacefully into democracies, but totalitarian Marxist ones cannot."

In 1982 the continuing turmoil in the Middle East thrust the Reagan administration into a new crisis. Israel had invaded Lebanon to destroy Palestine Liberation Organization units that were staging raids on northern Israeli settlements. Israeli troops easily overran much of the country, but in the process the Lebanese government disintegrated. Reagan agreed to commit American troops to an international peacekeeping force.

Tragedy resulted in October 1983 when a fanatical Muslim crashed a truck loaded with explosives into a building housing American marines in Beirut. The building collapsed, killing 239 marines. Early the next year, Reagan removed the entire American peacekeeping force from Lebanon.

Four More Years

A sitting president with an extraordinarily high standing in public opinion polls, Reagan was nominated for a second term at the 1984 Republican convention without opposition. The Democratic nomination went to Walter Mondale of Minnesota, who had been vice president under Carter. Mondale electrified the country by choosing Representative Geraldine Ferraro of New York as his running mate. An Italian American and a Catholic, Ferraro was expected to appeal to conservative Democrats who had supported Reagan in 1980 and to win the votes of many Republican women.

Reagan began the campaign with several important advantages. He was especially popular among religious fundamentalists and other social conservatives, and these groups

were increasingly vocal. Fundamentalist television preachers were almost all fervent Reaganites and the most successful of them were collecting tens of millions of dollars annually in contributions from viewers. One of these, the Reverend Jerry Falwell, founded the **Moral Majority** and set out to create a new political movement. "Americans are sick and tired of the way the amoral liberals are trying to corrupt our nation," Falwell announced in 1979.

During the first Reagan administration, the Moral Majority had become a powerful political force. Falwell denounced drugs, the "coddling" of criminals, homosexuality, communism, and abortion, all things that Reagan also disliked. Falwell also disapproved of forced busing to integrate schools. In addition, Reagan favored government aid to private schools run by church groups, something dear to the Moral Majority despite the constitutional principle of separation of church and state.

Success of the Republican "Southern Strategy" In 1968, Kevin M. Phillips, a key Nixon strategist, proposed a "southern strategy" to create an "emerging Republican majority." Many doubted that the South, which had long been opposed to the party of Lincoln, could be won over. But in presidential elections from 1968 to 1988, far more southern counties voted Republican than Democratic.

Reagan's support was also drawn from blue collar workers and white Southerners, constituencies that had been solidly Democratic during the New Deal and beyond. The president's personality was another important plus—voters continued to admire his informal yet firm style and his stress on patriotism and other "traditional" virtues.

Most polls showed Reagan far in the lead when the campaign began, and this remained true throughout the contest. Nothing Mondale or Ferraro did or said affected the president's popularity. On election day he got nearly 60 percent of the popular vote and lost only in Minnesota, Mondale's home state, and in the District of Columbia. Reagan's Electoral College margin was overwhelming, 525 to 13.

Reagan's triumph, like the two landslide victories of Dwight Eisenhower in the 1950s, was a personal one. The Republicans made only minor gains in the House of Representatives and actually lost two seats in the Senate.

"The Reagan Revolution"

Reagan's agenda for his second term closely resembled that of his first. In foreign affairs, he ran into continuing congressional resistance to his requests for military support for his anticommunist crusade. This was particularly true after Mikhail S. Gorbachev became the Soviet premier in March 1985. Gorbachev seemed far more moderate and flexible than his predecessors. He began to encourage political debate and criticism in the Soviet Union—the policy known as *glasnost* (openness)—and he sought to stimulate the stagnant Soviet economy by decentralizing administration and rewarding individual enterprise (*perestroika*).

Gorbachev also announced that he would continue to honor the unratified SALT II agreement, whereas Reagan, arguing that the Soviet Union had not respected the limits laid down in the pact, seemed bent on pushing ahead with the expansion and modernization of America's nuclear arsenal. Reagan sought funds to develop an elaborate system of missile defenses. He referred to it as the **Strategic Defense Initiative (SDI)**, although it was popularly known as Star Wars, a reference to the 1977 George Lucas film. SDI would consist of a network of computer-controlled space stations that would detect oncoming enemy missiles and destroy them with speculative high-tech weaponry.

When the president realized that the Soviets were eager for an agreement to limit nuclear weapons, he ceased referring to the Soviet Union as an "evil empire." In October 1986 he met with Gorbachev in Iceland in search of an agreement on arms control. The chief sticking point was SDI. Gorbachev proposed instead the elimination of all nuclear weapons—including SDI. Reagan, however, was determined to push Star Wars, and the summit collapsed.

Congress balked at the enormous cost of Star Wars. Expense aside, the idea of relying on the complex technology involved in controlling machines in outer space for national defense suffered a further setback in 1986, when the space shuttle *Challenger* exploded shortly after takeoff, killing its seven-member crew. This disaster temporarily put a stop to the program.

Reagan's basic domestic objectives—to reduce the scope of federal activity, particularly in the social welfare area; to lower income taxes; and to increase the strength of the armed forces—remained constant. Despite the tax cuts already made, congressional leaders of both parties agreed to the Income Tax Act of 1986, which reduced the top levy on personal incomes from 50 percent to 28 percent and the tax on corporate profits from 46 percent to 34 percent.

Watch the Video

Ronald Reagan on the Wisdom of the Tax Cut at **myhistorylab.com**

Reagan advanced another of his objectives more gradually. This was his appointment of conservatives to federal judgeships, including Sandra Day O'Connor, the first woman named to the Supreme Court. By 1988 Reagan had appointed three Supreme Court justices and well over half the members of the federal judiciary.

The New Merger Movement

During the Reagan years, the nation began to climb out of the recession of the 1970s. Reagan's policies helped, though often in unpredictable ways. Reagan's relaxed regulation of Wall Street helped precipitate a frenzy of corporate mergers. Deregulation provided the context for the merger movement, but the person most responsible for it was Michael Milken, a shrewd stockbroker of the firm of Drexel Burnham Lambert. Milken specialized in selling "junk bonds," the debt offerings of companies whose existing debts were already high. He persuaded savings and loan associations, insurance companies, pension funds, and other big investors to buy these junk bonds, which, though risky, offered high interest rates. The success of his initial ventures prompted Milken to approach smaller companies, encourage them to borrow immense sums by floating junk bonds, and use the proceeds to acquire larger firms.

In 1985 Ronald Perelman, an aggressive entrepreneur, employed this strategy to perfection. He had recently obtained control of Pantry Pride, a supermarket chain with a net worth of about $145 million. Now he sought to acquire Revlon, a $2 billion cosmetics and health care conglomerate. With Milken's help, Pantry Pride borrowed $1.5 billion and used that capital to buy Revlon. He then paid off Pantry Pride's $1.5 billion in junk bonds ("junk" because the debt so greatly exceeded the $145 million value of Pantry Pride) by selling huge chunks of Revlon. Then he integrated the food component of Revlon into Pantry Pride.

The bond purchasers profited handsomely from the high return on the junk bonds, and Perelman made a fortune from his new food conglomerate. That same year the R. J. Reynolds Tobacco Company purchased Nabisco for $4.9 billion. Three years later this new giant, RJR Nabisco, was itself taken over by Kohlberg, Kravis, Roberts, and Company for $24.9 billion.

Workers at a Nike factory in Indonesia insert soles into sneakers.

During the frenzied decade of the 1980s, one-fifth of the *Fortune* 500 companies were taken over, merged, or forced to go private; in all, some 25,000 mergers and acquisitions were successfully undertaken; their total value was nearly a half-trillion dollars. To make their companies less tempting to cash-hungry raiders, many corporations took on whopping debts or acquired unprofitable companies. By the late 1980s, many American corporations were wallowing in red ink. Debt payments were gobbling up 50 percent of the nation's corporate pretax earnings.

Read the Document

Paul Craig Roberts, *The Supply-Side Revolution (1984)* at **myhistorylab.com**

"A Job for Life": Layoffs Hit Home

Most corporations coped with the debt in two ways: They sold assets, such as factories, offices, and warehouses; or they cut costs through layoffs. U.S. Steel, whose rusting mills desperately needed an infusion of capital, instead spent $5 billion to acquire Marathon Oil of Ohio; that decision meant that nearly 100,000 steelworkers lost their jobs. No firm was immune, nor any worker secure. During the 1980s, the total number of employees who worked for *Fortune* 500 companies declined by three million; nearly one-third of all positions in middle management were eliminated.

Many of the jobs went abroad, where labor costs were lower and unions nonexistent. In 1984 Nike moved sewing operations to Indonesia, where it could hire female workers for fourteen cents an hour. In 1986 the chassis for the Mustang, long a symbol of American automotive style, was built by Mazda in Hiroshima, Japan.

Towering mountains of private corporate debt nearly were overshadowed by the Everest of public debt held by the federal government itself. Reagan's insistence on a sharp cut in personal taxes and a substantial increase in military expenditures produced huge—and growing—annual federal deficits. When Reagan took office, the total federal debt was $900 million; eight years later, it exceeded $2.5 *trillion*.

Corporate Restructuring

Although few perceived it at the time, the economy was undergoing a transformation of historic dimensions. Much as the depression after 1893 had strengthened the nation's economy by wiping out thousands of inefficient steel and machinery firms, the seismic

BILL GATES

"Project Breakthrough! World's First Minicomputer Kit to Rival Commercial Models." This headline in the January 1975 issue of *Popular Electronics* triggered the neurons in Bill Gates's brain. In an instant, he perceived that the revolution had begun. Most earlier computers cost hundreds of thousands of dollars, filled room-sized air-conditioned vaults, and were found in university science centers, government agencies, and corporate headquarters. But this kit cost only $397. The computer (its name—*Altair*—came from a planet in the TV series *Star Trek*), could fit on a desktop. Gates believed that computers like this would soon be as much a part of life as telephones or automobiles. Armed with the slogan, "A computer on every desktop," Gates resolved to become the Henry Ford of the computer revolution (and to become, like Ford, immensely rich). He was twenty years old.

Gates recognized Altair's fatal flaw: It did little more than cause a few lights to blink in complex ways. It lacked internal instructions to convert electrical signals into letters and numbers. He determined to write instructions—the software—to make the personal computer useful. Gates and Paul Allen, a school friend, telephoned Ed Roberts, the president of MITS, manufacturer of the Altair. They told him they had written operating software for the machine. Roberts was skeptical. Scores of programmers had made such claims, he said, but none had actually done it. He told them to bring their software to the company headquarters in Albuquerque, New Mexico, within two months. Allen and Gates were euphoric, but not for long: They had not even begun to write a program for the Altair.

The boys had met in 1967 at Lakeside, an elite private school in Seattle, when Gates was in seventh grade, Allen in ninth. That year, the Lakeside Mothers Club had bought time on a digital training terminal that connected by phone to a company that leased a mainframe computer. Within weeks of its installation, this computer had become Gates's life. He remained in the terminal room after school and late into the evenings, breaking only for Coke and pizza. "He lived and breathed computers," a friend recalled.

Gates learned programming by writing programs and seeing what worked. His first was for playing tic-tac-toe. He also designed a program for student schedules at Lakeside. He placed "all the good girls in the school" (and very few males of any kind) in his own classes—an early manifestation of his penchant for defeating competitors by conniving to eliminate them.

Bill Gates as a young CEO at Microsoft.

Although his father was a wealthy corporate attorney and his mother a prominent socialite, Gates was preoccupied with making money. In high school he took a job tabulating automobile traffic data; this required that he count the holes in a roll of paper punched out when automobiles passed over a hose. He designed a computerized machine to count and analyze the data and he formed a company, Traf-O-Data, to build and market the device. But, Traf-O-Data failed to attract many customers—most municipalities and highway departments lost interest when they learned that the company was run by high school students.

Gates and Allen completed the program just hours before Allen boarded the plane to Albuquerque. (Allen went because he was older and presumably a more credible "corporate" spokesman.) The next morning, Allen fed long rolls of punched yellow paper tape—the software—into an Altair while company executives looked on skeptically. For fifteen minutes the machine clattered away. Misgivings mounted. Then the teletype printed the word, "READY." Allen typed, "PRINT 2 + 2." The teletype spat out "4." The program worked. Gates and Allen had a deal.

Gates dropped out of Harvard and formed a partnership with Allen. They called their company Microsoft and moved to Albuquerque. They wrote operating programs for personal computers introduced by Apple, Commodore, and Radio Shack. Soon money was pouring into Microsoft. In 1979 they moved Microsoft to Bellevue, Washington, near Seattle. Then came the blockbuster.

In 1980 IBM, the world's foremost manufacturer of mainframe computers, belatedly entered the home computer market. IBM approached Gates to write the operating software for its new, state-of-the-art personal computer. IBM intended to keep the computer's specifications secret so that other manufacturers could not copy its design, but Gates shrewdly proposed that IBM make its specifications public. Doing so would allow the IBM personal computer to become the industry standard, giving IBM the edge in developing peripherals—printers, monitors, keyboards, and various applications. IBM agreed. Now Gates's software, called Microsoft-Disk Operating System (MS-DOS), would run every IBM personal computer as well as every computer made by other companies according to the IBM specifications. In a single stroke, Gates had virtually monopolized the market for PC operating software.

Microsoft's sales jumped from $7.5 million in 1980 to $140 million in 1985. Then Microsoft moved into software applications: word processing, accounting, and games. By 1991, Gates was the wealthiest man in the world. In 1994, he and his wife established the Bill and Melinda Gates Foundation; by 2010, it had assets of over $33 billion and gave nearly $2 billion annually to charitable causes, especially education.

Questions for Discussion

- Intelligence, ambition, business sense, or all three? In what ways did Bill Gates's triumph parallel Andrew Carnegie's a century earlier?
- What was the main prerequisite for Gates's triumph?

economic upheavals after 1973 toppled many inefficient manufacturers but created the foundations for more efficient global conglomerates. As weeds grew in the parking lots of the factories of the "Rust Belt" of the Midwest, new technology industries sprouted in the "Silicon Valley" of California, along Route 128 outside of Boston, and in booming cities such as Seattle, Washington, and Austin, Texas.

By the end of the Reagan era, the economy consisted of two separate and increasingly unequal components: a battered sector of traditional heavy industry, characterized by declining wages and diminishing job opportunities; and an advancing high-tech and service sector dominated by aggressive, innovative, and individualistic entrepreneurs. (See American Lives, "Bill Gates.") The older corporations that survived the shakeout of the 1980s were leaner and better equipped to compete in expanding global markets.

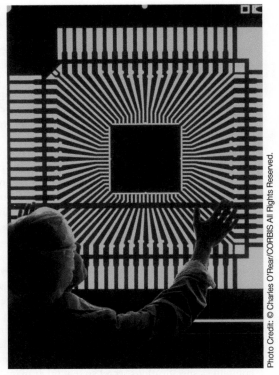

A worker studies a lighted diagram of an integrated circuit at a California computer factory.

Yet American society was becoming as fractured as the "bipolar" economy from which it drew sustenance. The Reagan tax cuts had disproportionately benefited the wealthy, as had the extraordinary rise of the stock market. Conversely, the economic transformation struck low- or semiskilled wage earners hardest. At the end of Reagan's second term the standard of living of the poorest fifth of the population (40 million people) was 9 percent lower than it had been in 1979, while that of the wealthiest fifth had risen about 20 percent.

Rogue Foreign Policy

Especially during his second term as president, Reagan paid little attention to the details of administration. Thus two major initiatives unfolded of which Reagan himself claimed little knowledge.

The first concerned Nicaragua. In 1979 leftist rebels had overthrown the dictatorial regime of Anastasio Somoza. Because the victorious Sandinista government was supported by both Cuba and the Soviet Union, Reagan was determined to force it from power. He backed anti-Sandinista elements in Nicaragua known as the Contras and in 1981 persuaded Congress to provide these "freedom fighters" with arms.

But the Contras made little progress, and many Americans feared that aiding them would lead, as it had in Vietnam, to the use of American troops in the fighting. In October 1984 Congress banned further military aid to the Contra rebels. Reagan then sought to persuade other countries and private American groups to help the Contras (as he put it) keep "body and soul together."

⬥⬥◦─Read the Document

Reagan, *Support for the Contras (1984)* at **myhistorylab.com**

Marine Colonel Oliver North, an aide of Reagan's national security adviser, devised a scheme to indirectly funnel federal money to the Contras. He inflated the price of U.S. weapons, sold them to Iran[1], and secretly transferred the profits to the Contras. This plainly violated the congressional ban on such aid.

When North's stratagem came to light in November 1986, he was fired from his job with the security council. Reagan insisted that he knew nothing about the aid to the Contras. Critics pointed out that if he was telling the truth it was almost as bad since that meant that he had not been able to control his own administration.

Meanwhile, the Soviet invasion of Afghanistan in 1980 enraged Charles Wilson, a Democratic congressman from Texas. (Wilson, a womanizer, heavy drinker, and alleged cocaine-user, was played by Tom Hanks in the movie, *Charlie Wilson's War* [2007]). Wilson persuaded his colleagues to allocate money for the *mujahideen*, Muslim warriors who were trying to drive the Soviets out of their country. Within several years the Afghan tribes, especially Islamist radicals known as the Taliban, were covertly receiving hundreds of millions of dollars in weapons. Muslim insurgents ambushed convoys, mined roads, and engaged in various acts of terrorism. Soviet casualties increased, as did the cost of the war. Soviet generals began referring to the war in Afghanistan as "our Vietnam." In 1989 the Soviets pulled out; in 1996 the Taliban took over Afghanistan and instituted a radical Islamic state.

Assessing the Reagan Revolution

Reagan was not an able administrator; the **Iran-Contra affair** and financial scandals of his administration did not stick to him because he was seldom close enough to the action to get splattered by it. He articulated, simply and persuasively, a handful of concepts—chiefly the "evil" character of Soviet communism, the need to get government off people's backs—and in so doing created a political climate conducive

Photo Credit: Pascal Manoukian/ Sygma/Corbis.

Mujahideen in Afghanistan stand on top of a Soviet helicopter they shot down with U.S.-supplied Stinger missiles in the early 1980s.

---

[1] Earlier in the Iran-Iraq war, when Iran appeared on the verge of defeating Iraq, Reagan had provided $500 million a year in credits to allow Iraq's Saddam Hussein to buy armaments. If either Iran or Iraq won decisively, it could control the flow of Middle Eastern oil. The United States therefore preferred a stalemate.

to change. Reagan was directly responsible for neither of the great transformations of the late twentieth century—the restructuring of American corporations and the collapse of the Soviet Union. Yet his actions and, indeed, his failures to act indisputably influenced them. His decision to increase military spending and undertake the fantastically expensive SDI ("Star Wars") forced Gorbachev to seek an accommodation with the United States. Reagan's tax cuts precipitated unimaginably large federal deficits, and deregulation unloosed a sordid pack of predators who preyed on the economy. Yet the ensuing Darwinian chaos strengthened those corporations that survived and gave them the muscle to prevail in emerging global markets.

The Election of 1988

The issues that had dominated American politics for over a decade—the Soviet threat, the energy crisis, stagflation—were gone. The presidential election of 1988 initially lacked focus. The selection of Vice President George H. W. Bush as the Republican nomination was a foregone conclusion. Bush, the son of a Connecticut senator, had served as a pilot during World War II and then settled in Texas, where he worked in the family's oil business and became active in Republican politics. From 1971 to 1973 he served as ambassador to the UN and from 1976 to 1977 as director of the CIA. As Republican presidential hopeful, he trumpeted his experience as vice president.

The Democratic race was far more complicated but scarcely more inspiring. So many lackluster candidates entered the field that wits called them "the seven dwarfs." But eventually Governor Michael Dukakis of Massachusetts, stressing his record as an efficient manager, accumulated delegates steadily and won the nomination.

During the campaign, Bush attacked Dukakis as a liberal governor who had been soft on crime. Lee Atwater, campaign manager for Bush, produced and aired a television advertisement showing prisoners, many of them black, streaming through a revolving door. Dukakis's attempts to shift the focus away from crime failed. The presidential campaign became, in effect, a referendum on crime in which Dukakis failed the toughness test. Bush won 54 percent of the vote and carried the Electoral College, 426 to 112.

George H. W. Bush as President

In 1989 President Bush, having attacked Dukakis for being soft on crime, named a "drug czar" to coordinate various bureaucracies, increased federal funding of local police, and spent $2.5 billion to stop the flow of illegal drugs into the nation. Although the campaign generated plenty of arrests, drugs continued to pour in: As one dealer or trafficker was arrested, another took his place. Bush also worked to shed the tough image he had cultivated during the campaign. In his inaugural address he said that he hoped to "make kinder the face of the nation and gentler the face of the world." He also displayed a more traditional command of the workings of government and the details of current events than his predecessor. At the same time he pleased right-wing Reagan loyalists by his opposition to abortion and gun control, and by calling for a constitutional amendment prohibiting the burning of the American flag. His standing in the polls soared.

The Collapse of Communism in Eastern Europe

One important reason for this was the flood of good news from abroad. The reforms instituted in the Soviet Union by Gorbachev led to demands from its Eastern European satellites for similar liberalization. Gorbachev responded by announcing that the Soviet Union would not use force to keep communist governments in power in these nations. Swiftly the people of Poland, Hungary, Czechoslovakia, Bulgaria, Romania, East Germany, and the Baltics did away with the repressive regimes that had ruled them throughout the postwar era. Except in Romania, where the dictator Nicolae Ceausescu was executed, all these fundamental changes were carried out peacefully.

Almost overnight the international political climate changed. Soviet-style communism had been discredited. A Soviet attack anywhere was almost unthinkable. The Cold War was over.

President Bush profited from these developments immensely. He expressed moral support for the new governments but he refrained from embarrassing the Soviets. At a summit meeting in Washington in June 1990 Bush and Gorbachev signed agreements reducing American and Russian stockpiles of long-range nuclear missiles by 30 percent and eliminating chemical weapons.

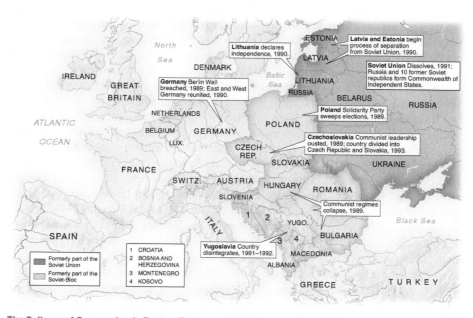

The Collapse of Communism in Eastern Europe When Gorbachev withdrew Soviet troops from Eastern Europe, the communist regimes there collapsed rapidly. The Soviet Union itself disintegrated.

In 1989 President Bush sent troops to Panama to overthrow General Manuel Noriega, who had refused to yield power when his figurehead presidential candidate lost a national election. Noriega was under indictment in the United States for drug trafficking. After temporarily seeking refuge in the Vatican embassy in Panama, he surrendered to the American forces and was taken to the United States, where he was tried, convicted, and imprisoned.

Meanwhile, in the Soviet Union, nationalist and anticommunist groups demanded more local control of their affairs. President Gorbachev, who opposed this breakup, sought compromise, backing a draft treaty that would increase local autonomy and further privatize the Soviet economy. In August, however, before this treaty could be ratified, hard-line communists attempted a coup. They arrested Gorbachev, who was vacationing in the Crimea, and ordered tanks into Moscow. But Boris Yeltsin, the anticommunist president of the Russian Republic, defied the rebels and roused the people of Moscow. The coup swiftly collapsed. Its leaders were arrested, the communist party was officially disbanded, and the Soviet Union itself was replaced by a federation of states, of which Russia, led by Yeltsin, was the most important. Gorbachev, who had begun the process of liberation, found himself without a job.

The War in the Persian Gulf

Although Reagan had provided economic assistance to Saddam Hussein of Iraq to prevent Iran from winning the Iran-Iraq war, few in the administration were enthusiastic about the Iraqi dictator. For years Saddam had been crushing the Kurds, an ethnic minority in northern Iraq that sought independence. In 1987 the U.S. State Department reported on his "widespread destruction and bulldozing of Kurdish villages." In March 1988, after Kurdish rebels had supported an Iranian advance into Iraq near Halabja, a mostly Kurdish city, Saddam's troops dropped mustard gas, sarin, and other chemical weapons on the city. Some 5,000 civilians died.

In August 1990, Saddam launched an all-out attack on Iraq's tiny neighbor to the south, the oil-rich sheikdom of Kuwait. Saddam hoped to swallow up Kuwait, thus increasing Iraq's already large oil reserves to about 25 percent of the world's total. His soldiers overran Kuwait swiftly, then systematically carried off everything of value they could bring back to Iraq. Within a week Saddam annexed Kuwait and massed troops along the border of neighboring Saudi Arabia.

The Saudis and the Kuwaitis turned to the United States and other nations for help, and it was quickly given. In a matter of days the UN applied trade sanctions against Iraq, and at the invitation of Saudi Arabia, the United States (along with Great Britain, France, Italy, Egypt, and Syria) moved troops to Saudi bases. Many Muslims opposed the presence of non-Muslim troops on Saudi soil; but the Saudi ruling family overruled them, fearing an Iraqi invasion.

By November, Bush had increased the American troops in the area from 180,000 to more than 500,000, part of a larger UN operation. On January 17, the Americans unleashed an enormous air attack, directed by General Norman Schwarzkopf. This air assault went on for nearly a month, and it reduced much of Iraq to rubble. The Iraqi forces, aside from firing a number of Scud missiles at Israel and Saudi Arabia and

President Bush on the Gulf War at **myhistorylab.com**

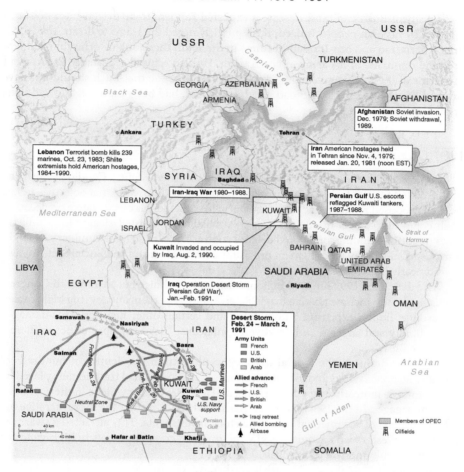

The Middle East In February 1991, combined U.S., British, French, and Arab armies drove Saddam Hussein from Kuwait and invaded Iraq.

setting fire to hundreds of Kuwaiti oil wells, simply endured the rain of destruction that fell on them daily.

On February 23 Bush issued an ultimatum to Saddam: Pull out of Kuwait or face an invasion. When Saddam ignored the deadline, UN troops (most under U.S. command) attacked. Bush called the assault "Desert Storm." Between February 24 and February 27 they retook Kuwait, killing tens of thousands of Iraqis. Some 4,000 Iraqi tanks and enormous quantities of other military equipment were destroyed.

Bush then stopped the attack, and Saddam agreed to UN terms that included paying reparations to Kuwait, allowing UN inspectors to determine whether Iraq was developing atomic and biological weapons, and agreeing to keep its airplanes out of "no-fly" zones over Kurdish territory and other strategic areas. Polls indicated that about 90 percent of the American people approved both the president's management of the **Persian Gulf War** and his overall performance as chief executive. These were the highest presidential approval ratings ever recorded.

President Bush and most observers expected Saddam to be driven from power in disgrace by his own people. Indeed, Bush publicly urged the Iraqis to do so. The Kurds in northern Iraq and pro-Iranian Muslims in the south then took up arms, but Saddam used the remnants of his army to crush them. He also refused repeatedly to carry out the terms of the peace agreement. This led critics to argue that Bush should not have stopped the fighting until Baghdad, the Iraqi capital, had been captured and Saddam's army destroyed.

Deficits

The huge cost of the Persian Gulf War exacerbated the federal deficit. Candidate Bush had promised not to raise taxes. As president he recommitted himself to that objective; in fact he even proposed reducing the tax on capital gains. But like his conservative predecessor, Bush could not control the deficit. Congress obstinately resisted closing local military bases or cutting funding for favored defense contractors. Reducing nonmilitary expenditures, especially popular entitlement programs such as Medicare and Social Security, also proved nearly impossible.

The deficit for 1992 hit $290 billion. Bush had no choice but to join with Congress in raising the top income tax rate from 28 percent to 31 percent and levying higher taxes on gasoline, liquor, expensive automobiles, and certain other luxuries. This damaged his credibility and angered conservative Republicans. "Read my lips," critics muttered, "No more Bush."

Another drain on the federal treasury resulted from the demise of hundreds of federally insured savings and loan institutions (S&Ls). S&Ls had traditionally played an important role in nearly every community, and a secure if sleepy niche in the economy: home mortgages. In the 1980s Congress permitted S&Ls to enter the more lucrative but riskier business of commercial loans and stock investments. This attracted a swarm of aggressive investors who acquired S&Ls and invested company assets in high-yield but risky junk bonds and real estate deals.

In October 1987 the stock market crashed, rendering worthless the assets held by many of the S&Ls. Hundreds were plunged into bankruptcy. In 1988 Michael Milken, the junk bond "guru," was indicted on ninety-eight charges of fraud, stock manipulation, and insider trading. He pleaded guilty, agreed to pay $1.3 billion in compensation, and was sent to jail. Drexel Burnham Lambert, his investment firm, filed for bankruptcy. The junk bond market collapsed.

Because S&L deposits were insured by the federal government, taxpayers were forced to cover the losses. The reserve fund for such purposes—$5 billion—was quickly exhausted. In 1991 Congress allocated $70 billion to close the failing S&Ls, liquidate their assets, and pay off depositors. The Justice Department charged nearly a thousand people for criminal involvement in a mess that, according to most estimates, would eventually cost taxpayers $500 billion.

During the preceding two decades, the American nation, like the automobiles that stretched for blocks in line to buy gasoline during the oil embargo, had been running on empty. The federal government was deeply in debt. Corporations had exhausted their cash reserves. Workers lived in fear of the layoff or bank foreclosure notice. Gone were the fanciful expressions of an earlier era—long and wide-bodied chassis, roaring

V-8 engines, sweeping tail fins, chromium grills like the jaws of a barracuda. Most cars had become simple boxes, trimmed with plastic, whose efficient four-cylinder engines thrummed steadily.

The nation's aspirations, like its cars, had become smaller, more sensible. Politicians muted their rhetoric, rarely issuing grandiose declarations of war against some intractable foe of humanity. Corporate executives spoke of "downsizing" firms rather than building them into empires. And the American people increasingly hunkered down in their own private spaces, which they locked up and wired with alarms.

Milestones

1973	Israel, aided by United States, defeats Egypt and Syria	1981	Iran releases U.S. hostages
1973–1974	Arabs impose oil embargo		Reagan appoints Sandra Day O'Connor to Supreme Court
1974–1976	Gerald Ford serves as president after Nixon's resignation	1981–1988	War persists between Iran and Iraq
1975	North Vietnam defeats South Vietnam; Saigon is renamed Ho Chi Minh City.	1984	Reagan is reelected president
		1985	Mikhail Gorbachev becomes premier of the Soviet Union
1976	Jimmy Carter is elected president	1986	Reagan secretly sells arms to Iran to finance Nicaraguan Contras
1978	Egypt and Israel sign Camp David Accords		
1979	Jerry Falwell founds the Moral Majority	1988	Republican George H. W. Bush elected president
	Muslim militants seize U.S. Embassy in Tehran, Iran	1989	Gorbachev allows Eastern European nations to establish independent democratic governments
	United States recognizes People's Republic of China		
1980	Soviet troops invade Afghanistan	1990	Iraq invades Kuwait
	U.S. rescue mission in Iran fails	1991	UN forces, led by the United States, drive Iraqi forces from Kuwait
	Ronald Reagan is elected president		
1980s	Entrepreneurs' merger movement leads to huge corporate debt		Soviet Union is dissolved; Boris Yeltsin becomes president of Russia

✓● Study and Review at www.myhistorylab.com

Review Questions

1. The introduction to this chapter suggests that cheap oil and gas have long been prominent in American politics. How did the oil shortage of the 1970s affect politics? What was its impact on the economy? In what sense was "stagflation" weird?

2. Did Carter realize his hopes for a foreign policy based on "constant decency"?

3. How did Reagan contribute to corporate restructuring? What was the impact of the merger movement on the American economy generally? What new industries emerged in the late 1980s and 1990s?

4. Why did the Soviet Union collapse? What role, if any, did Reagan play in its demise?

5. Why did George H. W. Bush go to war with Iraq? Why, having defeated the Iraqi army, didn't he seize Baghdad and remove Saddam Hussein from power?

Key Terms

Camp David Accords
Iran-Contra affair
Iranian hostage crisis

Moral Majority
Organization of Petroleum Exporting Countries (OPEC)
Persian Gulf War

Reaganomics
stagflation
Strategic Defense Initiative (SDI)

From Boomers to Millennials

((•●─[Hear the Audio at myhistorylab.com

Why do you go to college?

Every year since 1966, the UCLA School of Education has surveyed nearly a quarter of a million first-year college students. The college-aged Boomers of the late 1960s were not much different from Millennials in 2009. Then as now, the great majority regarded themselves as "middle-of-the-road" in politics.

But the past forty years have witnessed a widening gulf between Boomers (born from 1946 to 1964) and Millennials (born after 1980). One example relates to life goals. According to the survey, when Boomers were in their freshman year of college, about three-fourths believed that "acquiring a meaningful philosophy of life" was "essential" or "very important." Only a third attached similar importance to "being well off financially." But forty years later the percentages had been nearly reversed. Over three-fourths of the Millennials entering college in 2009 believed that "being well off financially" was "essential" or "very important" while only a third thought it equally important to acquire "a meaningful philosophy of life." (The figures do not add up to 100 percent because respondents could give opinions for more than one statement.) Millennials are far more likely to seek wealth, while Boomers were more likely to seek "a meaningful philosophy of life."

One explanation is that Boomers came of age during a period of unprecedented economic growth. They were free to ponder the meaning of life because they rarely worried about finding a decent job. They could imagine brave new worlds of gender revolution and institutional transformation, of liberal treatment of criminals and immigrants, of a broader reform of society as a whole.

But the protracted recession after 1973 changed the way people looked at things. An infusion of new peoples, a liberalization of attitudes, and a transformation of institutions all suggested that society was becoming unhinged. A period of retrenchment was in order. Marriage and the family were to be preserved in familiar forms; tougher laws must be passed and criminals punished.

Through it all, the sphere of public life contracted; private concerns—such as making money—took precedence over grand social schemes. And public spaces receded as people retreated to their cars and homes, where they could interact with Facebook friends and virtual realities.

The New Immigration

A Pew poll in 2008 unearthed another major attitudinal difference between Boomers and Millennials. When asked whether immigrants strengthened the country with

◉ See the **Map**

Immigration to the U.S., 1945–1990 at **myhistorylab.com**

their hard work and talent, or burdened it because they took jobs, housing, and healthcare, the Boomers overwhelmingly (50 percent to 30 percent) regarded immigrants as a burden, while Millennials overwhelmingly (58 percent to 32 percent) thought immigrants strengthened the country. One reason for the attitudinal change is that a far higher proportion of Millennials are themselves immigrants or the children of immigrants.

Since 1924, immigration to the United States had been governed by a quota system that ensured that the distribution of new immigrants mirrored the nation's existing ethnic patterns. But the Immigration Act of 1965 eliminated the old system. It instead gave preference to immigrants with specialized job skills and education, and it allowed family members to rejoin those who had immigrated earlier. In 1986, Congress offered amnesty to illegal immigrants who had long lived in the United States and penalized employers who hired illegal immigrants in the future. Many persons legalized their status under the new law, but the influx of illegal immigrants continued. Together, these laws enabled more than 25 million to immigrate to the United States from 1970 to 2000.

Asians, many of whom possessed skills in high-tech fields, benefited most from the abandonment of the "national origins" system. Of the 9 million Asians who immigrated to the United States during these years, most were from China, South Korea, India, Pakistan, and the Philippines. Following the defeat of South Vietnam and the Khmer Rouge takeover of Cambodia, some 700,000 South Vietnamese and Cambodians received refugee status.

From 1970 to 2000 the largest number of immigrants were Latinos, sometimes called Hispanics (16 million). By 2000, the Latino population of the United States (35 million) for the first time exceeded African Americans (34 million). The overwhelming majority of these Spanish-speaking immigrants

Dolores Huerta and César Chávez, leaders of the United Farm Workers, discuss their 1968 strike of grape pickers. They are framed by photographs of Robert Kennedy, campaigning for the Democratic nomination for president, and Mohandas Gandhi, leader of the non-violent protest movement that won independence for India in 1947.

Photo Credit: Arthur Schatz/Time Life Pictures/Getty Images.

were Chicanos—Mexican Americans who settled in the Southwest. (Of the nation's 35 million Hispanics, 11 million lived in California, and nearly 7 million in Texas; over 42 percent of the population of New Mexico was Latino.) In addition, several million Puerto Ricans came to the mainland United States, most of whom settled in well-established Puerto Rican neighborhoods in northeastern cities. About a million Cuban immigrants arrived in Florida during these years.

Read the Document
LBJ Immigration Act of 1975 at myhistorylab.com

But immigration was far more complex than the aggregate data suggest. Dearborn, Michigan, headquarters of the Ford Motor Company, is in many ways the prototypical American city. Yet nearly a third of its 100,000 residents are Arab-speaking immigrants from Lebanon, Iraq, Yemen, and Palestine.

About 10,000 Sudanese, refugees from a genocidal war in Africa, have flocked to Omaha, Nebraska, to work in its meatpacking plants. Nearly as many Bosnians, refugees from a civil war in the Balkans, have settled in Boise, Idaho.

In many communities, the new immigrants became a significant political force. Latinos elected Latino mayors in Los Angeles, Miami, Denver, and San Antonio. César Chávez, a pivotal figure in the history of Mexican Americans (Chicanos), succeeded in bringing tens of thousands of Mexicans into his United Farm Workers union. In a series of well-publicized strikes and boycotts, Chávez and the UFW forced wage concessions from hundreds of growers in California, Texas, and the Southwest.

But the infusion of immigrants generated concern. In 1992 Patrick Buchanan, campaigning for the Republican nomination for president, warned that the migration of "millions of illegal aliens a year" from Mexico constituted "the greatest invasion" the nation had ever witnessed. By then, about one-third of the Chicanos in the United States had arrived without valid visas, usually by slipping across the long U.S. border with Mexico. Of particular concern was the fact that the Latino poverty rate—which hovered around 10 percent—was twice the national average. In 1994 California passed Proposition 187, which made illegal immigrants ("undocumented aliens") ineligible for social services, public education, and nonemergency medical services. (The U.S. Supreme Court struck the law down as an infringement of federal powers. In 2001 the Supreme Court ruled that immigrants were entitled to all the protections the Constitution afforded citizens.)

In *Who Are We?* (2004), Harvard political scientist Samuel P. Huntington warned that the massive infusion of Latinos could "divide the United States into two peoples, two cultures, and two languages." Population projections showed that by 2050 whites might become a minority. But Huntington's dichotomy was too simple. Although immigrant groups often lived in distinct neighborhoods—Mexicans on one block and Hondurans on the next—they increasingly reached across national boundaries. Local restaurants offered wide assortments of ethnic fares, outdoor festivals attracted all peoples, and popular music featured a fusion of styles. Most important, immigrants increasingly ceased to think of themselves as belonging to a particular ethnic group. In 2000, nearly 7 million Americans identified themselves as "multiracial."

Read the Document
Illegal Immigration Reform and Immigrant Responsibility Act of 1996 at myhistorylab.com

BARACK OBAMA

Not many thirty-three-year-olds write a memoir. But Barack Obama, who intended to write a book on race relations, instead explored the meaning of his young life.

The facts were clear enough. He was born on August 4, 1961, in Honolulu, Hawaii. His mother was Stanley (Ann) Dunham, whom a friend described as "Kansas white." His father, Barack Obama, Sr., was a Luo tribesman from Nyanza Province, Kenya, who had come to the University of Hawaii on a program to educate potential leaders of newly independent African nations. The couple had met in a Russian-language course at the university the previous year. Within a few months, Dunham was pregnant. Obama told her that he had been married in Kenya but had since divorced. Ann and Obama married in February, 1961. She was eighteen when she had Barack, Jr.

Her husband, however, had lied. Not only was he still married to a Kenyan, but he had one son by her with another on the way. In 1962, after graduating from Hawaii, he went to Harvard to pursue a graduate degree, leaving Ann and their son in Hawaii. When she went to visit him at Harvard, she brought the infant along. The trip went badly. Her husband had not told his friends about her or his wife in Kenya. Ann returned to Hawaii; it would be another ten years before she or her son saw his father again.

Ann and her son moved into her parents' two-bedroom apartment in Honolulu. She returned to college and her parents often took care of the boy, whom everyone called Barry. Several years later Ann divorced Obama—by then he had taken yet another wife—and she married an Indonesian geologist at the University of Hawaii. In 1967, Ann, her new husband and six-year-old Barry moved to the outskirts of Jakarta, Indonesia, where the family lived in a stucco house on a dirt lane. Chickens and ducks ran around the back-yard and two crocodiles lived in a fenced-in pond on the property. Obama's mother had always encouraged her son to adapt to different peoples, but soon her thinking shifted. Now she realized the vast chasm separating the prospects of young people who grew up in Indonesia compared to the United States.

She enrolled in a correspondence course for elementary school children in the United States. At four each morning, she awakened Barry and together they worked through the materials. After he had completed fourth grade in Jakarta, she sent him to Honolulu to live with her parents, promising to follow within a year.

Barry's grandfather arranged for the boy to attend the elite Punahou Academy. He was one of the few African Americans in the school. When some boys teased him about living in the jungle, he invented stories about how his father was a warrior and an African prince. Obama nearly persuaded himself that this fiction was true.

When his father showed up in Honolulu for a month-long visit, Barry was appalled. What would he tell his friends? But he was also confused. His long-absent father proceeded to boss Ann and her parents

Stanley (Ann) Dunham with her son, Barack Obama, age two.

and demanded that Barry work harder in school. When Barry's teacher invited his father to give a lecture on Africa, Barry was mortified. But his father's talk was smooth and gripping. Barry's friends were impressed. His father left soon afterwards. Barry never saw him again.

As a teenager, Barry excelled at basketball; his senior year, he was on the Punahou team that won the state championship. He also wrote poetry. But he lacked motivation and managed only a B– average as a senior. He spent most of his time hanging out with slacker friends. Privately, he brooded over his father's estrangement. He coped with doubts about himself by using marijuana, booze, and cocaine. When one of his friends was busted for drug possession, Obama knew it could have been him.

His first two years at Occidental College in California were more of the same. He did little work. He was nevertheless popular with nearly everyone, navigating among different social groups with ease. "He was a hot, nice, everything-going-for-him dude," one friend recalled. "You couldn't help but like him." But issues of race weighed upon him and his black friends. After some of them teased him for using the name Barry, he began to ask people to call him Barack.

After his sophomore year, Obama transferred to Columbia University in New York. Denied campus housing as a transfer student, he lived in cheap apartments in Harlem. Then something changed. He studied, ran three miles a day, often fasted on Sundays, gave up drinking and drugs (cigarettes proved more difficult), and kept a journal to record his thoughts and poetry.

Late in the fall of his senior year, he received a phone call from Africa. His father was dead. He had been drunk and drove his car into the stump of a gum tree. Even in death, his father remained a mystery to Obama.

Obama later dreamt that he was on a long bus ride that ended up at a jail. He went in and saw his father in a cell, naked but for a cloth around his waist. As Obama entered the cell, his father teased him for being so thin. Obama embraced him and wept. His father then said that he had always loved his son.

When Obama awakened, he was crying.

Perhaps young Barack had at last reconciled with his absent father, enabling him to march toward his destiny with the singular purposefulness that became his trademark. Or perhaps he sensed that he would have to create a meaningful life through achievement of his own.

Whatever the reason, he did achieve. In 1985, after graduating from Columbia, he took a job as a community organizer in Chicago and established job training programs in schools, fought to remove asbestos in housing projects, and campaigned against drug dealers. Then he was admitted to Harvard Law School, named to the *Harvard Law Review*, and elected its president, the first black to hold this prestigious position. Afterwards he returned to Chicago to write a book; it became *Dreams from My Father* (1995), a memoir from which much of this account is taken. (The publisher has refused permission for any quotes from that book to appear in this text.) He taught constitutional law at the University of Chicago while working for a black law firm with strong connections to Chicago politics. In 1996 he ran for the Illinois state legislature and won. It was the beginning of a meteoric ascent in American politics that culminated in Obama's election as president in 2008.

Questions for Discussion

- President Barack Obama identifies himself as black. Do you agree? What is the definition of race in the contemporary United States?
- What explains Obama's transition from being an indifferent student in high school and college to a disciplined achiever?

The Emergence of Modern Feminism

"Boomers"—from the phrase "baby boom"—got that name because so many of their generation were born after World War II, when returning soldiers were reunited with their girlfriends and wives, and when ample job opportunities made it easier to raise families. Boomers' parents married earlier and had children sooner after marriage than at any other time in the twentieth century. By the late 1950s, the birthrate of the United States approached that of teeming India.

An important force in the early lives of Boomers was Dr. Benjamin Spock's *Common Sense Guide to Baby and Child Care.* First published in 1946, Spock's manual sold 24 million copies during the next quarter century. Spock's book guided young parents through the common medical crises of parenthood—ear infections, colic, chickenpox—and also counseled them on psychological issues. A mother's most important job, Spock insisted, was to shore up her children's sense of self by providing continuous support and affection. Women were naturally attuned to nurturing and childcare. Those women who entered the aggressive "men's world" of work would be at odds with their psychological inclinations.

Television picked up on this theme and hammered away at it each week in sitcoms such as Robert Young's ironically titled *Father Knows Best* (1954–1962) and Jackie Gleason's equally ironic take on working-class marriage, *The Honeymooners* (1953–1962). Repeatedly irascible or befuddled patriarchs blundered into family matters, only to be gently eased out of harm's way by their understanding and psychologically savvy wives.

But the reality of the postwar woman was more complicated. Economic expansion generated many new jobs, especially in the burgeoning corporate bureaucracies and retail stores. Women were in high demand because they would work for lower wages than men. Many took jobs, ignoring Spock and cultural conventions. In 1940, only one

Paid Workforce, 1950–2005, by Gender The number (and percentage) of wage-earning women increased rapidly after 1960. In 1950, for example, fewer than one-third of the paid work force consisted of women; by 2006, the proportion had increased to nearly half.

in four civilian employees was female, one-third of them married. Three decades later, four in ten paid employees were women, two-thirds of them married.

Working women were acutely aware of the fact that men in similar jobs were paid more and had better opportunities for advancement. Women noticed, too, that minorities had improved their situations by fighting publicly. Increasingly activists for women's rights adopted similar strategies; they were the founders of the modern women's liberation movement.

One of its leaders was Betty Friedan, an activist journalist in the labor movement during the 1930s and 1940s who shifted to gender issues in later decades. In *The Feminine Mystique* (1963), Friedan argued that advertisers, popular magazines, and other "authorities" brainwashed women into thinking that they could thrive only at home. They were wrong, Friedan insisted. According to her survey of her classmates at Smith College, many housewives were troubled with vague but persistent feelings of anger and discomfort.

The Feminine Mystique provided what later came to be known as "consciousness raising" for thousands of women. Over a million copies were quickly sold. Friedan was deluged by hundreds of letters from women who had thought that their unease and depression despite their "happy" family life were both unique and unreasonable. Many now determined to expand their horizons by taking jobs or resuming their education.

Friedan had assumed that if able women acted with determination, employers would recognize their abilities and stop discriminating against them. As feminists were outlining plans to strengthen women's claims to fair treatment in the workplace, they won an unexpected victory. In 1964, during a debate on whether to ban racial discrimination in employment, Virginia Senator Howard Smith, seeking to scuttle the law, proposed that women also be protected from discrimination in hiring and promotion. Several congresswomen immediately endorsed the idea and proposed an amendment to that effect. This became Title VII of the Civil Rights Act of 1964.

In 1966 Friedan and other feminists founded the **National Organization for Women (NOW)**. "The time has come for a new movement toward true equality for all women in America and toward a fully equal partnership of the sexes," the leaders announced. In 1967 NOW came out for an equal rights amendment to the Constitution, for changes in the divorce laws, and for the legalization of abortion, the right of "control of one's body."

The **Equal Rights Amendment (ERA)**, which would make it unconstitutional to deny equal rights "on account of sex," had been proposed by the National Woman's party in 1923; by the late 1930s it appeared headed for adoption by Congress. But Eleanor Roosevelt and other women's groups killed the amendment, fearing it would rescind laws that protected poor women and their children. By the late 1960s, however, NOW's campaign for the ERA was yielding dividends. In 1971 the House of Representatives approved the ERA and the Senate followed the next year. By the end of 1972, twenty-two states had raced to go on record to ratify the amendment: What politician could prudently oppose equal rights for women? At the outset of 1973, only sixteen more states needed to ratify ERA before it was added to the Constitution.

View the Image

Jimmy Carter Signs the House of Representative Resolution for the Equal Rights Amendment, 1972 at **myhistorylab.com**

Feminist activists soon turned to another major goal: legalization of abortion. The Constitution made no reference to abortion. But during the nineteenth century botched surgical abortions that killed many women prompted the American Medical Association to call for the "general suppression" of the practice. By 1900, every state except Kentucky had passed antiabortion laws. Most states granted exceptions when the woman had been impregnated by rape or incest or when a doctor thought it necessary to save the woman's life. In 1967, for example, Governor Reagan of California, an opponent of abortion, signed a law allowing doctors to perform abortions if childbirth would "gravely impair the physical or mental health of the mother." The number of legal abortions in California increased from 5,018 in 1968 to more than 100,000 by 1972.

In 1970, however, feminist activists persuaded the Hawaii legislature to repeal its criminal abortion statute, the first state to do so. Later that year, another battle was waged in New York. It pitted feminists, liberals, and the medical establishment against conservatives and the Roman Catholic Church. The state assembly repealed its antiabortion law by a single vote. Feminists regarded this as a crucial but sobering victory. If a liberal state such as New York had barely mustered a majority in favor of abortion rights, how long would it take for the campaign to prevail elsewhere?

Roe v. Wade

The question soon became moot; the United States Supreme Court took the decision out of the hands of state legislatures. A key factor was a new concept in constitutional law: the "right to privacy." In the nineteenth century, the Catholic Church had persuaded many state legislatures to ban dissemination of information on contraceptives and birth control. Connecticut was one such state. But in 1961 Estelle Griswold, head of Planned Parenthood in Connecticut, opened a birth control clinic to challenge the law. In the case of *Griswold v. Connecticut*, the Supreme Court, headed by Earl Warren, struck down the Connecticut statute, contending that it violated couples' "right to privacy." While conceding that no such term appeared in the Constitution, the Court held that various other constitutional provisions—such as freedom of speech and press and prohibitions against unreasonable searches—together provided an "umbrella" of privacy-related rights. This "right to privacy" protected people from unwarranted intrusions by the state.

Then, in 1969, Norma McCorvey asked her doctor for an abortion. She was unmarried, unemployed, twenty-five years old, and pregnant. Her doctor refused. Abortion, he told her, was illegal in Texas unless performed to save the woman's life. McCorvey's lawyer encouraged her to challenge the law. She consented, using the pseudonym "Jane Roe," and her lawyer filed suit against Henry Wade, the Dallas County prosecutor.

In 1973, after McCorvey had the baby, the U.S. Supreme Court rendered a decision in *Roe v. Wade*. Rejecting any "single" theory of life, the justices maintained that a fetus did not have a "right to life" until the final three months of pregnancy, when it could likely survive without the mother. Until then, the mother's right to "privacy" took precedence. The state could not prevent a woman from having an abortion during the first six months of pregnancy. Most abortions were no longer illegal. A major goal of the feminists had been achieved almost overnight.

The *Roe v. Wade* decision resulted in a rapid expansion of abortion facilities. From 1973 to 1980, the number of abortions performed annually increased from 745,000 to 1.5 million. Abortion had become the nation's most common surgical procedure. The new feminist movement had prevailed on a number of issues that would have been unthinkable a decade earlier.

Read the Document

Roe v. Wade (January 22, 1973) at **myhistorylab.com**

State Laws on Abortion Prior to *Roe v. Wade* **(1973)** Prior to *Roe v. Wade*, only Hawaii, Alaska, and New York had legalized abortion. Louisiana, Pennsylvania, and New Hampshire prohibited all abortions, while every other state allowed abortions only in cases of rape or incest or to preserve the life of the woman.

Conservative Counterattack

But the *Roe v. Wade* decision also energized a grass-roots conservative movement against abortion, often supported by the Catholic Church, the Mormons, and Protestant groups such as Falwell's Moral Majority. The right-to-life movement endorsed the presidential campaigns of Ronald Reagan and George H. W. Bush, whose Supreme Court appointments generally favored the right-to-life position. In *Webster v. Reproductive Health Services* (1989) and *Planned Parenthood of Southeastern Pennsylvania v. Casey* (1992), the Supreme Court allowed states to impose certain con-

ditions, such as tests of viability and waiting periods, before abortions could be performed. But well into the twenty-first century, *Roe v. Wade* remained the law of the land.

Conservatives were more successful in contesting the ERA, which seemed headed to prompt ratification. In 1973 Phyllis Schlafly, a former vice president of the National Federation of Republican Women and publisher of a conservative newsletter, spearheaded a nationwide campaign against ratification of the ERA. She argued that it would subject young women to the military draft, deprive divorced women of alimony and child custody, and

Phyllis Schlafly drew much of her support from working-class women who were left vulnerable by the recession after 1973.

289

make married women legally responsible for providing 50 percent of household income. As the recession after 1973 dragged the economy down, Schlafly's words struck a responsive chord among anxious housewives and low-wage-earning women who doubted they could survive the recessionary economy on their own. The ratification campaign lost momentum and stalled, falling just three states short. By 1980, the ERA was dead.[1]

The Rise of Gay and Lesbian Rights

The rhetoric of "minority rights" and the example of activists in other movements during the 1960s encouraged gay rights activists to demand that society cease harassing and discriminating against *them*. In 1969, New York City police raided the Stonewall Inn, a popular gay bar in Greenwich Village and arrested the occupants—most of them gays—for "solicitation" of illegal sexual acts. The crowd outside threw rocks and bottles and the police were forced to retreat. The Stonewall riot lasted for several days and marked a turning point in the history of gays and lesbians. No longer would gays in Greenwich Village remain "in the closet"—hidden from view. Public advocacy of their cause strengthened it immeasurably.

Read the Document

The Gay Liberation Front, Come Out (1970) at **myhistorylab.com**

Gay activists embarked on numerous campaigns to eliminate discrimination against gays. Gay psychiatrists challenged the American Psychiatric Association's longstanding judgment that homosexuality was a treatable mental illness. In 1973 the association's board of directors agreed to remove homosexuality from the standard manual of psychiatric disorders. Disgruntled traditionalists challenged the decision and forced the directors to put the matter up for a vote of the entire membership. In 1974 the members upheld the directors. The next year the American Psychological Association concurred. Homosexuality was not a mental illness.

Gay and lesbian activists also filed suits to eliminate discrimination against gays in education, housing, education, and employment. In response to such pressures, the U.S. Civil Service Commission rescinded its ban on hiring homosexuals. Now gays chose to run openly for public office. In 1977, Harvey Milk, the first openly gay man to run for office in California, was elected supervisor in San Francisco. The next year he led the fight against a California law that would fire gay teachers. Former California governor Ronald Reagan opposed the bill as a violation of human rights, as did President Jimmy Carter; the proposition was defeated by a million votes. Three weeks later Milk was assassinated; he became a martyr to the gay rights movement.

Photo Credit: Daniel Nicoletta.

Harvey Milk was the first openly gay candidate to be elected to office in California.

---

[1]Various Supreme Court decisions, such as *Reed v. Reed* (1971), struck down laws that failed to provide "equal protection" of men and women or applied arbitrary standards in making legal distinctions between the rights of men and women.

AIDS

But by the late 1970s, as gays were openly acknowledging and celebrating their sexual identity, many were being struck down by a new disease. World health officials had spotted the outbreak of yet another viral epidemic in central Africa; but no one noticed that this virus had mutated into a more lethal strain and was spreading to Europe and North America. On June 5, 1981, the Centers for Disease Control (CDC) alerted American health officials to an outbreak of a rare bacterial infection in Los Angeles. What made the outbreak distinctive was that this particular infection had struck five healthy young men. All were homosexuals. Within months, all died.

By 1982 the CDC called this new disease **acquired immunodeficiency syndrome (AIDS)**. The CDC learned that AIDS was caused by the **human immunodeficiency virus (HIV)**, a lethal virus that destroys the body's defenses against infection. HIV spreads when an infected person's body fluids come in contact with someone else's. By the end of 1982, the CDC had documented 900 cases of AIDS; the disease was increasing exponentially. In June 1983, when the federal budget approached $1 trillion, Congress finally voted $12 million for AIDS research and treatment.

Not until 1985, when the square-jawed romantic actor Rock Hudson confirmed that he was dying of AIDS, did the subject command widespread public attention. President Reagan, an old friend of Hudson's, publicly acknowledged that the disease constituted a grave health crisis. Congress approved Reagan's call for a substantial increase in AIDS funding. But Reagan's appeal was belated and insufficient. By then, nearly 21,000 Americans had died; by 1999, the total number of AIDS-related deaths approached 400,000.

The AIDS epidemic affected public policy and private behavior. Fear of the disease, and of those who suffered from it, exacerbated many people's homophobia. But the AIDS epidemic also forced most people to confront homosexuality directly and perhaps for the first time, and thus contributed to a deeper understanding of the complexity of human nature. Gay and lesbian organizations, the vanguard in the initial war against AIDS, continued to fight for social acceptance and legal rights.

In this electron microscopic photograph, two human immunodeficiency virus (HIV) cells, in different stages of budding, are emerging from an infected T-lymphocyte human blood cell (pink). The HIV cell that has almost broken free includes RNA (green—the cell's genetic code) and it will reinfect other T-cells. T-cells are part of the body's immune system.

Photo Credit: National Institute for Biological Standards and Control (U.K.)/Science Photo Library/ Photo Researchers, Inc.

Publicly Gay

Although gays had always served in the military—Milk had been an officer in the navy during the Korean War—they were technically banned. In 1992 President Bill Clinton had promised to end the ban on gays and lesbians in the armed services, but when the Joint Chiefs of the armed forces and a number of important members of Congress objected, he settled for a policy known as "don't ask, don't tell," meaning that such persons would be allowed to enlist only if they did not openly proclaim their sexual preferences. In 2010 Congress voted to openly admit gays and lesbians to the armed forces.

Another long-term objective was same-sex marriage. Why, gay and lesbian couples asked, should they not be allowed to adopt children or receive the legal protections and benefits of marriage? Conservative groups argued that religious texts and moral traditions had defined marriage as heterosexual. In 2006 conservatives, backed by President

Table 1 **Gender Activist Victories and Conservative Responses**

Year	Activist Victory	Consequence	Conservative Response (after 1972)
1964	Title VII, Civil Rights Act of 1964	Prohibited employers from discriminating on account of sex; enforced by federal government	
1965	*Griswold v. Connecticut*	Supreme Court asserted a "right to privacy" to allow dissemination of information on birth control	
1972	Equal Rights Amendment (ERA) approved by Congress	Extended the equal rights protections of Fourteenth Amendment to women	Phyllis Schlafly inaugurated "Stop ERA" campaign (1973), which blocked ratification
1973	*Roe v. Wade*	Supreme Court legalized most abortions	Jerry Falwell's Moral Majority founded; helped elect Ronald Reagan president (1980); named more conservative Supreme Court justices
2000	Vermont recognized same-sex unions	Paved way for a half-dozen states to approve same-sex marriage	George W. Bush-backed proposed constitutional amendment to limit marriage to heterosexuals narrowly defeated in Senate (2006)

George W. Bush, proposed an amendment to the Constitution that would define marriage as "a union between a man and a woman." The measure fell just short of passage in the Senate.

In 2000 Vermont became the first state to recognize same-sex civil unions, providing gay and lesbian couples with some of the legal rights of marriage. In 2004 Massachusetts was the first state to recognize same-sex marriage; within the next five years, a half dozen states passed similar laws. When Washington, DC approved a same-sex marriage law, the Catholic Archdiocese of Washington, DC protested the decision by revising health care benefits of its agencies to avoid covering same-sex couples. But by 2010, according to most opinion polls, a solid majority of Americans favored same-sex marriage. And by a hefty margin, Millennials were far more likely to endorse same-sex marriage than any other age group, including Boomers.

Crime and Punishment

Civil rights protesters who intentionally violated laws rather than work within the law to change it; feminists who flouted conventional gender roles and asserted a right to abortion; gays and lesbians who claimed a right to serve openly in the military and enter into same-sex marriages—all were evidence, at least in the opinion of some, that the nation had lost its moral bearings. Such misgivings had spiked in the late 1960s, as antiwar protests closed down college campuses and race riots ravaged cities. Violent crime increased. Many called for restoration of "law and order." During the 1970s and 1980s conservative activists, borrowing strategies from activist movements on the left, succeeded in implementing many of the goals of the "law and order" movement. They elected officials who passed tougher laws, hired more police, and built additional prisons.

The shift toward capital punishment was symptomatic. No criminal had been executed since 1967. The practice simply had fallen from favor. But in response to the

Narcotics policemen in Bridgeport, Connecticut, arrest a suspect for selling crack near housing projects in 1994.

●◀●─│Read the Document

*United States of America v.
Timothy James McVeigh—
Sentencing (August 14, 1997)*
at **myhistorylab.com**

conservative demand for tough legislation against criminals, legislators rewrote capital punishment statutes in light of the *Furman* decision, depriving juries of discretion in sentencing. The Supreme Court upheld these laws and capital punishment resumed in 1976. Since then, over a thousand convicts have been executed.

Another manifestation of the crackdown on crime was the increase in the nation's prison population. In 1973 the nation's prisons—state and federal—held about 200,000 convicts. By 1990 the number of prisoners exceeded 750,000, and by 2004, 2 million. This required the construction of a 1,000-bed prison every week. In 1995, for the first time, states spent more on prisons than on higher education. By 2010, the United States incarcerated more people than any country in the world, except perhaps communist China, which did not disclose such information.

Crack and Urban Gangs

Several factors intensified the problem of violent crime, especially in the inner cities. One was a shift in drug use. During the 1960s marijuana had become commonly available, especially on college campuses; this was followed by cocaine, which was far more powerful and addictive but so expensive that few could afford it.

During the 1980s growers of coca leaves in Peru and Bolivia greatly expanded production. Drug traffickers in Colombia devised sophisticated systems to transport cocaine to the United States. The price of cocaine dropped from $120 an ounce in 1981 to $50 in 1988.

Still more important was the proliferation of a cocaine-based compound called "crack" because it crackled when smoked. Many users found that it gave an intense spasm of pleasure that overrode all other desires.

The lucrative crack trade led to bitter turf wars in the inner cities; dealers hired neighborhood youths, organized them into gangs, armed them with automatic weapons, and told them to drive competitors away. A survey of Los Angeles county in the early 1990s found that more than 150,000 young people belonged to 1,000 gangs. Violence had become a fact of life. In 1985, before crack had seized hold of the inner city, there were 147 murders in Washington, DC; in 1991, the figure skyrocketed to 482.

Black on black murder had become a significant cause of death for African Americans in their twenties. In 1988 Monsta' Kody Scott, who at age eleven pumped shotgun blasts into rival gang members, returned after prison to his Los Angeles neighborhood. He was horrified: Gangs no longer merely shot their rivals but sprayed them with automatic weapons, seventy-five rounds to a clip, or blew them away with small rockets. By 2010, 30 percent of African American men in their twenties were in prison, or on probation or parole.

Violence and Popular Culture

Conservatives—and plenty of liberals—were also dismayed by the violence of popular culture. They cited as proof the lurid violence of the movie industry, pointing out that in *Public Enemy*, reputedly the most violent film of the 1930s, and *Death Wish*, a controversial vigilante fantasy of 1974, the body count reached eight. But three movies released during the late 1980s—*Robocop, Die Hard*, and *Rambo III*—each produced a death tally of sixty or more, nearly one every two minutes. The trend culminated in *Natural Born Killers* (1994), director Oliver Stone's unimaginably violent "spoof" of media violence. Television imitated the movies as the networks crammed violent crime shows into prime time. In 1991 an exhaustive survey found that by the age of eighteen, the average viewer had witnessed some 40,000 murders on TV.

A new sound called "rap" then emerged from the ghetto. Rap consisted of unpredictably metered lyrics set against an exaggeratedly heavy downbeat. Rap performers did not play musical instruments or sing songs so much as convey, in words and gestures, an attitude of defiant, raw rage against whatever challenged their sense of manhood: other young males; women, whom they derided in coarse sexual epithets; and the police. Predictably, raps such as "Cop Killer" and "Illegal Search" contributed to the charge that rap condoned violence and crime.

The appeal of rap quickly spread beyond black audiences. When Dr. Dre (Andrew Young), founder of a gangsta rap group and head of a record firm, discovered that whites bought more rap CDs than blacks, he promoted the career of a young white rapper, Eminem. Born Marshall Bruce Mathers III, Eminem attracted attention with songs such as "Murder, Murder," "Kill You," "Drug Ballad," and "Criminal." He bashed women, gays, his wife, and nearly everyone else. His lyrics were of such surpassing offensiveness that he became an overnight celebrity and instant millionaire. His fans, whom he treated with scorn, were delighted by the universality of his contempt. The list of those suing him included his mother.

By the 1990s improvements in computer graphics led to the development of increasingly realistic—and violent—video games. "Grand Theft Auto," which by 2005 had sold over 35 million copies and generated over $2 billion, was the subject of a *60 Minutes* special. Journalist Ed Bradley described the game this way: "See a car you like? Steal it. A cop in your way? Blow him away." Bradley recounted the story of Devin Moore, an eighteen-year-old who played the game "day and night" for years. On June 7, 2003, he stole a car; when apprehended he grabbed a gun, killed three policemen, and fled in a police cruiser. When finally caught he said, "Life is like a video game. Everybody's got to die sometime."

America, it seemed, had become seemingly filled with menace. At night, few ventured downtown and many avoided public places. Car alarm systems became standard. The popular phrase—"your home is your castle"—took on an eerie reality. Americans reinforced doors with steel, nailed windows shut, and increasingly hunkered down in their own private spaces, which they locked up and wired with alarms.

From Main Street to Mall to Internet

In 1960 civil rights protesters picketed six stores in Richmond, Virginia. Within several decades, all of the stores had closed. So had most of the luncheonettes, 5 & 10 cent stores, bus stations, and community swimming pools that had been sites of civil rights protests during the late 1950s and early 1960s. Civil rights leaders targeted such facilities because they sought equal access to public spaces downtown, where community life was transacted. There people worked, bought clothing and cars, got their hair cut and cavities filled, paid taxes and filed for driver's licenses, ate meals and brokered deals, watched movies and attended ball games, and engaged in countless other activities. Thirty years later, however, many downtown business districts had been all but abandoned.

In 2007 a storm approaches the mostly abandoned main street of Robert Lee, county seat of Coke County, Texas.

Some blamed the civil rights movement itself. Inner-city protests and the desegregation of city schools, they said, caused many whites to flee to the suburbs. Others cited the rise in crime in the late 1960s. But "white flight" commenced in the late 1940s, long before the civil rights movement and busing disputes, before the race riots and crack infestations. Postwar federal policies played a major role in the demographic upheaval that transformed the cities and gave rise to the suburbs. The G. I. Bill of 1946 offered veterans cheap home mortgages. Real estate developers bought huge tracts of land and built inexpensive houses designed especially for returning

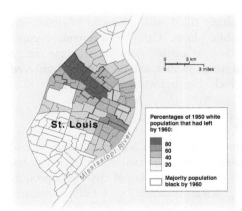

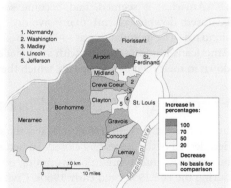

Racial Shifts in St. Louis during the 1950s During the 1950s, the white population of St. Louis declined by more than 200,000, while the black population increased by 100,000. Much of the central core was almost entirely black.

Growth of Suburban St. Louis, 1950–1960 During the 1950s, the suburban townships in St. Louis county west of the city gained nearly 300,000 people, an increase of 73 percent. More than 99 percent of the suburban residents were white.

veterans. Postwar lending policies of the Federal Housing Authority also contributed to the rise of the suburbs, chiefly by rejecting loans in older residential urban areas. Eisenhower's decision to pump money into highway construction (rather than subways and railway infrastructure) also contributed to the growth of suburbs.

Retailers followed consumers, renting space in strip malls along the busy roadways that reached out to the suburbs. Then came the shopping malls. In 1946 there were only eight shopping malls in the nation; by 1972, over 13,000. Mall managers anchored their complexes with national retailers such as Sears and JCPenney. Because such companies bought in large quantities, their stores out-priced locally owned competitors on Main Street. Main Street faded. By the 1980s, retailers such as Sam Walton took the logic of price competition several steps farther. He dispensed with the customary amenities of shopping—attractive displays, pleasant décor, professional salespeople—and built "big box" stores that were little more than shopper-accessible warehouses. Then came another shift. Early in the twenty-first century, shoppers who wearied of pushing carts through dimly lit warehouses and standing in line to pay now had an alternative: They could shop via the Internet, which by 2010 accounted for nearly 10 percent of all retail sales.

Within a half century, shopping had not only become more private, but it also was less social. Big-box stores replaced commissioned salespeople with low-paid checkers. In the past decade improvements in scanner technology allowed retailers to dispense even with checkers. And an increasing number of online consumers shop at home. Increasingly, shopping entails no social interaction whatsoever.

A similar shift from public interaction to private pursuits has characterized many other daily activities. For much of their lives, Boomers regularly visited local banks to make deposits and cash checks. But during the recession of the 1970s banks closed many branches and in subsequent decades hundreds of banks were merged. More branches were closed and tens of thousands of tellers laid off. Rather than drive to distant branches and wait in long lines, banking customers learned to use ATMs and bank online. Banking for Boomers had been a social occasion; for Millennials it became an interaction with a machine.

By the 1970s and 1980s, many service sector jobs had disappeared: milkmen who delivered fresh dairy products; door-to-door salespeople who demonstrated cosmetics, appliances, and encyclopedias; "service station" attendants who pumped gas and checked the oil; bakery owners and candy makers who sold goods they had made themselves. Then in the 1990s, person-to-person interactions in daily life occurred even less frequently. With the advent of the Internet and improved software, many people became their own travel agent, tax preparer, financial adviser, grocer, cosmetician, medical assistant, and bookseller.

From Community to Facebook

Religious institutions have long constituted the bulwark of communities, and the postwar period witnessed a remarkable expansion. By 1990, membership in all churches and synagogues surpassed 148 million, an increase of 60 million during the previous four decades. (The total population during the period increased by nearly 100 million.) With the large influx of Hispanic immigrants, membership in the Roman Catholic Church more than doubled. Membership in mainstream Protestant churches generally declined, but rose solidly in fundamentalist and evangelical churches, such as the Southern Baptist, Pentecostal, Holiness, Assemblies of God, and Church of God in Christ. The Jehovah's Witnesses and the Mormon Church grew as well. In 1990 two-thirds of all Americans reported that they belonged to a church, the highest percentage by far among the major industrial nations of the West.

But the membership numbers were misleading. Since 1970, church attendance among persons younger than sixty has declined about 20 percent. The UCLA survey cited in the introduction to this chapter found that in 1968, 9 percent of entering college freshmen said they never attended church; by 2000, that percentage had more than doubled. By the 1970s, moreover, millions of Americans went to church by turning on the TV. "Televangelists" such as Rex Humbard, Oral Roberts, Jerry Falwell, Pat Robertson, and Jim and Tammy Bakker founded their own churches and educational institutions, supported by direct appeals to viewers. A few established their own colleges, such as Falwell's Liberty University, Oral Roberts University, and Robertson's CBN University (renamed Regent University in 1990). A number of scandals involving prominent televangelists caused disillusionment and widespread defections. On the other hand, the rapid spread of cable television greatly increased the number of available channels, enabling scores of new evangelists to reach out to viewers. Community-based ministers saw congregations shrink; thousands of churches closed their doors for good. Some churches devised "healing rituals" to ease their abandonment of formerly sacred space.

Participation in team sports fell at about the same rate as church attendance. By the first decade of the twenty-first century, more young people played basketball and soccer than in the past, but far fewer played softball, baseball, football, tennis, and league bowling. The fields on which young Boomers often spent much of their lives had been sold to developers or fenced in and locked.

The lack of exercise among Millennials became a source of national concern. In 2010 Surgeon General Regina Benjamin announced that one in three American children was obese. One reason, Benjamin explained, was that youngsters between ages eight to eighteen averaged seven hours and thirty-eight minutes a day on electronic media—watching TV, talking on cell phones, playing video games, and logged into the Internet. That year, First Lady Michelle Obama inaugurated a nationwide antiobesity campaign named—appropriately—"Let's move!"

Some Millennials exercised *while* engaged with electronic media. (Multitasking became a redundant adjective for the Millennial generation.) Since 2000, membership in gyms skyrocketed. And often Millennials could be seen pounding away on treadmills or other exercise machines, staring at TV monitors or listening to music with an earpiece. Not all Millennials are sedentary; but many are nearly always plugged in.

The rise of online learning is an illustration of the transformation of social activities into solitary Internet pursuits. By 2009, over 4 million Americans enrolled in online courses, twice as many as in 2003. For many, especially full-time employees, ease of access compensated for the lack of face-to-face contact with other students. Tim Scott, a twenty-five-year-old clerk in a drugstore who enrolled in technology courses at the University of Phoenix, explained, "This is pretty much the only way I could get a college degree." Online education spread to all walks of life. Some people took courses to learn new languages and career skills, such as "Dental Anthropology," "Clown Education," or

"Golf Course Management." Others logged in to learn new hobbies, such as "building a kayak," "paragliding in the Alps," or "Salsa dancing." Employees were required to take mandatory online courses on company policies and sexual harassment. Although surveys suggest that most online learners prefer classes in which they interact with real people in a classroom, the fact was that often regular classrooms had themselves become anonymous and impersonal. As Harvard Professor Clayton Christensen observed, "Anything beyond the 10th row in a large lecture hall is distance learning."

One reason distance online education took off was that it spared commuting students the hassle of driving to college and finding parking. Such experiences underscored the extent to which cars had become the predominant mode of transportation, another shift from the earlier social context of mass transit to the mostly solitary experience of driving. Bus and train ridership was declining well before the advent of the Boomers; but the postwar population shift to the suburbs accelerated the ascendancy of cars over mass transit. As more drivers—nearly always alone—clogged the highways, traffic jams grew longer. By 2005, the average American spent thirty-eight hours a year stuck in traffic. Although many found repose within the solitary confines of a car, others coped with the loneliness of driving by chatting on their cell phones or texting friends. (A Pew poll in 2010 found that one in three texting teenagers did so while driving a car.)

The postwar suburban home itself was conceived as a private refuge from the hustle and bustle of downtown. But over time suburban homes became still more private. Newer houses were set farther back from the curb; high fences and thick hedges discouraged the over-the-barbecue conviviality of the 1950s suburbs. By the 1990s, many well-to-do people moved into privately owned "gated communities," surrounded by high fences and patrolled by private security guards. Only residents and specified guests were allowed in.

The trend toward increased privacy could be seen even within the home. Young Boomers generally ate dinner in a family dining room and played cards and board games afterwards in the living room. By the mid 1950s, television-watching had become a family affair, and a child's dreaded punishment was to be sent to his or her room after dinner. During the 1980s and 1990s, however, homes became larger and families smaller. Most Millennials had their own bedrooms. By 1975 fewer than half of Americans ate dinner with their whole family; and by 2000, that fraction had slipped to one-third. Family members instead retreated to their own rooms to watch their own television shows or log onto the Internet. (In 2010 the average number of TV sets per household—2.93— exceeded the number of *people* per household—2.88.) For Millennials, the worst punishment was to be deprived of the Internet or their Blackberries.

Millennials withdrew to the privacy of their rooms in order to socialize. David Greenfield of the Center for Internet Studies explained that the Internet was "a socially connecting device that's socially isolating at the same time." For their part, most Millennials thought the Internet improved social relations. "I've outsourced my social life exclusively to Facebook," one Millennial explained in 2009. "My time on Facebook substitutes for face time and has made my life more organized and efficient." In 2010 Facebook reported that the average college student had over 400 Facebook friends. Plenty of users greatly exceeded this average, prompting Facebook in 2008 to rule that friendship rosters would be capped at 5,000. Social connections in excess of 5,000, Facebook officials reasoned, were probably not "actual friends." While bemoaning the cutoff, Jeffrey Wolfe, a real estate broker in San Francisco with 4,447 friends, conceded that keeping up with them could be demanding: "Normally I start hitting it about 10 o'clock at night, and if I do it right, I can be done by 1 a.m."

Some worried that Millennials spent so much time attending to their own circle of Facebook friends (however great in circumference) or logging onto sites dedicated to Lady Gaga, labrador retrievers, or Legos, that they often failed to encounter people with ideas or perspectives different from their own. But others endorsed the Internet as an ideal if somewhat odd way to meet strangers and exchange opinions. *Second Life*, a virtual 3D world populated by some 18 million "residents," was among the innumerable interactive games that allowed strangers to converse and imaginatively interact. In 2009 Linden Lab, the San Francisco company behind the concept, noted that *Second Life* residents had logged over a billion hours on the site and spent a billion dollars buying unreal things (mostly clothing and cars) for their virtual personas, or avatars. One Stanford researcher explained how he had experienced "the most sexually charged non-sexual experience I've ever had" when his avatar was propositioned by another avatar in a "private room" (!).

Virtual communities possessed both the advantages and disadvantages of anonymity. "On the Internet, no one knows you're a dog," as a *New Yorker* cartoon's canine narrator remarked. A 2001 study found that half of the female Avatars in *Second Life* were actually men. Anonymity may help protect people who wish to articulate ideas and explore behaviors that might generate disapproval in "real" settings.

But the anonymity of the Internet also carries risks. Sexual predators target teen chat rooms and social-networking sites. Anonymity, too, allows people to vent frustrations, prejudices, and spite without concern for consequences. In 2006, Lori Drew, a mother in O'Fallon, Missouri, sought to teach a lesson to Megan Meier, a fourteen-year-old whom Drew believed had been spreading rumors about Drew's daughter. Drew created

In *Second Life*, a multi-player online game, these two avatars engage in virtual courtship.

a fictitious MySpace persona of a sixteen-year-old named "Josh," who friended Meier, gained her confidence, and acquired her secrets. But then "Josh" turned on Meier, advising, "The world would be a better place without you." Twenty minutes later, Meier hanged herself in her bedroom closet.

Drew was convicted of a misdemeanor for violating the terms of her MySpace agreement; but a federal judge set the ruling aside: Violation of an Internet agreement did not constitute criminal behavior. State legislatures in Missouri and California immediately passed "anti-cyberbullying" laws. In 2009 Congresswoman Linda Sanchez introduced the "Megan Meier Cyberbullying Prevention Act," but constitutional experts predicted that such laws would be struck down as infringements on free speech and privacy rights.

But what did privacy mean? During the previous four decades, Boomers and Millennials had repeatedly debated and redefined the concepts of private and public. Feminists had asserted a "right to privacy," including a right to an abortion; but the Moral Majority had insisted on the superior "right to life" of the fetus. Gays and lesbians had sought freedom from government harassment; but they also sought public acceptance through adoption of same-sex marriage laws and open acknowledgement of their service in the military. President Reagan and conservatives campaigned to "get government off our backs" and yet they expanded the government's role in prosecuting behavior deemed deviant or immoral. And if public physical spaces were disappearing, Millennials increasingly participated, often from the solitude of a bedroom or study, in a bogglingly public world of the Internet, blithely posting their innermost thoughts (and sometimes photos) on social networking sites.

Greying of the Boomers

On January 1, 2011, when the first Boomer turned sixty-five, nearly one-seventh of the American population was over sixty-five, the customary retirement age. Demographic projections indicated that by the time the Millennials reached sixty-five, one-fifth of the population would be over sixty-five.

The aging of the nation's population had serious economic implications. A substantial proportion of the nation's wealth was shifting from economically productive purposes (educating the young, building and maintaining infrastructure, and creating new businesses and technology) to the less productive task of providing health care and pensions for the elderly.

In 1980, sixty-year-old John A. Garraty, co-author of this book, completed his first twenty-six-mile marathon in New York City. He completed his last marathon when he was seventy-two.

Photo Credit: Courtesy of John A. Garraty, Jr.

Of particular concern was the viability of Social Security, the New Deal program that provided pensions for the elderly. In theory, workers and employers paid into the Social Security Trust Fund; when workers retired, they would draw their "savings" from the Trust Fund. But under pressure from seniors—the highest-voting proportion of the population—Congress increased old-age benefits. As of 2010, the Social Security Trust Fund had $2 trillion in assets, but the projected cost of Social Security by 2050 exceeded $7 trillion. The difference would have to be covered by the contributions made by working Millennials, many of whom worried that the fund would be gone by the time they retired. A 2009 poll by the American Association of Retired Persons (AARP) found that only 31 percent of Americans between the ages of eighteen and thirty-nine believe that Social Security will be available to them on retirement.

Medical advances during the late twentieth century led to an increase in the life span: An American born in 1900 could expect to live to be fifty, while one born in 2000 was projected to live to seventy-seven. But this good news further complicated the transition from Boomers to Millennials.

Compounding the difficulty were attitudinal differences between the generations, such as those cited elsewhere in this chapter. The 2008 Pew poll also found that 75 percent of Millennials had profiles on a social networking site, compared to 30 percent of Boomers; that 38 percent of Millennials had a tattoo, compared to 15 percent of Boomers; and that 23 percent of Millennials had body piercings other than an ear lobe, compared to fewer than 1 percent of Boomers. How Millennials will treat aging Boomers is anyone's guess.

Milestones

Year	Event	Year	Event
1946	Dr. Benjamin Spock publishes *Common Sense Guide to Baby and Child Care*	1969	Stonewall riots mark public assertion of rights of homosexuals
1947	Construction begins on Levittown, New York, first tract-house suburb	1973	Supreme Court legalizes abortion in *Roe v. Wade*
1960	FDA approves sale of birth control pills	1979	Jerry Falwell founds the Moral Majority
1963	Betty Friedan publishes *The Feminine Mystique*	1982	Center for Disease Control identifies new disease, AIDS
1965	Congress passes Immigration Act that ends "national origins" quotas	1989	Supreme Court limits abortion rights in *Webster v. Reproductive Health Services*
	Supreme Court affirms "right to privacy" in *Griswold v. Connecticut*	2000	Vermont recognies same-sex unions
	César Chávez organizes boycott to support grape pickers	2010	Michelle Obama introduces anti-obesity campaign

✓ •─[Study and Review at **www.myhistorylab.com**

Review Questions

1. The introduction to this text argues that young Boomers were more inclined to look for a "meaningful philosophy of life," while young Millennials were more interested in being "well-off financially." Do you agree? What evidence from the chapter supports your position? What refutes it?

2. What accounted for the emergence of modern feminism in the 1960s? Did it succeed in changing gender roles and if so, how? What explained the emergence of gay and lesbian activism?

3. What were the main components of the conservative movement after 1970? How did it influence culture and society?

4. How did the cultural shift from "downtown" to the suburbs change society more generally? In what sense has life become more or less "private"?

Key Terms

acquired immunodeficiency syndrome (AIDS)

Equal Rights Amendment (ERA)
human immunodeficiency virus (HIV)

National Organization for Women (NOW)

Shocks and Responses: 1992–Present

From Chapter 32 of *American Destiny: Narrative of a Nation*, Combined Volume, Fourth Edition.
Mark C. Carnes and John A. Garraty. Copyright © 2012 by Pearson Education, Inc. Published by
Pearson Prentice Hall. All rights reserved.

Shocks and Responses:
1992–Present

((•—[Hear the Audio at myhistorylab.com

What will happen to you?

"**T**HOSE WHO FAIL TO LEARN FROM THE PAST ARE DOOMED TO REPEAT it"—This cliché, a favorite of history teachers, contains some truth. The book you are reading, for example, provides some solid guidance: Governments that ignore the wishes of the people probably won't long endure; wars are easier to start than to stop; and investments that seem to be "too good to be true" probably are. But apart from such common-sense observations, history provides few clues about the future.

The first decade of the twenty-first century proves this point emphatically. In 2000 Americans were mostly optimistic, and for good reason. After the dissolution of the Soviet Union in 1991, a new era of peace was dawning. Successive American presidents reduced the nation's armed forces by nearly a million men and women; defense spending (as a proportion of the GNP) was nearly cut in half. Three decades of deficits had come to an end: In 2000 the U.S. Treasury operated at a $250 billion *surplus*. The Congressional Budget Office projected a $4 *trillion* federal surplus for the coming decade.

It didn't happen. The terrorist attack of September 11, 2001 shattered hopes for peace. Within two years, American soldiers were fighting fierce battles in Afghanistan and Iraq. By the end of the decade, over 5,000 U.S. servicemen and women would be dead.

By then, too, an economic earthquake had nearly toppled the nation's major financial institutions. By late 2008 political and economic leaders were spending trillions to prop up banks, investment houses, and insurance firms that "were too big to fail." The federal deficit for the decade approached $4 *trillion*.

More bad news was to come. In early 2010 an oil rig owned by British Petroleum blew up, killing eleven and releasing millions of barrels of oil into the Gulf of Mexico. President Obama called it the nation's worst environmental disaster ever.

By then, *Time* magazine had already pronounced these years "The Decade from Hell." But no one had any inkling of this in 1992.

A New Face: Bill Clinton

William (Bill) Clinton was born William Jefferson Blythe IV, but his father died in a car accident before he was born. Though his stepfather was an abusive alcoholic, at age fifteen Bill legally took his stepfather's name. He graduated from Georgetown, won a Rhodes scholarship to study at Oxford University, and graduated from Yale Law School. He returned to Arkansas and was soon elected state attorney general.

In 1977 Clinton and his wife, Hillary Rodham, joined with James McDougal, a banker, to secure a loan to build vacation homes in the Ozarks. But the development, which they named Whitewater, eventually became insolvent. McDougal illegally covered the debts with a loan from a savings and loan company he had acquired. In 1989 the savings and loan failed, costing the federal government $60 million to reimburse depositors. In 1992 federal investigators claimed that the Clintons had been "potential beneficiaries" of McDougal's illegal activities.

By this time Clinton, now governor of Arkansas, was campaigning in the New Hampshire primary for the Democratic nomination for president. Few voters could make much sense of the financial mess known as the "Whitewater scandal," nor did they have much opportunity to do so: Another, far more explosive story threatened to sink the Clinton campaign. It came out that Clinton had for many years engaged in an extramarital affair with one Gennifer Flowers; Clinton's standing in the polls tumbled.

Watch the Video

Bill Clinton Sells Himself to America: Presidential Campaign Ad, 1992 at **myhistorylab.com**

Hillary Rodham Clinton appeared with her husband on CBS's *60 Minutes* to address the allegations. Bill Clinton indignantly denied Flowers's statements but then issued an earnest if ambiguous appeal for forgiveness. "I have acknowledged causing pain in my marriage," he said. "I think most Americans will know what we're saying; they'll get it." Clinton was right, early evidence of his ability to address the American people directly, but on his own—carefully worded—terms. He finished second in New Hampshire, captured most of the remaining primaries, and won the Democratic nomination with ease. His choice of running mate—Senator Al Gore of Tennessee, a Vietnam veteran, family man, and environmentalist—helped the ticket considerably.

Young Bill Clinton (left) shakes hands with President John F. Kennedy. "The torch has been passed to a new generation of Americans," Kennedy had declared in his inaugural. "Ask not what your country can do for you—ask what you can do for your country," JFK added. Thirty years later, Clinton's inaugural echoed Kennedy's: "Today, a generation raised in the shadows of the Cold War assumes new responsibilities," Clinton declared. "I challenge a new generation of young Americans to a season of service."

Photo Credit: Getty Images, Inc – Liaison.

The Election of 1992

While Clinton tiptoed through a minefield of personal scandals, President George (Herbert Walker) Bush rested secure in the belief that, after crushing Saddam Hussein and the Iraqi army in the Gulf War, the 1992 election campaign would be little more than a victory lap. But he encountered unexpectedly stiff opposition within the Republican party. Patrick Buchanan, an outspoken conservative, did well enough to alarm White House strategists. Then Ross Perot, a billionaire Texan, announced his independent candidacy. His platform had both conservative and liberal planks. He would avoid raising taxes, and cut government spending by "getting rid of waste." He also supported gun control, backed a woman's right to an abortion, and called for an all-out effort to "restructure" the health care system.

Polls quickly revealed that Perot was popular in California, Texas, and other key states that Bush was counting on winning easily. At the Republican convention in August, Bush was nominated without opposition.

On election day, more than 100 million citizens voted. About 44 million voted for Clinton, 38 million for Bush, and 20 million for Perot. Clinton was elected with 370 electoral votes to Bush's 168. Perot did not win any electoral votes.

A New Start: Clinton as President

Watch the Video
Bill Clinton First Inauguration at **myhistorylab.com**

Clinton first used his executive authority to strengthen the Supreme Court majority in favor of upholding the landmark case of *Roe v. Wade*. The majority included three conservative justices who had been appointed by Reagan and Bush. Clinton appointed Ruth Bader Ginsberg, a judge known to believe that abortion was constitutional. Clinton indicated that he would veto any bill limiting abortion rights.

The first major test of the president's will came when he submitted his first budget to Congress. He hoped to reduce the deficit by roughly $500 billion in five years, half by spending cuts, half by new taxes. The proposal for a tax increase raised a storm of protest. Even so, the final bill passed by the narrowest of margins. Clinton rightly claimed a victory.

He then turned to his long-awaited proposal to reform the nation's expensive and incomplete health insurance system. A committee headed by his wife had been working for months with no indication that a plan acceptable to the medical profession,

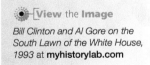

View the Image
Bill Clinton and Al Gore on the South Lawn of the White House, 1993 at **myhistorylab.com**

the health insurance industry, and ordinary citizens was likely to come from its deliberations. The plan that finally emerged seemed even more complicated and possibly more costly than the existing system. It never came to a vote in Congress.

Emergence of the Republican Majority

The Whitewater scandal, which Clinton had managed to brush aside during the campaign, gnawed at his presidency. Public pressure forced Attorney General Janet Reno to appoint a special prosecutor. She named Kenneth W. Starr, a Republican lawyer, to investigate Whitewater and other alleged misdeeds of the Clintons.

More troubles followed. Paula Corbin Jones, a State of Arkansas employee, charged that Clinton, while governor, had invited her to his hotel room and asked her to engage in oral sex. Clinton's attorney denied the accusation and sought to have the case dismissed on the grounds that a president could not be sued while in office. The case commenced a tortuous route through the courts.

Eager to take advantage of Clinton's troubles, Republicans looked to the 1994 congressional elections. Led by Congressman Newt Gingrich of Georgia, they offered voters an ambitious program to stimulate the economy by reducing both the federal debt and the federal income tax. Federally administered welfare programs were to be replaced by block grants to the states. Many measures protecting the environment, such as those making businesses responsible for cleaning up their waste, were to be repealed.

On election day, the Republicans gained control of both houses of Congress. Under the firm direction of Gingrich, now Speaker, the House approved nearly all of the provisions of this **Contract with America**. This appalled Clinton, who vetoed the 1995 budget drafted by the Republicans. When neither side agreed to a compromise, the government for a time ran out of money and shut down all but essential services.

The Election of 1996

The public tended to blame Congress, and particularly Speaker Gingrich, for the shutdown. The president's approval rating rose. But the main issue of the day was the economy, and the upturn during and after 1991 benefited Clinton enormously. By the fall of 1996, unemployment had fallen well below 6 percent, and inflation below 3 percent. Clinton was renominated for a second term without opposition.

A number of Republicans competed in the presidential primaries, but after a slow start Bob Dole of Kansas, the Senate majority leader, won the nomination. His main proposal was a steep reduction of the deficit and a 15-percent income tax cut. Pressed to explain how this could be done without drastic cuts in popular social programs, especially Social Security and Medicare, he gave a distressingly vague reply.

On election day Clinton won an impressive victory, sweeping the Northeast, all the Midwest except Indiana, the upper Mississippi Valley, and the Far West. He divided the South with Dole, who carried a band of states running north from Texas. Clinton's Electoral College margin was substantial, 379 to 159. The Republicans, however, retained control of both houses of Congress.

Clinton Impeached

Although President Clinton steadfastly denied allegations of womanizing, in January 1998 a judge ordered him to testify in Paula Corbin Jones's lawsuit against him. Jones, who sought to strengthen her suit by showing that Clinton had a history of propositioning women, also subpoenaed a former White House intern. Her name was Monica Lewinsky.

Lewinsky and Clinton were separately asked if they had had an affair, and each denied the charge. When word of their alleged relationship was leaked to the press, Clinton declared in a TV news conference, "I did not have sexual relations with that woman, Miss Lewinsky."

Unbeknown to the Clintons, however, Lewinsky had been confiding to Linda Tripp, a former White House employee, and Tripp had secretly tape-recorded some twenty hours of their conversations. Tripp turned these tapes over to special prosecutor Starr, whose investigations of the Clintons' roles in the Whitewater scandal had broadened into a more general inquiry. In the tapes Lewinsky provided intimate details of repeated sexual encounters with the president. Clinton and Lewinsky appeared to have lied under oath. Starr threatened to indict Lewinsky for perjury. In return for immunity from prosecution, she admitted that she had engaged in sexual relations with the president and that he and his aides had encouraged her to give misleading testimony in the Jones case.

When called in August to testify on videotape before the Starr grand jury, Clinton conceded that he had engaged in "inappropriate intimate contact" with Lewinsky. But he insisted, "I have not had sex with her as I defined it." When pressed to supply his own definition, he responded with legalistic obfuscation: "My understanding of this definition is it covers contact by the person being deposed with the enumerated areas, if the contact is done with an intent to arouse or gratify." Because Clinton had not intended to arouse or gratify Lewinsky, he had not "had sex" with her. He allowed that this definition was "rather strange."

●●●–[Read the Document

Bill Clinton, Answers to the Articles of Impeachment at **myhistorylab.com**

Clinton's testimony infuriated Starr, who made public Lewinsky's humiliatingly detailed testimony and announced that Clinton's deceptive testimony warranted consideration by the House of Representatives for impeachment.

But throughout Clinton's legal battles, opinion polls indicated that two in three Americans approved of his performance as president. Buoyed by the vibrant economy, most Americans blamed the scandal on the intrusive Starr nearly as much as the evasive Clinton. The November election proved disastrous for the Republicans, who nearly lost their majority in the House.

Clinton's troubles, however, were by no means over. Republican leaders in the House impeached Clinton on the grounds that he had committed perjury and had

Photo Credit: APTV/AP Wide World Photos.

A seemingly anonymous well-wisher from the crowd greets President Bill Clinton. When Clinton was later investigated for having an affair with Monica Lewinsky, a former White House intern, this photograph of the two surfaced. Clinton's lack of discretion struck many as self-destructive.

obstructed justice by inducing Lewinsky and others to give false testimony in the Jones case. The vote closely followed party lines.

The impeachment trial in the Senate began in January 1999. Chief Justice William Rehnquist presided. The Republicans numbered fifty-five, enough to control the proceedings but twelve short of the two-thirds necessary to convict the president and remove him from office. Democrats, while publicly critical of Clinton's behavior, maintained that his indiscretions did not constitute "high crimes and misdemeanors" as specified in the Constitution for removal from office. They prevailed. The article accusing Clinton of perjury was defeated by a vote of fifty-five to forty-five; on the article alleging obstruction of justice, the vote was fifty to fifty. Clinton remained president.

Clinton's Legacy

One reason why Clinton survived was the health of the economy. Few wanted to rock the ship of state when it was stuffed with cash. Until the final months, the Clinton years coincided with the longest economic boom in the nation's history. Clinton deserves considerable credit for the remarkable prosperity of the era. His reducing the federal deficit drove interest rates down, spurring investment and economic growth. By August 1998 unemployment had fallen to 4.5 percent, the lowest level since the 1960s; inflation had eased to a minuscule 1 percent, the lowest level since the 1950s. In 1998 the federal government operated at its first surplus since 1969. In the 2000 fiscal year, the surplus hit $237 billion.

Clinton also supported globalization of the economy. He successfully promoted the **North American Free Trade Agreement (NAFTA)** to reduce tariff barriers; Congress approved NAFTA in 1993. But the new global economy harmed many. Some union leaders bitterly asked how their members could compete against convict labor in China or sweatshop workers in Indonesia or Malaysia. Others complained that the emphasis on worldwide economic growth was generating an environmental calamity. International protests against the World Trade Organization culminated in the disruption of its 2000 meeting in Seattle, when thousands of protesters went on a rampage, setting fires and looting stores.

Clinton's record in foreign affairs was mixed. In 1993 he failed in an effort to assemble an international force to prevent "ethnic cleansing" by Serbian troops against Muslims in Bosnia, formerly part of Yugoslavia. In 1999 critics predicted another debacle when Clinton proposed a NATO effort to prevent General Slobodan Milosevic of Yugoslavia from crushing the predominantly Muslim province of Kosovo, which was attempting to secede. But after several months of intense NATO bombing of Serbia, Milosevic withdrew from Kosovo. Within a year, he was forced out of office and into prison, awaiting trial for war crimes before a UN tribunal.

Clinton labored, as had his predecessors in the White House, to broker peace between Israel and the Palestinians; like his predecessors, he failed. In 1993 Yitzhak Rabin, Israeli prime minister, and Yassir Arafat, leader of the Palestine Liberation Organization, signed an agreement preparing for a Palestinian state. But extremists on both sides shattered the fragile accord. In 1995 Rabin was assassinated by a Jewish zealot. Palestinians, enraged by the construction of Israeli settlements in Palestinian territory, stepped up their campaign of suicide bombings. Israel retaliated with tank and helicopter attacks on suspected terrorist strongholds. The negotiations collapsed. Arafat unleashed a new wave of uprisings, and hardliners, headed by Ariel Sharon, took charge of Israel. Violence intensified on both sides.

Whatever the successes and shortcomings of his administration, the Clinton presidency will always be linked to his relationship with a White House intern and the impeachment proceedings that ensued. Though by no means the first president to stray from matrimonial propriety, Clinton's behavior, in an era when the media thrived on scandal, was symptomatic of an almost willful self-destructiveness.

The Economic Boom and the Internet

A significant part of the prosperity of the 1990s came from new technologies such as cellular phones and genetic engineering. But the most important was the development of a revolutionary form of communication: the Internet.

In the early 1990s, Tim Berners-Lee, a British physicist working at a research institute in Switzerland, devised the software that became the grammar—the "protocols"—of the Internet "language." With this language, the Internet became the World Wide Web (WWW), a conduit for a stream of electronic impulses flowing among hundreds of millions of computers.

The number of Web sites increased exponentially. In 1995 Bill Gates's Microsoft entered the picture with its Windows operating system, which made the computer easy to use. It created a Web browser—Microsoft Internet Explorer—and embedded its software in the Windows 95 bundle.

"Venture capitalists," independent investors seeking to fund emerging "tech" companies, sensed a glittering new economic frontier somewhere down the Internet super-highway, and they poured billions into start-up dot-coms. In 1999 some 200 Internet companies "went public," selling shares in the major stock exchanges. They raised $20 billion easily. In the spring of 2000, with the stock market still surging, a selling wave hit the tech stocks and spilled over to other companies. Stock prices plummeted. In all, some $2 trillion in stock funds disappeared. As the 2000 election approached, many feared that the economy was nearing a recession.

The 2000 Election: George W. Bush Wins by One Vote

During the 2000 campaign, Vice President Al Gore secured the Democratic nomination and chose as running mate Senator Joseph Lieberman of Connecticut, an observant Jew and outspoken critic of Clinton during the impeachment proceedings.

The leading contender was George W. Bush, son of former President Bush. Like his father, Bush graduated from Yale and worked in the family oil business. He headed a group that bought the Texas Rangers baseball team. Although some doubted Bush's abilities, his visible success with the Rangers catapulted him into Texas politics. An effective and personable campaigner, he was elected governor in 1994. Six years later he defeated Senator John McCain of Arizona in a battle for the Republican nomination for president. Bush selected as running mate Dick Cheney, who had served as defense secretary in his father's administration.

The main issue was what to do with the federal surplus, which by some projections would soon exceed $1 trillion. Bush called for a substantial tax cut; Gore wanted to increase spending on education and shore up the Social Security system.

Gore, though knowledgeable, seemed stiff, and he occasionally indulged in self-serving bombast, as when he claimed to have "invented" the Internet. Bush's principal offense was against the English language. "Rarely is the question asked," he once declaimed, "Is our children learning?" His poetic flights of fancy did not stay long aloft, as when he evoked American aspirations for "wings to take dream" and endorsed economic growth to "make the pie higher." However exaggerated or garbled their messages, the candidates spent a record $1 billion getting it to the voters.

Having been inundated with advertisements, many on election night breathed a sigh of relief that the election was finally over. They were wrong. By midnight it appeared that Bush had 246 electoral votes, and Gore, 267, with 270 necessary to win; but Florida, with 25 electoral votes, had not been decided. As returns trickled in, the television networks reversed themselves and declared Florida—and the election—"too close to call." Bush's lead there was 1,784 out of nearly 6 million cast.

After a machine recount, Bush's margin in Florida was reduced to several hundred votes, with Democrats complaining that a punch-card ballot used in some communities was confusing, depriving Gore of thousands of votes; worse, the machines routinely failed to count incompletely punched ballots. Gore's lawyers demanded that the ballots in several predominantly Democratic counties be counted by hand. Republicans countered that Democrats had no right to change voting procedures after the election. They demanded that the hand recounts cease.

The entire election ended up in the courts. On December 12, more than a month after the election, the Supreme Court ruled by a five to four vote that the selective hand recounts violated the Constitution's guarantee of equal protection. Bush's victory stood.

Nationwide, Gore received 51 million votes, Bush, 50.5 million.

The New Terrorism

After the fall of the Soviet Union, American military might seemed unassailable. Military dictators who had been kept afloat by the Soviets or the Americans—and often from both simultaneously—now were obliged to seek the support of the people they had long ruled. This further destabilized the Middle East. The military leaders of Egypt and hereditary rulers of Saudi Arabia, for example, sought to retain the support of Islamic clerics while refraining from accepting an Islamic theocracy—direct rule by Islamic rulers. Arab leaders cultivated popular support by denouncing Israel, which refused to return land seized in the 1967 war. Insofar as Israel relied ultimately on American support, Arab rage was increasingly directed at the United States.

During these years, Islamist terrorists emerged throughout the Middle East, usually in response to the repression of radical Islamic clerics. In 1998 a new figure surfaced from among such groups: Osama bin Laden, son of a Saudi oil billionaire. In 1998, bin Laden published a *fatwa*—a religious edict—to Islamic peoples throughout the world: "To kill Americans and their allies, both civil and military, is an individual duty of every Muslim who is able . . ." By now, bin Laden was protected by an extremist Islamic group, the Taliban, that ruled Afghanistan. (The United States had provided military assistance to the Taliban in its ultimately successful campaign to drive the Soviet Union out of the country a decade earlier.) Six months later, bin Laden's terrorist organization—al-Qaeda—had planned and ordered the bombings of the U.S. embassies in Nairobi and Dar es Salaam in Africa, which killed hundreds of people.

September 11, 2001

At 8:40 on the morning of September 11, 2001, Madeline Amy Sweeney, an attendant on American Airlines Flight 11, placed a cell phone call from the galley of the plane to her supervisor in Boston. In a whisper, she said that four Arab men had slashed the throats of two attendants, forced their way into the cockpit, and taken over the plane. She gave him their seat numbers so that their identities could be determined from the passenger log. The supervisor asked if she knew where the plane was headed. She looked out the window and noted that it was descending rapidly. "I see water and buildings." The water was the Hudson River, and the buildings were the skyscrapers of lower Manhattan, foremost among them the 110-story twin towers of the World Trade Center.

The hijackers pushed the throttle to full, and the Boeing 767 was traveling at 500 miles per hour at 8:46 when it slammed into the ninety-sixth floor of the north tower. A fireball, fed by 10,000 gallons of jet fuel, instantly engulfed eight or nine stories.

Fifteen minutes later a second airliner came into view over Manhattan harbor, banked sharply, and plowed into the eightieth floor of the south tower. New York mayor Rudolph Giuliani, who had raced to the scene, asked Fire Chief Peter Ganci, "What should I communicate to people?" "Tell them to get in the stairways," Ganci replied. "I think we can save everyone below the fire." The World Trade Center employed 50,000. As thousands fled the buildings, hundreds of firefighters, Ganci among them, charged up the stairs to rescue those who were trapped.

At 9:30 the White House received word that another hijacked airliner was barreling toward Washington, DC. Secret Service agents rushed Vice President Cheney to an emergency command bunker far below the White House. At 9:35 the airliner plunged into the Pentagon and burst into flames. Cheney telephoned President Bush, who was in Sarasota, Florida. The nation was under attack. Bush authorized the Air Force to shoot down any other hijacked airliners. A few minutes later a fourth hijacked airliner crashed into a field in Pennsylvania after passengers had declared their intention— again by cell phone—to retake the plane.

While television viewers absorbed these shocks, they watched as the upper floors of the World Trade Center towers blackened, like charred matches. At 9:59, the south tower collapsed, followed by the north tower a half hour later, pulverizing millions of tons of concrete and glass and enveloping lower Manhattan in choking dust. Nearly three thousand lay dead in the mountain of rubble, including Chief Ganci and 350 firemen; several hundred more perished at the Pentagon and in the crash of the airliner in Pennsylvania.

Teams of four or five Arabic-speaking men had hijacked each of the planes. Several of the hijackers were quickly linked to the al-Qaeda terrorist network run by bin Laden, who had previously been indicted (but not captured) for the 1998 bombing of U.S. embassies in East Africa and the 2000 attack on the USS *Cole*. Bin Laden operated with impunity in Afghanistan.

A second jetliner approaches the south tower of the World Trade Center on September 11, 2001. The north tower had already been hit and was engulfed in flames and smoke.

That evening President Bush addressed the nation. He spoke simply and with force. "We will find these people," he said of the terrorists. "They will pay." Any government harboring the terrorists—an obvious reference to the Taliban—would be held equally responsible for the attack.

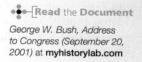

George W. Bush, Address to Congress (September 20, 2001) at **myhistorylab.com**

Several weeks later, Bush declared that bin Laden would be taken "dead or alive." The president also offered a $25 million reward for his death or capture, an evocation of swift frontier justice that suited the national mood. Within the United States, thousands of Arabs were rounded up and detained; those with visa and immigration violations were imprisoned.

Then more trouble arrived at the capital, this time in the mail. Several letters addressed to government officials included threatening messages and a white powder consisting of billions of anthrax spores, which could prove fatal if touched or inhaled. Thousands of government employees took antibiotics as a precaution, but some spores had seeped out of the envelopes and killed five postal workers and mail recipients.

Bush responded to these multiple threats by creating a Cabinet position, the Office of Homeland Security, and naming Pennsylvania Governor Tom Ridge to direct it. Repeatedly Ridge issued vague warnings of imminent terrorist attacks. How exactly Americans were to protect themselves, he did not say.

America Fights Back: War in Afghanistan

Bush had declared a **war on terror**, a war unlike any other the nation had fought. Al-Qaeda had secret terrorist cells in many countries. Bin Laden was ensconced in remote Afghanistan, protected by thousands of Taliban soldiers who had inflicted heavy losses on Soviet invaders in the 1980s. The source of the anthrax letters proved even more problematic, because the spores resembled a strain developed in American military laboratories.

Bush's challenge was all the greater because of his own stated opposition to ill-defined and far-flung military operations. He had chastised the Clinton-Gore administration for "extending our troops all around the world." He underscored his reticence for such ventures by naming Colin Powell secretary of state. Powell, who had been sobered by his experiences in Vietnam, maintained that U.S. troops should only be deployed when their political objective was clear, military advantage overwhelming, and means of disengaging secure. This became known as the Powell doctrine, and Bush had endorsed it during the campaign. But the proposed war against terror adhered to none of its precepts. Now such scruples did not matter; the president had little choice but to fight.

Powell urged European, Asian, and even Islamic states to crack down on terrorist cells in their countries and to provide assistance in the U.S. military campaign against the Taliban; he also persuaded anti-Taliban factions within Afghanistan to join forces to topple the regime. On September 20 Bush ordered the Taliban to surrender bin Laden and top al-Qaeda leaders; when the Taliban refused, Bush unleashed missiles and warplanes against Taliban installations and defenses.

For several weeks, Taliban soldiers cowered in bunkers as bombs thudded nearby; but they defended their positions when anti-Taliban forces attacked. Then small teams of elite American soldiers, armed with hand-held computers and satellite-linked navigational devices, joined with anti-Taliban contingents, marking Taliban positions with laser spotters and communicating with high-altitude bombers. These planes, circling at 30,000 feet, dropped electronically guided bombs on Taliban troops with uncanny (but not infallible) accuracy. Within weeks the Taliban were driven from power. Only one American soldier was killed by hostile fire. The United States had won the first battles in the war against terror.

The Second Iraq War

In January 2002, after the Taliban had been crushed, President Bush declared that he would not "wait on events while dangers gather." The United States would take "preemptive actions"—war—against regimes that threatened it. He identified Iran, North Korea, and Iraq as an **axis of evil** that warranted scrutiny. Immediately after September 11, he secretly initiated plans to attack Iraq, ruled by Saddam Hussein.

Secretary of State Powell advised Bush not to attack Iraq. If Saddam were driven from power, Powell warned, Bush would become "the proud owner of 25 million people—you'll own it all." Vice President Cheney, Defense Secretary Donald Rumsfeld, and others in the administration insisted that the Iraqis would welcome liberation and embrace democracy.

In September, Bush sought congressional support for an attack on Iraq. "The Iraqi regime possesses chemical and biological weapons," he declared, adding that Saddam also sought nuclear weapons. Congress voted overwhelmingly for the war appropriation.

Bush then called on the United Nations to join the United States. That Saddam had used chemical weapons during the Iran-Iraq war and also against the Kurds was beyond dispute; but following Saddam's defeat in 1991, UN inspectors had destroyed thousands of tons of Iraqi chemical weapons. They doubted that more such weapons had been stockpiled. Bush saw this as proof that Saddam had hoodwinked the inspectors. When the Security Council delayed taking action, Bush formed a coalition to oust Saddam. The United States was joined by Great Britain, Italy, Spain, and a few other countries.

On March 20, 2003, American missiles and bombs pounded Saddam's defenses. The "Shock and Awe" campaign to liberate Iraq had begun. Two armored columns roared across the Kuwaiti border into Iraq, passing burned-out Iraqi tanks from the first Gulf War. British forces moved along the coast toward the oil port of Basra. Television reporters, perched atop Humvees and armored personnel carriers, provided live coverage. The first night, American units advanced halfway to Baghdad.

On April 4, the U.S. Army seized the Baghdad International Airport. The next morning, some 800 American soldiers in tanks and armored vehicles blasted their way into downtown Baghdad. While some Iraqis poured into the streets to celebrate, others looted offices, museums, stores, and hospitals. Saddam disappeared and his government evaporated. By mid-April, the Pentagon declared that major combat operations had come to an end.

"Mission Accomplished" proclaimed the banner on the USS *Abraham Lincoln*, where on May 1, 2004, President George W. Bush declared, "Major combat operations in Iraq have ended." But the war continued for years.

Photo Credit: AP Wide World Photos.

But Iraq was in chaos. There were too few U.S. troops to preserve order. Islamist radicals, enraged by the American occupation, joined with Saddam's supporters in ambushing occupation forces. The insurgents rammed trucks filled with explosives into police stations, wired cell phones to artillery shells, and detonated them as Americans approached. Others sabotaged oil pipelines and power generators.

2004: Bush Wins a Second Term

The war became the main issue of the presidential campaign. In December 2003 American soldiers captured Saddam, hiding in an underground bunker. Bush's approval rating soared.

By January, however, Senator John Kerry, a Democratic senator from Massachusetts, was gaining in the polls. The son of a diplomat and a graduate of Yale, Kerry appeared accomplished and steady. He had commanded a patrol boat during the Vietnam War and was decorated for courage under fire. In April, he won the Democratic nomination. He chose Senator John Edwards of North Carolina, a wealthy trial lawyer, as his running mate.

In Iraq, the situation deteriorated further. In April the *60 Minutes* news program revealed that American captors had tortured Iraqi captives in the Abu Ghraib prison. Photographs of American soldiers, including women, taunting naked Muslim men fueled the insurgency. Casualties mounted. The cost of the occupation spiraled upward. Worse, American forces failed to find any Iraqi weapons of mass destruction.

At the Democratic convention in July, Kerry emphasized his military service in Vietnam. He criticized Bush for attacking Iraq before capturing Osama bin Laden, who remained at large. He also chided the president for initiating war with insufficient international support, and not sending enough troops to preserve order and rebuild Iraq.

Bush mobilized conservatives and religious fundamentalists by proposing a constitutional amendment that would define marriage as the union between a man and a woman. Kerry endorsed gay rights but endlessly qualified earlier statements in support of same-sex marriage.

Republicans also portrayed Kerry as opportunistic. If Kerry and Edwards thought the war was a mistake, why did they vote for the original war resolution in the Senate? During a debate with Bush, Kerry conceded that he had "made a mistake" in explaining his position on Iraq. "But the president made a mistake in invading Iraq. Which is worse?"

The election, one of the most divisive in recent decades, brought 12 million more voters to the polls than in 2000. Kerry received 57 million votes, 3 million more than Ronald Reagan in his 1984 landslide. But Bush got over 60 million, a record. He also prevailed in the Electoral College, 286 to 252.

Crime: Good News and Bad

The crime wave of the 1980s subsided during the 1990s. By 2009, the homicide rate nationwide was 40 percent below 1991. In many big cities the decline was astonishing. In 1990, for example, 5,641 felonies were committed in New York City's twenty-fourth precinct, near Central Park; in 2009 the number of felonies there had declined to 987.

But if urban crime was down, violence repeatedly jolted the nation. On April 20, 1999, two teenagers wearing trench coats and armed with automatic weapons went on a rampage at Columbine High School in Littleton, Colorado. Before shooting themselves to death, they killed twelve students and a teacher and wounded more than thirty. On October 2, 2006, a thirty-two-year-old truck driver took a dozen Amish schoolgirls hostage and shot and killed six of them. A week earlier, in two separate incidents, a gunman took six girls hostage at Platte Canyon High School at Bailey, Colorado, and shot and killed one; and a fifteen-year-old student at Weston High School in Cazenovia, Wisconsin, shot and killed his principal.

Perhaps inspired by these attacks, a deranged student at Virginia Tech in February 2007 bought a .22 caliber Walther P22 pistol on the Internet. The next month he bought a Glock 19 rapid-fire semiautomatic pistol and acquired ammunition from online vendors and from Wal-Mart and Dick's Sporting Goods. On April 16 he went to another dorm and shot and killed a female student and the resident advisor. After reloading, he entered Norris Hall, an engineering building, chained all three entry doors closed, climbed the stairs to the second floor, and walked up and down the hallway, taking aim at students and teachers and shooting them. Then he put a pistol to his head and committed suicide. The shooting spree at Norris lasted less than ten minutes: He shot over sixty people, killing thirty-three.

The massacre at Virginia Tech was the worst mass killing in recent American history. But each year, about 14,000 Americans are killed with guns. The spate of shootings reignited a heated debate. Proponents of gun control deplored the easy access to such lethal weapons. The National Rifle Association and other defenders of the right to bear arms, affirmed by the Second Amendment to the Constitution, blamed criminals for the mayhem. They insisted that law-abiding citizens needed guns to defend themselves from such evildoers. In 2010 the Supreme Court struck down municipal laws banning handguns in Chicago and the District of Columbia (*McDonald v. Chicago*).

Hurricane Katrina

The Bush presidency was largely shadowed by two events over which he initially had little control: the terrorist attack of September 11, 2001, and Hurricane Katrina, which swept across Florida and into the warm waters of the Gulf Coast in August 2005. On the morning of August 28, the National Weather Service released so dire a warning about Katrina—"devastating damage," "most of the area will be uninhabitable for weeks"— that some broadcasters refused to read it, thinking it might be a hoax. State and federal officials ordered mandatory evacuation of the Louisiana coastline.

Millions fled in their cars, clogging the highways. But of the half million residents of New Orleans, 100,000 remained, many of them poor African Americans who lacked access to automobiles. As rain started to fall that evening, some 10,000 took refuge in the New Orleans Superdome stadium.

Early the next morning Katrina crashed ashore. Within minutes, it destroyed nearly every building in Plaquemines Parish. Winds approaching 150 miles per hour ripped two holes in the Superdome. By afternoon, the hurricane had moved north, dumping more water along the way, swelling the rivers, streams, and canals that emptied into the Gulf. Within hours, rising waters spilled over the banks and collapsed canals. Then the levees at Lake Pontchartrain broke.

Photo Credit: Thomas Dworzak/Magnum.

Downtown New Orleans after Hurricane Katrina.

By that evening, much of New Orleans was underwater. Some 25,000 people crowded into the Superdome. Food and water grew scarce. Fights broke out. When officials locked the Superdome's doors, the thousands left outside went to the nearby Convention Center, surged past security guards, and took possession of the complex.

Over the next three days, the situation worsened. Over a million people had been displaced from their homes. In the heat and humidity, dead bodies, sewage, rotting food and plants, and factory effluents combined to form a fetid and toxic inland sea. The Convention Center, which now housed 20,000, descended into anarchy. There were reports of rape and murder. Throughout the storm-devastated region, looting became widespread; public order collapsed.

"Mr. President, we need your help," declared Louisiana Governor Kathleen Blanco. But TV crews arrived on the scene long before assistance from the Federal Emergency and Management Agency (FEMA). Television viewers were outraged to see footage of the dead floating in pools of filth or abandoned in wheelchairs.

Yet Michael Chertoff, secretary of Homeland Security (which oversaw FEMA), expressed satisfaction with its efforts. "Considering the dire circumstances that we have in New Orleans, virtually a city that has been destroyed—things are going relatively well," he declared. By then, more than 1,300 were dead.

Many shared in the blame. For decades, engineers had warned that the levees and canals in New Orleans could fail, but little was done to strengthen them. Environmentalists had complained of the overdevelopment and erosion of the coastal marshes and wetlands whose vegetation sponged up excess water, but their warnings, too, had been mostly ignored. Officials in New Orleans had neglected to devise an evacuation plan for those without cars; worse, one-sixth of the police force abandoned the city before the storm struck. In Washington, FEMA director Michael Brown was so worried about making a mistake that he failed to do much at all—the worse mistake possible. Bush erred in publicly complimenting the beleaguered FEMA director: "Brownie, you're doing a heck of a job," a statement so obviously at variance with public perception that it became an instant joke. Within a week Brown was demoted; soon afterward he resigned.

Katrina was not the worst natural disaster in the nation's history. In 1900 a hurricane destroyed Galveston, then the largest city in Texas, killing 10,000. In 1906 an earthquake hit San Francisco, ignited hundreds of fires that burned 500 blocks of the city, and killed 700—a larger proportion of the population than perished in Katrina. But apart from Katrina's terrible human toll, the hurricane pointed up the nation's vulnerability. If Homeland Security could not get buses or water to New Orleans in a timely fashion, how could it protect the nation from determined terrorists or respond effectively should they mount another attack?

Iraq Insurgency and Bush's "Surge"

Bush faltered during Katrina partly because he was distracted by Iraq. Insurgents blew up police stations and marketplaces; saboteurs destroyed power facilities and cut oil pipelines; and rival religious sects, tribes, warlords, and criminal gangs pushed the country toward anarchy.

While coalition forces attempted to halt the violence, political officials laid the foundations for a new Iraqi government. On June 28, 2004, the coalition transferred nominal authority to an Iraqi Governing Council whose chief task was to organize the

In 2006 an Iraqi tribunal convicted Saddam Hussein of murdering his own people and sentenced him to death by hanging. What might have been a defining moment in the emergence of a new Iraq was marred when he was rushed to the gallows and taunted by his executioners.

election of a National Assembly to draft a constitution. On January 30, 2005, nearly 8 million Iraqis went to the polls, almost two-thirds of the eligible voters.

The election, though fraught with irregularities, offered a glimpse of the democratic Iraq that Bush hoped would initiate a broader transformation of the Middle East. But the election also underscored the divisions within Iraq. In the north, the Kurdish majority won most of the seats, but Kurdish leaders sought to form their own state and secede. In the south, the Shiites forged strong ties to the radical Islamic clerics who ruled Iran. The Sunnis dominated the region around Baghdad. Post-Saddam Iraq was on the verge of fracturing into separate nations.

Complicating matters further was the decision by terrorists to wreck the new government by driving a deeper wedge between Sunnis and Shiites. On February 22, 2006, insurgents blew up the golden dome of the Askariya Mosque in Sammara, a Shiite shrine. Enraged Shiites attacked Sunni mosques and clerics, triggering an endless cycle of reprisals. Some Iraqi military and police officers formed extralegal death squads to eliminate Sunni leaders and terrorize their followers. Sunni militias responded in kind.

In the fall of 2006, an Iraqi tribunal convicted Saddam of killing 148 Shiites, the first of several planned trials to chronicle his regime's genocide. But on December 30, 2006, the Iraqi government dispatched Saddam to the gallows. Instead of marking the triumph of law over tyranny, the executioners resembled the Shiite death squads: Hangmen taunted Saddam and chanted the name of Muqtada Al Sadr, a Shiite cleric whose militias caused much of the chaos.

Attacks on security forces and civilians intensified and casualties mounted. As the 2006 U.S. congressional elections approached, the war was costing $2 billion a week; the annual U.S. deficit soared to a half trillion dollars. Democrats, most of whom had voted for the war, increasingly withdrew their support. Some Republicans, too, defected from the president's position.

THREE HEROES

On March 20, 2003, American, British, and NATO forces commenced the assault to drive Saddam Hussein from power. It marked the beginning of the second Gulf War, also known as "Operation Iraqi Freedom." Saddam was swiftly driven from power, but by March 20, 2010, the seventh anniversary of the war, Americans were still fighting in Iraq and Afghanistan. By then, over 5,000 United States service personnel had died, including over 100 women; over 25,000 had been wounded. The following soldiers are a random sample of that group, chosen because they died on the March 20 anniversary of the onset of the war.

Francisco ("Paquito") Martinez, 20

"Paquito" Martinez was born on December 16, 1984, in San Juan, Puerto Rico. He was the son of Francisco Martinez, an army soldier and air force airman, and Carmen R. Hernandez. In 2000 Paquito moved to Ft. Worth, Texas, where he joined his father, "Paco," and his stepmother Maria. His father worked as a computer software engineer. Paquito enjoyed skateboarding, drawing, poetry and Web design. An "army brat," he vowed never to follow his father into military service. But several months after graduating from Eastern Hills High School in 2002, "Paquito" enlisted. He thought he might eventually go into computer-based graphic design.

Francisco G. Martinez.

In 2003 he was stationed in Korea. The next year he was sent to Iraq. He soon had doubts about the war. "I will serve myself, my family, my friends, and my loved ones," he blogged. "I won't serve my country, nor will I serve its leaders."

Later that year he completed a video entitled "Peacefull." Grass sways before a distant hill. In editing the video, Martinez drained it of color. The text is sparse:

> *take this time to breathe*
> *open your mind*
> *feel your worries flow free*

Then a monarch butterfly, in dazzling yellows and orange, wafts across the scene.

> *life is what you make of it*

On March 20, 2005, while on patrol in Tamin, Iraq, a sniper shot Martinez in the hip, severing an artery; despite trauma surgery, he died within an hour.

Curtis E. Glawson Jr., 24

Curtis E. Glawson was born on June 10, 1982, in Detroit, Michigan. His parents—Yolanda and Curtis Sr.—were both career soldiers. As a child Curtis traveled with his parents from one base to another in Germany, New Mexico, Georgia, and Alabama. He learned to adapt to different people and cultures and made friends quickly; his smile was electric.

Glawson was fast and agile and he excelled in sports. When not engaged in football, baseball, basketball and running, he enjoyed sports-related video games. He was a passionate fan of all Detroit (and Michigan) sports teams. Friends called him Mr. ESPN.

Curtis E. Glawson Jr.

In 2000 Glawson graduated from Daleville high school in Alabama, near Fort Rucker. He immediately enlisted in the army. That fall he was sent to Fort Jackson, South Carolina, where he received advanced training in mechanics. Certified as a light truck mechanic, he was subsequently stationed in Afghanistan, Uzbekistan, and Korea.

In Korea, he met Hyunjung Jang; the couple married at the United States embassy in Seoul in September, 2005.

In February, 2007 he was sent to Baghdad in Iraq. Once, when his unit made a wrong turn, they encountered a group of preteens armed with AK-47 automatic weapons. Although he grew increasingly nervous about his missions, he relished his work. When his mother urged him to beg off dangerous assignments, he replied, "No, momma, I can't do that. I have a job to do."

On the morning of March 20, 2007, Glawson was sent to retrieve a truck that broke down in the outskirts of Baghdad. He went out, fixed it, and brought it back to the motor pool. Later that afternoon, his platoon sergeant asked if Curtis could rescue another disabled vehicle in a dangerous sector. "I'm good to go, sergeant," Glawson replied. "Are you sure?" the officer asked, looking him in the eye. "Always ready, sergeant," Glawson replied.

That journey proved to be his last. As the road wound toward the dusty hills outside Baghdad, an **improvised explosive device (IED)** blew up his vehicle. Glawson was killed instantly. He wanted to be remembered as a loving son, husband, brother, friend, and dedicated soldier.

Daniel J. Geary, 22

Daniel Geary was born on September 12, 1986, the son of Michael Geary, machine foreman, and Agnes Geary, machine operator, in Rome, New York. Daniel was the fourth of seven children. When he was eight, he smelled smoke and pulled his four-year-old sister from a room that was engulfed in flames.

Photo Credit: Agnes Geary.

Daniel J. Geary.

As a teenager, Geary enjoyed paintball, working on his Chrysler Sebring, and bowling. At sixteen, he bowled his first perfect game. He attended Rome Free Academy, a public high school, but dropped out a few weeks before graduation. For a time, he was unsure of what to do with his life. He landed a job at the Turning Stone Casino in Rome, owned by the Oneida Indians. Several months later, however, he resolved to get his diploma. "I was never more proud of him," his mother recalled. In 2006 he returned to school, joined the officer training program, and decided on a career in the military. In June, shortly before receiving his diploma, he enlisted in the Marines and soon subscribed to its motto wholeheartedly: *semper fidelis* (always faithful).

In September, Geary reported to Camp Lejeune, North Carolina, where he met his fiancée. In November, 2008, after a tour of duty on a ship in the Indian Ocean, he was sent to Kandahar, Afghanistan. He was impressed by the mountains that towered above ancient valleys. "Other than people trying to shoot me and blow me up," he told his mother, "you can't believe how beautiful it is over here."

On March 19, 2009, he was part of a team of Marines that caught an enemy bomber near a police station. The next day the team returned to the station to encourage the local police to work harder to capture insurgents. While the others were meeting inside, Geary stood guard, manning a machine gun in a Humvee. Then a car with police markings came through the gate, approached the Humvee and blew up, killing Geary instantly.

Question for Discussion

■ These three soldiers are among the millions who contributed to the American destiny but whose names so often are missing from historical accounts. What other unsung heroes are missing from this book?

When the midterm votes were counted, the Republicans were decisively defeated. Democrats now controlled Congress—and the budget. Several days after the election Bush dismissed Defense Secretary Rumsfeld, acknowledging voter "displeasure with the lack of progress in Iraq." But the president vowed to remain. "America's going to stand with you," Bush promised Iraqi leaders.

Democrats named Nancy Pelosi Speaker of the House of Representatives, the first woman to hold that position. Insofar as the speaker follows the vice president in chain of succession, Pelosi became the highest-ranking woman ever to hold office in the United States. In January 2007, when Bush called for a modest increase in troop levels in Iraq, Pelosi and some prominent Democrats opposed the measure. The Democratic leadership in Congress voted to reduce funding for the war, actions Bush vetoed.

In January, 2007 Bush named General David Petraeus to command a "**surge**" in American troop levels in Iraq. The troops were to remove insurgents from a region, establish military control over it, and build stronger ties with the Iraqi people. Initially, Petraeus made little progress. The losses among American military personnel mounted (see American Lives, "Three Heroes"). Petraeus shifted more military tasks to the Iraqis and reduced operations that would likely lead to high civilian casualties. He also worked to bring former Sunni leaders into the Iraqi government. By the spring of 2008, the violence in Iraq had declined; the "surge" appeared to be working.

2008: McCain v. Obama

By the spring of 2008 John McCain, a Republican senator from Arizona, was far ahead in the race for the Republican nomination. McCain had piloted a navy fighter-bomber during the Vietnam war. After his plane was shot down over North Vietnam, he was held as a prisoner-of-war for six years; occasionally he was tortured. Now seventy-one, McCain if elected would be the oldest person to serve as a first-term president. Although McCain's positions were similar to those of Bush, McCain had often criticized the president and described himself as a "maverick."

Watch the Video

The Historical Significance of the 2008 Presidential Election at myhistorylab.com

True to his own label, he surprised pundits by naming Sarah Palin, the little-known governor of Alaska, as running mate. Her youth (forty-four) counterbalanced McCain's age. Palin also exhibited a down-to-earth feistiness. She was a new type of feminist: a former beauty queen who hunted and fished; an ardent defender of traditional family values who pursued an extravagantly ambitious career.

Among Democrats, Hillary Clinton, now a senator from New York, emerged as front-runner. But she was soon eclipsed by Barack Obama, a first-term senator from Illinois. Clinton had voted for the war in Iraq while Obama opposed it; otherwise they agreed on most issues. Obama won the Democratic nomination and named Joe Biden, a senator from Delaware, as his running-mate.

During the general election McCain pointed out that Obama had failed to serve even a single full term as U.S. senator: Obama, he claimed, was unqualified for the presidency. But McCain's choice of Palin deprived McCain of his strongest issue. Palin had served as governor for only two and a half years; before that she was mayor of tiny Wasilla, Alaska. When critics questioned her experience in foreign affairs, her breezy reply—"You can actually see Russia from land here in Alaska"—cast doubt on McCain's judgment.

Obama criticized the Republican administration for waging war against Iraq, thereby diverting resources that might have crushed the main 9/11 culprits: the

Taliban in Afghanistan and Osama bin Laden, who remained at large. Obama proposed moving troops from Iraq to Afghanistan. He also advocated a major expansion of federally backed health care. McCain sought to send more troops to Iraq: The "war on terror" did not allow retreats. He also criticized Obama's health-care proposal as a major step toward socialized medicine.

As the campaign was heating up, a tremor rocked the foundations of the global economic system. Alarming financial news pushed the campaign out of the headlines.

Photo Credit: Scott Weiner/Retna Ltd./Corbis.

Republican candidates John McCain and Sarah Palin campaign at Franklin & Marshall University in 2008.

Financial Meltdown

The fault lines of the 2008–2009 crisis extended to the 1990s. At that time the economy appeared to have recovered from the recession that began in 1973. But while the stock market soared, wages lagged far behind. By 2005, for the first time since the Great Depression, the American people spent more than they earned. Mostly they bought houses. But how, without savings, could they afford down payments? Politicians, bankers, and financial "wizards" had devised several solutions. In 2002 President George W. Bush declared that the government should "encourage folks to own their own home." Homeowners, he believed, were more responsible citizens than renters. Leaders in both parties advocated easier lending requirements and prodded the huge federally owned mortgage companies to issue more mortgages. Private mortgage companies followed suit. They reasoned that as house prices increased, the ability of homeowners to repay loans mattered less: A repossessed house could be sold for more than the original mortgage loan.

Granted easier credit, millions of Americans for the first time bought homes. In 1994, 64 percent of U.S. families owned homes; by 2004, the percentage had increased to

Table 1 Causes of the 2008–2009 Financial Crisis

Consumers exhaust savings to buy houses
The president and Congress call on federally owned mortgage companies to relax lending requirements
Global investment bankers devise complicated bundles of mortgages and market them globally
Credit-rating agencies grade these mortgage investments as solid and AIG insures them
Lending banks issue mortgages greatly in excess of available reserves
Millions of homeowners fall into debt and cannot make mortgage payments
Collapse of mortgage investments brings down investment banks
Capital evaporates, leading to layoffs and threatening a second Great Depression

69 percent, the highest ever. Housing prices soared. Many homeowners bought bigger ones—"McMansions," in the slang of the day.

Soon banks and mortgage companies had exhausted their capital. Large international investment banks such as Goldman Sachs, Lehman Brothers, and Bear Stearns more than filled the void. They bought tens of thousands of mortgages from the original banks and lending institutions. Lending banks used this revenue to loan out more mortgages— thereby generating more profits (and bonuses). International investment firms chopped up the mortgages like sausages, clumped them into complicated investment bundles, and sold the bundles to investors worldwide. Credit-rating companies, such as Moody's and Standard and Poor's, pronounced the bundles to be sound investments. And many investors bought insurance from the American Insurance Group (AIG) to protect them if the bundles somehow went bad. AIG, perceiving little risk, failed to set aside much money to cover potential losses.

By late 2008, however, millions of homeowners were swamped with bills they could not pay. Total household debt in the United States exceeded $14.5 *trillion*—twenty times more than in 1974. Nearly 10 percent of all American mortgages were delinquent or in foreclosure. Goldman Sachs quietly placed bets that the mortgage bundles it had mass-marketed would lose their value!

Investors suddenly caught on and dumped their mortgage bundles. Panic selling hit financial markets worldwide. Almost overnight, Bear Stearns collapsed and Lehman Brothers went bankrupt. The Dow Jones Industrial Average plunged from over 14,000 to under 9,000; stocks lost $8 trillion. Pension funds, corporate reserves, and personal accounts for retirement and college education lost one-third of their value. AIG, swamped with claims, neared bankruptcy. Its failure would take down many of the world's major banks and investment firms.

Nearly all banks and investment houses ran low on capital; many struggled to stave off bankruptcy. Few could make new loans. But most businesses, hospitals, schools, state and municipal governments relied on short-term loans, which were repaid as revenues came in. In the absence of these customary loans, few employers could pay bills or cover payrolls. A global calamity loomed.

In the final months of 2008, Bush and his chief financial advisers raced to avert catastrophe. Ben Bernanke, head of the Federal Reserve and a scholar of the Great Depression, pleaded with Congress to authorize over $700 billion to buy up the "toxic" mortgage bundles, an indirect way of preserving the banks and global investment firms that had issued them. He also proposed to pump hundreds of billions directly into Goldman Sachs, AIG, and scores of other investment banks. Such companies, he warned, were "too big to fail." Congress seethed at using taxpayers' money to bail out avaricious corporate executives; but political leaders could not risk a second Great Depression.

"Yes We Can": Obama Elected President

The economic crisis caught nearly everyone by surprise. Much of the blame fell on Republicans, whose support for deregulation of financial markets dated from the Reagan era. McCain was especially hurt by the economic meltdown. On September 15, 2008, the day after Lehman Brothers declared bankruptcy, McCain downplayed the crisis, claiming "The fundamentals of our economy are strong." Within a few hours, the stock market fell 500 points. He appeared to be out of touch.

Obama's oft-repeated (albeit vague) insistence on change now acquired new meaning. When confronted with "impossible odds," he insisted, "Americans have responded with a simple creed: Yes we can." The nation was ready for change. On election day, Obama won by over 8 million votes; his victory in the Electoral College was by a 365 to 173 margin.

Obama's victory stunned foreigners. Nelson Mandela, the black leader of the movement that toppled white rule in South Africa, claimed that Obama's election inspired everyone who wanted "to change the world for a better place." Gordon Brown, prime minister of Great Britain, called Obama's election "a moment that will live in history as long as history books are written."

Obama as President

Only a few weeks after Obama, his wife Michelle, and their two daughters had moved into the White House, he was awarded the Nobel Prize "for his extraordinary efforts to strengthen international diplomacy and cooperation between peoples." Abashed at receiving an award in the expectation that he would earn it, Obama gave the $1.4 million prize to charity. Nevertheless, Obama's intentions of changing the course of American foreign policy were evident. He closed CIA-run secret prisons and banned torture and other means of coercion during interrogation of suspected terrorists. He named Hillary Clinton secretary of state and promised to work more closely with the international community.

In Iraq, Obama proceeded cautiously. He asked Robert Gates, secretary of defense under Bush, to remain in that capacity in his administration. He also announced a plan to withdraw most American troops from Iraq by the fall of 2010.

During his first months as president, however, Obama was mostly absorbed in the financial crisis. Despite repeated promises of change, he retained many of Bush's chief financial advisers; nearly all were Wall Street insiders. Critics grumbled that it made little sense to ask those who had broken the economy to put it back together. But Obama had little choice. No one else understood the complicated mathematical models on which modern trading was based; unfortunately, few Wall Street executives understood them either. Macroeconomics, some economists maintained, had become an elaborate exercise in chaos theory.

By late March 2009 the Dow Jones had fallen below 6,600, down from 14,000 seventeen months earlier. Chrysler declared bankruptcy, followed by General Motors several months later. Huge layoffs ensued. Unemployment rose steadily, surpassing

President-elect Barack Obama, his daughters, and wife, Michelle, celebrate his victory in November, 2008.

Photo Credit: Tannen Maruty/epa/Corbis.

Watch the Video
The Connection Between Obama & Lincoln at
myhistorylab.com

327

SHOCKS AND RESPONSES: 1992–PRESENT

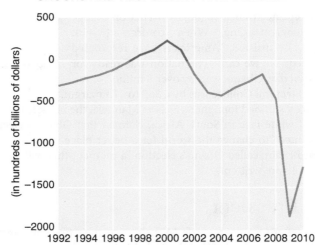

Annual Federal Deficit (and Surplus), 1992–2010 After years of deficits, the federal government operated at a $250 billion surplus in 2000. But the war on terror after 9/11 resulted in massive deficits, which were exacerbated by the financial meltdown after 2008.

10 percent for the first time in several decades. Obama pumped another $700 billion into the struggling economy.

Then word leaked out that hundreds of millions of dollars had been paid in bonuses to executives of Goldman Sachs, AIG, and many of the big banks that had been saved by federal bailouts. Obama railed against their ill-timed greed and slapped the companies with nuisance taxes, but he could do little else. He needed the big financial institutions to help jolt the economy back to life.

By the fall of 2009, the strategy appeared to be working. Employment increased and the stock market rose. Some banks repaid their government loans. Talk of economic collapse abated, partly because predictions varied widely. Some economists insisted that once the stimulus money had been exhausted, employment, wages, and prices would again fall and the nation would slip into a recession—or worse. Others pointed to the projected $1.8 trillion deficit for 2009 and predicted rampant inflation. Insofar as no one had forecast the financial meltdown of 2008–2009, most political leaders discounted *all* economic predictions and simply hoped for the best.

Health Care Reform

By 2009 nearly everyone agreed that medical costs had spun out of control. In 1990, per capital medical expenditures were $3,000; by 2009, they exceeded $8,000. That year, though nearly 18 percent of the nation's gross domestic product went for medical care, some 46 million Americans lacked any coverage whatsoever. When struck by serious illness, they were denied treatment or were hit with staggering bills. More than half of the nation's personal bankruptcies were precipitated by illness.

Obama's goal was twofold: to provide health care to Americans who lacked it and to reduce health care costs. Some advocated a government-run system, such as Franklin Roosevelt had done with old age pensions through Social Security. Many European governments operated health care systems along similar lines. But opposition

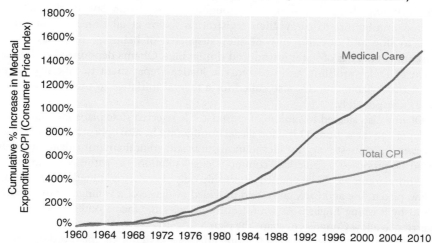

Price Increases - CPI vs. Medical Care (Cumulative % Increase)

The Increasing Cost of Health Care, 1960–2008 (% increase) By the 1990s, health care cost increases greatly exceeded the increase in the Consumer Price Index.

to socialized medicine in the United States was intense. Polls showed that few Americans wanted their doctors to be employees of the federal government.

Supported by Democratic leaders in Congress, Obama proposed a system that combined private and public health insurance. Elderly and poor Americans would continue to be covered by the government; private insurers would continue to insure millions of Americans, but they could not kick people out of their systems when they became ill; companies with more than fifty employees would be required to provide health care insurance for employees and their families or else face stiff penalties; most other persons would be eligible for publicly supported health insurance.

Republicans almost uniformly denounced the plan; they insisted that Americans did not want the federal government to control health care. Republicans instead recommended tax incentives or state initiatives to encourage private employers to broaden coverage. Republicans added that the federal government, with a looming annual deficit of $1.8 trillion, would be hard-pressed to pay for Medicare in the future; to embark on a major new commitment was madness.

The Democrats, despite strong majorities in both houses of Congress, were themselves divided on Obama's plan. The final compromise provided for his reform to be phased in over ten years at a cost of $1 trillion, and coverage would not be universal: By 2019, 24 million people would still lack health insurance, about a third of them illegal immigrants.

In March 2010, Congress approved the measure—the vote in the House was 220 to 207. No Republican voted for the bill. Obama had nevertheless engineered the first major health care reform since 1965, when President Lyndon Johnson signed Medicare into law.

Immigration Reform

Buoyed by this success, Obama turned to immigration. Early in his presidency, he strengthened border security to cut down on illegal immigration from Mexico, an action that angered Mexican leaders. Yet illegal immigration persisted. In 2010

Arizona governor Jan Brewer, complaining that "the majority of illegal trespassers" were "bringing drugs in," signed the toughest immigration law in the nation. It required immigrants to carry alien registration forms at all times and authorized police to stop and question anyone they suspected of being an illegal immigrant. Legislators in dozens of states introduced similar bills. Obama denounced such laws as a form of racial profiling and ordered the Justice Department to take legal action against the Arizona bill. He also called for a federal initiative to prevent states from acting "irresponsibly."

Obama also steered toward a compromise. He rejected state plans for rounding up and deporting the nation's 11 million illegal immigrants; he also opposed liberal proposals to declare an "amnesty" against illegal immigrants and grant them immediate citizenship. Instead he proposed a "practical, common-sense" solution—a "pathway to citizenship." Illegal immigrants would be granted citizenship only after they admitted they had broken the law, paid a fine and back taxes, and provided evidence of a willingness to assimilate, such as by learning English. As with health care reform, Obama outlined few specifics, preferring to allow Congress to shape the plan.

Republicans bristled; without more effective policing of the border, Obama's "reform" would encourage more illegal immigrants to pour into the country. Many complained that Obama was courting Hispanic voters just a few months ahead of the 2010 congressional elections. The prospects for quick passage of comprehensive immigration reform seemed poor.

Environmental Concerns and Disaster in the Gulf

During his first weeks in office, Obama had pledged a "new era of global cooperation on climate change." Nearly everyone assumed that he intended to push for ratification of the 1997 agreement, signed by more than 130 nations at Kyoto, Japan, to reduce emissions of carbon dioxide and other atmospheric pollutants. The Senate had opposed the Kyoto accords because developing nations—including China, the worst air polluter in the world—were exempted from its costly provisions. President Clinton never submitted the treaty for ratification. In 2001, President George W. Bush withdrew the United States from subsequent negotiations. But in 2006 the mayors of over 200 U.S. cities, struggling with smog and air pollution, signed a Climate Protection Agreement pledging to meet the Kyoto targets for greenhouse gas reductions by 2012. But if Obama intended to move in the direction of the Kyoto agreements, the economic crisis of 2008–2009 changed his mind. With the nation's economy in recession, Obama thought it unwise to impose new environmental restrictions. In late 2009 he quietly withdrew support for an international arrangement on atmospheric pollutants.

By then, political economic realities had already caused Obama to backtrack on another environmental issue. Originally an opponent of oil drilling off the Atlantic coast, he changed his position during the 2008 presidential campaign: The nation needed cheap oil and gasoline. On April 21, 2010, disaster struck in the Gulf of Mexico. Workers aboard a British Petroleum (BP) oil platform forty-one miles off the coast of Louisiana were drilling for oil at a depth of 5,000 feet. The drill hit a pocket of methane gas under high pressure; it shot upward through the drilling pipe and exploded, blasting eleven workers from the platform and engulfing it in flames. Oil gushed from the damaged pipe, an upsetting image captured by underwater cameras and transmitted by streaming

Photo Credit: Tannen Maury/epa/ Corbis.

A brown pelican surveys the ecological damage caused by the BP oil spill in the Gulf of Mexico in 2010.

video on the Web. The world watched in horror as BP's repeated attempts to cap the well failed; weeks passed as hundreds of millions of gallons of oil spewed into the Gulf, fouling marshes and beaches, killing fish, birds, and aquatic life. Obama called it the "worst environmental disaster America has faced."

Pressure built on him to "do something." Exactly what was unclear. "He can't put on scuba gear and go down and stop this well," observed New York City mayor Michael Bloomberg, a Republican. Obama forced BP to set aside $20 billion to cover damage claims and sacked the director of the Minerals Management Service for failing to adequately inspect the off-shore platforms. He also declared a six-month moratorium on deepwater drilling, pending the inspection of existing platforms.

Opponents of the moratorium included both of Louisiana's senators and its governor, Bobby Jindal, who noted that the oil industry accounted for 17 percent of Louisiana's jobs and much of the state's revenue. Such opposition underscored the dilemma confronting a nation whose thirst for cheap oil was unquenchable. The exhaustion of oil reserves beneath the earth's landmass necessitated offshore drilling; but the environmental risks of deep-sea drilling were all too apparent.

Obama resurrected his campaign goal of promoting alternative sources of energy, such as solar and wind power. But such solutions seemed to lie far in the future. Whether the disaster in the Gulf of Mexico would reinvigorate the environmental movement remained to be seen.

Afghanistan, Again

The economic crisis and the environmental calamity in the Gulf of Mexico notwithstanding, Afghanistan loomed as the dominant issue for Obama's presidency. Few could have imagined such a development in December 2001, when the war in Afghanistan appeared to be over. The Taliban had been driven from power; most of

Photo Credit: David Goldman/AP Photo.

An Army helicopter arrives to evaluate soldiers wounded after their armored vehicle hit an improvised explosive device (IED) in the Tangi Valley in Afghanistan.

its leaders had been killed or captured or they had fled to Pakistan. Bush shifted his attention to driving Saddam Hussein from power in Iraq; a United Nations commission was given the task of building a new Afghan government.

In late 2001, the commission summoned Afghan leaders who eventually chose Hamid Karzai as interim leader of the nation. Karzai had helped channel American aid to the Taliban when it was fighting the Soviet Union; he later became a staunch opponent of the Taliban and worked with Americans to forge a coalition in opposition to it. As interim leader, Karzai relied on United Nations troops—one-half of them provided by the United States—to enforce the new government's authority.

For a time it appeared that a new Afghanistan was emerging. Hundreds of schools, hospitals, and roads were built; women were granted new rights. In 2004 Karzai defeated twenty-two opponents to become the first democratically elected president of the Islamic Republic of Afghanistan.

But much of the progress was illusory. Karzai's government was weak and riddled with corruption. In the southern sections of Afghanistan, Islamic radicals resurfaced and the former Taliban slipped back into the country, calling on Muslims to fight "infidel" troops. In the north, tribal leaders jockeyed to expand their power. Nearly everywhere, criminal militias vied for control of the lucrative opium trade.

The election scheduled for the fall of 2009 made matters worse. The first round was marred by voting fraud, which UN observers confirmed. During the final campaign the chief opposition candidate withdrew, charging Karzai's government with rigging the outcome. Karzai "won" by default. Enemies of Karzai's regime exploited the controversy.

By late 2009 Obama, who had opposed the "surge" in Iraq, sent another 30,000 troops to Afghanistan. American forces increasingly relied on drones—unmanned planes—to drop guided bombs on suspected enemies in Afghanistan and Pakistan. When the bombs missed the targets and killed civilians, riots ensued and UN casualties mounted.

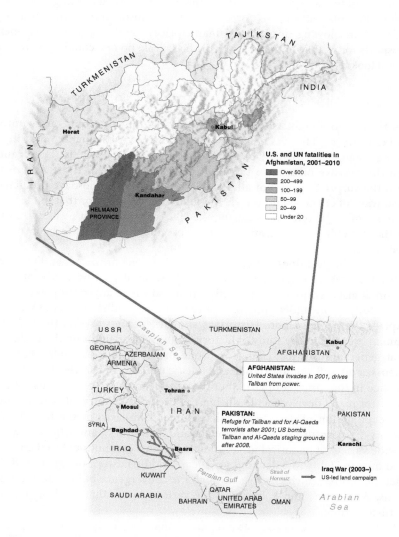

War in Iraq and Afghanistan, 2001–Present Since 2003, the United States has fought two major wars in Central Asia: in Afghanistan, first to drive the Taliban from power and later to suppress an insurgency; and in Iraq, first to crush Saddam Hussein and later to install a democratic government. In Afghanistan, American losses have been heaviest in the southern provinces bordering Pakistan.

For some time, General Stanley McChrystal, commander of the United Nations troops, had chafed at rules of engagement designed to limit civilian casualties. Obama's administration, McChrystal's aides complained to reporters for *Rolling Stone*, was weak and ineffective. The article appeared in June 2010, the month with the heaviest losses of the war. Obama sacked McChrystal for insubordination, replacing him with David Petraeus, architect of the "surge" in Iraq. "We have arrived at a critical point," Petraeus declared on July 4, 2010. "We are in this to win."

A month later secret government documents, leaked to the press, revealed that while Pakistan had pledged to support the war on terror, its intelligence service helped the Taliban plan attacks on American soldiers. Insurgents in Iraq and Afghanistan persisted in blowing up crowded marketplaces, mosques, and government offices. Prospects for victory in the region remained bleak; no one could even imagine what it would look like.

The Persistent Past and Imponderable Future

But the previous eighteen years had shown that human events rarely unfold in predictable ways. The 9/11 terrorist attack, the subsequent wars in Iraq and Afghanistan, the near-collapse of the economy in 2008–2009, Hurricane Katrina, and the massive oil spill in the Gulf of Mexico all shocked the American people. And the surprises were not all bad. No one in 1992 could have predicted that the tidal wave of crime would recede the following decade. For that matter, the relative absence of racial references during the 2008 campaign that resulted in the election of the nation's first African American president would have been unimaginable decades earlier.

But if the past does not enable us to predict the future, what do we ever "learn" from history? Consider an analogy with seismology, the study of earthquakes. Seismologists cannot predict exactly when and where any earthquake will strike, but their study of the underlying forces—the shift and collision of tectonic plates—helps explain the phenomenon. Historians similarly cannot predict the future course of human events. But the study of history can provide insights on the underlying forces that generate historical change. No one predicted, for example, that a particular deep-sea oil well would explode and release millions of barrels of oil into the Gulf of Mexico in the summer of 2010; but the American nation's voracious thirst for oil—a result of many developments during the previous century—led to the demand for the exploitation of deep-water oil resources. Similarly, in the first decades of the twenty-first century Americans fought and died in Iraq and Afghanistan because of a wide variety of historical forces, ranging from a commitment to democratic values and human rights to a demand for cheap Middle Eastern oil. History does not predict the future, which emerges through the convergence of infinite actions and reactions. But history can help reveal the various forces that are heaving beneath the surface of time.

This text was conceived as a reminder that the past is never truly past. It radiates through time. It touches our lives, just as what we do today will influence the future. By connecting to the past, we better understand ourselves and perhaps gain an inkling of what will become of us.

Milestones

1992	Democrat Bill Clinton is elected president
1993	Ruth Bader Ginsberg becomes second woman justice of the Supreme Court
1994	Republicans win control of both houses of Congress
	Congress defeats Clinton's health care reform plan
1996	Democrat Bill Clinton is reelected president; Republicans retain control of Congress
	Measure revamping federal welfare system is passed by Congress and signed by President Clinton
1998	The House of Representatives impeaches Clinton
1999	Clinton acquitted by Senate, Clinton remains in office
	NATO troops, including Americans, are sent to Kosovo to stop Serbian "ethnic cleansing"
	Gun violence in schools escalates; twelve die at Columbine High School in Colorado
2000	Republican George W. Bush is elected president when Supreme Court halts Florida recounts
2001	Terrorists hijack airliners and fly them into the twin towers of the World Trade Center in New York and the Pentagon, killing 3,000
	United States drives Taliban from power in Afghanistan
2002	President Bush prepares for war as he accuses Saddam Hussein of Iraq of developing weapons of mass destruction
2003	United States and United Kingdom attack and defeat Iraq and capture Saddam Hussein
2004	Republican George W. Bush is reelected president
2005	Hurricane Katrina devastates New Orleans and Gulf Coast region
2007	Democrat Nancy Pelosi becomes first woman Speaker of the House
2008	Deranged student kills thirty-three at Virginia Tech
	Democrat Barack Obama is first African American to be elected president
	Collapse of U.S. mortgage markets triggers global financial crisis
2009	Obama implements troop surge in Afghanistan
2010	Congress approves health care bill
	BP-owned rig explodes, killing eleven and spewing oil into the Gulf of Mexico
	Arizona passes law to crack down on illegal immigrants; national debate ensues
	Republicans take control of House of Representatives

✓ ●—[Study and Review] at www.myhistorylab.com

Review Questions

1. The introduction divides this chapter into two different narrative arcs: the first one—from 1992 to 2001—is mostly positive; the second, from 9/11 through 2010, is said to constitute—as *Time* magazine put it—"The Decade from Hell." What were the "positive" aspects of the period from 1992 to 2001? The "negative" components of the subsequent one? How is this characterization too simple?

2. Bill Clinton was hardly the first president to commit adultery. Why did his indiscretions lead to charges that resulted in an impeachment proceeding? Did his actions constitute "high crimes and misdemeanors"? What were the major achievements of the Clinton presidency?

3. The section of this chapter on the disputed 2000 presidential election is subtitled: "George W. Bush Wins by One Vote." What does that mean? Why did Bush win the election?

4. Why did Islamist terrorists attack on 9/11? Why did George W. Bush go to war against Afghanistan shortly afterwards? Why did he then invade Iraq? What issues in Iraq made it difficult to withdraw United States troops?

5. Hurricane Katrina was a natural disaster. To what extent, however, did human actions—and inactions—aggravate the calamity?

6. Why did global financial markets nearly collapse from 2008–2009? What caused the financial meltdown? What impact did it have on Americans?

7. What factors contributed to Barack Obama being elected president? What were the major elements of his health care reform act and how did he get it through Congress?

8. Why did Obama send American troops back into Afghanistan?

Key Terms

axis of evil
Contract with
America
improvised explosive
device (IED)

North American Free
Trade Agreement
(NAFTA)

"surge"
war on terror

Index